The Peter Martyr Library
Volume Four

Philosophical Works

Hardcover originally published in 1996
by Truman State University Press, Kirksville, Misssouri,
jointly with
The Thomas Jefferson University Press and Sixteenth Century
Journal Publishers, Inc. Kirksville, Missouri, U.S.A.
The Peter Martyr Library, Series One, vol. 4
Sixteenth Century Essays and Studies, vol. 39

Paperback edition published 4/1/2018
Moscow, ID
The Davenant Press

ISBN-13: 978-0-9995527-6-6
ISBN-10: 0-9995527-6-7

Cover design by Rachel Rosales, Orange Peal Design

To
Thomas F. Torrance
Doktorvater and friend,
who introduced me
to Peter Martyr

Contents

PART FIVE *ba* FREE WILL AND PREDESTINATION

Abbreviations Used in this Volume

BDB   *The New Brown, Driver & Briggs Gesenius*. Oxford: Oxford University Press, 1907; reprinted 1981.

BIB   *A Bibliography of the Writings of Peter Martyr Vermigli*. John Patrick Donnelly and Robert M. Kingdon, with Marvin W. Anderson. Kirksville, Mo.: Sixteenth Century Journal Publishers, 1990.

CHGM *The Cambridge History of Later Greek and Early Medieval Philosophy*. Edited by A. H. Armstrong. Cambridge: Cambridge University Press, 1967.

CHRP   *The Cambridge History of Renaissance Philosophy*. Edited by C. Schmitt and Q. Skinner. Cambridge: Cambridge University Press, 1988.

COR   Peter Martyr Vermigli. *In Selectissimam S. Pauli Priorem ad Corinthios Epistolam ... Commentarii*. Zurich: C. Froschauer, 1551.

CP   *Common Places of Peter Martyr Vermigli*. "Translated and partly gathered" by Anthony Marten. London, 1583.

CR   *Corpus Reformatorum*. Edited by Karl Gottlieb Bretschneider and Heinrich Ernst Bindseil. Halle, 1834–.

CSV   John Patrick Donnelly. *Calvinism and Scholasticism in Vermigli's Doctrine of Man and Grace*. Leiden: Brill, 1976.

DEF   Peter Martyr Vermigli. *Defensio Doctrinae veteris & Apostolicae de ss Euch. ... adv. Stephani Gardineri*. Zurich: C. Froschauer, 1559.

DIAL   Peter Martyr Vermigli. *Dialogue on the Two Natures in Christ*. Translated and edited by J.P. Donnelly. Peter Martyr Library, 2. Kirksville, Mo.: Sixteenth Century Journal Publishers, 1995.

DM   Peter Martyr Vermigli. *The Life, Early Letters and Eucharistic Writings of Peter Martyr*. Translated by G. E. Duffield and J. C. McLelland. Oxford: Sutton Courtenay Press, 1989.

ETH   Peter Martyr Vermigli. *In Primum, Secundum, et Initium Tertii Libri Ethicorum Aristotelis ad Nicomachum*. Zurich: C. Froschauer, 1563.

EW   Peter Martyr Vermigli. *Early Writings: Creed, Scripture, Church*. Translated by M. Di Gangi and J. C. McLelland, edited by J. C. McLelland. Peter Martyr Library, 1. Kirksville, Mo.: Sixteenth Century Journal Publishers, 1994.

GEN   Peter Martyr Vermigli. *In Primum Librum Mosis Qui Vulgo Genesis Dicitur Commentarii*. Zurich: C. Froschauer, 1569.

Inst.   John Calvin. *Institutes of the Christian Religion* (1559). 2 vols. Edited by J. T. McNeill and F. L. Battles. Philadelphia: Westminster Press, 1960.

IUD   Peter Martyr Vermigli. *In Librum Iudicum ... Commentarii*. Zurich: C. Froschauer, 1561.

LC   Peter Martyr Vermigli. *Loci Communes Petri Martyris Vermilii*. London: R. Masson, 1576; Basle: P. Perna, 1580–1582 (3 vols.).

NE   Aristotle. *Nicomachean Ethics*, in R. McKeon, ed. *The Basic Works of Aristotle*. New York: Random House, 1941.

PG   *Patrologiae Cursus Completus. Series Graeca*. Edited by J. P. Migne. Paris, 1857–.

PL   *Patrologiae Cursus Completus. Series Latina*. Edited by J. P. Migne. Paris, 1844–.

PMIR   *Peter Martyr Vermigli and Italian Reform*. Edited by Joseph C. McLelland. Waterloo, Ont.: Wilfred Laurier University Press, 1980.

PML   The Peter Martyr Library, series 1. Edited by J. P. Donnelly and J. C. McLelland. Kirksville, Mo.: Sixteenth Century Journal Publishers, 1994-.

PMRE Marvin W. Anderson. *Peter Martyr: A Reformer in Exile (1542–1562): A Chronology of Biblical Writings in England and Europe*. Nieuwkoop: De Graaf, 1975.

PPS   Peter Martyr Vermigli. *Prayers from the Psalms*. Translated and edited by J. P. Donnelly. Peter Martyr Library, 3. Kirksville, Mo.: Sixteenth Century Journal Publishers, 1996.

REG   Peter Martyr Vermigli. *Melachim Id Est, Regum Libri Duo Posteriores cum Commentariis*. Zurich: C. Froschauer, 1566.

ROM   Peter Martyr Vermigli. *In Epistolam S. Pauli Apostoli ad Romanos ... Commentarii*. Basel: P. Perna, 1558.

SAM   Peter Martyr Vermigli. *In Duos Libros Samuelis Prophetae ... Commentarii*. Zurich: C. Froschauer, 1564.

SCG   Thomas Aquinas. *Summa Contra Gentes*. Rome: Marietta, 1952.

ST   Thomas Aquinas. *Summa Theologiae*. Rome: Marietta, 1952.

VWG   Joseph C. McLelland. *The Visible Words of God: An Exposition of the Sacramental Theology of Peter Martyr Vermigli*. Edinburgh: Oliver and Boyd, 1957.

WA   Martin Luther. *Werke. Kritische Gesamtausgabe* [Weimar-Ausgabe]. 107 vols. Weimar, 1883–.

General Editors' Preface

$\mathcal{T}$HE PETER MARTYR LIBRARY presents a series of English translations of the chief works of Peter Martyr Vermigli (1499–1562) together with scholarly notes and introductions. Martyr spent most of his adult life as an Augustinian Canon in Italy before he converted openly to Protestantism and fled Italy in 1542. Almost no writings survive from his Italian years. Very quickly his early lectures on the Old Testament at the Strasbourg Academy (1542–47) earned him a reputation for erudition and clear thinking. He spent his next six years as Regius Professor of Theology at Oxford, where he lectured on Romans and First Corinthians until the accession of Queen Mary drove him back to Strasbourg. There he lectured on Judges as well as Aristotle's Nicomachean Ethics. Increasing pressure from Lutheran pastors who controlled the Strasbourg church led Martyr to transfer to Zurich in July of 1556. Aside from a trip to France to participate in the Poissy Colloquy of 1561, Vermigli spent his last six years at Zurich, lecturing on the books of Samuel and Kings. There Vermigli also published controversial works against Richard Smith on celibacy, against Stephen Gardiner on the eucharist, and against Johann Brenz on the two natures of Christ. During his twenty years in northern Europe he also wrote many lesser works. By his death he was widely regarded as the most acute and learned Reformed theologian after John Calvin. The posthumous publication of several biblical commentaries only enhanced his reputation, and the demand for his works remained strong until 1630.

This is the fourth volume in The Peter Martyr Library. The first volume brings together two of Martyr's early writings and a later apologetic for his apostasy. The second volume is a translation of his Dialogue on the Two Natures in Christ, which Martyr wrote some sixteen months before his death. It is Vermigli's finest controversial work. The third volume, Sacred Prayers Drawn from the Psalms of David, presents the reformer leading his students at Strasbourg in prayer. These three volumes are fairly short; most subsequent volumes in the series will be considerably longer.

This fourth volume brings together several treatises of Martyr, which illustrate how philosophy and theology interact in his writings.

Vermigli's use of medieval and Renaissance Aristotelianism to under-gird and defend biblical teaching and Reformed theology has been a subject of keen interest for scholars during the last thirty years. Both of the general editors of this series have written on the problem. Vermigli's training in philosophy at the University of Padua was stronger than similar training received by either Luther or Calvin, and Aristotle plays a more prominent role in Vermigli's theological works than in Luther's or Calvin's. Yet Vermigli clearly based his theology on Scripture; he saw Aristotle and philosophy as useful allies for Christian theology, not foundation stones. Although the writings gathered in this volume are explicitly theological, they all illustrate the interplay of faith and rea-son, of theology and philosophy. A later volume in this series will trans-late Vermigli's commentary on Aristotle's Ethics, his only explicitly philosophic work. The writings in the present volume show Vermigli's actual use of philosophy in his theological works. Here philosophy plays a subordinate role, but one more prominent than in the writings of Calvin. Vermigli then stands midway between, on the one hand, Luther and Calvin and, on the other, his own disciple Girolamo Zanchi and the neo-scholastics who dominated the Reformed theology in the early seventeenth century.

John Patrick Donnelly, S.J.
Joseph C. McLelland

Translator's Preface

$\mathcal{T}$HIS VOLUME is one of two in the Peter Martyr Library devoted to philosophical writings. The other is the commentary on Aristotle's *Nicomachean Ethics*. The present selection consists of the preface to that commentary, scholia from Martyr's biblical commentaries, a lecture on free will, and three summaries. While all concern topics on the agenda of philosophy, some are more explicit than others. In "Dreams" for instance, Martyr has before him two of Aristotle's minor works, and in "Providence" he deals with themes familiar in Cicero. The material in this book raises the question of Martyr's role in the debate about "Reformed Scholasticism." Obviously this volume is a contribution to that discussion inasmuch as Martyr's explicit teaching on the relation of philosophy to theology has not hitherto been explored in its own terms. Brian Armstrong thought that my first work on Martyr (1957) struggled "to rescue him from the charge of scholasticism." Some forty years later I still prefer a modified form of the thesis about both the nature and the origins of the scholastic development in Protestant orthodoxy, as I argue in the introduction to the present volume. I take pains to note Vermigli's conscious or unconscious references to both Aristotle and Aquinas; there are many places where similar references to Bucer, Calvin, and Zwingli are in order. In my opinion, Peter Martyr remains essentially Augustinian in theology, so that his attitude toward philosophy is seen to be a form of Aristotelianism measured and controlled by a scriptural and theological standard.

Complex issues surround the history of philosophy in the sixteenth century. Late medieval and Renaissance philosophy forms one of the most subtle debating grounds in Western intellectual history. The rapidly changing theology of the same period is part of the story, revealing the questions disputed by Scholastics as well as the renewal of biblical and patristic authority achieved by Humanism, Reform, and Counter-Reform. Peter Martyr was part of that story; his own philosophical and theological training forced him to take the measure of the new thinking. This constraint drove him into exile, moving from Italy to Strasbourg, thence to England and back to Strasbourg, and finally to Zurich: four occasions of controversy and debate. If his calm argument of weighty problems seems to deny this turbulent context, it is because his spirit was strong and his humor (as he himself might say) phlegmatic.

The philosophical dimension of Peter Martyr's thought has been well explored by John Patrick Donnelly, S.J., especially in *Calvinism and Scholasticism in Vermigli's Doctrine of Man and Grace* (Leiden: Brill, 1976). I acknowledge my debt to his research and publications in preparing this volume, and for his translation of the "De Resurrectione," which he provided. Two research assistants should be acknowledged for their contribution to this enterprise: Leszek Wysocki of the Classics Department of McGill University checked my translation against the original Latin. Since he is also translating Martyr's *Ethics* commentary for a future volume, he kindly allowed me to use his translation for the first selection. Dr. George Harper of Westminster, South Carolina, formerly of Presbyterian College, Montreal, processed the text through its various stages of revision; Ms. Samieun Khan prepared the final copy. Our college librarian, Mr. Dan Shute, assisted with Hebraic terms and Rabbinic references. The manuscript was read by J. P. Donnelly, Edward Furcha, Frank A. James, and William Klempa. Without the help of these colleagues the work would have been much more onerous and less reliable. Thanks are also due to the Zurich Zentralbibliothek for the facsimiles of title pages included in this volume.

Two points of style should be noted. In general, translators seek the mean between literalism and paraphrase, or "stencil" and "aureate" forms of speech. The former is easy, the latter much more demanding. In Martyr's case we have a Latin that is clear but dense and often convoluted. His writing bristles with connectives, superlatives, subordinate clauses, and the like—simple for literal translation but awkward when one seeks a modern and more colloquial rendering. Professor Donnelly provides helpful comments on the procedures followed in his translation of Martyr's *Dialogus* (volume 2, xxiv-xxv), including the problem of verifying references. In correspondence he has also noted the problem of choosing proper terms for such common words as *pius*, *impius*, and *ratio* as well as *homo*, with its special problem of gender identity, as noted below. Related to this is Martyr's frequent use of the passive voice (which we often turn active) and his overuse of the connectives *ergo*, *igitur*, *autem*, *praeterea*, *unde*, *nec*, and the like. What this volume offers is a somewhat free translation that seeks to convey the sense of the original sentence-by-sentence rather than word-by-word. The attempt is not without its risks. Long ago Rufinus commented on Jerome's translation of Origen's *De Principiis*: "I find that he is so enamored of his own style that he pursues a still more ambitious objective, namely, that he should be the creator of the book, not merely its translator." In Martyr's case, my hope is that the actual body survives as quite recognizable but with added comeliness.

A more specific problem today concerns inclusive language. In the case of sixteenth-century material this is not easily solved. Our procedure was explained in the introduction to volume 1. We state there: "While we try to use inclusive language wherever possible, it is anachronistic to change the masculine in historical documents, particularly since an inclusive intention seems clear in most cases" (p. 26). Therefore, while we try to translate according to contemporary standards, we recognize that the canons of integrity of text and elegance of phrase must predominate.

The dedication signifies my debt to Thomas F. Torrance. In our initial interview forty-five years ago to discuss my doctoral program, I expressed my wish to study a Reformed theory of knowledge. He suggested Vermigli's sacramental theology as a good—if surprising—way to proceed. It proved to be just that; this book shows part of the reason why. At last I am able to provide further evidence, with gratitude.

Joseph C. McLelland

Montreal
The Feast of Peter Martyr
29 April 1996

Peter Martyr Vermigli, from frontispiece printed in London by John Day in 1564

Peter Martyr Vermigli's Philosophical Works

Translator's Introduction

FLORENCE, PADUA, AND BEYOND

"A man has arrived from Italy who is quite learned in Latin, Greek, and Hebrew and well skilled in the Scriptures; he is about forty-four years old, of serious demeanor and keen intelligence. His name is Peter Martyr."[1] The year was 1542; threat of Inquisition had driven Pietro Martire Vermigli (1499–1562) from his native land, never to return. His career as Protestant Reformer for the next twenty years took him to three cities and identified him with three leading figures in the drama of Reform: Strasbourg and Martin Bucer, Oxford and Thomas Cranmer, Zurich and Henry Bullinger.

Recent research on Vermigli reveals the thorough grounding in philosophy, theology, and languages that he received in Italy, notably at Padua between 1518 and 1526. He was a Florentine who studied at Padua, and these two streams of philosophy—Platonic and Aristotelian—meet in his own formation. Most significant for the present work is the state of Aristotelian teaching in those years, which relates to the question of Martyr's own philosophy and its role in the development of Reformed Scholasticism.[2] Aristotle was the good luck of Thomist theology; Thomas Gilby, speaking of Thomas Aquinas

---

[1] Bucer to Calvin, 28 October 1542: *Calvini Opera* XI.c.450. For Martyr's life and work, see Philip McNair, "Biographical Introduction," EW 3–14.

[2] See "Reformed Scholasticism" on page xxvii, below, and J. C. McLelland, "Aristotelianism," in *Blackwell Encyclopedia of Late Medieval, Renaissance and Reformation Thought*, forthcoming.

in relation to the new stature of Aristotle as "*Philosophus* ... symbol for ambitious and confident rationalism," writes: "Before this St. Thomas neither stood on the defensive nor beat a retreat; it was no threat but a promise, and one very much to his liking."[3] Similarly, Vermigli welcomed Aristotelian philosophy as the gift of fundamental reasoning in both logic and ethics.

Renaissance thinkers enjoyed a revival of three classical systems: Platonism, Aristotelianism, and Neoplatonism; in general the Renaissance discovery of the human microcosm is informed by all three, along with the revival of occult and alchemical ideas.[4] In 1518, Peter Martyr was received into the Paduan monastery of S. Giovanni di Verdara, the celebrated academy of the Lateran Congregation; Vittorio Cian called it "Pantheon of Humanists." Its library formed a fitting environment for the salon of resident and visiting scholars, including Pietro Bembo.[5] While the University of Padua no longer enjoyed the heady days of Pomponazzi, a new generation of teachers was enhancing its name and modifying its tradition. Their *via antiqua* offered a harmonious view of reason and revelation, with its concomitant positive assessment of philosophy. Such harmony did not obtain throughout the university since Neo-Peripateticism based on humanist and philological methods was absent from the faculty of theology. The latter provided for masters both *in via Thomae* and *in via Scoti*. What was common to philosophy and theology, however, was the humanist thesis that our capacity is not sufficient for eternal truth, with its consequent focus on human problems and concerns.

Certain assumptions exist concerning the freethinking, even atheistic, views of Renaissance Italians. Antonio D'Andrea calls this "the myth of Italy"; Paul Oskar Kristeller considered "Paduan Averroism" a "misleading name."[6] Still, it was Paduan Averroism that informed John Calvin's Genevan enemies, the Libertines. Calvin regarded their errors as deriving in large part from the

---

[3]ST 1a.Q1, trans. Thomas Gilby (London: Eyre & Spottiswoode, 1964) 1:49.

[4]See E. Cassirer, *The Individual and the Cosmos in Renaissance Philosophy* (Philadelphia: University of Philadelphia, 1983) 16–18. Cf. P. O. Kristeller, *Renaissance Thought and Its Sources* (New York: Columbia University Press, 1979).

[5]For the material in this paragraph see Philip McNair, *Peter Martyr in Italy* (Oxford: Clarendon Press, 1967) 86–115. Philosophers from the local university also frequented the monastery, including Genua and his son Marcantonio (the latter was Vermigli's professor) and the Averroist Nicoletto Vernia, who willed his own books to the monastic library; ibid., 94 ff.

[6]A. D'Andrea, "Geneva 1576–78: The Italian Community and the Myth of Italy" in PMIR 53 ff.; P. O. Kristeller, *Renaissance Thought: The Classic, Scholastic and Humanist Strains* (New York: Harper, 1961) 37; G. H. Williams, *The Radical Reformation*, 3d ed., Sixteenth Century Essays and Studies, 15 (Kirksville, Mo.: Sixteenth Century Publishers, 1992) 63 ff.

idea of universal intellect and pantheistic determinism.[7] In any case, we may regard Padua as a center of speculative thinking. The word "speculation" implies the radical analysis associated with Lorenzo Valla as well as the skepticism of Agrippa von Nettesheim. Sextus Empiricus had been rediscovered and classical skepticism reintroduced. Martyr himself seemed to escape the negative thrust of the Paduan experience. He resisted the Italian antitrinitarians, for instance, not least because he considered their speculative theology a risky pursuit for fallible minds. More important is the continuing debate between (Platonic) rationalism and (Aristotelian) voluntarism. The former assumes that one always chooses what one perceives to be the good (e.g. *Prot.* 352B); the latter allows greater strength to desire or affection, which often conflicts with reason, the product of which is a person of weak will.[8]

In the selections to follow, Peter Martyr shows himself debtor to both Aristotle and Thomas Aquinas. His regard for the Philosopher is high: "After Plato came Aristotle, a man of singular genius, who subjected all the relevant material to methodical analysis and arranged it with the greatest accuracy.... The school of Peripatetics sprang from Aristotle; it had fewer errors than any other school, and flourishes to this day" ("Philosophy and Theology," §3, p. 12 below). Martyr describes the relation between philosophy and theology in positive terms, the first grounding and supporting the second while the second governs use of the first. His approach is cosmological rather than ontological; he echoes the "five ways" of Aquinas, but insists that the key is not demonstration through argument but the development of universal and inchoate knowledge.[9] Martyr's method follows a careful order, based on the Scholastic tradition of the *quaestio disputata;* although neither so precise nor consistent as the late medieval development had been, Martyr works steadily through *objectum* to *respondeo.* He is not behind in appreciating the need for clarity of reason; judgment involves "compounding and dividing."[10] This in turn entails categories and predicables, and the range of analytic tools honed by Aristotle and adapted by Aquinas. Drawing on this rich heritage, Martyr does not shrink from the subtleties of syllogistic reasoning, rational demonstration, analogical predication, or a complex epistemology. He is painstaking

---

[7]E.g. John Calvin, "On the Libertine View That a Single Immortal Spirit Comprises Everything, and What Pestilence Is Hidden under This View," *Against the Fantastic and Furious Sect of the Libertines Who Are Called "Spirituals"* (1545) chap. 13, cited by B.W. Farley, ed., *Treatises against the Anabaptists and against the Libertines* (Grand Rapids: Baker Book House, 1982).

[8]*Akratēs*, "incontinent" in standard translation, *NE* VII.2.1145b21ff.

[9]E.g. "Nature and Grace," §3, p. 20, below; cf. ST 1a.Q2, art. 3: Utrum deus sit; *Inst.,* 1.3.1.

[10]Timothy McDermott, ST 1a, 2–11 (London: Eyre & Spottiswoode, 1964) 175: see app. 2, "Logical Preliminaries," 174–180.

in arranging argument and counterargument (e.g. "Author of Sin"); he organizes his arguments in syllogistic form ("Free Will," §11) and mounts them according to the Philosopher's fourfold causality ("Philosophy and Theology" §1). He credits Plato also with identifying first and second causes ("Resurrection" §55); for Vermigli as for Aquinas, grace does not destroy nature but crowns it ("Free Will" §8). So far the case for labeling Vermigli as Reformed Aristotelian seems clear. But there is more to consider, as we argue below.

Martyr's eight years at the University of Padua involved a solid grounding in both philosophy and theology. Padua exemplified "one of the sixteenth century's most important philosophical characteristics, the development of a revivified Aristotelianism."[11] The Aldine *editio princeps* of Aristotle was published in Venice 1495–1498; Niccolò Tomeo began to teach Aristotle from the Greek texts in 1497. In Vermigli's student days the dominant figure was Marcantonio Genua, noted for his innovative treatment of Aristotle's *De Anima*.[12] Advancing beyond the received Arabic commentaries, Genua went back to the Greek commentator Simplicius; the new Paduan Aristotelians were dubbed "Simpliciani." But Averroism continued, if less problematic than the medieval "Latin Averroism" that separated philosophy from theology and so incurred the rejection of theologians. Martyr also knew the Aristotle of Albertus Magnus and Thomas, whose critical reading departed from that of "*the* Commentator."[13] Where Averroës could say, "The doctrine of Aristotle is the supreme truth, because his intellect was the limit of human intelligence,"[14] Martyr regards revelation as the proper limitation of reason. Like Aquinas, our Reformer brings a scriptural test to Aristotle, particularly on the moot questions of Renaissance debate. Most important at Padua were the twin concerns of the *De Anima*, which had been handled in detail by Thomas in his own commentary, namely the unity of the agent intellect and the immortality of the soul.[15]

[11]CHRP 69–70.

[12]See CHRP 523ff.

[13]As Aquinas dubbed Averroës; see ST 1a.Q3, art. 5, obj. 2.

[14]Quoted in E. Gilson, *History of Christian Philosophy in the Middle Ages* (New York: Random House, 1955) 220.

[15]See *Aristotle's De Anima in the Version of William of Moerbeke and the Commentary of St. Thomas Aquinas*, trans. K. Foster and S. Humphries, intro. by Ivo Thomas (London: Routledge and Kegan Paul, 1951; New Haven: Yale University Press, 1951, 1965) esp. 18ff., "The Averroist Issue"; also available as a computer program: Past Master series (Pittsboro, N.C.: InterLex Corp., 1992). Aquinas had settled the problem raised by the Arab interpreters of Aristotle as to whether the active intellect is part of the individual soul by declaring the soul immaterial and therefore immortal: e.g. SCG III.43, *De Unitate Intellectus,* III.

THE INTELLECT: ONE AND IMMORTAL

Hellenistic thought is characterized by its sense of duality, the *chorismōs* between matter and spirit, as in the mortal and immortal soul of Plato's *Timaeus*, or the intellect as the true self distinct from the moral personality in Aristotle's *Nicomachean Ethics*.[16] Plotinus in turn rejected the Stoic material soul by showing the connection of impassibility with incorporeality.[17] So the relation among intellect, immateriality, and immortality was well developed. It is this conceptual scheme that involves The One of both Plato and Aristotle, a simplicity or unicity that transcended every determination or limitation. Alexander Aphrodisias (ca. 200 CE), the leading Greek interpreter of Aristotle, had taken his master's noetics as implying an Intelligence that is both active and omnipresent.[18] An obvious and fateful question is posed by this development of doctrine: is there an individual intellect that is an immortal soul?

Renaissance discussion of human being found its starting point in Aristotle's teaching on the intellective soul in *De anima* III.4–5. The Philosopher's psychology parallels his cosmology: humanity is microcosm, "an ordered unity at the summit of whose structure stands a transcendent intellectual principle" or "separable reason."[19] He distinguishes two factors in nature, one potential and one productive, and "these distinct elements must likewise be found within the soul." The productive mind is "separable, impassible, unmixed, since it is in its essential nature activity … this alone is immortal and eternal…."[20] How should one interpret the key texts? Two crucial and related questions arise: how does an immaterial and incorruptible soul act in a material subject, the rational in the irrational? And, did Aristotle intend to argue for personal immortality, based on the intellective soul?

To the first question Aristotle himself answered that natural bodies that have life are composite: the body is the subject matter, and the soul is *the form of the body*. Martyr adopts this formula in arguing for the unity of body and soul: soul is "motor," "the drive and form of the body"; this determines his doctrine of resurrection.[21] It also engages him in debate with the commentators on Aristotle. Some had argued that both passive and active intellects are part of individual souls, while Alexander Aphrodisias, as noted, placed the

---

[16]*Timaeus* 69; cf. *NE* 1177b–1178
[17]See CHGM 223 ff.
[18]See CHGM 116 ff., "Aristocles and Alexander Aphrodisias."
[19]A. H. Armstrong, *An Introduction to Ancient Philosophy* (London: Methuen, 1947) 91.
[20]*De Anima* III.5.430a10 ff.
[21]Aristotle, *De Anima* II.1.412a17 ff.; Martyr, "Image," §§1–2; "Resurrection," §31; cf. Aquinas, SCG II.70, 78, etc.

passive intellect within the soul, but considered the active intellect to be a separate Existent.[22] The Muslim commentators provoked sharp debate; Aristotle emerged from his Arabic eggshells smelling of determinism. This posed the familiar problem of "coherence" for Renaissance scholars, as they attempted to reconcile contingency and necessity. Avicenna (980–1037) posited a universal Agent Intelligence, related to Platonic emanationism; but he also granted individual immortality.[23] Averroës (1126–1198) reasoned that the unicity of the Intellect implied one agent intellect for all, a monopsychism that denied individual immortality. Or so Christian interpreters understood him: they equated intellect with soul, whereas Averroës himself followed the Koran: what is predicable of the one is not thereby predicable of the other.[24] The development of Latin Averroism in thirteenth-century France, exemplified by Siger of Brabant, had pitted philosophy against theology and provoked the Condemnation of 1277, as well as responses from Albert and Aquinas.[25]

John Patrick Donnelly observes that "Aristotle's brief and obscure comments on the agent intellect have generated more controversy than any short nonbiblical passage in the history of western thought." He adds that while Martyr himself uses the technical term only once, he "talks about the possible intellect hundreds of times."[26] Martyr accepts the Aristotelian-Thomistic epistemology in which our external senses receive from the outside world images (*species, imagines*) that are transferred to internal senses and thence to the intellect. Such theory of knowledge is little different from that of Augustine, of course, who sees *memoria* as the storehouse of *species*.[27] The intellect conceives them as universals, likened by Martyr to a mirror, showing "how the forms or images existing in the mind make extramental objects really (*reipsa*) present in

---

[22]See SCG II.62. "Against the Opinion of Alexander about the Possible Intellect."

[23]Avicenna pursued Porphyry's problem of abstract Ideas or *intelligibilia* to posit a universal essence. See his *Metaphysica* IX.4, in M. Horton, *Das Buch der Genesung der Seele* (Frankfurt a. M.: Minerva, 1960); cf. L. E. Goodman, *Avicenna* (London: Routledge, 1992) 61ff., 127–128.

[24]*Averrois Cordubensis Commentarium Magnum in Aristotelis de Anima Libros*, III.4. See O. N. Mohammed, *Averroës' Doctrine of Immortality: A Matter of Controversy* (Waterloo, Ont.: Wilfrid Laurier University, 1984) 9–10, 84ff.; and B. H. Zedler, *Saint Thomas Aquinas: On the Unity of the Intellect against the Averroists* (Milwaukee: Marquette University, 1968) introduction. [We use the traditional form "Koran," rather than the proper "Qur'an," in harmony with earlier usage.]

[25]Albert had refuted Averroës in *De Unitate Intellectus contra Averroem* (1256) and Aquinas in *De Unitate Intellectus contra Averroistas* (1270); see Gilson, *History of Christian Philosophy*, 387–427.

[26]CSV 86. The single passage is DEF 630. The argument that external objects are effectively made present to us is used by Martyr against Stephen Gardiner to support the Reformed doctrine of sacramental presence; see n. 28, p. xxv, below.

[27]E.g. *De Trinitate* XI.3.6, 10.17 (PL 42.988–989, 997–998).

the mind" apart from their physical substance.[28]

The second question is: Does Aristotle's "separable, impassible, unmixed" part of the human soul entail immortality? Thomas had said yes, Duns Scotus perhaps. Pietro Pomponazzi argued that it is either individual or immortal, but not both; he agreed with Thomas in rejecting the Averroistic unity, but considered the Thomist doctrine of immortality to be rationally indemonstrable; Tommaso di Vio Cajetan had argued the same point in his 1509 commentary on the *De Anima*.[29] Marcantonio Genua, Martyr's Paduan professor, added a third, "habitual," intellect to the epistemological formula: "Whenever the rational soul speculated on the *species* contained in the habitual intellect, imagination produced the relevant *phantasmata*." He also represents the "real breakthrough of Neoplatonism into Renaissance psychology," with the Platonic category of "participation" modifying Aristotelian structures of form and matter.[30] Jacopo Zabarella (1533–1589) illustrates the "shift of emphasis from the ontological to the operational aspects of intellection."[31] Thus do epistemology and anthropology meet in the development of Paduan Aristotelianism.

Peter Martyr treats the problem of the intellective soul and its immortality in several places, notably the scholia *De Homine* and *De Resurrectione*, translated in this volume. Here he rejects the Averroist separate *agens intellectus* with immortality as absorption into the world soul, noting that some philosophers accept and others reject immortality (§§16, 72). He follows Aristotle and Aquinas when discussing the soul as "form of the body," and the role of the intellective soul in knowledge.[32] On the former point he echoes the

[28]CSV 87. Donnelly cites the key passages in ETH 170, SAM 165v, and IUD 92v, for which he provides the original, including the key sentence: "Vis in nobis intelligendi, quam philosophi appellant possibilem, ut Aristoteles ait, potest fieri omnia..." (DEF 630).

[29]See J. H. Randall, introduction to Pomponazzi's "Immortality of the Soul," *The Renaissance Philosophy of Man*, ed. E. Cassirer, P. O. Kristeller, and J. H. Randall (Chicago: University of Chicago Press, 1948) 257–279. Pomponazzi reasons that "the soul is essentially and truly mortal, relatively and improperly immortal," and concludes that "the question of the immortality of the soul is a neutral problem" (chap. 15). Thomas Gilby, in ST 1a.Q1, 76, remarks that Thomas "accepted the philosophical implications of the unity of the human soul as the substantial form of the human body despite the apparent threat to its spirituality and immortality."

[30]CHRP §15 ("The Intellective Soul, " by Eckhard Kessler), pp. 524ff.; also *Aristotelismo padovano e filosofia aristotelica, Atti del XII convegno internazionale di filosofia* 9 (Florence: Sansoni, 1960).

[31]CHRP, 533; see P. Petersen, *Geschichte der Aristotelischen Philosophie im Protestantischen Deutschland* (Leipzig: F. Meiner, 1921) 196ff.

[32]See J. P. Donnelly, "Calvinist Thomism," *Viator: Medieval and Renaissance Studies,* vol. 7 (Berkeley: University of California Press, 1976) 441–55. Martyr's teaching runs parallel to the more detailed exposition of Aquinas in SCG II:49–90.

Theologian: *intellectus sive anima intellectiva, est forma corporis*.[33] As to the latter, the complex and subtle "theory of the concept" in Thomistic epistemology shows through Martyr's occasional references to the human way of knowing objects, our intellect as individual and *capax dei*, against the Arabic commentators.[34] For Thomas, the *intellectus agens* acts on the *species sensibilis*: it "abstracts the intelligible species from phantasms ... taking the specific nature without individuality, the image of which informs the passive intellect."[35] Peter Martyr shares such "moderate realism," in which intellect is privileged over will in grasping reality.[36] But he can also applaud Clement of Alexandria's apophatic terminology, thus following Aquinas in treating negations with respect, even privilege.[37] In short, to define Martyr as "Thomist" requires qualification not only as to the unscholastic dimensions of Aquinas's own thought, but also because of Martyr's disagreements with Thomas.[38]

Martyr seems to have emerged from Padua without succumbing to Genua or to Scotism, endorsing Thomistic theory while acknowledging the "popular Aristotelianism" based on the practical rather than speculative works—the *Ethics* and *Politics* rather than the *Physics* and *Metaphysics*.[39] This was the sort of philosophy that Martyr helped introduce into the Reformed school; in fact it simply reflects the general antimetaphysical bent of the Renaissance.[40] Our anthology of selected "philosophical works" illustrates

---

[33]ST 1a.Q76 (*De unione animae ad corpus*) art. 1, resp.; cf. ST 1a.QQ 77ff. on the *potentia animae*; *De Unitate Intellectus*, I.12, III.60.

[34]E.g. "Nature and Grace" §3, p. 20, below, "Visions" §3, p. 140, below. On Aquinas see P. Rousselot, *The Intellectualism of Saint Thomas* (London: Sheed & Ward, 1935) 46ff., 86ff. Gilson, *History*, 225, notes that Albert the Great accepted Averroës' own formulation of "the process of abstractive knowledge," for which "the fact that Averroës had posited the agent Intellect as a separate substance was irrelevant...."

[35]ST 1a.Q85, a1, ad 4; see M. C. D'Arcy, *Thomas Aquinas* (London: Benn, 1930) 216–226.

[36]"Medieval 'voluntarists' attribute to will that acquisition of reality by a process of tranformation into itself, which St. Thomas regards as the exclusive privilege of the intellect"; see Rousselot, *Intellectualism of Saint Thomas*, 13n. See E. Caird, *The Evolution of Theology in the Greek Philosophers* (Glasgow: MacLehose, Jackson, 1923) 1:13: "Does the Primacy Belong to Reason or to Will?," 350ff.

[37]Clement, *Strom*. V.12; Martyr, "Visions" §12. For Aquinas, see ST 1a.Q 13, art. 12 ad 1: "In the things of God negations are true, and affirmations are defective"; and SCG III.39, 49: negation "is the *proper* knowledge of God obtained by demonstration." Cf. Rousselot, *Intellectualism of Saint Thomas*, 94.

[38]See Donnelly, "Calvinist Thomism," 442ff.

[39]So Donnelly concludes, providing tables of statistics for Martyr's references, and an account of his marginalia in the copies of Aristotle he owned, now in the university library of Geneva; see CSV 22–23.

[40]See W. J. Bouwsma, "Renaissance and Reformation: An Essay on Their Affinities and Connections," in *A Usable Past* (Berkeley: University of California Press, 1990) 225ff.

the careful handling of philosophical terms and concepts familiar to Renaissance Aristotelianism, drawing on the method known as Scholastic, while maintaining the priority of scriptural revelation over reasoning.

"Reformed Scholasticism"

Was Peter Martyr a founding father of that phenomenon known as "scholasticism" within the developing Reformed theology? A contemporary of his, Joseph Scaliger, stated: "The two most excellent theologians of our times are John Calvin and Peter Martyr, the former of whom has dealt with the Holy Scriptures as they ought to be dealt with—with sincerity I mean, and purity and simplicity, without any scholastic subtleties.... Peter Martyr, because it seemed to fall to him to engage the Sophists, has overcome them sophistically, and struck them down with their own weapons."[41] This methodological judgment should be related to the question of naming Martyr Aristotelian and Thomist. As we have seen, he abandoned neither his early Aristotelianism nor the Thomist theology that built on the Philosopher's groundwork.[42] Returning to Strasbourg from Oxford in 1553, for instance, he began lecturing on Aristotle's *Nicomachean Ethics,* alternating with Girolamo Zanchi's on the *Physics*. And we noted above certain distinctive elements in his theological method that borrow from Aristotle and Thomas. If this is the whole story, one might ask if he too should be counted among the so-called scholastics.

The thesis that "the nonscholastic theology of Calvin" was displaced by "elements of scholasticism" introduced largely by Zanchi, Martyr, and Beza has been advanced strongly by Brian Armstrong.[43] That thesis has been

[41]Quoted by B. B. Warfield, "John Calvin the Theologian" in *Calvin and Augustine*, ed. S. G. Craig (Philadelphia: Presbyterian and Reformed Publishing, 1956) 481, who himself contrasts Calvin with Zwingli the "speculative theologian" and Martyr the "scholastic theologian" among the Reformers.

[42]Donnelly, CSV 202, puts the question and answer like this: "Does Martyr's scholasticism have affinities to any party? Yes. Martyr cannot fairly be called a Thomist, yet his scholasticism stands far closer to Thomism than to any other major school of the Middle Ages"; Donnelly's description of scholasticism has been grouped with Brian Armstrong and Jill Kraye and duly criticized by P. C. Holtrop: "It removes 'scholasticism' too much from the early Reformers, and does not recognize that this movement continued from late medievalism through the Reformation and into the next centuries"; see P. C. Holtrop, *The Bolsec Controversy on Predestination, from 1551 to 1555* (Lewiston: Edwin Mellen Press, 1993) 1:27–28 and 40, nn. 93–94.

[43]B. A. Armstrong, *Calvinism and the Amyraut Heresy* (Madison: University of Wisconsin Press, 1969). Armstrong draws on the view associated with Otto Ritschl, *Dogmengeschichte des Protestantismus* (Göttingen: Vandenhoeck & Ruprecht, 1900), Ernst Bizer, *Frühorthodoxie und Rationalismus* (Zurich: EVZ-Verlag, 1963) and Walter Kickel, *Vernunft und Offenbarung bei Theodor Beza* (Neukirchen: Neukirchener Verlag, 1975). Their view concerns not only methodology but whether

disputed in particular by Richard Muller and Philip Holtrop. Muller questions the identity of "scholasticism" with "a use of Aristotelian philosophy, a pronounced metaphysical interest, and the use of predestination as an organizing principle in a theological system." Muller further notes that the exaltation of Calvin as "chief codifier" of Reformed doctrine ignores the collegial work of Bullinger, Musculus, Vermigli, and others.[44] Holtrop reinforces both points, and accuses Armstrong of near hagiography in regard to Calvin, drawing on the work of Ian McPhee to relieve Theodore Beza of the charge of scholastic innovator.[45] Without pursuing the debate further, we attempt to clarify its chief terms, in particular "scholasticism," "Aristotelianism," and "Calvinism," in order to assess Martyr's place and role in the alleged development.

Scholasticism has suffered from a supposed contrast between medieval and Renaissance thought, popularized by Jacob Burckhardt: *Humanism* was the new philosophy of Renaissance and displaced scholasticism. Paul Oskar Kristeller led the critique against such a simplistic historiography, arguing that the Renaissance is too complex to be summarized in terms of mere discontinuity. Humanism itself is plural in ideas and ideals, and can be either Platonist or Aristotelian.[46] When Reformation historians identify periods of "orthodoxy" subsequent to the original Reformers—notably Calvin, Beza, Andreas Musculus, and Martyr—they run a parallel risk in implying a method of system-building, or more narrowly, "the rational justification of religious belief."[47] Muller provides a definition that rescues the term from merely pejorative meaning: "the technical and logical approach to theology as a discipline

---

predestination functions as the "central dogma" of emergent Calvinism. See both R. A. Muller, *Post-Reformation Reformed Dogmatics*, 2 vols. (Grand Rapids: Baker Book House, 1987), and Holtrop, *Bolsec Controversy*, for surveys of the material; see also G. Lewis, "Geneva 1541–1608" in *International Calvinism 1541–1715*, ed. M. Prestwich (Oxford: Clarendon, 1985) 39–70, particularly for Beza and Calvin; cf. J. C. McLelland, "Peter Martyr Vermigli: Scholastic or Humanist?" PMIR 141–151.

[44]R. A. Muller, *Post-Reformation* 1:18. Cf. R. A. Muller, *Christ and the Decree: Christology and Predestination in Reformed Theology from Calvin to Perkins* (Grand Rapids: Eerdmans, 1988) 11ff.

[45]Philip C. Holtrop, *Bolsec Controversy*, 1:3ff.; in the foreword, H. Oberman refers to W. Bouwsma's thesis of "the dichotomy between Calvin the forward-looking humanist and Calvin the anxiously conservative dogmatician" (xviii). See also I. McPhee, "Conserver or Transformer of Calvin's Thought? A Study of the Origin and Development of Theodore Beza's Thought" (Ph.D. dissertation, University of Cambridge, 1979).

[46]P. O. Kristeller, *Renaissance Thought: The Classic, Scholastic, and Humanist Strains* (New York: Harper & Bros., 1961); scholasticism was rejected because it failed the test of eloquence and did not maintain the patristic consensus on church government and sacraments; cf. C. Trinkaus and H. Oberman, eds., *The Pursuit of Holiness in Late Medieval and Renaissance Religion* (Leiden: Brill, 1974).

[47]A. E. McGrath, *Reformation Thought: An Introduction* (Oxford: Basil Blackwell, 1988) chap. entitled "Scholasticism and the Reformation," 50ff. Cf. Holtrop, *Bolsec Controversy*, 27ff.

characteristic of theological systems from the late twelfth through the seventeenth century ... [is] not necessarily allied to any particular philosophical perspective nor does it represent a systematic attachment to or concentration upon any particular doctrine or concept as a key to theological system."[48]

Think of Aquinas himself, in what sense the term "scholastic" might apply: "To the Augustinians of the day his rationalism and empiricism, particularly with respect to the singleness of the human soul as a form in matter and the dependence of intelligence on sense, verged on materialism and earned episcopal condemnation after his death. Yet ... he treated St. Augustine as his greatest authority among the Fathers and Doctors of the Church, and his doctrine of grace is completely Augustinian."[49] It is one thing to use philosophical categories because one assumes that reason is entirely capable of religious truth; it is quite another to use rational argument because grace completes nature. Aquinas makes the difference clear upon beginning his theological *Summa*: "Sacred doctrine proceeds by argument" insofar as theology moves from articles of faith to their necessary corollaries, for unlike reason, faith finds its rationale in the authority of revelation.[50] This "Thomistic" axiom reflects Augustine, whose famous example was learning about Logos from philosophy but requiring revelation to learn that the Logos was incarnate.[51] Moreover, Thomas's famous "five ways" or arguments for the existence of God occupy only a few pages in his huge work; if philosophers have extracted them for their own purposes, theologians should have more regard for the original context and intention. (Philosophers are always on the lookout for other philosophers; they do not expect to be surprised by prophets.) Aquinas also credits rational argument with a special ability to refute error, "since the contrary of a truth can never be demonstrated."[52] Such medieval scholasticism must be seen in its Augustinian dress: "Fundamental to the program of the *Sentences*, and to that of its commentators during the twelfth and thirteenth centuries, was the reaffirmation of Augustine.... [T]he inspiration for a

---

[48]Muller, *Post-Reformation Reformed Dogmatics* 1:18. A typology of the degrees of orthodoxy is provided at 1:14 ff. The final clause refers to the thesis associated with Alexander Schweitzer that predestination constitutes the *Centraldogma* of Calvinism.

[49]Gilby, ST, 56.

[50]ST, 1a.Q 1.1.7, ad 2: "The first principles of this science are the articles of faith ... The whole of a science is virtually contained in its principles."

[51]PL 32.740–741 (*Conf.* VII.9.13–14).

[52]ST 1a.Q 8 (utrum haec doctrina sit argumentativa). Cf. Gilby "Theology as Science," ST, app. 6, 67–87. Such defensive use of philosophical argument is clear from Martyr's "Resurrection" and "Whether God is the Author of Sin" especially; it recalls Scaliger's adverb in describing Martyr's method: "sophistically."

transition from a speculative to a soteriological view of grace—even though he had in fact been the source of both."[53]

As to the Reformers, Calvin may prefer enthymeme and Martyr syllogism, but both have been identified with the dialectico-rhetorical tradition; it seems that to focus on methodology begs the question.[54] Calvin's own eclectic method and use of Plato, Aristotle, and Stoic sources is similar to Martyr's.[55] Martin Bucer of Strasbourg, so influential on both Calvin and Martyr in their formative years, embodies the problem of definition. Bucer was a Dominican and therefore a Thomist; yet his subsequent Humanism did not destroy his "scholastic" nurture but helped direct it into more biblical and pragmatic ways. As for Peter Martyr, he remained a faithful Augustinian. Philip McNair remarks, "Of the three A's who contended for the mastery of his mind, Aristotle outrivaled Averroës, but Augustine outclassed them both: in the life of this Augustinian, Augustine was to remain to the end his favorite reading after the Bible."[56] We see this especially in Martyr's polemic against those contemporaries he considered Pelagian (much like Gregory of Rimini against the *Pelagiani Moderni*); here he quotes the Father's anti-Pelagian works at length, along with his disciple Prosper of Aquitaine—sometimes ad nauseam. Moreover, Martyr is always the kerygmatic theologian, even in polemics. In the preface to his huge work against the transubstantiation of Stephen Gardiner, almost a catena of patristic quotation, he states: "We are not debating the Ideas of Plato, or the Atoms of Democritus, or the Intermundes of Epicurus, or the Enteleches of Aristotle—but the Body and Blood of the Son of God, by which our redemption is paid in full...."[57] The root question, of course, concerns the role of *analogia entis* in the transition from nature to grace, whether a diastasis intervenes to render the natural reason impotent for saving knowledge. Such a break seems as clear for Martyr as for Calvin, so that "natural

---

[53]J. Pelikan, *The Growth of Medieval Theology (600–1300)*, The Christian Tradition, 3 (Chicago: University of Chicago Press, 1978) 270, 275; cf. ibid., "Natural Theology and the Scholastic Method," 284ff.

[54]Q. Breen, *Christianity and Humanism* (Grand Rapids: Eerdmans, 1968) chap. 4, "John Calvin and the Rhetorical Tradition"; C. Vasoli, "*Loci Communes* and the Rhetorical and Dialectical Traditions," PMIR 17–28.

[55]See J. C. McLelland, "Calvin and Philosophy," *Canadian Journal of Theology* 11/1 (1965): 42–53; Charles Partee, *Calvin and Classical Philosophy* (Leiden: Brill, 1977) 59, notes that despite his liking for Plato, Calvin at times prefers Aristotle: "Plato, in some passages, talks nobly of the faculties of the soul; and Aristotle, in discoursing on it, has surpassed all in acuteness"; see *Psychopann.*, CO 5.178.

[56]McNair, *Peter Martyr in Italy*, 94.

[57]DEF Praefatio.

theology" serves only to render us inexcusable.[58] Donnelly notes that while Martyr "defends and elaborates revealed truth with the aid of Aristotle," the formal syllogism "has far less importance for him than for later Calvinists such as Zanchi and Pierre du Moulin." Thus he is a transitional figure or stepping stone to seventeenth century scholasticism; he is both humanist and scholastic.[59]

Aristotelianism tends to mean a fall from biblical theology into static categories of formal logic. The Italian Aristotelians particularly are blamed for the development of Reformed theology from a dynamic, biblical exposition to a static, metaphysical system.[60] While this is perhaps true in some cases, it requires considerable modification in itself, and particularly when applied to Martyr. For one thing, Aristotle offers more than formal logic—his modal categories are equally important, while his work on motion provides a more dynamic dimension to his thought. Moreover, he is a source not only of dialectic but also of *rhetoric*. Martyr's penchant for figurative language is as Aristotelian as are his moral and practical goals. A good example is found in Martyr's preface to his commentary on Romans. Assessing the charge of Jerome that Paul's speech was hurried and careless—"not words but thunder"—he states: "When we affirm that Paul's writings do not lack eloquence—although he did not seek it; it followed him as he spoke—we do not mean to scare people away from the study of good arts. Rather we advise them to apply themselves to them with diligence, so that later when they come to teach Christ in earnest, they may help them even when they are not thinking of them." Not only do his figures of speech suggest the rhetorical tradition; commenting on Rom. 8:28 ("We know that in everything God works for good") he says: "In a sense we are like players in a comedy, in which even though the beginning and middle scenes are full of trouble, it concludes with a joyful and

---

[58]Martyr is explicit in rejecting the *analogis entis*: "Nature and Grace" §5, and "Visions" §14. See Muller, *Post-Reformation Reformed Dogmatics*, 1:5, "Natural and Supernatural Theology," 167 ff., who concludes that Martyr agrees with Calvin on the result of natural knowledge, that it renders us inexcusable. Bullinger modifies this position in allowing that "the Gentiles could have made use of the natural knowledge of God if they had wished"; see E. J. Platt, "The Seventeenth Century Remonstrant Appeal to Bullinger on the Issue of the Natural Knowledge of God, " in *Gericht Verleden*, ed. W. Nijenhuis, C. G. F. de Jong, and J. van Sluis (Leiden: J. J. Groen, 1991) 115–128.

[59]CSV 199 ff. The final chapter is entitled "From Padua to Zurich: The Limits of Martyr's Scholasticism" (196–207). In light of Oberman's revision of the traditional thesis that Occam was the "foster father of Protestantism," Donnelly, CSV 204–205, states: "The striking thing about the rise of Reformed scholasticism is that its roots in medieval scholasticism run heavily to Thomism, hardly at all to nominalism."

[60]B. A. Armstrong, *Calvinism and the Amyraut Heresy*, 38–39, stresses the influence of "Italian Aristotelians" on the emerging scholasticism, taking as example the fact that Beza once ordered a work of Pomponazzi's.

happy ending. But the faithless are like players in a tragedy—it seems holy and glorious at first but has a dreadful and mournful end." In short, he is scholastic in his use of argument that involves Aristotelian logical categories, but this keeps him well within the Thomistic program shaped by Augustine's theology of grace. Moreover, in Martyr's case we must also take the measure of the *schola Augustiniana moderna* recently investigated by Heiko Oberman, Alister McGrath and Frank James.[61] The crucial figure in this area is Gregory of Rimini (d. 1358), known to Vermigli as a famous general of his order and one skilled in the doctrine of predestination. Again, the essential influence is Augustinian; indeed, the Augustinian heritage itself demanded new ways out of "the dilemma posed by the doctrine of predestination, and, for that matter, out of the paradox of the eucharistic presence."[62]

Calvinism presents a similarly complex history. It is a simplistic term, rightly criticized for its concentration on one historical figure.[63] It reduces the significance of Ulrich Zwingli's independent reform, as well as that of Bucer, whom Wilhelm Pauck designates "the father of Calvinism."[64] In the thesis about Reformed scholasticism, Calvin himself must not be separated and exalted so that he represents a pristine Reformed theology over against Beza, Martyr, and Zanchi.[65] At an earlier stage of the discussion, Donnelly stated: "Jerome Zanchi was the most thoroughgoing and influential in pioneering Calvinist scholasticism, Theodore Beza was the best known and most prolific, but Peter Martyr was the first and the inspiration of all who came after."[66] As we have maintained, all three figures may be seen in a better light than merely the cause of a fall from Calvin's theology of grace. Beza's *Tabula praedestinationis* and Zanchi's *De praedestinatione sanctorum* present a more coherent but less nuanced view of predestination than either Calvin or Martyr. Beza has been blamed for raising predestination to the "central dogma" of Reformed

[61]See H. A. Oberman, *The Harvest of Medieval Theology* (Grand Rapids: Eerdmans, 1967) 196ff.; H. A. Oberman and F. A. James III, eds. *Via Augustini: Augustine in the Later Middle Ages, Renaissance and Reformation* (Leiden: Brill, 1991); McGrath, *Reformation Thought* 55–56, 60–61. Their work marks a considerable advance over that of Gilson, *History of Christian Philosophy* 502–503.

[62]Pelikan, *Growth of Medieval Theology* , 95ff., "The Claims of Reason."

[63]E.g. CSV 1, "to designate this complex movement *Calvinism* obscures almost as much as it illuminates"; cf. Muller, *Post-Reformation Reformed Dogmatics*, 22: "The viewpoint of the twentieth century, which has selected Calvin as the chief early codifier, must be set aside…"; and P. Collinson, "England 1558–1640" in *International Calvinism 1541–1715*, 214: "'Calvinist' is a stereotype and too blunt an instrument for any discriminating purpose."

[64]W. Pauck, ed. *Melanchthon and Bucer* (London: SCM, 1969) 85, 99.

[65]Holtrop, *Bolsec Controversy*, 5ff., 35 n. 26, takes a harsher view than Muller of both Calvin and Beza.

[66]CSV 207. That was written in 1976, as was Donnelly's "Calvinist Thomism." His views must be seen today in light of the more recent work of Muller and Holtrop.

theology as well as for introducing supralapsarianism; moreover, his *syllogismus practicus* is charged with replacing objective grace by subjective faith.[67] Yet there is another side to the debate.[68] Indeed, the idea of *gemina praedestinationis*, a single divine will embracing both elect and reprobate, is found in Luther, Zwingli, and Calvin; Karl Barth discusses this example of "two species within the one genus" and terms it a "fatal parallelism."[69] Girolamo Zanchi, in turn, locates predestination within the divine attribution—he also loves the formal syllogism.[70]

In this question of continuity and discontinuity, all three of our terms—scholasticism, Aristotelianism, and Calvinism—require further exploration. One of the ironies in this subject is that Peter Martyr, an Augustinian theologian and biblical exegete who produced no systematic theology and whose method is more analytic than synthetic, became famous as an author of *loci communes*, because his scholia were later extracted by Robert Masson and organized in the traditional four classes.[71] Before turning to the question of how Martyr's philosophy relates to his biblical norm, we must pursue the theme of Reformed Scholasticism into its test question.

PROVIDENCE AND PREDESTINATION

One formal test of scholasticism—it provides evidence of both methodological principles and theological axioms—is the relative positioning of the

[67]E.g. R. T. Kendall, *Calvin and English Calvinism to 1649* (Oxford: Oxford University Press, 1979) 29ff. Calvin rejects the practical syllogism; see Calvin, *Inst.*, III.2.38, 24.4.

[68]See Muller, *Christ and the Decree*, 79ff., 110ff. His analysis of the *Tabula* shows it to be less speculative and systematic than is usually assumed. Armstrong, *Calvinism and the Amyraut Heresy*, 39, regards an extreme portrait of Beza's scholasticism—notably Walter Kickel's *Vernunft und Offenbarung bei Theodor Beza*—as "overdrawn" through concentration on Beza's systematic works; see n. 43 above.

[69]Karl Barth, *Church Dogmatics*, 4 vols. in 13 (Edinburgh: T. & T. Clark, 1961–1969), ii, 2, 17.

[70]Zanchi follows a Thomist method but has "an Augustinian, perhaps Scotist rather than a Thomist leaning" (Muller, *Christ and the Decree*, 111); cf. Donnelly, "Calvinist Thomism," 444ff. Both Muller and Donnelly criticize the work of Otto Gründler, *Die Gotteslehre Girolami Zanchis und ihre Bedeutung für seine Lehre von der Prädestination* (Neukirchen-Vluyn: Neukirchener Verlag, 1965). Gründler limits his analysis to the relation between divine attributes and election, whereas other works illustrate the infralapsarian intention. McNair, *Peter Martyr in Italy*, 228–229, uses a 1565 letter of Zanchi describing the Martyr of their Lucca days, indicating an influence evangelical rather than scholastic.

[71]Even though Masson was following the example of Calvin's *Institutio* (Praef. to LC, *editio princeps*, 1576). See Muller, *Christ and the Decree*, 57ff. on "Vermigli's Loci Communes." As example, in Karl Barth's only reference to Martyr, when discussing the place of Scripture in confessional preambles of the Reformation, he includes "the *Loci* of Peter Martyr (1576)" within the "older orthodox dogmatics" as being less ardent than Calvin and later Lutherans in placing "the Scripture principle at the very peak of their theological system"; see Barth, *Church Dogmatics* I.2.460.

doctrines of providence and predestination within systems of doctrine. The medieval tradition regarded predestination as falling within the scope of universal divine governance: it is *pars providentiae*. Such inclusive providence entails a *decretum generale* and in turn a determinating will for everyone's destiny. Thomas Aquinas employed a fateful phrase, *quaedam pars providentiae*, of significance in the case of Peter Martyr.[72] The identical words appear in our second "Summary" (*De providentia et praedestinatione*), constituting the chief reason for rejecting Martyr's authorship, as we shall see. Frank James has described the "causal matrix" of predestination, for which "the conceptual *locus classicus*" is Rom. 8:28–30 (which includes the Augustinian favorite, "called according to his purpose"). James claims that Vermigli follows Gregory of Rimini in breaking with the "Thomist inclination to view predestination as *pars providentiae*."[73] The point at issue is whether election belongs to the doctrine of creation along with providence, or to the doctrine of God.

The two scholia making up Martyr's locus *De Providentiae* contain statements reflecting the Thomist tradition. The first (from the Strasbourg lectures on Genesis, ca. 1545) states: "In providence we see predestination, which brings so great a comfort to the godly as to strengthen them greatly" (§2); the second (from the Zurich lectures on Samuel, 1556–1557) concludes: "In this question we have in a sense established the roots and foundations of predestination." These assertions, bracketing in time the predestination scholium, pose a question. Was Martyr ambiguous, or does he see the two as related in a sort of dialectic?[74]

John Calvin is the standard for comparison in the debate on Reformed scholasticism. He joined the two doctrines in the 1539 *Institutes*, but by the definitive 1559 edition they are quite separate: providence belongs to the doctrine of creation, predestination to the doctrine of God. Yet his teaching on providence is much like Martyr's. In the *Institutes* Calvin stresses "the care of God for the whole human race, and especially his vigilance in the government of the church, which he favors with more particular attention" (1.17.1).

---

[72]ST 1a.Q 23, 1c.

[73]Frank A. James, III, "Juan de Valdés before and after Peter Martyr Vermigli: The Reception of *Gemina Praedestinatio* in Valdés' Later Thought" in *Archiv für Reformationsgeschichte* 83 (1992): 180–208, esp. 196ff. James' thesis is that during Martyr's triennium in Naples, 1537–1540, he influenced Juan de Valdés in developing a doctrine of predestination, and one of soteriological nature in line with the late medieval Augustinianism of Gregory of Rimini. Cf. James, "A Late Medieval Parallel in Reformation Thought: *Gemina Praedestinatio* in Gregory of Rimini and Peter Martyr Vermigli," *Via Augustini: Augustine in the Later Middle Ages, Renaissance and Reformation* ed. F. A. James III, and H. A. Oberman (Leiden: Brill, 1991) 157–188.

[74]See the translator's introductions to the sections on "Providence, Miracles, and Responsibility, " pp. 169 ff., and "Free Will and Predestination," pp. 263 ff.

He is sensitive to the complex causality involved: God has "due regard to second causes in their own place" (1.17.6). Thus we can reconcile human deliberation with divine providence, "the eternal decrees of God form no impediment to our providing for ourselves" (1.17.4). It appears that the two doctrines are parallel or even connected in a single logic of divine willing. The problem is that "theologians have generally maintained that Calvin denied a 'general providence.'"[75] This is because Calvin rejected any formal or mechanical determinism, even one of divine law. "For we do not with the Stoics imagine a necessity consisting of a perpetual chain of causes ... but hold that God is the disposer and ruler of all things" (1.16.8). Thus God's will is "the best of all reasons" and his counsel always "in accordance with the highest reason." This rationality remains hidden, however, "concealed in the purpose of God," so that we are called to "entertain such reverence for his secret judgments, as to esteem his will the most righteous cause of everything that he does" (1.17.1). Now it might be argued that the distinction, so large in Calvin's mind, is in fact moot. For one thing, no obvious empirical difference could exist between events caused in one way rather than the other. Eyes of faith discern a divine will, but verification remains elusive, bound by necessity to the circle of faith. Such circular reasoning is not wrongheaded, but it calls in question the strength of any distinction drawn between two kinds of divine willing. The twin doctrines of providence and predestination pose two questions for philosophers and theologians alike. One is the problem of evil, the other that of the relationship between necessity and free will, as difficult in the case of divine as human being.

Zwingli wrote the first Reformation treatise on the subject (1530), in which he blends rationalistic argument with biblical motifs. "Providence is the enduring and unchangeable rule over and direction of all things in the universe." So comprehensive is this oversight—*perpetuum, immutabile, universarum*—that secondary causes are "not properly called causes," and a "soft" determinism obtains.[76] Divine foreknowledge includes events as they will happen; they do not happen because God foresees them. Predestination is for Zwingli the presupposition and not the corollary of providence. It is based completely on God's will as "principal Cause," "the work of will" rather

---

[75] B. Farley, *The Providence of God* (Grand Rapids: Baker Book House, 1988), 152, referring to Langdon Gilkey, Wilhelm Niesel, and Richard Stauffer.

[76] CR 93.3 (*De Prov.* 84, chap. 2); see Farley, *Providence of God,* 143 ff.; McGrath, *Reformation Thought,* 86 ff.: despite the existential as well as theological dimension of Zwingli's doctrine, it breathes the air of (Senecan) fatalism.

than wisdom, goodness, and so forth, "otherwise God's gift and disposition would seem to depend upon our acts."

Zwingli's successor Henry Bullinger places "providence" before "creation" in the Second Helvetic Confession of 1556, a document in which Martyr probably shared, in its initial preparation at least.[77] Bullinger rejects the Epicurean restriction of providence as well as the Libertine use of the doctrine as an excuse for license.[78] In his *Decades* sermon on the subject, Bullinger reflects a similar view. Its title reads: "That God is the creator of all things, and governs all things by his providence: Mention is also made of the goodwill of God towards us, and of predestination."[79] After dealing with providence and its reassuring teaching on divine care he writes: "The doctrine of the foreknowledge and predestination of God, which has a certain likeness [*cognationem*] with his providence, no less comforts godly worshippers of God." Exploring scriptural texts for his homiletical purpose, he sums up by noting the connection among "creation, the governing of all things by God's divine providence, ... God's goodwill towards us" and predestination. He concludes with a eulogy to God's universal care and goodwill, "whose providence has reached already to the very whole, whatsoever it is. To this God be all glory." It seems that Martyr may be identified with this line of thought, in which the governing will of God includes both the universal care of all and the special grace towards the elect. Perhaps it is not so much a question of how providence and predestination are placed in the theological curriculum as how the all-encompassing divine will makes its choices among the creatures under its care. That is, if "election" is viewed as a special case of God's general provision through grace, does this contradict a theology of grace?

Karl Barth thinks so. He states: "The root of the doctrine of predestination is to be found in the being of God. But the doctrine of providence has no corresponding root of which this may be said."[80] Yet Barth's own insistence on creation as external basis of covenant and covenant as internal basis of creation suggests a more complex view. He admits that the Reformation was "a kind of

---

[77]See Donnelly, "Three Disputed Tracts," 44.

[78]Bullinger revised the work during 1562, when he expected to die of the plague. It was Martyr's own final year and he embraced it warmly. See P. Jacobs, "Dir Lehre von der Erwählung in ihrem Zusammenhang mit der Providenzlehre und der Anthropologie im Zweiten Helvetischen Bekenntnis," in J. Staedtke, ed., *Glauben und Bekennen: 400 Jahre Confessio Helvetica Posterior* (Zurich: Zwingli Verlag, 1966) 258–277.

[79]*The Decades of Henry Bullinger,* 4 vols,. ed. Thomas Harding (Cambridge: Cambridge University Press, 1849–1852) 4:3; I have modernized the language slightly.

[80]Barth, *Church Dogmatics* III.3.XI, §48.1: "The Concept of Divine Providence," 5.

rebirth of the Christian belief in providence," and that knowledge of such lordship "can only be compared to the category of axiomatic knowledge." He proceeds to describe the conception of a providential God as an act of faith: "In its substance the Christian belief in providence is Christian faith, i.e. faith in Christ." Comparing the two doctrines he concludes: "We have not to reckon with a parallelism of the two sequences, but a positive connexion between them...."[81] Here is Barth's typical reluctance to specify parallelism, for example between philosophy and theology, while admitting connections. His alternative is the unbalanced dialectic familiar throughout the *Church Dogmatics*.[82] The divine coordination of "creaturely occurrence" is subordinated to the covenant of grace, so that any *analogia entis* is replaced by an *analogia fidei et revelationis*. But is this subordinate relation different in kind from that intended by Zwingli, Bullinger, and Martyr?

The Augustinian-Reformed emphasis on divine willing as the chief divine attribute drives towards the disjunctive syllogism of All or Nothing, placing the weight of argument on the relative role of divine and human choice in the operations of grace and faith.[83] Such a perspective from the isolated will tends to represent reality, as Clifford Geertz has argued, as "a thing of imperatives to be responded to, of wills meeting wills ... a realm of prophets not philosophers."[84] In fact Peter Martyr grasps the problem better than most; discussing responsibility for sin he states: "So it is concerning the will and God: our will does all, and God does all, but one is the first cause and the other secondary" ("Author," §22). This escapes the causal matrix by positing a *con*junctive operation of wills.

The Reformers seized on this moral dimension of their Augustinian heritage to develop a theology of willing and unwilling, of choice and rejection. Perhaps this was an advance over the metaphysical categories of much medieval speculation; perhaps also it was inevitable given the historical

---

[81]Barth, *Church Dogmatics* III.3.XI, §48.14, 16, 39ff.

[82]Barth's paradigm case is articulated in *Schicksal und Idee in der Theologie* (Dortmund lectures, 1929), in *The Way of Theology in Karl Barth,* ed. H. M. Rumscheidt (Allison Park, Pa.: Pickwick, 1986), 25ff., where he explores the possibilities of realism (something is *given*) and idealism (it is given to *us*) for theological epistemology. He rejects both temptations, to settle for either *Wirklichkeit* or *Wahrheit*, the dilemma of heteronomy and autonomy; seealso J. C. McLelland, "Philosophy and Theology—A Family Affair (Karl and Heinrich Barth)" in *Footnotes to a Theology,* ed. H.M. Rumscheidt (Waterloo, Ont.: Wilfrid Laurier University Press, 1974) 30–52.

[83]See J.C. McLelland, *Prometheus Rebound: the Irony of Atheism* (Waterloo, Ont.: Wilfrid Laurier University Press, 1988) 54ff. ("Classical Theism") 281ff. ("The Paradox of Omnipotence").

[84]C. Geertz, "Local Knowledge: Fact and Law in Comparative Perspective" in *Local Knowledge, further essays in interpretive anthropology* (New York: Basic Books, 1983) 167–234, is in fact discussing the Islamic concept of *haqq*; a distinct parallel exists between this and the Reformed stress on the will.

moment of Renaissance and Reform where the foundations of virtue were at risk and the will needed to be secured. In this sense Reformed thought was correct in identifying predestination as a corollary of grace and not a special case of continuing creation, that is, providence. But the price was high, for now nature and grace oppose one another in a battle of wills. It takes considerable logical footwork for Martyr and his colleagues to preserve the human freedom that divine grace requires for its integrity as the essential form of God's love.

Philosophy and Scripture

"We do not follow philosophy, but the word of God," Martyr once wrote, near the end of his life, to John Sturm. For "we listen to the voice of nature so long as it is not against its Author." He refers to the debate on the ubiquity of Christ's body, and insists that the divine power does not "imply a contradiction."[85] This principle reflects Martyr's governing thesis: philosophy and theology are harmonious, but the final arbiter is Scripture. He takes explicit note of the Pauline warning (Col. 2:18) "Beware lest anyone prey on you through philosophy and empty deceit," interpreting it not as referring to "true philosophy" deriving from the knowledge of creation, but philosophy "corrupted by human invention and the bitter disputes of philosophers" ("Philosophy and Theology," §4). Their error lay in failing to respect the natural limits of creaturely knowledge. The Pseudo-Dionysius, for example, cannot be the biblical Areopagite of Acts 17:34, because his writings "contain the doctrine of vain philosophy rather than pure Christian doctrine, and lack all edification."[86] Aristotle passes the Reformed test of edification because he refuses ontological speculation in behalf of practical reason. Where he does contradict Scripture, Martyr stoutly opposes him. "We don't agree with the sayings of Aristotle because of the author but because we consider some of his axioms true, in the same way that Paul quoted certain verses of the poets. But when the Philosopher was mistaken and taught something contrary to religion, we support him least of all and even oppose his errors utterly."[87] For example, Aristotle's teaching that moral virtue is acquired through habitual action is rejected because of Christian teaching that theological virtues are inspired by the Spirit. Martyr's interests in commenting on the *Nicomachean Ethics* "centered rather on defining the areas of agreement and disagreement

---

[85]LC, appendix, 1144 ff. (May 1562, *Ep. Ad amicum quendam ... de causa eucharistia*).
[86]De Missa, IUD 1:33 (LC 4.12) translated in DM 305.
[87]Orothetes in DIAL 14; see also CSV 46.

between the *Ethics* and the Gospel."[88]

In the previous section we noted Martyr's use of philosophy as theology's preparation and auxiliary. He is clear on the difference between knowledge gained by each. The goal of the one is happiness gained through human powers, while the other seeks the image of God. Our first selection, introducing his commentary on the *Nicomachean Ethics*, makes it clear that even Aristotle cannot teach us the remission of sins, faith, and justification, or Christ ("Philosophy and Theology," §6). Above all, our texts illustrate Martyr's thesis of a twofold knowledge of God, one ineffectual and the other salvific, across a range of problems in the intersection of philosophy and theology.[89] The point is made forcefully towards the end of "Resurrection." Throughout this work Martyr has used philosophy as handmaid in exploring the body-soul relationship. He adds: "The teachings of nature are not to be reshaped except when they contradict the word of God.... We follow the Magisterium of the sacred writings..." (§65).

We noted above Peter Martyr's negative response to the Arabic interpreters of Aristotle. A more positive influence is that of the Rabbinic commentators on the Jewish Bible. Only recently are scholars exploring this dimension of Jewish exegesis in the Reformation.[90] When Martyr was doing his exegesis he worked from the Bomberg Rabbinic Bible (1525), which provided him with the traditional (Masoretic) Hebrew text and the Targum, both of which Bomberg printed with the commentaries of medieval Rabbis bordering them. Most frequent are those of Ibn Ezra (1089–1164) and Rashi (1040–1105). David Kimhi (1160?–1235) is as much a favorite of Martyr as of Calvin;[91] at times Martyr also cites Gersonides (1288–1344). This remarkable Jewish influence bears on philological aspects of Martyr's biblical work as well as his interpretation itself. He seeks the "literal" meaning, dealing cautiously with allegory. Of tropes he is careful; as one would expect, they prove crucial in his sacramental theology, in the manner of Zwingli and the Reformed school. In general we might say that the "holy writings" that constitute his authority

---

[88]Jill Kraye, "Moral Philosophy," in CHRP 346.

[89]See Muller, *Post-Reformation Reformed Dogmatics,* 22: "Twofold and Threefold Knowledge of God: The Necessity of Supernatural Theology" 1:173ff.

[90]E.g. L. I. Newman, *Jewish Influence on Christian Reform Movements* (New York: AMS Press, 1966). Dr. Dan Shute, librarian of the Presbyterian College, Montreal, is working on this subject in relation to his translation of Martyr's commentary on Lamentations for the PML. His is the credit for the references here and in footnotes throughout regarding the Bomberg Bible as well as moot points of Hebrew translation.

[91]John Calvin, *Commentary on the Book of Psalms* iv.326: "David Kimhi, the most correct expositor among the rabbis...."

over philosophy include the Hebrew Bible as providing testimony to divine providence over God's people and therefore confidence in his own turbulent age. The first love of this professor of Hebrew is evident in his commentaries on Old Testament books, replete with historical type and moral lesson for his own time, and with scholia affording opportunity to exposit their complex *scopus*.

We can see this style developing, from the early commentary on Lamentations (Strasbourg, 1543) to the final series on Samuel and Kings (Zurich, 1556–1562). The first is cautiously technical, the last are theological, replete with scholia, even though they maintain concern for the Hebrew text, as the "Resurrection" treatise shows. Peter Martyr's role in the story of Rabbinical and Reformed exegesis remains to be told. One item concerns the commentary on Kings, from which the treatise "Resurrection" is taken for this volume. Its editor had to work from Martyr's manuscript and dictated notes.[92] As we will see, Martyr used Hebrew text and Rabbinic commentary aplenty; but it becomes evident that its editor was unsure of his own Hebrew.[93] John Wolf completed the unfinished final seventeen chapters. His pages show his knowledge of Hebrew, for he was a respected exegete among his peers.[94] This suggests that an unknown editor must be held guilty, despite the prestige of the Froschauer publishing firm. Further research is required on that generation of Hebraists and their editors, their mutual influences, and whether Martyr should be placed within the "Rhenish school of exegesis."[95]

Selection of Texts

Any selection of Peter Martyr's writings illustrative of his understanding and use of philosophy poses two sorts of problem. One is that he uses metaphysical and logical categories regularly, chiefly from Aristotle, although Plato and Cicero are cited frequently. This means that a selection of texts is exemplary rather than definitive, except for more explicit treatments of the relation between philosophy and theology or passages in which he deals with philosophers or their opinions. Our first selection is the obvious example, taken from

---

[92]See BIB 82.

[93]See "Resurrection," §§26ff. in the translation that follows.

[94]E.g. letter from Bishop Parkhurst, August 21, 1566: "For the learned commentaries of yourself and Martyr on the two books of Kings, I thank you.... You will do well to publish your discourses upon Deuteronomy, Judges, Ruth, etc..."; letter LII, *Zurich Letters*, 2d series (Cambridge University Press: Parker Society, 1845) 127. Cf. letter LXXX, 199, regarding Wolf's commentaries on Ezra and Esther.

[95]See B. Roussel, "De Strasbourg à Bâle et Zurich: Une école rhénane d'exégèse" in *Revue d'histoire et de phil. rel.* 68 (1988): 19–39; he includes Martyr in his overview; Gerald Hobbs, "Strasbourg et l'école rhénane d'éxègése (1525–1540): 2. l'hébreu, le Judaisme et la théologie,"*Bulletin de la Société de l'Histoire de Protestantisme Français* 135/1 (1989): 42–53.

Martyr's commentary on Aristotle's *Nicomachean Ethics*. Another is the little scholium on dreams, which deals with the same material as two treatises by the Philosopher. Our series of texts attempts to provide both kinds of example, explicitly philosophical and some theological treatments of familiar philosophical topics, such as providence and free will.

A second kind of problem is that most of Martyr's scholia are found in his biblical commentaries: "*loci* or scholia, digressions in the form of systematic tracts which pepper Martyr's commentaries."[96] While there is "no methodological difficulty," as Donnelly puts it, in extracting Martyr's philosophical comments and arranging them systematically, there is the danger that when used out of context—as Masson did when he cast them in the form of *loci communes*—they read like academic reflections rather than spin-offs from theological work. In this they resemble the earlier *observationes* of Martin Bucer's commentaries, no doubt one model for Martyr, along with the *Loci* of Philip Melanchthon and Musculus.[97] For instance, when the topic of providence is removed from the biblical narrative of Genesis, or miracle from that of Judges, each loses Martyr's own scriptural perspective. So there remains a certain ambiguity of the topical method of handling Martyr's work—which the present volume may even reinforce!

Our texts range in nature and length from the brief scholium on the *imago Dei* to the major treatise on resurrection. The eleven selections are grouped into five sections according to subject. Separate introductions discuss textual and historical data, with summary of content. Martyr is unrelenting in maintaining his text without a break. Masson introduced sections for his *Loci Communes*, repeated in all subsequent editions, and these are included. Marginalia (not necessarily by Martyr himself) have been used to supply subheadings for each article, while original pagination is indicated in brackets within the text. Our base texts have been the first edition where possible, or later collated with the *editio princeps*. In Martyr's case we are fortunate in that he produced a limited corpus, and that it has been examined recently by Marvin Anderson, John Patrick Donnelly, and Robert Kingdon and well documented in *A Bibliography of the Works of Peter Martyr Vermigli* (1990). Their expertise makes the preparatory work of the translators of our series a much simpler task, and on their behalf as well as my own I express our gratitude.

---

[96]CSV 60.

[97]See Irena Backus, "Church, Communion and Community in Bucer's Commentary on the Gospel of John," in D. F. Wright, ed., *Martin Bucer: Reforming Church and Community* (Cambridge: Cambridge University Press, 1994) 63. For Musculus (1497–1563) see Muller, *Christ and the Decree*, 47ff.

LOCI COMMVNES

D. PETRI

MARTYRIS VER-

MILII, FLORENTINI, SACRARVM
LITERARVM IN SCHOLA TIGVRINA
Professoris : ex varijs ipsius authoris scriptis, in vnum
librum collecti, & in quatuor Classes distributi.

*QVAM multa ad priorem editionem accesserint, ex admoni-
tione quamprima pagina exhibebit, faci-
lE Lector deprehendet.*

Omnis Scriba doctus ad regnum cælorum, similis est homini patrisfami-
liâs, qui profert ex thesauro suo noua & vetera. MAT. XIII.

LONDINI
Excudebat Thomas Vautrollerius
Typographus. 1583.
CVM PRIVILEGIO REGIÆ MAIESTATIS.

PART ONE

Reason and Revelation

IN PRIMVM,

SECVNDVM, ET INI-
TIVM TERTII LIBRI ETHI-

CORVM ARISTOTELIS AD NICOMA:
CHVM, Clariss. & doctiss. viri D. PETRI MARTY:
ris Vermilij, Florentini, Sacrarum literarum in
Schola Tigurina Professoris, Commentarius doctissimus.

HVIC *accessit Index rerum & verborum locupletissimus.*

TIGVRI

Excudebat Christophorus Froschouerus Iunior,
Mense Augusto, Anno M. D. LXIII.

Title page from the first edition of the
Commentary on Aristotle's Nicomachean Ethics (1563)

About the Translation

Reason and Revelation

PETER MARTYR'S INTRODUCTION to his commentary on Aristotle's *Nicomachean Ethics* provides an excellent statement of his position on the classic question of the relationship of reason and revelation.[1] Martyr's aim is to compare the *Ethics* with the Gospel. While the two systems of morality agree that virtuous habits must issue in action, they differ on whether virtue comes from habit or from Holy Spirit. "Vermigli's purpose in making such comparisons was not merely academic: he wanted to use them in order to demonstrate the superiority of Christian to pagan morality."[2] He begins by distinguishing revealed and acquired knowledge, that is, theology and philosophy, adding the Philosopher's own distinction between theoretical and practical knowledge. The speculative intellect is distinguished from the practical by its different goal. Speculation includes metaphysics, physics, and mathematics, and aims at contemplation. The practical intellect, on the other hand, issues in action.[3] Martyr denies the superiority of theoretical knowledge, arguing that theology is practical because it fulfils theory and serves the human goal of happiness (*eudaimonia*, felicitas). Since this is an introduction to commentary on Aristotle's chief ethical work, it considers the meaning of

---

[1]*In primum, secundum et initium tertii libri Ethicorum Aristotelis ad Nicomachum.... Commentarius doctissimus* (Zurich: C. Froschauer, 1563) 436 pp. The commentary breaks off after III.2. Andreas Hyperius completed the rest of the commentary and published *Meditationes Ethicae sive Aristotelis Ethicorum NIKOMAXEIΩN explicatio per D. Petrum Martyrem Vermilium ... et D. Andream Hyperium* (Lichtenstein: Nicholas Erbenius, 1798). See BIB VIII.1–3.

[2]CHRP 346.

[3]See Aristotle *Metaphysics* VI.1.1026a18 ff.; CSV 88.

"Nicomachean" and "ethics," the origin of moral philosophy among the Greeks, and the best method of analysis. He discusses (§4) the hindrance posed by Paul's warning in Col. 2:8 to beware of philosophy. "True philosophy," however, is acceptable because it derives from "knowledge of created things" and leads to conclusions about "the justice and righteousness that God implanted naturally in human minds." Aristotle remains within these limits and, therefore, does not teach "empty deceit."

Philosophy stands to theology as reason to revelation: the one is good but imperfect, the other complementary and effective in securing virtue and consummating human life. Martyr's *famulus,* Giulio Santerenziano, wrote the preface to the *Ethicorum* in which he sums up the role of philosophy as *ancilla theologiae*: "We join philosophy to its queen, theology, not as equal in place and rank but as a modest and submissive handmaiden." Our first selection sets the stage for Martyr's treatment of a variety of themes intrinsic to the agenda of sixteenth-century philosophy as handled by a biblical scholar. It is ironical, if understandable, that one who was professor of Hebrew and whose biblical commentaries form the bulk of his productivity should be known either as polemicist of sacramental theology or as Reformed scholastic.

*   *   *

THE TOPIC OF NATURAL THEOLOGY is treated, as may be expected, at the opening of Martyr's commentaries on Genesis and Romans. The lecture series on Genesis was offered at Strasbourg during the 1542–1547 sojourn, while Romans was exposited at Oxford during the 1547–1553 period. Like Calvin before him,[4] Martyr seizes on the Pauline passage on general revelation as providing sufficient grounds that no one is excused from believing in a creator. God "continually holds open the book of creation before our eyes"; these symbols convinced natural philosophers of the existence of God (§2). And in "our own nature" we have excellent qualities that provide analogies for higher truth, the theme of "know thyself" familiar in Plato and Augustine (§4). Martyr follows Stoic epistemology in holding that God has implanted notions or *prolepseis* in our minds (§3). He makes a point of rejecting the "idle" gods of Epicurus (§5), in line with his insistence on the superiority of practice over theory in understanding divine grace. As will be seen in later texts, this results in an effective calling and willing and a human response of gratitude and good works.

---

[4]John Calvin, *Comm. in Ep. ad Rom.* (1540); cf. *Inst.* I.5.15.

Briefly put, natural reason yields knowledge that is reliable but incomplete, especially as to divine existence and the moral law. Such general revelation equips us with wisdom and ability in arts and science, sufficient to maintain order, promote good government, and advance civilization.[5] Only another kind of knowledge, revealed and scriptural, suffices for salvation through knowledge of the Gospel. Martyr's exegesis of Rom. 1:19ff. provides a full statement of his position.[6] Working from the Pauline text, Martyr notes that some philosophers argued for divine existence and even certain attributes, although such knowledge is "so vague and weak that it avails only to make men inexcusable." In fact he scolds philosophers, notably Aristotle and Cicero, for not communicating this knowledge to ordinary people. Martyr is explicit and consistent on the Reformed doctrine of *sola scriptura*: "Faith has joined with it the divine inspiration and power of the Holy Spirit so that it apprehends truth effectively." Against Cicero he states, "It is enough for us to be assured of this by Scripture."

---

[5]E.g. "Philosophy and Theology," §§3, 7; cf. Calvin, *Inst.* II.2.12–17. The same point occurs in regard to freedom of the will; on this topic Martyr reiterates the benefits of natural knowledge, e.g. "Many good laws propounded by Lycurgus, Solon, Numa, and others testify sufficiently that human power may do much in these civil affairs, at least in regard to justice." (*De lib. arb.,* ROM 7:25, LC 2.2.3). Cf. "Free Will," §5 below: "Ethnic histories also show that Scipio, Pompey, Caesar, Cato, and Cicero did many things exceptionally well, speaking, commanding, and acting for the well-being of their countries and the cause of public good, though they were then strangers from Christ." In the former passage Martyr adds that Pompey, Cato, and Cicero found their plans going wrong, and in despair attributed it to Fortune.

[6]ROM fols. 409–431 (1:16). A translation by Frank A. James, III, is forthcoming in the PML. See also M. V. Anderson, "Peter Martyr on Romans," *Scottish Journal of Theology* 26 (1973): 401–420, and idem, "Pietro Martire Vermigli on the Scope and Clarity of Scripture," *Theologische Zeitschrift* 30 (March–April, 1974): 86–94; also CSV 51ff. Cf. the parallel in Calvin, *Inst.* II.2.18–21.

Vermigli's Introduction
to the Commentary
on the Nicomachean Ethics

Philosophy and Theology

[THE NATURE OF PHILOSOPHY]

1. [*1*] All our knowledge is either revealed or acquired. In the first case it is Theology, in the other Philosophy.[1] The word *philosophia* is a compound. Some say that wisdom [σοφία] is the knowledge of everything that exists. But since wisdom consists only of certain and firm knowledge, it can by no means include everything, for particulars are unknown—accidents and contingencies cannot be known on account of their impermanence.[2] Others hold that philosophy is the knowledge of things both divine and human. But we find great variety among the divine and the human: celestial bodies, constellations,

---

[1]On the *duplex notitia,* see also ROM 1:19 and 7:15, COR 1:21, PPS Ps. 19(2), and "Visions," §1, p. 138, below. Charles Partee, *Calvin and Classical Philosophy* (Leiden: Brill, 1977)44, provides an excellent survey of the discussion of twofold revelation/knowledge in Calvin's thought.

[2]Cf. Plato *Republic* VI.484–485, 500c.

In primum, secundum et initium tertii libri Ethicorum Aristotelis ad Nicomachum.... Commentarius doctissimus (Zurich: Froschauer, 1563) Praefatio, fols. 1–10. Selected paragraphs appear in LC/CP 1.1.5–11. We include the LC section numbers, with the original foliation in brackets. My translation is based on one kindly supplied by Leszek Wysocki of the Classics Department, McGill University.

elements, minerals, plants, and animals. They ascribe heaven to God because it is eternal, saying that lesser things are unsuitable for human beings, since they are corruptible. But where will they place mathematics?[3] So it seems that philosophy should be defined as a capacity given by God to human minds, developed through effort and exercise, by which all existing things are perceived as surely and logically as possible, to enable us to attain happiness [*felicitas*].

All the kinds of causes are there:[4] the form, that is a capacity; the matter in which it resides, that is the human mind and reason; whatever it apprehends as objects, namely all that exists that is knowable not simply and absolutely but as certainly as possible; agency is also involved there, since God is clearly the author. He endowed our minds with light, and planted the seeds from which the principles of all knowledge arose. That is why Cicero said in book 1 of the *Tusculan Disputations* that "philosophy is the gift and invention of the gods."[5] This is also conceded by Lucretius, even though he was an Epicurean.[6] Since assured knowledge of all things is more desired than expected, and more easily loved than possessed, and since the more we reach toward it the more we are inflamed with it, for this reason it is called "desire of wisdom," *philosophia*. The author of this term was Pythagoras, who had come to Phlius and conversed with its tyrant Leo. Marveling at Pythagoras's genius and eloquence, Leo asked which art or science he professed. Pythagoras would not say that he was "wise," but that he was "devoted to wisdom," that is, a "philosopher."[7]

2. [2] Thus defined, philosophy is divided into active and contemplative, both of which Aristotle investigated as the subject required.[8] They differ inasmuch as contemplation [θεορετικὸν] only observes, while action [πρακτικὸν] does what is known. Therefore, they are distinguished as to their ends: theory rests in the very contemplation of things, since it cannot create them. Like-

---

[3]See p. 9, n. 14 below.

[4]For Aristotle's concept of fourfold causality (formal, material, efficient, final) see *An. Post.* II.11.94a20ff.; *Phys.* II.3.194b16ff.; *Meta.* V.2.1013a24ff.

[5]Cicero *Tuscul. Disp.* I.21.

[6]Lucretius *De Rerum Natura* IV.10ff: "Hear me, illustrious Memmius–a god; / Who first and chief found out that plan of life / Which now is called philosophy...."

[7]Pythagoras of Samos (b. ca. 582 BCE), one of the so-called seven sages of ancient Greece; he left no written record.

[8]Martyr has in mind Aristotle's *NE* book 10: contemplative is superior to active knowledge because it is self-sufficient; the minimum of necessities to survive make do. This allows likeness to God, since "perfect happiness is a contemplative activity" and "the activity of God, which surpasses all others in blessedness, must be contemplative." Cf. Aristotle *Meta.* VI.1.1025b25; *Topics* VI.6; also Jill Kraye, "Aristotelian Ethics," in CHRP 325ff.

wise, practice observes, but only insofar as it may express what it knows in action. Clearly we see two operations in man, for he thinks and then acts. God not only understands himself, being happy and perfect in himself, but also creates by his providence and rules what he has created; even so is human happiness considered to be twofold. The one we may call action [πρακτικὸη], of which Aristotle writes in book 1. The other, far more perfect and admirable, is contemplation, which he discusses in book 10. Thus it is obvious that man may approach to a small degree the likeness of God, if this is accomplished through such double felicity.[9] That is why Plato in his *Phaedo* said that philosophy is "likeness to God, according to human capacity."[10] Nor is the distinction between practice and speculation the same as that between the operations of our will and intellect respectively, as some think.[11] This is not admissible, since the sciences are distinguished by their objects. If anyone examines the matter more diligently, he will see that it must be taken in regard to objects of the understanding. For they have God and nature as their cause, and so would pertain to the speculative genus, since we cannot create them by our own will. Those other things of which we are the cause, which we are able to will and to choose, belong to the practical faculty.

Which of the two is superior remains to be seen. The common and accepted belief is to prefer the speculative to the active, for action is subjected to contemplation, and not the reverse. And no one doubts that whatever is subject to something else is less worthy. They also object that the theoretical genus belongs to action, since we behold nature so that we may love its author, and we seek to perceive God in order to honor him. For this reason some call our theology practical. But those who reason like this are wrong. A science is called practical not because it is accompanied by some action but because the very same object is attained that was known beforehand.[12] When we contemplate nature and heaven, even if worship and the love of God follow, we cannot call such knowledge active, since what we contemplate is not something produced. No one can create heaven and nature, so that all the results of such contemplation are said to happen by accident. Not all who contemplate these things love or cherish God; on the contrary, they are most

[9]Cf. SAM, introduction: prophecy corresponds to theory, history to practice.

[10]Plato, *Theaetetus* [sic] 176B: "The way of escape lies in becoming as like God as possible." Cf.Plato *Tim.* 90D.

[11]e.g. Aristotle *NE* III.2.1112a15ff.

[12]See §5, p. 14, below; Donnelly, CSV 88, remarks, "Martyr disagrees with both Plato and Aristotle and awards pre-eminence to the practical intellect"; cf. Aquinas, ST I.4 resp., "Sacra tamen doctrina comprehendit sub se utramque.... Magis tamen est speculativa quam practica"; Gregory Nazianzen *Orat.* XX.12; PG 35.1080B: "*Praxis* is the ladder to *Theoria.*"

often alienated from him. Thus the works which result from that knowledge, and our theology itself, seek to know God [3] more and more so that in heaven we can look closely at him face to face. Christ our Savior confirmed this belief, saying: "This is eternal life, that they know you the only true God, and Jesus Christ whom you have sent."[13]

This distinction applies not only to philosophy but also to our minds; thus some minds are called practical and others contemplative. But it is not as if there were two powers or faculties of the mind, for they are called so relatively, depending on whether they concern themselves with action or contemplation.

Speculative philosophy is divided into three parts:[14] when things are averse to and quite separate from matter, such as God or intelligence, they constitute metaphysics; when they are so closely connected with matter that they cannot be defined without it, they are accordingly physics; or they take a middle course when they cannot exist without matter—iron or wood, etc.— yet can be defined and understood without it, such as mathematics.

[PRACTICAL PHILOSOPHY]

3. Such matters could be defined further, but I will refrain from doing so, and distinguish practical philosophy by providing the rules that refer to the life and upbringing of one person or many. If an individual is concerned, it is ethics; if more than one is concerned it is important whether they are many or fewer. If fewer, the subject is domestic economy; if more, it is politics. But where do we put the arts? These are included under the third kind of the practical; they pertain to politics, and are not to be excluded from the category of wisdom. For art is "a system of devices exercised for some end which may be useful in anyone's life."[15] Two things are clear in this definition. First, that art is a means that relates to knowledge through which some things are understood with certainty, through trial and experience. Thus it cannot be removed from wisdom. Nor can we doubt that those who invented these arts or excelled in them were called wise by the ancients; accordingly, Bezalel and Oholiab are called wise in Scripture.[16] On the other hand, we say that this

---

[13]John 17:3.
    [14]See Aristotle *Meta.* III.2.997b20, VI.1.1026a18: "There must, then, be three theoretical philosophies, mathematics, physics, and what we may call theology."
    [15]See *NE* II.4.1105a21ff. Cf. Aristotle, *Meta.* A(1).981a.5: "Now art arises when from many notions gained by experience one universal judgment about a class of objects is produced."
    [16]Ex. 36:1. Cf. Josephus *Antiq.* III.8.4: "Bezalel and Oholiab appeared to be the most skilful of the workmen"; Calvin, *Inst.* 2.2.16.

knowledge is practical because its objects are known through practice, and through its devices something is provided and effected which leads to a pleasant life. So ropedancers, jugglers, and others of this sort who provide nothing useful for human life are not masters of an art but should be called impostors and triflers.

The arts may be divided into those which produce some work and those which are fulfilled by their own act. From this it follows how we should judge dialectics, for it should itself be considered among the arts, and it brings about things most useful in life.[17] Hence it is not to be separated from wisdom, [4] since it is the method, the instrument, and the way by which we claim wisdom for ourselves, and the way should not be cut off from its goal. In this manner in his *Prior Academics*, Cicero made distinctions within philosophy, so that in part it concerns life and morals, in part nature and higher subjects, or else the art of discussion, which idea he owes to Plato.[18] Galen does not differ from this opinion. Also, it should be noted that from these authors of philosophy more is gained for the world than from Ceres, who gives us fruit, or Bacchus, from whom we receive wine, or Hercules, who rid the world of monsters. These have to do with aspects of physical life, but philosophy nourishes and instructs the very soul.

In these books of practical philosophy, the first of which we have at hand, namely *Ethics*, stands out from the entire corpus like the book *On Physical Hearing*.[19] In the latter the fundamentals of the natural sciences are described; in the former you will find the first principles of economics and politics. Therefore, we will interpret this book before any other treatise. We may acknowledge that ethics has borrowed something from physics, for example the discussion of the parts of the mind or the rule that the same effects are found in the same minds, and that on these principles it bases many of its premises and draws numerous conclusions. Yet it cannot be considered an auxiliary science, because physics and ethics are quite unlike in kind, and this is not characteristic of auxiliary sciences, where the subject of a superior science must include that of an inferior.

---

[17]Classical dialectics was a discipline preparatory to theoretical philosophy (theology, physics, mathematics) or what today we would call formal logic. Whereas the Middle Platonist Albinus harmonized Plato and Aristotle, in his *On Dialectic*, Plotinus "is content to summarize Plato's statements about *dialektikē* and to distinguish it sharply from Aristotelian logic"; see CHGM 68, 235. Aristotle's methodological propaedeutic to his theoretical works was regarded by his school as the general instrument (*organon*) for all science; in modern terms the Organon includes his logical works.

[18]Plato *Academica I*, 5; cf. Plato, *Soph*. 253.

[19]The *De Audibilis* is now ascribed to Strato (d. 269 BCE).

Ethics takes it name from *to ethos* [ἀπὸ τὴ ἤθους], that is, "custom." And *ethos* comes from the verb "to be accustomed" [ἐθίζω] with "epsilon" changed into "eta"; for the only way for us to acquire morals and good habits is by custom.[20] That whole book is concerned, moreover, with the human: how one becomes endowed with virtues, and attains the happiness which may be acquired in this life. Hence Plato in the *Theaetetus* called this part of philosophy "the greatest harmony"[21]—not as if it dealt with sounds, voices, or lyres, but because it is concerned with the harmony of the parts of the mind with reason. It is not difficult to see what method of teaching Aristotle uses. He distinguishes and defines, and uses almost every kind of argument. Sometimes he uses examples, sometimes induction, occasionally enthymemes, at times that perfect form of reasoning called syllogism, and even demonstrative syllogism, although rarely, since the nature of morals is shaky and uncertain.[22] Frequently he uses comparisons and sometimes explanations, but these "a posteriori" and almost never or very rarely "a priori," as causes.

The discoverers of this part of philosophy are said to have been Pythagoras, Socrates, and Plato, while all the philosophers of earlier times— Parmenides, Melissus, Anaxagoras, Democritus, Empedocles, and Hippocrates—were wholly preoccupied with the examination of nature. Socrates was the first to have focused in earnest on establishing the principles of the moral life. Before him, the seven Greek sages at times spoke reasonably about [5] what constitutes the good life—Solon, Pittacus, and others—but what they had to say were merely aphorisms; even though elegant and famous, they contained nothing elaborate or complete. After Plato came Aristotle, a man of singular genius, who subjected all the relevant material to methodical analysis and arranged it with the greatest accuracy. He was born seven years after Rome had recovered from the Gauls. His place of birth was Stagyra in Thrace, a village otherwise obscure except that he was its citizen. His father was Nicomachus, by profession a physician whom King Amyntas, the father of Philip, esteemed on account of that profession. For a time, Aristotle was a pupil of Socrates, and of Plato for a full twenty years.[23] Alexander of Macedon was educated as Aristotle's pupil; he used to say that he owed

---

[20]Aristotle, *NE* II.1.1103a16 ff.: "moral virtue comes about as a result of habit, whence also its name *ethikē* is one that is formed by a slight variation from the word *ethos*."

[21]Perhaps *Phaedo* 93–94 on the soul as giver of harmony.

[22]Aristotle analyzes these types in his two *Analytica*. Discussing "logical and probable reasons," Martyr, ROM 8:38, notes: "Probable arguments cannot by themselves persuade completely, but when joined to firm and demonstrative reasons make something more evident"; cf. "Reformed Scholasticism," p. xxvi, above.

[23]Aristotle (384–322 BCE) spent twenty years (368/7–348/7) in association with Plato's academy in Athens. He was never a pupil of Socrates (d. 399).

more to Aristotle than to King Philip his own father, for Philip merely made him live, whereas Aristotle made him live well and happily. In thanks to his teacher, he restored Stagyra, which Philip had destroyed, and raised it to better political shape than it had before it was overthrown. The school of Peripatetics sprang from Aristotle: it had fewer errors than any other school, and flourishes to this day.[24]

[The Nicomachean Ethics]

This *Ethics* is called Nicomachean because it was dedicated to Nicomachus, the author's son, just as was Cicero's book *De Officiis*. Both Aristotle and Cicero were great writers, yet neither of their sons matched the parent in teaching and fame. I know that there were several people who thought that Aristotle's son Nicomachus wrote these books, since he was the first to receive the teaching from his father, and afterwards collected the writings and put them in one volume. Suidas holds that Nicomachus wrote ten books on morals, but whether these are one and the same is most doubtful. Cicero also (in book 5 of the *De Finibus*) seems to assume that Nicomachus composed these books. The *Magna Moralia* are extant, and so is what is called the *Eudemean Ethics*, but they are not to be compared with this treatise.[25]

The position of this moral teaching in relation to other sciences was established by the ancients so that someone who had already gone through grammar, rhetoric, and dialectics would then turn to moral subjects. For if the mind is inflamed with desire and overwhelmed by vice, it is unsuitable for mathematics or for divine and human contemplation, since such matters require a calm and peaceful mind. Among these moral subjects, the first place is surely held by ethics, then economics, and finally politics. I see this order as circular. Through ethics, those who are its students will, one by one, become good. If they prove upright, they will raise good families; if the families are properly established, they will in turn create [6] good republics. And in good republics, both law and administration will aim at nothing less than each

---

[24]Aristotle taught in an Athenian home that featured a covered walking place (*peripatos*), hence the school name Peripatetic. The Renaissance revival of Aristotelianism was marked at Padua, where Martyr studied under Pomponazzi's successor, Genua. See p. xxii above.

[25]Suidas, *Lexicon*, c. 950. Modern opinion held that Nicomachus probably edited his own course of ethics, and Aristotle's friend Eudemus another, called Eudemian; see W. D. Ross, *Aristotle* (London: Methuen, 1923) 14. Confusion arose because the Nicomachean and the Eudemian ethics share three books, probably originally from the former. The *Magna Moralia* is a later Peripatetic compilation based on the Eudemian. Anthony Kenny, *The Aristotelian Ethics: A Study of the Relationship between the Eudemian and Nicomachean Ethics of Aristotle* (Oxford: Clarendon, 1978), argues that Aristotle's mature moral theory appears in the *Eudemian* and not the *Nicomachean Ethics*.

becoming a good citizen, for they have eyes for the spirit as well as the body, and will take care that citizens live according to virtue.[26]

Therefore, as far as our method of analysis is concerned, let us accept the following outline of these ten books. First, the goal of human life is discussed, being defined in book 1, where it is taught that happiness is the carrying out of perfect virtue.[27] This requires a consideration of the nature of virtue, which occurs in book 2, in which the virtues are first dealt with—not yet those of the intellect, but those which pertain to moderate desires; it is then asserted that virtue is the state between excess and defect.[28] In book 3, the principles of virtue are taught: voluntary, involuntary, choice, and that sort of thing.[29] A detailed discussion of particular virtues begins specifically with courage, and to this matter all of books 4 and 5 are devoted. After that, in book 6, Aristotle examines those capacities which enrich the reason or the intellect, that is, prudence, industry, skill, and many others of this order. Book 7 is about the virtue of heroism, which far surpasses those already mentioned, and about temperance and intemperance, neither of which truly belongs to the category of virtue or vice. Books 8 and 9 treat of friendship. Book 10 contains an elaborate discussion of pleasure. The book ends with a discourse on true and absolute happiness, which is based on contemplation, especially of things divine. For my part, I will apply the following reasoning and form of interpretation. First, I will analyze the text of Aristotle; second, I will explain the scope and proposition of a chosen passage, with its proof; third, I will study its meaning and comment on terms which may require exegesis; fourth, I will expose to view any doubts that have arisen; and last, I will note and discuss those passages which agree or disagree with Scripture.

[A WARNING FROM SAINT PAUL]

4. Now I can easily proceed to the exposition of Aristotle, except that a certain hindrance must first be removed. It consists of what Paul said in Colossians 2: "Beware lest anyone prey on you through philosophy."[30] Truly, with

---

[26]See Aristotle *Pol.* 1.2ff. for these distinctions. Aquinas *Comm. ad loc.*, followed Eustratius in describing the tripartite division according to subject matter, with the names *monastica, oeconomica,* and *politica* (cited in CHRP 304).

[27]NE I.8.1098b30. Ευδαιμονία means happiness or well-being; Martyr translates it by "foelicitas."

[28]NE I.6.1106b25, *affectus moderandos*: Aristotle's doctrine of *metriopatheia* tempered the Stoic *apatheia*. Cf. ROM 1:24, "The Peripatetics judged that the wise man should not be completely without affections; they allowed those that were moderate."

[29]Martyr's own commentary breaks off at the beginning of book 3.

[30]Col. 2:8.

such words he seems to frighten Christians away from the study of philosophy, but I am sure that if you properly grasp the meaning of the Apostle's statement you will not be disturbed. Since true philosophy derives from the knowledge of created things, and from these propositions reaches many conclusions about the justice and righteousness that God implanted naturally in human minds, it cannot therefore rightly be criticized: for it is the work of God, and could not be enjoyed by us without his special contribution.[31] What Paul censured is that philosophy corrupted by human invention and by the bitter disputes of philosophers. If they had remained within limits and discussed only what creaturely knowledge has revealed about God and nature by the most certain reasoning, they would not have strayed from the truth. [7] Hence the Apostle says: "By this philosophy," i.e. "empty deceit" by epexegesis;[32] then he adds: "which has its origin in human tradition and is inspired by cosmic forces." That the universe is eternal was taught by human beings, not by lower creatures. Nature did not show the universe to be composed of the random conjunction of atoms; this was conceived by empty speculation. Stoic fate and impassibility [ἀπάθεια], the perpetual doubt of the Academics, the motionless and idle deities of the Epicureans—who would question that such ideas are "empty deceit?" They dreamed of the community of property, of wives openly traded, of pleasure as the highest good, and of gods worshipped in vulgar ways; yet they did not learn such things by any natural illumination or by practical principles known in themselves by sure reasoning. Surely these things are poisons and corruptions by which the devil, through evil men, perverts that gift of God, philosophy. This polluted and spoiled philosophy is what Paul wishes to avoid.

[THE BIBLICAL CRITERION]

5. Now we must see how what we have so far discussed agrees with Holy Scripture. There also we have active and contemplative knowledge. The things in which we believe and which are contained in the articles of faith pertain to contemplation [θεωρητικὸν] since we perceive them but do not create them, and although they are not included within knowledge they are nonetheless understood. What is contained in the laws, deliberations. and exhortations should be referred to practical knowledge. So far these matters agree, yet they also differ, for in philosophy action [πρακτικὸν] precedes contemplation

---

[31]See "Nature and Grace," p. 18 ff., below.
[32]per ἐπεξηγήσις: Martyr mixes Latin and Greek to render Col. 2:8: "Philosophy and empty deceit … according to the elemental spirits of the universe."

[θεωρητικòν] because, as it is said, we can contemplate neither God nor nature by human powers unless our emotions are first at rest.[33] But in Scripture speculation comes first, since we must first believe and be justified through faith.[34] Afterwards, good works follow, which occur more abundantly the more frequently we are renewed by the Holy Spirit. That is what Paul shows in his letters: for first he deals with doctrines, only afterwards coming to moral instruction and principles for living. So also were the children of Israel first gathered in Egypt under the faith of one God the Deliverer: afterwards in the desert, they received laws that refer to practical knowledge. The same order was kept in the Decalogue. First it is said, "I am the Lord your God," which belongs to faith or theoretical knowledge. Afterwards there follow precepts that look to the works commanded by God. The cause of this difference is that human contemplation is gained by study and diligent reflection; therefore, moderation of emotion is required. But what we believe is received by the inspiration of God and so there is no need of those preparations. According to human reason, men should first do righteous deeds before there is justification. But the order of divine sanctification is established far otherwise; first we believe, and afterwards are justified, then [*8*] the powers of our minds are restored by the Spirit and by grace, and finally just and honest deeds follow.

6. The goal of philosophy is that we reach that beatitude or happiness which can be acquired in this life by human powers, while the goal of Christian devotion is that the image in which we are created in righteousness and holiness of truth be renewed in us, so that we grow daily in the knowledge of God until we are led to see him as he is, with face uncovered. From these *Ethics* we will not learn about the remission of sins, about fear and faith towards God, nor justification through faith, nor yet about Christ and similar things. Such matters are brought to light by God's will; they cannot be produced by natural knowledge from anything created. We do not deny that it often happens that these *Ethics* commend the same things as God commands in Holy Scripture. In such cases the topic is the same but not its form, properties, and principles; for here the rationale is different, as are the qualities and

---

[33]Aristotle *NE* X.7–8: Contemplation reduces bodily necessities to a minimum, as close as possible to the impassive deity whose likeness is sought.

[34]Aristotle *NE* X.7.1177a27ff., sees self-sufficiency and leisure as requirements for "the contemplative activity." For Augustine, on the other hand, contemplation of divine truth constitutes human blessedness: "The highest good is God; but God is the truth, and one enjoys truth by beholding it and resting in its contemplation"; for Aquinas, "the *verum* toward which the intellect aims is higher in rank than the *bonum* toward which the will strives"; see W. Windelband, *A History of Philosophy* (N.Y.: Harper & Bros., 1958) 1:286, 331. Cf. ST 2a2ae.8.3: intellectus est donum speculativus ... contemplatio Dei.

foundation, just as water from rain and from a spring is the same in substance while its powers, properties, and essentials are far different. One comes from the heat of heaven and the clouds and cold of the middle regions of the air, while the other is drawn through the subterranean channels of the earth and from the sea, and comes out sweet through filtering, or else by converting air to water from the cold of the place where the spring arises. Thus what Christians do occurs by the impulse of the Spirit of God, for those who act according to the Spirit are sons of God. What philosophers do about ethics happens under the guidance of human reason. They are urged to action according to what they judge to be honest and correct; but Christians because God judges so. The former think that they improve and perfect themselves if they act in this way; the latter think that if they act it is because one should be obedient to the divine. The former believe in themselves, the latter in God and the words of the law that he himself gave. The former labor from self-love [φιλαυτία] while the latter are driven by the love of the one God. From these numerous differences it happens that substantially the very same thing may be pleasing to God or damned by his judgment. Let this suffice concerning these differences and agreements between divine Scripture on the one hand and human philosophy on the other.

7. Let us return to the point from which we digressed, namely whether this discipline contradicts piety. I say that it is more against it than is astrology or the nautical or military arts, or else fishing and hunting, also the knowledge of human law which everyone understands as necessary for public administration. Jurisprudence forms its own laws and institutions out of propositions concerning the justice and goodness innate in our minds; moral philosophers analyze the same propositions and probe them minutely, so that they themselves might know them thoroughly, and also transmit them to others with great clarity. Thus among the Greeks wisdom is called *sophia* as if it meant "clarity" [σαφεία] and "wise" is *sophos* as if it meant "clear" [σαφής], no doubt because it clarifies its subject matter and makes it obvious. Therefore, those learned in the law may easily regard [9] their own science as part of philosophy, even if they judge virtue, honesty, and justice less severely in their legislation than philosophers do in their debates. For example, philosophy detests ingratitude in any human condition, but the laws do not punish it unless committed by children against parents, or by freedmen against their patrons. Human laws do not compel anyone to give his goods to the needy, but philosophy commends liberality and generosity towards all. What more should be said? In praise of this kind of philosophy Cicero exclaimed in *Tusculanus* 5: "O philosophy, guide of life, O explorer of virtue and expeller of vice! Without

you what would have become of me and even of human life itself? You have given birth to cities, you have called scattered human beings into the bond of social life, you have united them first of all in common dwellings, then in marriage, then in the ties of common literature and speech (you have discovered law) you have been the teacher of morality and order," etc.[35] Everyone acknowledges how splendid it is to know the power of herbs, rocks, metals, and medicines, nor do we deny this in the least. But does it not follow from all this that here is a worthy faculty by which human acts, choices, arts, methods, skills, virtues, and vices are to be perceived? What could be more noble than to know oneself? This we know in the first place through philosophy. We should also keep in mind what Plato said, that it may easily happen that ardent love for virtue is aroused in us if now and then its likeness meets our eyes.[36] On the other hand, the chief cause of our vices is that we could never see virtue with our own eyes.

The pleasure derived from this science is not small, to know within what bounds the illumination that nature sheds should confine itself, and how far it may extend itself in its own right. Moreover, the Christian religion is spurred by the knowledge of pagan ethics, for we understand through comparison how far those things taught in Scripture surpass philosophy. It is a common saying that when opposites are compared with one another they become clearer. Errors cannot be easily avoided unless they are first understood. Therefore, whoever knows both faculties will more easily avoid the mistakes of human philosophy, especially when properly demonstrated.[37]

[35]Cicero *Tuscul. Disp.* 2.5.2.

[36]Plato *Symp.* 210–211.

[37]The introduction concludes with a paragraph that provides "a shorter division of Aristotle's treatise," and features the governing concept of the end, τέλος.

Commentaries on Romans 1 and 1 Samuel 5

Nature and Grace

[NATURAL KNOWLEDGE OF GOD]

1. [30]*For what is known of God is manifest among them.*[1] The Greek reads τὸ γνωστὸν τοῦ Θεοῦ as if to say, "What may be known [cognobile] of God." This is said because there are many divine mysteries that we cannot reach naturally, such as that God would justify us freely, forgive our sins through Christ crucified, and restore these very bodies of ours to eternal happiness. These and the like are not taught us by nature. Therefore, Paul says "What can be known of God is made manifest in them." Here he declares what kind of truth it is that they withheld in unrighteousness; it was the knowledge of things divine that they attained by a natural light. Paul reduces all their knowledge to two principal points: the everlasting power of God, and his divinity.

They knew that God is most mighty by the very fabric of this world. They also knew by the beauty, appearance, and variety of things that such great power was ordered by the highest providence and wisdom. Moreover, the suitability and utility of created things taught them the divine majesty, which consists chiefly in acting well towards all. These are the gifts which God

---

[1]Rom. 1:19, the biblical text on which Martyr is commenting.

The topic *De Naturale Cognitione Dei* in Masson's LC I.2 is taken from two biblical commentaries. He used the commentary on Rom. 1:19, *In Epistolam S. Pauli Apostoli ad Romanos* (Basel: P. Perna, 1558) fols. 30–33 for §§1–6, and the commentary on Rom. 1:18, fols. 29–30 for §§7–9. Then follows material from 1 Sam. 5:12, from *In Duos libros Samuelis Prophetae* (Zurich: C. Froschauer, 1564) fols. 36v–36r for §§10–11.

bestowed on the heathen; but they abused the gifts of God. Thus the similitude used by Chrysostom fits them beautifully.[2] He speaks as follows: suppose a king gives a great sum of money to his servant to furnish his household and to enhance his splendor, so that his wealth and honor should be all the more evident. Suppose the worthless servant spends it all on pimps and harlots; does it not seem just and proper that this servant be punished? Just so did the wise among the heathen conduct themselves. When they received from God the clearest knowledge of things by which they should have worshipped and adored him, they turned it into the worship of rocks and wood and images. Therefore, the wrath of God was fierce against them with good reason.

[WHAT PHILOSOPHERS SAY]

2. By stating "It was manifest in them," and not "it was manifest in all," Scripture distinguishes wise men and philosophers from the crude and ignorant masses. Everything was not known to all alike; but it happened through the fault of these philosophers: they should have proclaimed what they knew to the people openly and forcefully. They failed to do what prophets and apostles did, but with proud mind kept these matters to themselves and in a sense hid them lest they be understood by all. In this regard the letter of Aristotle to Alexander [the Great] is much spoken of, in which he says that his *Physics* were produced [edita] by him as if they were not. For he seems to write as if to make things obscure by intention, lest they be understood by others.[3] Moreover, by their reasoning they defiled what they knew to be pure. When they understood that there is one God and concluded that he should be worshipped, they proceeded to reason among themselves as follows: Since it is improper for common folk to worship the highest divinity that is present everywhere (for they cannot apprehend it), it is better to divide it and assign it to images, heavenly signs, and other creatures. They also acknowledged that the nature of God is separate from all corporeal matter, that is, it is spirit and therefore to be worshipped in mind and spirit. But thinking the masses so crude when compared to themselves that they could not handle this, they introduced external rites and ceremonies devised from their own heads, by which those who performed them might think they had fulfilled divine

---

[2]Chrysostom, *Comm. in Ep. ad Rom., Hom.* III.2 (Rom. 1:19) (PG 60.412).

[3]Aristotle's works were divided into exoterica and esoterica. The former are the scientific (demonstrable) works, the latter are speculations communicated privately to disciples. The implication of secrecy has now been dropped; see *Encyclopedia of Philosophy* (1967): 1:152. Martyr has the same reference to Aristotle's method of private oral communication to disciples (*akroamatika*) in a letter to John Jewel, 15 August 1561; see PMRE 520–529.

service. So by their feeble reasons they corrupted what they recognized from creation in its purity, nor were they faithful to the truth that they knew.

They should rather have submitted to the highest power which they acknowledged, allowing themselves to be governed by the providence of God, trusting him in adversity. They did not do so, and to their shame fell into despair. In his later years Cicero cried out in a letter to Octavius: O that I had never been wise! And in his books *On the Nature of the Gods* he introduces Cotta, a high priest, who says that he wishes he could prove to himself the truth of the existence of the gods.[4] [*31*] Disbelieving those things of God which they knew by nature, they were not only evil toward him but also harmful toward their neighbors. Sometimes the more famous philosophers they were, the more infamous life they led. As the poet accuses them: "Careful the life they feign, but follow Bacchus vain."[5] Therefore, God's wrath raged against them. A schoolmaster cannot tolerate the negligence of a pupil he is diligently teaching who is meanwhile thinking and doing other things; even so does God behave toward us. For he continually holds open the book of creation before our eyes; he is always illuminating and calling us; but we regularly turn our minds away from his teaching, and are busy elsewhere. Therefore, God will cast us out as unworthy pupils, nor will he endure so great an injury with impunity.

[DIVINE REVELATION]

3. *For God has revealed to them*; we gather from this that all truth comes from God, for it does not spring from us. But there are two opinions about how it comes from God. Some say that it is because God has made those things by which we can perceive these truths. But others (whom I prefer) hold that God has planted *prolepseis* [προλήψεις] in our minds, that is, anticipations and notions through which we are led to conceive noble and exalted opinions about the divine nature.[6] These ideas of God naturally engrafted in us are daily confirmed and refined by the observation of created things. Others

---

[4]Cicero *Ep. ad Iul. Caes. Octavium*; *De Natura Deorum* I.21–22. Cotta desires "to have the existence of the Gods, which is the principal point in debate, not only fixed in opinion, but proved to a demonstration."

[5] Juvenal, *Sat.* 2:3. Here we use Juvenal, *Satirae* from *Juvenal and Persius*, trans. G. G. Ramsay, rev. ed., Loeb Classical Library (Cambridge: Harvard University Press, 1965).

[6]Stoic epistemology turned on a term of Epicurus' in which "repeated experiences preserved by memory give rise to 'anticipations' (*prolepseis*), which are equivalent to general notions or concepts"; *Encyclopedia of Philosophy* (1967): 3:3. Cicero *De Nat. Deorum* I.16, states: "An antecedent conception of the fact in the mind, without which nothing can be understood, inquired after, or discoursed on … what nation, what people are there who have not, without any learning, a natural idea, or pre-notion of a Deity?"

say, proudly and wickedly, that they have learned these truths from Aristotle or from Plato, giving no thanks whatever to God for them. To be sure, these men were agents and instruments, but not authors. They speak much as an Israelite might, saying that he knew the truths of the law not through God but through Moses who was only God's mediator and messenger, relating to the people matters whose author was God. It should be noted that although God is a nature so separated from matter that he cannot be perceived by the senses, yet he regularly declares himself by symbols and what may be called sensible words. These signs which have declared God to us from the beginning are themselves creatures; when natural philosophers [Physici] studied them, they were led to knowledge of God on account of the wonderful properties and qualities of nature. Knowing the series of causes and their relation to effects, and clearly understanding that it is not proper to posit an infinite progression, they reasoned that they must arrive at some highest being, and so concluded that there is a God. Plato, Aristotle, and Galen have set forth these matters exceedingly well.[7]

We must not neglect the sacred writings: they also have described the same path to us. Christ sends us to the birds of the air, to the lilies and grass of the field, that we might acknowledge the singular providence of God in preserving those things which he created. Solomon commends the ant to us for imitation on account of his foresight, by which he prepares in the summer what he will need in winter. Isaiah says that the donkey knew the manger of its lord, and the ox his master, but Israel knew not its lord.[8] Thus it is clear that we may be taught many things by creatures. David composed a Psalm in which he states the same thing: "The heavens declare the glory of God."[9] Among other books of Holy Scripture which abound in this matter is the dialogue of the book of Job. For the speakers he introduces were heathen, so that the subject is handled by natural reasons alone. Much is spoken about the revolutions of heaven, about stars, the earth, the sea, light, winds, rain, thunder, lightning, snow, and ice; also of animals such as lions, deer, horses, and

---

[7]In this paragraph Martyr follows the cosmological argument, an induction from the contingency of worldly phenomena to God, stated classically in the first of Aquinas' five ways, ST Ia.2.46; cf. Plato *Laws* X; Aristotle *Phys.* 261a30, and *Meta.* XII.6.1071b4ff. Galen (129–ca. 199) accepted much of Plato's anthropology and Aristotle's epistemology. Martyr combines two concepts in the natural knowledge of God, innate notions or *prolepseis* and created effects that entail a transcendent Creator. Cf. Calvin, *Inst.* I.5.4: "proofs of his divinity" and "the seeds of divinity sown in the nature of man."

[8]Prov. 6:6; Isa. 1:3.

[9]Ps. 19:1.

Behemoth which many think to be the elephant, and finally of Leviathan the greatest beast of the sea.

4. All these matters are handled there so as to proclaim to us the eternal power and divinity of God. Among other things which especially reveal God to us is our own nature. For we are made according to his image and likeness, so that we resemble him most of all, especially in regard to the soul, where the foresight of things to come is reflected—justice, wisdom, and many other of the noblest qualities; also the knowledge of what is right and honest, and what wrong and unclean. Seeing that humanity and the soul did not arise by themselves but depend on God, it follows that we should by no means deny the very thing we owe to God himself, but yield it to him as its chief and principal author. Thus we may conclude that God foresees everything that is done, and is a just judge of our deeds, to whom honest things are as pleasing as evil are displeasing. I know that Cicero in his third book, *On the Nature of the Gods,* labors to overthrow this argument, by which we would prove that the things we consider most excellent in us must not be denied to God.[10] But let him argue whatever he wants; it is enough for us to be assured of this by Scripture. It is written in Psalm 94: "He who planted the ear, shall he not hear? Or he who formed the eye, shall he not see?"[11] We learn from this not to withhold from [32] the divine nature whatever is perfect and absolute in us. Moreover we see that our consciences naturally detest the evil we have done, and on the contrary enjoy and applaud our good deeds. Since this is engrafted in us by nature, we are taught the divine judgment to come, a condemnation which so terrifies our mind that sometimes it courts madness; on the other side, it rejoices through hope of a judgment of acceptance and reward from that tribunal. We could also reason from many other such matters, but they may be easily gathered from the writings of both Scripture and philosophers. Therefore, I will add nothing more; I count it sufficient to have said that nothing may be found in the world so abject or lowly that it gives no witness to God. The poet said, "All things begin and end in Jove."[12] So long as it endures, whatever is in the world has the power of God hidden under it. If this is discovered through inquiry and knowledge of nature, God will be revealed to us.

[10]Cicero *De Natura Deorum* III.15.
[11]Ps. 94:9.
[12]Vergil *Ecl.* 3.60: *Iovis omnia plena.*

[CONTRARY ARGUMENTS]

5. Other places of Scripture seem to disagree with this saying of the Apostle's, denying knowledge of God to the wicked. We read in the Psalms: "The fool has said in his heart, there is no God"; we also have: "None on earth understand, or seeks God."[13] Not to make a lengthy recital, it says in the first chapter of Isaiah: "Israel has not known me."[14] But this difference may be reconciled as follows. Convinced by created things, as Paul says, the wicked confess that there is a God, but afterwards affirm such things about his nature and properties that it may well be inferred that God does not exist. Epicurus for instance said that there are gods, but removed them from all activity, care, and providence, so that he ascribed to them a completely idle happiness.[15] When it is said that there is a God but that he has no concern for human affairs, does not punish or hear those who call upon him and so on, it appears that they allowed a god in name only. Therefore, Scripture denies that they knew God. For the true God is not such as they imagine him to be; so far as receiving help or enjoying the divine assistance are concerned, for them he was just as if he were not, since they neither called upon him nor looked for aid or support from him. Moreover, some of them were so evil that they tried to convince themselves that God does not exist. They could not succeed, since their mind contradicted them and their conscience strove against them; even so, Scripture judges them by their efforts and says they did not know God.

Finally, we should understand that knowledge of God is of two kinds.[16] One is effectual, by which we are so changed that we try to express what we know in works; Scripture ascribes this knowledge of God to the faithful alone. The other is frigid, by which we do not become better people. For we do not show through our works that we know what in fact we are doing. Paul speaks of this kind of knowledge when he says: "Since they did not see fit to acknowledge God," etc. And Christ will say to many who boast of his gifts and knowledge, "I do not know you."[17] Since knowing God in this way brings no results, Scripture rejects it so much that not once does it give it the name of divine knowledge, but insists that God does not know the wicked because this is the way they are.[18]

---

[13]Pss. 10:4, 14:1–2.

[14]Isa. 1:3.

[15]The gods of Epicurus "do nothing. They are embarrassed with no business; nor do they perform any work. ... nothing can be happy that is not at ease"; Cicero, *De Natura Deorum* I.19.

[16]On the *duplex notitia* see p. 6, n. 1, above.

[17]Rom. 1:28; Matt. 7:23.

[18]In the commentary the new paragraph begins here; the CP follows, numbering it 8. The LC begins para. 6 with "What Paul says...."

6. *Therefore, they are without excuse*. The Greek is εἰς τὸ εἶναι αὐτοὺς ἀναπολογήτους. God did not reveal such natural knowledge for this purpose alone, but it follows from our own fault. What Paul says here seems to disagree with what is often expressed when we discuss works and grace. If it is true that by our own strength and free will we cannot even fulfil the law which we know, how will such people be said to be inexcusable? If what we say is true, they might easily be excused, because they knew this law by a natural light but lacked the strength to fulfil what they knew; therefore, they do not seem inexcusable. But Paul deals only with the excuse that could be made from ignorance. The weakness that is introduced now would not have been acknowledged by the heathen, for they ascribed everything to free will. Therefore, they would not have said they were lacking in strength; all that remained to excuse them was ignorance. Paul now cuts off this defense from them, leaving them branded inexcusable by their own judgment. To admit that they were too weak while knowing what they should do would have proved Paul's point. Knowledge of natural law did not make them better, because even if the law is known it cannot change us nor give us strength to act rightly; therefore, we must run to Christ. Because he knew that the Gentiles did not seek that excuse, he rejected what he saw as an obvious objection, that is, ignorance.

Nor can we admit the other excuse, from lack of power. For such weakness came by our own fault, that is through sin. Besides, they could not have been excusable [33] since they did not do even the little that lay within their power, namely the outward acts of which they were aware. For we are not so destitute of strength through sin that we cannot do much by outward works; in this respect they showed themselves worst of all. We conclude that they were without any excuse. Nor could they object that they were forced to act sinfully against their wills. Therefore, since they did what was evil both knowingly and willingly, they had no excuse. We should not think that God gave them this excellent natural knowledge in order to render them without excuse. That arose through their own fault, although divine providence made full use of their depravity to illustrate God's glory and righteousness. This much they profited from their sins, that the very doctrine and knowledge which they attained brought them to judgment and condemnation. Thus it follows that we should not be deterred from teaching even though we see that people become no better, since by that doctrine the very things happen that God ordains for us. At the least this benefit occurs: if men are not converted by God they will be condemned by their own judgment and witness. What God wills above all appears to be so that when he condemns and punishes it will be just.

The teaching which the traitor Judas received from Christ was useful to him at the end when he condemned himself, saying: "I have sinned in betraying innocent blood."[19] The wicked are driven so far that they are finally condemned by their own sentence. Those who should have benefited from the teaching are deeply harmed by it, as we read in the prophet Isaiah, chapter 6, when it is said: "Make the heart of this people blind, dull their ears, and shut their eyes, lest they should see, hear and understand, and be converted, and I should heal them." Likewise the heart of Pharaoh was more and more hardened by the word of Moses.[20]

7.[21] The reason why they are without excuse is declared in these words: *Who withhold the truth in unrighteousness.*[22] [29] They attained enough truth to understand how to act toward God and their neighbors; yet they held this truth down in unrighteousness. The Hebrews did the same in regard to the truth God revealed to them through the law. Since both they and the others have been severely punished, what should those who profess to be Christian hope for, who keep such a great light of the Gospel to themselves, without bearing fruit? Surely they will become the most miserable of all. This teaches us that those who boast of Christ and yet live wickedly, in the end surpass all others however evil, in corruption and vileness. The truth is in a sense held captive within those who understand it but do not express it in deed and in life. It is bound and tied with chains of evil lusts which break out of the lower parts of our spirit, darkening the mind and enclosing familiar truth in a dim prison. God illuminates it in our minds, but through evil lusts it is quite overshadowed. We must not think, as Chrysostom warns us, that it can experience any change in itself (for truth by its nature is unchangeable), but whatever disturbance does occur harms our own mind and soul.[23] In two words Paul handles what Aristotle in his *Ethics* treats at length when he discusses the unstable person,[24] asking how the rash individual descends to vices even though he has a right opinion in his mind. And he answers that this happens because he is too much moved by a particular good that is presented to the senses. Its weight oppresses even the better part, so that he yields to desires and does not do his duty of reflecting effectively on the truth which he had earlier come to

---

[19]Matt. 27:4.

[20]Isa. 6:10; Ex. 7:13.

[21]CP §9.

[22]Rom. 1:18. At this point the LC topic reverts to earlier commentary, fols. 29–30.

[23]Chrysostom *Hom. in Rom.* III.1 (on Rom. 1:18): Error varius, veritas una (PG 60.412).

[24]Aristotle *De Incontinente*, *NE* VII, esp. 3. 1146bff. Aristotle's question is "action with and without knowledge" (1147b18).

know. The Poet affirms of Medea, "I see the better and approve; I follow what is worse."[25]

Paul teaches us all this when he says: "The wicked hold down the truth of God in unrighteousness." The truth strives as much as it can to break forth into action, but is hindered by lust. At the beginning of the *Ethics* it is written: the better part of the soul always encourages and exhorts to better things.[26] For God and nature have so framed us that we wish to express what we know in deeds. When this does not happen we are reproved by our own judgment. Here are the marvellous powers of conscience, which can never be completely at rest when faced with the most serious offenses.

[TWO KINDS OF KNOWLEDGE]

8.[27] Strictly speaking, to withhold the truth in unrighteousness is to refuse God's calling, which by its truth recalls us constantly to him. Thus whenever we attain truth through study or observation of things, it will be most profitable to us to ask ourselves immediately why God calls us through that truth which he presents to our minds. By unrighteousness the Apostle understood in general whatever sin we commit against God or others. So Paul speaks of that truth which is naturally engrafted in us, as well as what we obtain by our own study. Both teach us the highest things concerning God, nor can the injustice we commit blot it out of our minds. Yet the scholars of the Academy tried to teach the same thing, when they contend that nothing can be determined by us with certainty. Therefore, they would not have us embrace anything as if we are sure of its truth, but want us to consider everything uncertain and doubtful. Similarly the Epicureans try to delete from our minds those things concerning God imprinted in us by natural preconception.[28] But neither of these could achieve what they sought. Whether they wish it or not, these truths still remain in men's minds, although tragically held down in wickedness.

---

[25]Ovid *Metamorph.* 7.20–21, where Medea soliloquizes: "Video meliora proboque / Deteriora sequor." Calvin, *Inst.* II.2.23 uses the same quotation.

[26]Aristotle *NE* 1102b14ff.: "The rational principle ... urges them aright and towards the best objects."

[27]CP §10.

[28]Naturali anticipatione, i.e. the concept of *prolepsis*; see p. 20, n. 6 above. Cf. P. Merlan, "The Later Academy and Platonism" in CHGM 53ff. In the classical age, the distinction between appearance and the Real led Sophists and Skeptics to embrace a radical empiricism culminating in the materialism of Epicurus and his disciple Lucretius.

9.[29] You may ask how it happens that the truth we have by faith is stronger for proceeding to action than the truth perceived by nature. Surely this does not happen because one truth by itself and taken on its own is stronger than another. Truth has the same nature on both sides; the difference arises from the ways and means by which it is perceived. Natural strength is corrupt, weakened and defiled through sin, so that the truth which it grasps has no effect. But faith has joined with it the divine inspiration and power of the Holy Spirit so that it apprehends truth effectively. Hence the difference is not in truth itself but in the means[30] by which we embrace it. This is why it happens that there we are changed but here we remain the same as before. We have a striking testimony to this in the Gospel. Christ set before the young man what he should do to obtain salvation. Hearing this, he was not persuaded [30] to believe, but went away sorrowful.[31] He trusted to natural powers, and therefore, asked the Lord what he might do to obtain eternal life. On the other hand, when Matthew heard the call he embraced it with such great faith that he left his money and customers at once in order to follow Christ.[32] Also when Zaccheus, who had been greedy for profit, heard that the Lord planned to visit him, he received him into his house wholeheartedly, even offering at once to distribute half his goods to the poor and to restore fourfold to those he had previously defrauded.[33] The whole difference consists in the faculty by which truth is apprehended. This should not be taken to deny that more than we know through nature is revealed to us by the Scriptures, the New as well as the Old Testament. But we have drawn a comparison between the same truth when known by nature and when perceived by faith.

10.[34] Aristotle teaches in his *Rhetoric* that it is a valuable testimony to have our affairs judged by our enemies.[35] So it is most telling to hear in the book of Samuel how the Philistines, the worst enemies of Jehovah, witnessed to his power, declaring it so great that they could not withstand it. Nor did they seek natural causes of the diseases that afflicted them, even though there were such causes of the sores and hemorrhoids and dysentery.[36] But when they saw that they were all struck by the same disease at once, they immediately believed that they were oppressed by the hand of the God Jehovah. So

[29]CP §11.
[30]The original commentary adds *et instrumenta*, which is followed by CP but not LC.
[31]Matt. 19:22.   [32]Matt. 9:9.   [33]Luke 19:6.
[34]The next two sections are from SAM 5:12, fols. 36r–v; the CP inserts them above as §§6–7.
[35]Aristotle *Rhetorica* 1372b19, 1373a18.
[36]1 Sam. 5:6–7.

God forced them to confess his name against their will. Similarly, after Pharaoh had suffered various plagues, he at last cried out: "I have sinned against Jehovah and against you: entreat God on my behalf." [37] Nebuchadnezzar and Darius, having pondered what God did for Daniel, openly confessed that he is the great God, and proclaimed under harsh penalty that no one should blaspheme or speak evil of his name. [38] Julian the Apostate, otherwise a most evil man, was constrained at his death to acknowledge the power of Christ, saying: "You have conquered, Galilean." [39] Demons were also driven to the same confession when they witnessed, exclaiming that Jesus Christ is the holy one and son of God, and recognizing that he came ahead of time to destroy them, and that they well knew both Christ and Paul. [40] For the same reason it is evident that the ark of the Lord was not taken by the Philistines in vain, and that the Jews were carried away captive to Babylon so that some worship and knowledge of God should shine at least briefly among foreign nations. Many measures that seem hard and extreme often have worthy results; but what they will come to we cannot perceive before the outcome [καταστροφή]. So we should not judge the works of God until the fifth act. For if we guess according to the beginning or middle, it would be like wishing to reconstruct a statue of Phidias from one finger. All parts of the body must first be studied if we want to attain knowledge of the harmony and symmetry of the whole work. Because we often neglect this procedure, the result is that we sorrow, lament, blame, and blaspheme what we don't know.

11. The Philistines arrived at some knowledge of God through their victory and capture of the ark, though not so great that they were renewed to eternal life. So we should consider that God offers himself for human perception in two ways. [41] On the one hand we see his mercy and clemency, on the other his power and severity. Most of the Philistines felt the strength and power of Jehovah, for they were vessels of wrath, fit for destruction. They did not see his compassion and mercy through Christ; therefore, they fled from and despised his appearance in the ark, as if he were a tormentor and cruel judge, and did not return to him. They drove the ark away, and did not resume the true worship of God by forsaking their idols. In the same way, when Christ came into the world to bring us salvation, the devil opposed him,

---

[37]Ex. 9:27–28.

[38]Dan. 3:29, 6:26.

[39]*Vicisti Galilæe*, the dying words ascribed to the emperor Julian (331–363); he had been reared in the Christian faith but reverted to paganism.

[40]Matt. 8:19; Acts 19:15.

[41]On the twofold knowledge of God, see p. 6, n. 1, above.

feeling his strength and power, saying: "Why are you come to destroy us?" When the Gadarenes lost their pigs through a miracle, they did not accept or worship Christ, but when they met asked him to leave their coasts.[42] Some write that the divine countenance is of two kinds, one pleasant and loving that he presents to the devout, the other dreadful and fierce, in which he is perceived by the wicked. But we need not imagine God to have two faces or two heads. God is always the same, bearing one kind of face, although he is not always perceived the same by all: for the faithful behold him one way, and the unfaithful another.[43]

---

[42]Mark 1:24; Matt. 8:34.

[43]Anthony Marten added two further sections for his English translation of this topic, one from GEN preface, §12; and another from the NE preface §13; see "Philosophy and Theology" §6, p. 15; §2, para. 2, p. 20 above. The former distinguishes knowledge of God "in three ways" [tribus rationibus]: in heaven, natural knowledge, and faith. But "the power of faith must always be added to the contemplation of creatures" if we are not to miss the divine "power, wisdom, and goodness," citing Heb. 11:3, "by faith we understand that the worlds were made."

¶ The commentarie of Ma-
ster Peter Martyr vpon the
Booke of Iudges.

Here be some whiche deuide the ho-
ly scriptures into foure parts, and ascribe some
bokes as wel of the old testament as of the new,
to lawes, some to histories, some to prophecies,
and other some agayne to wisdome. But it is
not meete so to deuyde the bookes of the holye
scripture one from an other, bicause that in the
bokes of Exodus, Leuiticus, Numeri, and Deu-
teronomie, in which they appoynt lawes to be con-
teined, are founde almoste as many histories as
lawes. Besides that in the bokes which they as-
signe to prophetes, lawes of liuing vprightlye
are oftentimes written and clearely expounded.

Neither can we properly separate the bokes of Salomons other of þ kynd (which
they wil haue proper to wisdome) from lawes and prophecies. For there are in
them sentences here and there written, which seruing for the instruction of life,
haue also wout controuersie the nature of lawes. Furthermore for þ that in them
are very many secretes opened vnto the church by the inspiration of the spirite
of god, they poure vndoubtedly into the attentiue hearers, oracles of thinges to
come. It may easily be graunted, that all these thinges which they make mentio
of, are founde in the holy bookes: I meane the precepts of liuing, notable hysto-
ries, prophecies of thinges to come, and also moste wise sentences and sayinges:
but in such sort, that in maner in euery booke they are set forth vnto vs disper-
sedly, neither yet would I that these holy bookes should be deuided one from an
other by those endes and limittes.

I would rather thinke as the learned sorte doe also iudge, that whatsoeuer
thinges are conteyned in the holy Scriptures should be referred vnto two prin-
cipall heades, the lawe I meane and the gospell. For euery where are declared
vnto vs either the precepts of god of vpright liuing, or that we are exposed to
haue strayed from the vpright of weakenes or els of malice, þ gospel is layd forth
before vs, wherin by Christ that thing wherein we haue offended is pardoned,
and the strength and power of the holy ghost promised vs, to reforme vs agaíe
to the image of god, whiche we had loste. These two thinges maye we beholde
in all the bookes of Moyses, in the histories, Prophetes, and bookes appointed to wisdome, and that not onely in the olde Testamente, but also
in the newe, and they are not separated one from an other by bookes and
leaues, but by that maner which is now declared. And this is sufficient as touching the generall matter of the holy scriptures. But nowe the most peculiar-
ly speake of this booke, that we may vnderstand what thinges they be which are
entreated of in the same. And to the ende we may the more plainly vnderstande
this, it is needefull to call to memory those thinges which were spoken of in the
former bookes.

In Genesis is set forth the creation of the worlde, then howe of Abraham,
Isaac, Iacob and his twelue childré was engendred the people of god and how

C.i. they

PART TWO

Body and Soul

IN PRIMVM LIBRVM

MOSIS, QVI VVLGO GE-
NESIS DICITVR COMMENTARII
doctissimi D. Petri Martyris Vermilii Florentini, professoris diuinarum literarum in
schola Tigurina, nunc primum
in lucem editi.

Addita est initio operis Vita eiusdem à IOSIA SIM-
LERO *Tigurino descripta.*

PRAETEREA *accesserunt duo Indices locupletissimi Rerum
& verborum vnus, alter locorum communium qui
in his Commentarijs explicantur.*

Absit mihi gloriari nisi in cruce Domini nostri IESV CHRISTI
per quem mihi mundus crucifixus est & ego mundo.

TIGVRI

EXCVDEBAT CHRISTOPHORVS
FROSCHOVERVS M. D. LXIX.

Title page from Commentary on Genesis, printed in Zurich
by Christoph Froschauer, 1569

About the Translation

Body and Soul

THE IMAGE OF GOD (DE HOMINE). Two selections represent Martyr's teaching on human nature, particularly the relation between soul and body; they have been introduced above in relation to the special problem of the agent intellect. It is typical of Reformation anthropology to base the doctrine of human being on exegetical work. The first chapter of Genesis offers ideal material for exploring the human condition: its fall from nature and need of grace, its limited and spoiled grasp of the divinity present to everyone.[1] The kinds and degrees of such knowledge form the agenda for Martyr's scholium, raising the question of the relationship between body and soul. The soul is separable from the body, although it may "use" the latter; Augustine insisted on their unity.[2] Aristotle provided an alternative formula, "soul as form of the body." This is Martyr's line also: soul is *motor* and *forma* of body (§§1–2). On the *imago dei*, Martyr adopts a moderate position, rejecting the separation of "image" from "likeness," which identified the two with nature and quality respectively. He distinguishes the human soul from both immutable deity and animals. Disagreeing with Origen, he holds that body and soul are created together (§2). Like Aquinas, he follows Aristotle in regarding soul as the

---

[1]Peter Martyr Vermigli, *In Primum Librum Mosis, qui vulgo Genesis dicitur Commentarii doctissimi...* (Zurich: C. Froschauer, 1569) fols. 9 v–10 v, with supplemental material as noted in the translation. The commentary on Romans appears as a separate volume in the Peter Martyr Library.

[2]E.g. Plato *Ps-Alcibiades I* 129E ("a soul using a body"); Plotinus *Enneads* I.1.3; Augustine, *De civ. Dei* XIX.3.1. See E. Gilson, *History of Christian Philosophy in the Middle Ages* (New York: Random House, 1955) 74 ff., 593.

active cause of its body, created together with it.[3] Both Ibn Ezra and Aristotle assist his argument that the divine breathing is an enabling power—an argument applicable also to resurrection (§3). The image consists in dominion over creatures, reflecting the divine governance (§5), which is not tyranny insofar as it shares in the renewal granted by grace: the "full image" is Christ (§6). Woman is the image of God compared to other creatures, but she is to obey man (§5). Finally, the androgynous myth of Jewish and Greek teaching is rejected (§8).

(4) DE RESURRECTIONE. This treatise reflects the fact that Aristotle's *De Anima* was a privileged text in Padua, and indeed in the emerging Renaissance psychology.[4] Although quoted directly only twice, it is clearly in Martyr's mind as he writes about Christian hope.[5] Whereas the Florentine Neoplatonism of Ficino had celebrated the immortality of the soul, the new "secular Aristotelianism" or "Paduan Averroism" denied that immortality can be demonstrated. Martyr holds that Aristotle did not believe in immortality, citing Tertullian and Gregory Nazianzen in support. Unlike Pomponazzi, he finds "greater suasive value in the moral arguments for immortality."[6] Denying that there are apodictic rational arguments for immortality, he develops a theological rationale through the analogy of resurrection as new creation, involving the same enlivening Breath expounded in the two scholia before us. It will be noted that as Martyr summons his arguments, most of his evidence is drawn from the Old Testament (§§20–52), although often it is a New Testament text referring back, as in the debate between Jesus and the Sadducees on Exodus 3:6, "I am the God of Abraham, Isaac, and Jacob" (§§20ff.). Martyr's linguistic and exegetical skills are on display as he deals with key passages in Job, Daniel, and elsewhere. He draws not only on church fathers, notably Augustine and Tertullian, but also medieval rabbis such as Kimhi (§31, etc.) and Gersonides (§49) as well as the Targum (§40).

Martyr's treatise *De Resurrectione* deals explicitly with the relation between reason and revelation. Echoing both Augustine and Aquinas, he asks whether reason can demonstrate resurrection. He answers that only probable reasons may be generated, since revelation alone can establish such a surpass-

---

[3]Aristotle *De Anima* II.1.412a20; Aquinas SCG II.68, 87. See CSV 90 ff. on the soul's origin and its relation to body.

[4]See CHRP 456 ff.

[5]The scholium on resurrection appears in the commentary on 2 Kings 4:37, based on Vermigli's last lecture series: *Melachim id est, Regum Libri Duo posteriores cum Commentarijs* (Zurich: C. Froschauer, 1566) fols. 214v–230v (LC/CP 3.15).

[6]CSV 96ff.; cf. CHRP 500ff.

ing phenomenon.[7] He takes this opportunity to discuss the nature of apodictic argument or proof. Some arguments resolve questions into self-evident
principia, chiefly mathematical formulae. Others may be reduced to such principles. Still others rest on necessary principles, but these are not evident in the
subalternate science that uses them, being demonstrable only in some higher
science.[8] Thus music borrows mathematical principles but does not itself
demonstrate them, whereas the arguments are apodictic to someone versed in
both. Similarly, arguments for resurrection are not apodictic for the philosopher because he cannot trace them back to natural causes, whereas the believer
knows their foundation in the word of God.

Martyr's use of "rational proof" is significant for his attitude towards
human reason and philosophy. If asked what is "natural," he would answer
that in terms of formal cause (in this case the union of soul with body) "the
term 'natural' is by no means to be rejected." But considering "the efficient
cause and its mode," nature is surpassed (§15). He cites examples of rational
proof, such as: something imperfect is incapable of eternal happiness; the soul
separated from the body is imperfect; therefore it must be reunited with the
body (§16). He admits that this syllogism is cogent for believers because of
scriptural evidence about the union of soul and body. Similarly, to argue to
bodily resurrection from the union of immortal souls with body satisfies faith
but not philosophy, which charges: "It takes something to be certain and evident that is obscure in the light of nature, namely that the soul continues after
death and is immortal." It will be seen that he stands in the Augustinian-
Anselmic tradition of *fides quaerens intellectum*; but as our Introduction notes,
Martyr is following Thomas closely here, identifying theology as a kind of science.[9] The believer is like someone who knows two disciplines, occupying the
stronger position because he understands the workings of both nature and
grace: "When the devout refer the conclusions that have been reached back to
the Word of God, undergirding and confirming them by tracing them back to
that Word, they hold them as apodictic, not indeed by natural knowledge but

---

[7]For the discussion of rational argument see "Resurrection" p. 52, §7 and §15, p. 58 ff. Aristotle had distinguished rigid demonstration (ἀπόδειξις) from the "dialectical" or controversial;
e.g., *An. Post.* I.1. 71a5 ff., I.33, 88b30 ff. Cf. CSV 47 ff. Calvin *Inst.* III.25.3, states: "while many of
the philosophers asserted the immortality of the soul, the resurrection of the body was admitted
by few. And though this furnishes no excuse, yet it admonishes that this truth is too difficult to
command the assent of the human mind."

[8]See "Resurrection" §15, p. 58, and p. 59, n. 41.

[9]Donnelly, CSV 48, comments on this passage: "A better example of residual Thomism in
Martyr's theology would be hard to find."

by faith, which depends wholly on the divine oracles."[10] By working from a revealed Word as axiomatic for knowledge, faith seeks an understanding which is wholly convincing, "apodictic" in a strict, if restricted, sense. Martyr is on his familiar ground of joining apodictic and probable reasons as allies in his task of defense and persuasion. Where apodictic reasons can be found, they function negatively, in refuting contrary arguments in the role of apologetics. But persuasion is higher on Martyr's agenda, still the preacher and pastor of his first career in Italy. Here the rhetorical devices of similitude, analogy, image, and other tropes are marshalled for a positive presentation of a doctrine that "surpasses nature."

---

[10]§15; cf. CSV 48.

Commentary on Genesis

The Image of God

[CREATION]

1. (22) When you hear that God has formed man, do not think only of outward parts or lineaments, but consider the inward parts—namely the veins, skin, and sinews, the gates and channels, the bones and marrow, in short all those means of our life that lie hidden within. I consider three chief subjects in the creation of mankind that are described in general, and now distinguished more closely as follows. First, consultation: "Let us make man." Second, "God formed him from dust." Third, "He breathed in his face the breath of life."[1] You will not read that this was done in the case of other living creatures. Yet elsewhere you may find the verb of making attributed to the

---

[1] Martyr's translation of Gen. 2:7 (fol. 97r) is: "Formaverat itaque Iehovah Deus hominem e pulvere terrae, inspiraveratque in faciem eius spiraculum vitae, et fuit homo in animam viventem." The Vulgate reads: "Formavit igitur Dominus Deus hominem de limo terrae, et inspiravit in faciem ejus spiraculum vitae, et factus est homo in animam viventem."

The scholium *De Homine* (LC 1.12.22-28, CP 1.13.22-28) consists of selections from *In Primum Librum Mosis ... Genesis ...*(Zurich: C. Froschauer, 1569), fols. 9v–10v on Gen. 2:7 (§§ 22–24), fols. 39v–40r on Gen. 9:4 (§25), and fols. 7r–v on Gen. 1:26 (§§27-28), with §26 from *In selectissimam D. Pauli Priorem ad Corinth ...* (Zurich: C. Froschauer, 1551) fol. 286r–v on 1 Cor. 11:7. The sections numbered 1–7 correspond to LC 22–28. §8 completes the Gen. 1:26 passage, fol. 7v. Our title "The Image of God" seems to suit the subject matter best.

37

heavens and other things, namely in Psalm 95: "His hands have formed the dry land"; Isaiah 45: "It is I that formed the light"; and Amos 7: "He formed grasshoppers." But it is not the last or least dignity of the human body that it stands upright. Thus Ovid: "While downward bend the beasts, / and stoop toward earth, / A face sublime to man he gave."[2]

And he formed him from earth.[3] For this reason the name of Adam is from "earth," as if you should say "Born-of-earth" [Terrigenam]. Some, however, say that it was from *Adam* [אדם] because that earth was "red."

First therefore the instrument is formed, that is the body: next the mover [motor] was added, that is the soul, to use it.[4] *In his face or nostrils*. For *Appaiim* [אפים] signifies nostrils first, then by the figure synecdoche the whole is taken for the part, for the countenance and face: here it may signify both. First the nostrils, because by breathing they especially indicate life. Then if you take it for the face, excellent signs of the soul and of life are revealed. Some consider the metaphor as taken from the formation of glass. By blowing through certain instruments they shape cups, bowls, and various kinds of vessels. In the same way you will observe a metaphor here, since God has no mouth, nor does he breathe, just as he has no hands by which he might frame the human body. But in these matters you should understand the divine power, his commandment and present strength. As to the words *Neshama* [נשמה] and *Nephesh* [נפש], sometimes they signify both wind and breath, sometimes they are taken for substance and the soul, because life is primarily maintained and signified by breathing. Moreover the Latin word *Anima* is derived from wind and breath. In Greek it is *anemos* [ἄνεμος]. It is also called by the Greeks *psyche* [ψυχή], from "cooling." Thus all these proper terms seem to have conspired together in naming the soul, that it should be called after breathing out.[5]

A double exposition, therefore, derives from the double meaning of the word, since it signifies both soul and breathing. First it says that the nostrils or face of the human body were breathed into by God's command, and so life and soul were received. That breath was not the soul, but a sort of sign that it would be planted in man from the outside, and that we should not expect a

---

[2]A paraphrase of Ovid *Metam.* 1:84–85; cf. Calvin, *Inst.* I.15.3. Dryden's translation is fuller: "… while the mute creation downward bend / Their sight, and to their earthly mother tend, / Man looks aloft, and with erected eyes / Beholds his own hereditary skies."

[3]Pulverem e terra (1569): LC (1580) has: Finxit autem e terra.

[4]On the soul as drive and form of the body, see n. 12 (p. 40), below.

[5]These sentences show a play on the verbs *respiro, conspiro, expiro*. The verb ψύχω means both "to breathe" and "to make cool." For the view that soul is a "cooling," see Plato *Crat.* 399D-E; Aristotle *De Anima* 1.2 405b; Tertullian *De Anima* 25 and 27; Origen *De Princ.* II.8.3; Augustine *De Anima* IV.12.18.

work of nature, as is the case with the souls of other living creatures. We read in the Gospel that Christ breathed on the Apostles and said: "Receive the Holy Spirit."[6] Yet that breath was not the essence of the Holy Spirit but its symbol, that he would come into their souls from without, by the work of Christ. Again, we can take that word for breath, saying that God breathed, that is, he made man to breathe like himself—after the body was made he gave him the power of respiration, so that being alive and endowed with a soul he might be admired. The second interpretation is to take that breath for the soul, given to us by God.[7] They say that *Neshama* [[נשמה]] signifies mainly the divine and rational, given to us by God. Where it is added, "Man was made a living soul," *Nephesh* [נפש] signifies sensible life, which other living creatures share. This clearly teaches us that a reasonable soul is given to us by God from above, and has with it all the power that other inferior creatures possess.

A double error is thus excluded.[8] We must not think that the soul is of the substance of God, for that is immovable and unchangeable [invariabilis et immutabilis], while the soul may become unhappy and appears to be quite changeable. Moreover it is not the breath of the nature and substance of a breathing person. Nor should it on the other hand be counted of the same quality and nature as that of brute animals, because understanding will never be found in them, as is said of the horse and the mule in Psalm 32, that there is no understanding in them.[9] If they had been endowed with the same kind of soul, other animals might think themselves wrongfully subject to humans. But this opinion does not need to be refuted by many reasons, since it displeased the noblest philosophers also.[10]

[SOUL AND BODY]

2.(23) There is disagreement as to whether all human souls were created by God at the beginning, or are made by him and placed in bodies in proportion as the order of nature seems to require. Some have thought that they were all created at the beginning, among whom many Jews are included: among us Origen is also considered of that opinion.[11] It seems that they were

---

[6]John 20:22.   [7]נשמה may mean divine breath, e.g. Job 4:9, Isa. 30:33.

[8]Cf. EW 95: Prop. 4.N.1. from Gen. 2: "The human soul is not of the substance of God, nor has it the same nature as the souls of brute beasts."

[9]Ps. 32:9.

[10]E.g. Aristotle *De Anima* I.5.410b8ff.

[11]Origen *De Princ.* 1:8.4 (PG 11.180). cf. EW, 95, 4.N.2, Martyr's proposition from Gen. 2: "The souls of men were not created at once from the beginning, but are created daily by God to be put into bodies"; also, in IUD 13:25, "de visionibus Angelis, " Martyr treats Origen's concept of the fall of souls into various bodies: "Origen speaks more like a Platonist than a Christian"; LC/CP 1.13.6.

led to this for the reason that a rational soul is incorruptible and so is not procreated from matter. Therefore they say that since they are made by God from nothing, we cannot say in truth that in respect of creation he rested the seventh day from all his work. But this opinion does not seem likely. Since the soul is the drive and form of the body, it seems that they should be produced together.[12] Moreover, are they idle or else doing something when they preexist bodily time? If you say that they are idle it seems absurd that things should be left so long without their function. But if they do something, it must necessarily be either good or evil. Yet Scripture in Romans 9 clearly denies it concerning Jacob and Esau: "Before they had done either good or evil."[13]

What counts more is the story of creation, which shows us that the soul was made at the very formation of the body. For no mention is made of it before, and the production of something so great would not have been kept silent; therefore when we read that it was inspired by him it must be understood as made by God. The argument about ceasing from all labor is refuted when we say that God is also at work either through the continuing governance of things [assiduam rerum administrationem], or else because whatever he makes is referred to the former, and of the same kind as things created in the first six days. Why the body was made first before the soul is answered by the fathers.[14] For if the soul had been introduced before the body, it might have been without a use, lacking the organ and instrument of its actions. But God observed this order, always to prepare first that by which things of greater value are to act; as soon as they are made they are brought forth to work. First the earth was uncovered from the waters, then the lights were made, which would exercise their power on the earth and its fruit. All the animals were made first, and the woods and plants of the earth. Last of all was mankind, to be set over all these things, that as soon as created they might have work to do. Similarly now, the body is first and then follows the soul, lest it should be idle. This divine purpose teaches us that it happens among us too that the more people excel, the more material for working is supplied to them, lest they should live fruitlessly.

---

[12]Actus et forma corporis: on soul as the form of the body, see Introduction, xxiii–xxiv.

[13]Rom. 9:11.

[14]Of the "two orthodox opinions, transducianism and immediate creation," Martyr chooses the latter on philosophical grounds, since Scripture gives no clear teaching; see CSV 91. Augustine favored the former.

3. (24) Ibn Ezra[15] says that since man was made a living soul he moved himself at once: the first man was not created to be weak like infants, who cannot guide themselves and walk. He is more like other creatures that walk as soon as they are born. Or else he showed signs of the presence of the soul, namely motion and sense. For these two (as Aristotle affirms) seemed to all the ancient philosophers to be the chief effects of the soul.[16] From this blowing of God upon the dust or clay of which the human body was composed—which we perceive to be strong enough to enliven immediately and give strength to all members—we gather a good argument for the facility of our resurrection. For if his spirit blows again upon the ashes of the dead, they will easily recover their souls, as described in chapter 37 of Ezekiel, where he shows that by the breath of the spirit of God those bones were quickened. That last renewing of bodies will far excel this, just as Paul called this first man of the earth earthy, and the latter he called both spiritual and heavenly.[17]

4. (25) Let us see how our assertion that the blood is the soul can be true.[18] The Manicheans cannot abide this in the Old Testament, and reprove it as a lie, for they completely reject the old books. They mock what is written in Genesis, Leviticus, and Deuteronomy with the following arguments. In 1 Corinthians 15 it is said: "Flesh and blood shall not inherit the kingdom of God"; therefore blood is not the soul, otherwise Paul would exclude souls from the kingdom of heaven. Further, in the Gospel Christ said: "Fear not those who kill the body, and cannot touch the soul":[19] if the blood is the soul, then surely when tyrants kill God's holy martyrs they abuse it, they shed it, destroy it, and so on. These arguments are refuted by Augustine against Adimantus in two respects.[20] In the Old Testament the sayings concern animals, but the arguments they bring out of the New Testament relate to a reasonable and human soul. Therefore their own reasoning has caught them unaware. But to disprove their first argument more thoroughly, notice that when Paul speaks of the resurrection to come, he means by flesh and blood that the condition of a mortal body will be removed from the saints at the

---

[15]Ibn Ezra (1089–1164), Franco-Spanish rabbinic commentator, who was included in the Bomberg Bible, which Martyr used in preparing his biblical commentaries; see Translator's Introduction, p. xxxix, above.

[16]Aristotle *De Anima* I.2.403b27: "Two characteristic marks have above all others been recognized as distinguishing that which has soul in it from that which has not–movement and sensation."

[17]I Cor. 15:47.

[18]This section is from GEN 9:4, "You shall not eat flesh with its life, that is, its blood."

[19]I Cor. 15:50; Matt. 10:28.

[20]Augustine *Contra Adimantum* 12.1 (PL 42.143–144).

resurrection. This is what those words declare: It is sown in corruption and mortality, but it shall rise again in the opposite conditions.

Consider that the life of animals as well as the human soul is called blood. That must be a figurative speech, to be interpreted by metonymy, in which the sign is put for the thing signified. In this way Augustine testified against Adimantus: "The Lord did not hesitate to say, This is my body, when he gave the sign of his body."[21] Since the blood is a sign of the soul's presence, it may be called the soul itself. Again, by the same figure the container is taken for its contents. For who does not know that the human soul is in one sense contained in the blood, which being spilled and consumed, cannot stay longer in the body? It is so joined to the body as to follow its affections and disturbances so long as we live in this life. Some have thought that we were prohibited from eating blood so that animal behavior would not be induced, for it is easily carried into our mind if we eat the blood of animals. I do not offer this as if I accept it as the reason why God gave that commandment, but to indicate the communion of man's soul with the body.

[THE DIVINE IMAGE]

5.(26) The beginning of Genesis teaches how man is the image of God, where it is written that God said, "Let us make man after our image and likeness, that he may have dominion over the birds of the air, the fish of the sea, and the beasts of the earth." This shows that the image of God consists in this, that he should be ruler over all creatures, as God is ruler over everything.[22] Augustine often refers this to the memory, mind, and will, which as faculties of the same soul represent (as he said) the three persons in one substance.[23] Yet this doctrine of Augustine rather shows the cause of the image. For man is not set above other creatures to have dominion over them for any other purpose than that he is endowed with reason, which reveals itself clearly by these three faculties. Nor is this the only place that the image of God is found. For it is not enough to govern and rule God's creatures well with memory, mind, and will, unless we understand, remember, and choose those things that are pleasing to God. If our mind remains infected (as it is) with sin, it will not have proper dominion, but will exercise tyranny over things instead. The image of God is the new man, who understands the truth of God and desires its righteousness. So Paul has taught us, when he writes to the Colossians: "Put on the new

---

[21]Augustine *Contra Adimantum* 12.3 (PL 42.144).

[22]Gen. 1:26; cf. EW 94, *Prop.* 3.P.1. on Gen. 1: "Man is said to be created in the image and likeness of God … his dominion over creatures is from God."

[23]E.g. Augustine *De Trin.* X.11.17 (PL 42. 982).

nature, which is being renewed in the knowledge of God, after the image of its creator."[24] Here we see that the knowledge of God is true and effectual, leading to an image of perfection. This is set forth more clearly in the letter to the Ephesians: "Put on the new nature, created in God's likeness, in true righteousness and holiness."[25] Our mind truly expresses God when it possesses the knowledge of God and is adorned with righteousness. For righteousness and the knowledge of divine things are nothing else than a sort of influx of the divine nature into our minds.

Perhaps you will argue that in the same way a woman is also the image of God. We say that if you compare her with other creatures she is the image of God, for she has dominion over them and has use of them. But in this instance you must compare her to man, and then she is not said to be the image of God, because she does not bear rule over the man but rather obeys him. Thus Augustine in the 13th chapter of his book *On the Trinity* said: "If it is understood of man and woman, insofar as they enjoy mind and reason, it is fitting that they should be according to the image of God; but when the woman is compared to man as to the actions and affairs of this life, she is not the image of God because she was created to be a helper of man." And in the same place he has another exposition, although allegorical. He said that we are called men because we contemplate God, and are rightly bareheaded because in this case we must persevere in ceaseless labor, for there is no end to the discovery of divine things. "But we are called women," he said, "when we descend with our thoughts to the care of earthly things. There we should have the head covered, because moderation must be practiced, and we should see that we do not plunge too far into worldly things."[26] But we must not rest on allegorical interpretation. The exposition that we gave before is clearer.

[THE NATURE OF "DOMINION"]

6.(27) The image of someone is the form by which it represents him. A similitude of someone is a quality by which it resembles him. What this image is may be put simply. Not only has a person the powers of understanding through which he is not far from God; he is also made with excellent, even divine, qualities, provided with justice, wisdom, mercy, temperance, and charity. Paul commends this image, to accomplish our renewal to that nature created by God in holiness and truth: Ephesians 4, Colossians 3, and 2 Corinthians 3. But the full image of God is Christ in his divine nature, and so much

[24]Col. 3:10.   [25]Eph. 4:24.
[26]Augustine *De Trin.* XII.7–12 (PL 42.1003ff.); cf. Augustine *Cont. Faustum Manicheam* XXIV.2 (PL 42.476).

as his human nature can possess of the divine likeness: Hebrews 1, Colossians 1, and Romans 8. Again, "This is my son with whom I am well pleased."[27] We were made to be like that: for we have intellect and are capable of divine perfections. So were we made, yet we cannot be restored to them without the help and example of Christ, who is the primary and true image. How much we are the image of God is seen by our happiness [foelicitate], which we share with God; I mean loving and knowing. But if you ask by what powers we rule over things, it is not by bodily strength: for in that respect most creatures exceed us. Therefore it is accomplished by reason, deliberation, and art, by which we not only mastered and controlled these creatures, but also move and change great objects. This power is best restored by faith: "You will tread on the adder and serpent": Psalm 91. Daniel was thrown to the lions. The Lord lived among wild beasts in the wilderness. Paul took no harm from the viper. Samson and David overcame lions.

A difficulty arises regarding dominion over animals: Why were these wild beasts made, that they should afflict humans? I answer, so that wicked sons might be chastened: after sin a scourge was required. Sin armed our own servants against us, so that the uprising of animals was inflicted by God, as Scripture testifies in Ezekiel 5: "I will send famine and wild beasts against you."[28] All of them appear gentle and tame to the just. Even now when they have rebelled, by divine mercy very few perish from them. If anyone is destroyed by them, two lessons are given us. It is an example of the severity of God, as with the Samaritans who were killed by lions, the children who were killed by bears because they mocked Elisha, and the disobedient prophet whom a lion killed.[29] Further, it shows how great is the majesty of God, that even wild animals revenge the injury done to him. Last, consider with me the goodness of God towards us, who has bound these harmful beasts within deserts and solitary places, so that they can wander only at night. Here also man may perceive his calamity after sin, that so noteworthy a creature can perish with the sting of one little scorpion or the bite of a mad dog. Yet despite sin wild beasts have not been able to shake off the human yoke completely; they fear and tremble at his sight; you see a child rule, beat, and threaten the greatest animals. In him they honor the image of God.

7. (28) This image is not properly meant in relation to the body, since God is not corporeal; yet it is not far from the likeness of God, for it assists us by expressing many similitudes of God lying hidden in the soul. Some

---

[27]Matt. 3:17.   [28]Ezek. 5:17.
[29]2 Kings 2:23 ff.; 17:2; 1 Kings 13:24.

Hebrews affirmed that this was also spoken concerning the body, if you regard those images and likenesses in which God revealed himself in order to be seen by Patriarchs and Prophets. For he appeared as the son of man. If we accept their reasoning we say that this was true rather because of the incarnation of Christ—such a body was given to man as God had already determined that his Word would take upon him.[30] As I have said, this is to be understood of the inward man, the soul, of which the body is the instrument and therefore not completely alien to that likeness. Thus you have the true knowledge of man: a creature of God formed in the image of his maker. From this statement we understand not only his rational nature but his properties and his end, namely happiness, that according to such a constitution he should live in those actions that express the image of God.

Both natural and human laws depend on this, so that this image may be restored and preserved, and man maintain free dominion. All virtues proceed from the excellent state and condition of human nature—to be just, valiant, and endowed with charity. From this condition of our nature we may conclude that virtues are naturally engrafted in us, and that the arguments by which Aristotle in his second book of ethics proves the contrary, take place in this our corrupted nature.[31] Consider also the goodness of God, that besides the excellent actions of virtue, human happiness requires an abundance of outward things, since they are instruments. For we do many things through riches or means; therefore at the beginning God adorned the first man with great wealth and sovereignty. By this condition man is admonished about his duty, the manner and form of all his actions. Whenever he is about to do anything, let him say to himself: will this reveal my Father? is this to live according to the image? We also learn how appropriate is our deliverance through Christ. For since our perfection consists in retaining the image of God obscured by the fault of our first parents, it was fitting that it should be again imprinted by Christ, that is by his Spirit, the lively image of God. We may learn from this the dignity of the Church of God, what kind of citizens it has and requires, namely such as are like God. When you hear that God created man you should remember the body, the whole artistry of all its organs, and the utilities and ornaments of its several members, and as for the soul, all the powers, qualities, and actions which are found in it.

8. It was said before, "To the image and likeness." This statement depicts one thing only, as I mentioned above, because two terms are used to say the

[30]Ezek. 1, Dan. 7, Isa. 1. Martyr refers to the concept of *logos incarnandus.*
[31]Aristotle *NE* 2.1.1103a15: intellectual virtue "owes its birth and growth to teaching ... while moral virtue comes about as a result of habit...."

same thing, and refer to the greater expression. I approve this opinion of the passage rather than that which judges "image" to relate to nature and "likeness" to property.[32]

Concerning other living natures, we do not know how many were made separately. But as to humanity, two were created at first, and in such a way that the female was taken from the male. From this we have evidence of both choice and love. Since plants and herbs are given the power of producing seeds they are able to propagate their kind; even so in us that function belongs to sexual differentiation, as it is said, "Male and female he created them." Adam was created first, through preconception [Anticipationem], when what happens later is recounted first. This may be referred to the first created man, so that afterwards the woman was taken from him: thus the capacity as it were is in him first. This explodes the Jewish fable, which Plato copied in the *Symposium*; they hold that the first man was twofold, both male and female, and the woman was created through no less than a splitting and division of one from the other.[33]

---

[32]Cf. Calvin, *Inst.* 1.15.3: "There is no small controversy concerning 'image' and 'likeness' among expositors who seek for a difference, whereas in reality there is none … whether they confine *zelem*, that is 'image,' to the substance of the soul, and *demuth*, that is 'likeness,' to its qualities." Partly because the LXX introduced a copula lacking in the Hebrew, Irenaeus in particular developed a dualism. Thus εἰκών refers to human nature that cannot be lost, whereas ὁμοίωσις refers to a lost likeness to be recovered through redemption. Free will belongs to the image and is therefore not lost through sin. The Scholastics built on this, interpreting the Vulgate *imaginem et similitudinem* in Aristotelian categories as *anima rationalis* and *spiritualis*, the latter capable of receiving and losing the *donum superadditum supernaturale*. See E. Brunner, *Man in Revolt* (London: Lutterworth, 1947), app. 1, "The Image of God in the Teaching of the Bible and the Church," 499–515, and T. F. Torrance, *Calvin's Doctrine of Man* (London: Lutterworth, 1949) 23ff.

[33]The androgynous myth (e.g. Hermaphroditus in Ovid, *Metamorphoses* 4.347-88) is described by Aristophanes in Plato *Symposium* 189E–191E. The midrash on Gen. 1:27 states that God created the first man as androgyne; thus Adam gave birth to Eve; see *Encyclopedia of Religion*, ed. M. Eliade (New York: Macmillan, 1986) 1:276ff.

Commentary on 2 Kings 4

Resurrection

[INTRODUCTION]¹

1. [*214v*] It is very difficult to believe in the article on the resurrection of the flesh because it is something far removed from human reason. Still, a conviction about it involves many chief points of Christian faith necessary for salvation. Those who are clearly and firmly convinced about the resurrection prepare themselves well for the last hour; those who are dying and are certain of a blessed resurrection can only be eager and joyous about being delivered from this life. In contrast, at that hour enormous anxieties rack, torment, and agitate those who are vacillating on this point, nor indeed do they know where to turn. Moreover, this solid conviction consoles us when death takes away our friends and relatives, as Paul taught the Thessalonians.² Besides this, we are armed against persecutions, hard luck, and the difficulties we must bear on account of the faithful confession of Christ's name. The holy martyrs suffer

---

¹The marginalia have been used to provide headings throughout; as usual, Martyr's sense of appropriate division and relative length is not always helpful to the reader, however patient. Numbers within the text so indicated [ ] are also marginalia.

²1 Thess. 4:13.

De Resurrectione: scholium from I Kings 4: *Melachim id est, Regum Libri Duo posteriores cum Commentarijs* (Zurich: C. Froschauer 1566) fol. 214v–230v; LC/CP 3.15. From the lectures of 1560–1562; after Martyr's death, John Wolf completed the last fourteen chapters. John Patrick Donnelly, S.J. kindly supplied a translation, which I have adapted to the style of this volume.

anything at all so long as they are assured that a blessed life will be restored to them. Remembering this also helps us to develop temperance, for we will easily restrain ourselves from unlawful pleasures when we trust that true and solid pleasures of soul and body will be awarded us. If this article is overturned, many main points of religion are destroyed. In 1 Corinthians, Paul says, "For if the dead are not raised, then Christ has not been raised,"[3] which is total nonsense. For he would be held in death right up to this moment, [215r] which is appropriate neither for God nor the redeemer of the human race. If he has not arisen, neither did he truly die; otherwise he would be held by death. Hence those who deny the resurrection of the dead likewise assert that Christ did not truly die; they do not want him to have had true human flesh but a phantasm, and to have died only in phantasy, that is, only in appearance.[4]

2. Seeing that a discussion of the resurrection of the flesh is useful and necessary, it is right for us to deal with it at some length. First, if it is asked why God ordained it, two reasons can be advanced. The first is in order to make his elect truly and perfectly happy. It is impossible to obtain true happiness in this life because no human actions, whether in theory or in practice [νεc θεωρητικά νεc πρακτικά], are found to be whole and perfect. For with regard to knowledge we are ignorant about much more than what we know. Noting this, Socrates used to say that one thing he knew was that he knew nothing. Moreover, our understanding of the few things we do know is very weak and slight. We can claim this not just about natural phenomena but also the things that the Spirit of God has revealed to us. On this point Paul said, "For our present knowledge is imperfect and our prophecy is imperfect" and "we see in a mirror dimly."[5] Our memory is weak and often fails us. Who can remember all the things they read and learn, or have taught and decided? Recent information pushes out old information, just as one nail drives out another[6] and as the waters upstream in a river push forward the waters below. Since our knowledge of things comes from either discovery or being taught, how many are found who enjoy the happy gift of discovery? How very many there are who are inept and slow to learn. So as regards theoretical matters we have in this world little to be happy about. In practical affairs we also fall far short since we either act wrongly or wander far from perfection in upright

---

[3]1 Cor. 15:16.

[4]Here Martyr seems to have in mind the ancient heresy of the docetists.

[5]1 Cor. 13:9, 12.

[6]*clavium clavo pellere*, a favorite of Martyr's, as of Erasmus in, e.g., *Adagia* 52.4 (*Op. omnia* II, col. 70).

acts. Our virtues are maimed and mutilated; therefore we cannot draw from them perfect and complete deeds. Next, mental troubles or emotions come into play which drag us hither and thither so that we cannot be totally focused on doing what is right. Besides, many troubles arise from the body itself which is weak and brittle as glass. For if one is troubled by diseases (which overflow in such numbers that they overwhelm the skill of doctors), or is wounded, cut or burned, goes hungry, or is hard pressed by misfortunes or hardships, or finally if one is sorely afflicted by poverty and need—what soul could avoid being upset, disturbed, and anguished? These and many other things show clearly enough that we must despair of perfect happiness while we live here.

3. Some people noticed this and therefore postponed the experience of supreme happiness to another life and thought it should be restricted to the soul alone; indeed, they felt the body would hinder it if it were brought back. Marcion, Basilides, Valentinian, the Manichees, and similar plagues labored under this error; they set up two principles, I mean a good god and a bad one. Since they considered the bad god the author of visible creatures, they also said that he was the creator of the body and flesh, and that therefore the soul, cut off from these things after death, would be happy, and that there was no need for restoring those things that do not promote happiness but hinder it. They also felt this same way who thought that the soul was joined to the body like a sailor linked to his ship and a moving object to the thing it moves. So they decided that after this life the joining of the soul to the body does not happen a second time. Just as sailors and those who move and push burdens do not repeat their earlier labors when they have accomplished their task and have acquired enough wealth, so they believed that once souls are set free from the wearisome governing of their bodies, they are not about to return to them. But they are making an enormous mistake. For this is not the right way to link the soul to the body. The soul is its form and perfection, and one person or ὑπόστασις results from uniting both of them together. Hence a propensity to take up their body again is left remaining in souls after death, and a very strong one. Plato seems not to be unmindful of this, and Pythagoras as well. For both of them propose μετεμψύχωσις, that is, if I may put it so, transmigration of souls [transanimationem].[7] For, as they wished, souls after death

---

[7]Plato, e.g. *Timaeus* 41E–42E, *Rep.* X.618ff.: Spirits choose by lot "a new cycle of life and mortality." Pythagoras taught the Orphic doctrine of unity and kinship of all life, hence the prohibition against meat and belief in transmigration, attributed to him first by anonymous Pythagoreans (P. Merlan in CHGM, 90). For critique see Justin Martyr, *Dial.* 4–5, Clement of Alexandria, *Strom.* vii.32.8 and Tertullian, *De Anima* 28ff.

are transferred into other bodies again. Because they do not take on the same bodies, this was called migration rather than resurrection.

4. There are some who posited a sort of resurrection, claiming that after the great year or perfect revolution of the heavenly orbits, all things would be restored as they are now, so that thirty-six thousand years from now we shall be the same persons in number and reality as at present—I myself will then be teaching in this place and you will be sitting here, just as I am teaching now and you are in attendance here. The argument for this opinion is astronomical: they posit (as Ptolemy taught) that the highest orbit of the heavens includes in itself three hundred sixty degrees and each star crosses one of them every hundred years. So it happens that after thirty-six thousand years every star should return to that same point from which it departed and began its motion.[8] Since the status and location of the heavenly bodies were established on the same basis which obtained in the beginning, they thought that all things would return to the same form they were then. I am aware that there were some of them who put off this restitution of things not to thirty-six thousand but forty thousand years. But I do not accept their reasoning. Indeed, both opinions are foolish and inept; they are refuted by Aristotle, who clearly asserts that it is impossible for things that perish to return the same numerically, regardless of the interval of time you want to posit.[9] But they could lie with impunity—for who could refute them after thirty-six thousand years, especially since from the foundation of the earth to our time six thousand years have not yet passed?

I pass over that a lie of this sort is contrary to the truth because the resurrection of the dead depends not on the heavenly bodies, not on the stars or degrees of the firmament, but on the will of God most high. Moreover, the sacred Scriptures assert that eternal life is conferred on the dead through the final resurrection so that they do not die anymore. But that sort of life cannot be looked for from the heavenly bodies. Nor would the beatitude of the saints be solid and lasting, since they would still worry that they might be reduced to the same labors and troubles which they suffered when they were here before. This is therefore a great mistake about the resurrection of the dead. There were Sadducees among the Hebrews who did not believe that the spirit existed and denied the resurrection of the dead.[10] Today too there are

---

[8]Martyr makes minor mathematical misstatements here, which the translator has corrected: tercentum sexaginta sex gradus. Cf. Origen *Contra Celsum* IV.67ff., V.20–21 on the Stoic doctrine of the succession of ages.

[9]E.g., Aristotle *Physics* VI.5, 229a7ff.

[10]Acts 23:8.

Libertines, who mock it and apply the scriptural treatment of the resurrection only to souls. During Paul's lifetime there lived Hymenaeus and Philetus, who claimed that the resurrection had already taken place by then.[11] Their teaching (as the Apostle says) was like a disease that has a wide pasture since the minds of the uneducated are easily taken in by these wicked opinions.

5. Another reason why God will restore the bodies of the departed to life depends upon his perfect justice, which is not manifest in this world. Often we see that at present the wicked abound in power and honors, overflow with wealth, and enjoy kind treatment; in contrast the devout and upright receive harsh treatment and labor under terrible burdens. These things could seem unjust if no other hope remained. Nor would it be fair if only the soul were to be either happy or afflicted with punishments since it had the body as its partner in performing both good and bad deeds. So it is just that it experience joys and punishments together with the body since it performed all actions through the body.

Among the Jews the rabbis put together a tale to teach this point, saying that some rich and powerful man planted a garden for himself with noble species of trees which bore splendid fruit.[12] To keep the fruit from being plucked, he assigned guards. Since one had to be on watch against the guards themselves, he employed two, such that one had excellent eyesight but was so lame that he could not walk at all; the other had good feet but was blind. When the lord of the garden went away, the wicked guards began to discuss between themselves how to eat the fruit. The blind man said, "I want some, but I can't see." The lame man said, "I see them but can't get at them." After long discussion they agreed that the blind man would lie on the ground and take the lame man on his back; since he could see he directed the blind man with his hand. Thus joined together they came to the trees and ate the fruit to their hearts' content. The lord of the garden returned and noting the damage that had been done, rebuked the guards. The lame man made the excuse that he could not have gone to the trees. The blind man said he could not have seen the fruit. Knowing their craftiness and trickery, the owner said, "You worked together, so I also will join you again and punish you together." So he tied the two together and punished them by beating and striking them both at once. That,

---

[11]2 Tim. 2:18.

[12]This story, which Martyr quotes almost verbatim, goes back to ca. 120–140 C.E. and is attributed to Rabbi Ishmael in Leviticus Rabbah, Wayikra, iv.5. It is translated in C. G. Montefiore and H. Loewe, eds., *A Rabbinic Anthology: Selected and Arranged with Comments and Introduction* (Cleveland: Meridian Books, 1963) 312–313. Thanks are due to Thomas Caldwell, S.J., of Marquette University for this reference.

they say, is the way it is with people. The soul knows, understands, and thinks but cannot by itself perform external works. The body in itself is stupid and does not think, but when it is urged and moved by the soul, is a suitable instrument for external actions. Since this is the case, reason and justice demand that after death they be joined again to receive punishments and rewards.

[OUTLINE OF THE TREATISE]

6. These statements have been made in a general way; in approaching the subject we divide this treatise into several chapters. First we bring forth reasons that seem to hinder and oppose the resurrection of the flesh. Second, we investigate its nature. Third, whether it can be proved and confirmed by human reasons, and indeed conclusive [ἀποδεικτικῶς] ones. Then we state the evidence from the divine letters of both Old and New Testaments; from these it is proved that the resurrection is sure to come and should be expected. Later we deal with its causes. In addition there are some remarks about the conditions and qualities of the risen. At the end we refute the arguments that seem to maintain that the resurrection is not going to happen. These I will review at the outset, not noting all of them but only the more important; from their refutation the other arguments can be easily solved.

[CONTRARY REASONS]

7. [1] First, as Porphyry used to say, for the happiness of our soul we should shun all bodies because they hinder and do not promote the contemplation and knowledge of God, where our happiness lies.[13] So it seems it should be laid down that souls cannot be perfectly happy if they are joined to bodies a second time. [2] Moreover [*216r*] even that is impossible, since the bodies have already been dissolved, they have disappeared into ashes, they have gone back to the original elements, even to prime matter. [3] Besides, it sometimes happens that a wolf eats a human being, a lion eats the wolf, birds eat the lion and then become food for other humans; therefore it is impossible to distinguish the flesh of the first person from that of later ones.[14] [4] This becomes much clearer if we look at *Anthropophagi*, men who eat only human flesh. Here it happens that the substances of the human bodies are mingled

---

[13]Porphyry (b. ca. 232), a founder of Neoplatonism. His emphasis on the One entailed reducing the soul's "vehicles" to appearances or parts of universal soul and intellect. Martyr's personal library included a copy of Porphyry's *Institutio* (CSV 212). See §67 below.

[14]For similar arguments, cf. Augustine, *De civ. Dei* 22.20; also, on Porphyry and Origen, see H. Chadwick, "Origen, Celsus and Resurrection," *Harvard Theological Review* 41 (1948) 88ff.

together on this basis. If there were a future resurrection of the dead, to whom should this flesh be attributed, the eaters or the eaten?

[5] We also see in nature that it is considered impossible to restore the same particular individual who has perished. Hence generation was established so that the arrangement of things may be continued, at least by the procreation of similar species. [6] When the soul is torn away from the body in death, it is not just accidents that are corrupted but the essential principles from which a human being is constituted, namely the body and also certain parts of the soul such as the nutrient and sentient faculties, which cannot exist outside the body. [7] Besides, when a certain quantity is cut in two it is no longer one in number; there are two quantities. If a motion that has been interrupted is repeated, it may be the same in kind but is distinguished from the first in number. While one is walking a mile, if he stops and rests a bit and later returns, could he say that the second walk is the same as the first? This is perceived not just as to length and movement and successive stages but also qualities and forms. For if someone enjoys health and falls into sickness, the previous health is ruined. But if the person later recovers, the health that takes over is not completely identical with the former state. Thus if bodies are to be restored with all that belongs to them, all their liquids, hair, and fingernails would be returned and their weight would be enormous. But if not everything is going to be restored but only certain things, no rationale can be assigned why this rather than that will be returned.

8. There are also many passages in the divine letters which oppose the resurrection, if they are taken *prima facie*. In Psalm 78 it is written that God punished the Jews in the desert to a certain degree, but did not want to pour out his full wrath against them. Because, it says, he remembered that they are flesh and like a soul that passes away not to return. If their souls do not return, there is no resurrection. It is also said in Psalm 115, "The dead do not praise you, Lord."[15] But if the souls of the dead do not celebrate the praises of God and those who have passed away are not going to proclaim them, there will be no resurrection. In the same Psalm it is stated, "The heavens are the Lord's heavens, but the earth he has given to the sons of men." If heaven has no relation to humans and they must dwell on earth and perish on it, there can be no hope for a resurrection. Solomon writes in Ecclesiastes 3, "For the fate of the sons of men and the fate of the beasts is the same; as one dies so dies the other. They all have the same breath." And he says, "Who knows whether the soul of Adam's sons go upward and the soul of the beast goes down?"[16] Chapter 14 of

---

[15] Pss. 78:38–39; 115:17.   [16] Eccl. 3:19, 21.

Job states that there is no common basis for humans and trees or plants; when these have been pruned they usually can sprout again, but a person who has died does not return.[17] It is also said that this future resurrection will be universal. But Daniel chapter 12 seems to describe a particular resurrection; he says, "Many of those who sleep in the dust of the earth shall awake."[18] But he would not have said "many" if all were to be awakened. Likewise it is written in the Psalm that the wicked will not rise at the judgment.[19] It is fitting that since the dead are to be restored to life through Christ, only those who are joined to Christ will receive this benefit. It follows that the wicked who are strangers to Christ should not be awakened. These are the arguments which are usually advanced against those who affirm the resurrection.

[DEFINITION]

9. Now let us proceed to our second topic by examining the items that contribute to the nature and definition of the resurrection. We will begin with the etymology of the name. The Greeks call it *anastasis* [ἀνάστασις]: in this word's composition the prefix *ana* is the same as *palin*, that is "again," as if it meant that something which had fallen were to stand again. Hence Damascene writing on this subject says that *anastasis* is "the second standing of the dead" [δεύτερος τῶν νεκρῶν στάσις].[20] The Hebrews call it תחיית המתים. For חיה is "to live"; so it is as if one should say, "the revivification of the dead." For them קרט means "to rise," from which they derive the term תקומת המתים,[21] that is, "the rising of the dead." קומה is also found among them, and צמידה from the verb צמד, "to stand."[22] Perhaps they have other words with this meaning, but these are the more commonly used and frequent among the rabbis. We will look at Latin terminology later.

10. As to substance: resurrection belongs to the predicament of action.[23] There are two main things to consider in actions, namely the agent and the subject itself into which the action is transferred by the agent. We take God to be the efficient cause of this action because no other cause in nature or in any

---

[17]Job 14:7, 9.   [18]Dan. 12:2.

[19]Ps. 1:6.   [20]John of Damascus *De fide orth.* IV.27 (PG 94.1220).

[21]The text is disordered. Before the pair of Hebrew terms we read *Heemanthicum*, an attempt at their transliteration but in the reverse order from Hebrew, i.e. *tecumat hametim* or such like. Anthony Marten gets the order right in CP: *Thechijath hammethim* (fol. 331 A). See "Selection of Texts," pp. xl–xli above concerning the editing of the work.

[22]The word צמידה is lacking and must be supplied if Martyr is alluding to a noun derived from the verb צמד, perhaps referring to Ezek. 37:10, where enfleshed bones "stand up" and constitute "a very great army."

[23]Cf. Aristotle *Topics* 1.9, 103b20ff.

sensate creature can be found with power to carry out the resurrection, as we shall discuss later in its place. Action is distinguished in many ways. One sort is physical [φυσική], such as generation, corruption, increase, [*216v*] decrease, alteration, and the like. Other actions are associated with practical knowledge, such as building, painting, plowing, metal casting, and the like. Still others look to the will, that is, to human choice, such as the works of virtues and vices. Actions are also distinguished because some are economic, some political, and others ecclesiastical. But resurrection finds its place nowhere in these distinctions. For all these we have mentioned somehow or other go back to nature. But the resurrection of the dead is an action completely supernatural; accordingly it is listed among those actions which surpass the powers of nature.

11. Now it remains for us to look into the subject that receives it. The only thing awakened is the human person who was extinguished by death. But a human person consists of two parts, as is clear to all; the soul, I mean, and the body. So we have to see whether the resurrection pertains to the soul or to the body. If we wish to speak strictly, bodies rise again but not souls. For that which fell after standing up is said to rise again. Souls do not perish together with the body but remain: therefore since they have not fallen they do not rise again. The sacred writings indicate that souls continue after their separation from their bodies. Christ said to the apostles, "Do not fear those who kill the body but cannot kill the soul."[24] But if the soul were extinguished with the body, the person who kills the body would also destroy the soul. Moreover Christ said to the thief, "Today you will be with me in paradise."[25] This would not happen if the soul were going to perish with the death of the body.

When the story of the death of Lazarus and the rich man is told in the Gospel, there is a clear explanation of what happens to human beings after death. Lazarus was carried up to the bosom of Abraham by the ministry of angels, but the rich man was carried down to the tortures of hell.[26] There are other testimonies about this proposition, but for the present let these suffice. Tertullian also taught in his fifth book against Marcion and in his book on the resurrection of the flesh that the resurrection is to be attributed to bodies.[27] He says that many rise who have not fallen earlier, such as bushes, plants, and the like, but none are said to arise again except those which fell after they had stood. The argument arises from an idiom of Latin speech, which distinguishes between "to rise" and "to rise again." He says that *cadaver* was derived

[24]Matt. 10:28.   [25]Luke 23:43.
[26]Luke 16:19–25.   [27]Tertullian *Adv. Marcionem* V.9 (PL 2, 523).

from *cadendo,* falling. Therefore he affirms the resurrection of bodies and not of souls.[28]

12. It should also be noted that the resurrection of the dead is a sort of new birth. For just as in the prior birth a person is produced consisting of a soul and a body, so in the resurrection, which is another birth, the person will be restored again. In Matthew chapter 19 it is written: "in the new world [ἐν τῇ παλιγγενεσίᾳ] when the son of man shall sit in his majesty."[29] Regeneration is now beginning as regards the soul, but then it will be completed as regards the body. There is then a sort of new birth. I said that in case it might be thought of as a new creation that comes from nothing and not from existing things, although in the divine writings it is not always understood in this sense. So the soul will return and impart its existence to the body just as it did before death. It will give the body not only its existence but will bring along with it all the human properties and communicate them to it. There will be some variation but not in essential principles; only the accidents will be changed, which can vary while the subject remains identical. If one set of qualities and affections belongs to children and another to youths and to old people, it is still the same person and the same man in childhood, youth and old age.

Thus we can define the resurrection of the dead this way: it is a new union of the soul with the body by the force or power of God, so that whole persons may stand before the last judgment and may receive rewards or punishments on the basis of their previous life. All the various kinds of causes are stipulated in this definition.[30] The formal cause is the union of soul and body, which also takes place as soon as humans are born, hence the addition of "new" or "repeated" [Nova seu Iterata], namely after death. We indicate the efficient cause when we state that it is to be done by divine force or power. The material cause is the soul and body which are again joined together. The final cause is so that the last judgment may be passed on a complete person.

13. We should, moreover, observe the important distinction between the death of humans that precedes the resurrection of the dead and the sort of death by which animals perish. For human death is called a separation of soul from body, since even if the body dies, the soul remains. This does not happen in animals, whose death involves soul and body together. Hence the statement of Solomon in Ecclesiastes, that the death of humans and beasts is the same, is not true unless understood in a general sense—namely that death comes to

---

[28]Tertullian *De Resurrectione Carnis* 18 (PL 2, 865).
[29]Matt. 19:28.
[30]For the Aristotelian fourfold causality see "Philosophy and Theology" §1, n. 4.

both of them.[31] But the sort of death is not the same for both groups. More will be said later about Solomon's statement. I mentioned it now so that we could understand how a different kind of death is laid down for animals and humans: if the resurrection of both is granted, it will not have the same form. Therefore even though we say that the body and not the soul will arise, still the resurrection will not take place without the soul, for it should be present.

In a sense the soul too can be said to rise again for two reasons. First, [*217r*] through death it somehow ceases to inform and direct the body, and in this respect it may be said to die. The other reason is that souls too are said to fall. Hence if rising belongs to someone who has fallen, souls too are understood as rising since in one sense they fall. Paul said to the Colossians, "If then you have been raised with Christ, seek the things that are above."[32] There is no doubt that he is speaking about the resurrection of souls, for those to whom he wrote this were still living. Likewise he says to the Romans that if Christ was raised through the glory of the Father, so you too should walk in newness of life. And to the Ephesians: "Arise from the dead, arise, and Christ shall give you light."[33] The book of Ecclesiasticus chapter 2, states: "Do not turn aside from God lest you fall." Likewise: "Let him who stands take heed lest he fall." Romans forbids judging another's servant: "It is before his own master that he stands or falls."[34] Since all these passages refer to souls, it seems that they have both fall and resurrection.

These are true statements, but we should know that the divine letters posit a twofold resurrection: a prior one, I mean, and a later one. In the former the soul arises from sins; in the later it recovers the body. At present we are talking about the later resurrection, so we said that it is proper to the body. Just as in the prior one the soul arises and not the body, so in this later one the body arises and not the soul.

14. We gather this twofold resurrection not only from the book of Revelation, where those who have a part in the prior resurrection are proclaimed to be blessed, but also from John's Gospel where the two are joined in the same passage, namely in chapter 5.[35] First Christ spoke there about the prior resurrection when he said, "The hour is coming and is now when the dead will hear the voice of God's son and who shall have believed." His statement that "The hour is coming and is now" indicates clearly enough that these words apply to the prior resurrection. No one would say that the hour of the later resurrection was then at hand. By "the dead who would live again if they had

---

[31]Eccl. 3:19.   [32]Col. 3:1.   [33]Rom. 6:4; Eph. 5:14.
[34]Sir. 2:7; 1 Cor. 10:12; Rom. 14:4.
[35]Rev. 20:6; John 5:25: qui crediderint (Vulg.: et qui audierint vivent).

believed in God's son" he understood those who were deprived of the spiritual life of souls because of their sins. Elsewhere Christ spoke about them: "Leave the dead to bury their own dead."[36] In Ephesians it states: "When you were dead through the trespasses and sins." He writes to Timothy about widows, "She who is a real widow, and is left alone, has set her hope on God and continues in supplications and prayers; whereas she who is self-indulgent is dead even while she lives."[37]

Indeed, we are all dead before justification by faith due to original sin and those sins that we add by our own free choice, and we stand absolutely in need of this resurrection of the dead. There is, however, an enormous difference between the earlier and later resurrection because the prior one applies only to the elect and those who are going to be made blessed forever. But the later resurrection applies to all, both wretched and joyful. On this point Christ continues in the same passage from John, saying, "Do not marvel at this; for the hour is now coming when all who are in the tombs will hear the voice of God's son and come forth, those who have done good to the resurrection of life, and those who have done evil to the resurrection of judgment."[38] Here there is mention of tombs, that is, of sepulchers. Then he said that the time will come; he did not add that it was then present. Just as there is a prior and a second death, so also there is a prior and a later resurrection. But as was said already, just now we are dealing only with the later resurrection.

[Rational Proofs]

15. It has been proved that the resurrection of the dead is an action from the class of things which depend on a miracle, not on nature.[39] So if one asks, "Is it something natural?" we answer like this: as regards the formal cause, which I said was the joining together of soul with body, the term "natural" is by no means to be rejected. It suits our human nature to have the soul joined to a body. But if the efficient cause and its mode are considered, they do indeed surpass nature. Thus it is that there is an easy answer to the third topic of this treatise in which the question was posed: are there arguments for the resurrection which are natural and conclusive [ἀποδεικτικῶς]? I say on that presupposition, since the thing itself surpasses all the power of nature, reasons of that kind cannot be found. There are indeed some that are fairly effective, but if they are examined more closely they are probable but not necessary

---

[36]Matt. 8:22.   [37]Eph. 2:1; 1 Tim. 5:5–6.
[38]John 5:28–29.   [39]See §10 (p. 54) above.

arguments, if we look to the nature of things.[40] To reveal the case more clearly, it should be noted that apodictic arguments are of two kinds. Some break down their questions to self-evident first principles in the nature of things. Arguments of this sort are so rarely found that only some few of them can be demonstrated in mathematics.

Other arguments do not rest at all on self-evident first propositions, yet the propositions to which they conclude may be traced back to those that are truly self-evident. Again, there are some arguments that rest on true and necessary principles but not ones evident in the science which uses them, but which are proved and truly known in a more lofty and higher faculty. This kind is commonly called a subalternate science.[41] For the musician proves and concludes some things about harmony and sounds from certain principles proved and formulated in mathematics. This sort of reasoning is apodictic, but only to someone skilled in both sciences, namely mathematics and music. It cannot be called apodictic to the other person, who is a musician only, because [*217v*] his analysis [ἀνάλυσις] does not arrive at self-evident first principles. This is the case in arguments for the resurrection of the dead. Some arguments about it are drawn from natural propositions that are highly probable. But if their principles were spelled out, physicists and those who work exclusively in the study of nature would not be convinced because they cannot see any analysis leading to the supernatural causes that bring about the conclusion and consistently assert it. When the devout refer the conclusions that have been reached back to the Word of God, undergirding and confirming them by tracing them back to that Word, they hold them as apodictic, not indeed by natural knowledge but by faith, which depends wholly on the divine oracles.

16. We now have to explain by what means philosophers and those who rely only on natural reason set themselves against arguments deriving from natural principles. Let me begin with those that seem more solid than the others. First they say that something imperfect is incapable of perfect happiness; the soul separated from the body is maimed and mutilated so that to gain happiness it must be united again with the body. Philosophers launch a two-pronged attack against this argument. Either they say that the part that has been torn from the other is imperfect when it draws some advantage and

---

[40]Martyr contrasts *argumenta necessaria* (apodictic, convincing) with *probabilia*. For the material in this section see Aristotle *An. Post.* I.2.II.19, and *NE* VI.3.

[41]The scholastics treated this topic under *de subalternatione scientiarum*; e.g. Aquinas in ST Ia.Q1.2 resp.a 5. ST Ia.1.2, Resp.: "quae procedunt ex principiis notis lumine superioris scientiae"; see Aristotle *An. Post.* I.10. 766b23.

perfection from the other. But it is the nature of the soul to bestow its goods on the body without receiving any perfection or utility from it. Therefore the absence of the body is no hindrance to its own happiness. Or they answer that it is enough for the soul's perfect happiness that the ultimate good is present to it; through it the soul understands perfectly and is engulfed in supreme pleasure. For this the body is not needed. But for believers the previous argument is strengthened by the divine writings because from them they know that the soul together with the body are thrown into hell by God; if he acts this way as regards punishments, he would do the same as regards rewards.

A second argument is put together like this: nothing against nature will last forever, but the permanent separation from the body is contrary to the human soul. But since souls are immortal and do not fall along with the body, they endure forever; and as it is natural for the soul to be the form of the body, it is contrary to its nature to be cut off from the body. If this separation cannot be perpetual, there is no alternative aside from its being reunited to the body. Against this argument the pagans might say that it takes something to be certain and evident that is obscure in the light of nature, namely that the soul continues after death and is immortal.

Not a few noble philosophers have thought very differently. Very learned men, Tertullian, I mean, and Gregory Nazianzen, charged Aristotle himself with thinking that the human soul is mortal; Alexander of Aphrodisias, no obscure Peripatetic, thought so.[42] Averroës in the Peripatetic school taught that there was only one human intellect which was linked to individual people through phantasms.[43] Hence the principle taken for granted, that the soul continues incorruptible after death, is doubtful and does not depend on matters that are self-evident and known in the nature of things. An argument built on it waffles and cannot be taken as solid. Avicenna in his *Metaphysics* says that the soul is joined to the body so that it might acquire for itself through the external senses both interior information and knowledge of things; once it has achieved this, there is no need for it to seek that union again.[44]

---

[42]Tertullian *De Anima* 12 (PL 2.707ff.); Gregory Nazianzen *Orat.* VII.20 (PG 35.781); Alexander Aphrodisias (2d century), most celebrated Greek commentator on Aristotle, "deals with the soul in terms of entelechy and, therefore, denies its immortality"; see P. Merlan in *CHGM* 121. His doctrine of the soul's mortality was adopted by Pomponazzi at Padua-; see Introduction, p. xxv.

[43]According to the received scholastic opinion, Averroës *In de Anima* III.4–5, taught a universal Intellect that contacts the individual through imagination; see also Introduction, p.xxiii; Aquinas, SCG II.59.

[44]Avicenna or Ibn Sina (980–1037) follows Aristotle *De Anima* I.1, the sixth book (*Liber sextus naturalium*) in the *Shifa* (*The Healing*) in seeing the soul as the form of its body; Gilson, *History of Christian Philosophy*, 198f,. 64 n. See L.E. Goodman, *Avicenna* (New York: Routledge, 1992) 160ff., and Introduction, p. xxiv above.

Others refute the argument for the resurrection more subtly and say that what is contrary to nature cannot be perpetual when the principles of its restoration survive in the natural order. But if they are completely done away with, no restoration is to be expected. They illustrate what they had argued with a rather clear analogy: they say that a tree that has been cut down lies flat contrary to nature; it may be restored if its roots survive vigorously because it sprouts a second time and is reborn. But if the roots are completely pulled out, their destruction will be permanent. Hence they assert that the soul torn from the body knows well that the prerequisites of second union no longer exist in the nature of things. Accordingly it is untouched by any desire for it, since the choice of our will is not drawn toward impossible things. Thus might the pagans respond to the argument. But believers employ and find comfort in this argument by confirming it with the word of God, which asserts the incorruptibility of our soul after death and concedes to God power and freedom to unite the soul with the body.

17. The third argument is usually derived from God's justice, which should allot punishment and rewards for acts performed in this life through the body. It would not seem fair that when these two, the soul and body, have acted together in union either rightly or wrongly, only one of them should be either punished or rewarded. Philosophers would moreover reply that it is not clear to them that the world is so ruled by God through his punitive and retributive justice that he takes account of individual persons, rendering to each one rewards or punishments. Perhaps they would grant a certain providence regarding the firm and constant motion of the heavens and the conservation of species, but they would deny that it exists for individuals.[45] They would add that sufficient rewards and punishments are built into good and bad actions themselves. For upright conduct brings a marvelous joy to the conscience that surpasses all external rewards. [*218r*] Likewise immoral conduct troubles people severely, nor can they escape the scourge of conscience which provides sufficient misery and unhappiness to punish them. Finally they would urge that it is enough that the soul itself either receives a reward or suffers punishment; there is no need to transfer these to the body, which is not the principal cause but only the instrument of actions. An analogy might be introduced about craftsmen. They are rewarded only if they produce a beautiful tapestry or a fine house. No compensation is given to the tools they used in weaving or building. If the work turns out badly, these instruments are not the least affected by punishment or condemnation. One does not smash a poisoned cup because some people died by drinking from it, especially if it

---

[45]See "Providence," §7 below.

were an elegant and precious vessel. Nor do they break or throw away a sword by which someone was killed, because these are instruments and not principal causes. Sometimes anger is so unbearable that poisoned chalices are destroyed and swords thrown away. Hence both things could and sometimes do happen—the argument is probable, not necessary.

Besides, a distinction should be added regarding means because some are united and some are separate. The body is the instrument of the soul and is conjoined to it. So it is no surprise if it is jointly punished or achieves remuneration. While we live here we see that evildoers have their hands cut off and eyes gouged out. Nor should we ignore the fact that this argument, which is deduced from God's justice and judgment, is not universal because infants are also revived, but they still should not be held accountable for the works which they do through their bodies. Paul seems to confirm this argument; after asserting the resurrection of the body, he says to the Corinthians, chapter 15, "Therefore, my beloved brethren, be steadfast, immovable, abounding in every good work, knowing that in the Lord your labor is not in vain."[46] But work is common to both soul and body. Therefore both will reap a profit. Almost all the Fathers used this sort of argument.

I have already reviewed what are the stronger arguments; I will now come to other, weaker ones in which we see not a proof of the resurrection but a kind of image.

18. As we see, people talk about days passing by and returning daily but in fact yesterday is not the same numerically as today. An analogy is also drawn from trees and plants. They seem to have died in winter but with the return of spring they sprout again, are adorned with leaves, send forth flowers, and at last produce fruit. But we should know that they were not really dead in winter—life continued in them still, although hidden. It could be replied to this that human life is also not completely taken away after death because it continues in souls, which still survive. Paul to a degree uses this argument in 1 Corinthians and shows that revivification comes after corruption when he says, "What you sow does not come to life unless it dies." He also shows that the previous scattering of seed causes various conditions for the new fruit, for he says, "You sow a kernel of wheat or some other grain; God gives it a body as he has chosen."[47] Therefore if renovation often comes immediately to creatures, what will happen to humans who count for much more before God than either trees or hay? For all were created for mankind's sake.

---

[46]1 Cor. 15:58.   [47]1Cor. 15:36ff.

They borrow an analogy from the Indian bird called the phoenix; Lactantius gives an elegant description of how it dies and is renewed.[48] They also bring forward the testimony of the Sibyls which confirms the resurrection of the dead.[49] And lest anything be missing, they weave in the fables of the poets who say that Hippolytus and Aesculapius were once raised from the dead.[50] They say that the poets told such fables because this dogma about the resurrection was once handed down by the Fathers. It was transformed by those fellows, or rather deformed, in their wretched poems. But this is not necessarily so, because not everything that they cooked up was borrowed or discovered by the holy Fathers. They wrote and made up things about centaurs, harpies, and chimeras which the saints never thought about. The image of sleeping people is also brought in, a daily occurrence for us. A person deep in sleep stops moving, does not walk, does nothing. After being roused, the same person returns at once to former activities. The analogy finds support in the way the Scriptures speak; they call death sleep and speak of the dead as sleeping.[51]

The unbelief of people who doubt that human bodies can be restored from corrupted ashes is reproved when they repeatedly see how various animals—mice, moles, frogs, and worms—are produced from corrupt and rotten matter. Sparkling gems are commonly collected from caves in the earth. Besides, who can look at seeds and see what will come forth from them with the passage of time? The seed of animals is a speck or drop of shapeless liquid where hands, feet, ears, eyes, head, and the like are invisible. Let us talk of the seed of the vine: its body is so small that it can hardly be held between two little fingers. Where are the roots in it, and the trunk of the roots, or the complex of tentacles? The shade [*218v*] of its foliage? Where the beauty of the grape clusters? Although that seed is very dry, from it winepresses overflow with floods of grape juice. These things happen daily in nature, so we should reflect

---

[48]*Phoenix*, attributed to Lactantius (PL 7, 277); cf. Tertullian *De Res. Carnis* 13 (PL 2, 857).

[49]The Sibyls were female prophets, first mentioned by Heraclitus. Most famous was the soothsayer of Cumae whom Aeneas consulted before descending into the lower world (*Aeneid* vi.10). She sold the Sybilline books to Tarquin the Proud; they were studied by the Romans to learn religious observances and predictions.

[50]Hippolytus, son of Theseus and Hippolyte, was restored to life by Aesculapius at the request of Artemis; Aesculapius, legendary Greek god of medicine, was skilled in healing and resurrecting, and himself rumored to have returned from death. Origen also defended the resurrection of Jesus as different from such "prodigious stories" designed to deceive the simple; see Origen, *Contra Cels.* II.55, trans. H. Chadwick (Cambridge: Cambridge University Press, 1965).

[51]John 11:11–13.

that whenever bodies are sent to the tomb, the seeds of the resurrection are being committed to the furrows for a second renewal.

Some of the dead were brought back by the prophets, by Christ, and the apostles.[52] It is even reported that some saints restored animals to their former life. It is written that Sylvester raised a dead bull. They say that the holy Germanus called back from the dead his donkey that had died and a calf that his family had eaten.[53] You may say that these are fables; I will not argue the point. Many things were mixed in with the lives of the saints which, even if their truth were allowed, do not make us grant that those animals were restored the same numerically. It could have been that it was not they themselves, but others like them were substituted. Still I would not say that this is impossible by an act of divine power. For he who created a man out of nothing doubtless has the power to restore him. Gregory wrote in book 6 of the *Moralia* that everybody should agree that it is far more difficult to create what did not exist than to restore what had existed.[54]

19. God can do all things which do not involve a contradiction, as they say in the schools.[55] For in general it is impossible for things to coexist when they cancel out and destroy each other. That does not, however, take anything away from God's omnipotence. For God is omnipotent even though he cannot sin or deny himself or make things that happened in the past not to be past events, nor make a human body while it exists not to be a human body, and make the number three not to be three. Such things are not impossible because of some defect in him but from the very contradiction in the things. The resurrection of the dead in no way belongs within this category. With regard to souls: they do not die but remain alive along with their powers and human properties. Hence those who die can be said to survive somehow in their property and root. Here is how Gregory the Great in his account of Job confirms this: in his story it is related that everything was restored to him twofold. Previously he had seven thousand sheep, fourteen thousand were restored to him; he had three thousand camels, he now has six thousand, and so on for the rest of his possessions. But he had only seven sons and three daughters. It is understood that the number of children was also doubled,

---

[52]1 Kings 17:20; 2 Kings 4:32ff., 13:21; Matt. 9:25; Luke 7:15; John 11:44; Acts 9:40, 20:10ff.

[53]Sylvester I, Pope (314–335), subject of the legendary *Vita beati Sylvestri*; Germanus I, Patriarch of Constantinople (715–730); the *Historia ecclesiastica et mystica*, of doubtful authenticity, is attributed to Germanus.

[54]Gregory the Great *Moralium Libri* (*Exp. in Lib. Job* 5:9) v.15.18 (PL 75, 738).

[55]E.g. Peter Lombard, *Sent.* 1.d.42, cap. 2; Aquinas, ST 1.25.3c: "He can do all things that are possible absolutely," i.e. in terms of logical possibility.

because as Gregory says, the previous seven still remained safe with God, wherefore he could be said to have fourteen.[56]

Since this is the situation, the whole difficulty of the resurrection seems to lie with the body. For when it becomes extinct, so that not even its footprints survive, it does not seem possible to restore it. Still, because it does not fade back into nothingness but is dissolved into the elements or into primary matter (as the philosophers say), then one should not deny that it is possible to extract it again from the same matter and the same elements. Indeed, even the souls of animals, although wiped out by death, are still not reduced to nothing. So the divine power can restore them from matter and from the elements. As is written in Romans, God calls the things that are not as if they are, nor is there anything that can resist his voice.[57] Just as all things were created by God's voice, so they can be restored by it. Let these considerations suffice — based on natural reason, they are, as we said, probable but not conclusive.

What is affirmed on this subject should also be understood regarding the other articles of faith. Things that are believed by someone cannot be known naturally by the same person.[58] But somebody might say, "We believe in one God, but his existence is deduced by natural reason." To this we answer that the philosopher did indeed arrive by physical investigation at one supreme principle, which the Greeks called *Theos* and the Latins *Deus*. But He is not the one whom Christian faith professes. We do not believe in one God simply and purely, but in him who created heaven and earth, and who has a Son and a Holy Spirit. These additions the philosophers in no way attained by their reasoning. Hence what the Apostle taught the Hebrews remains most true: "Faith is the conviction of things not seen."[59]

[OLD TESTAMENT]

20. Since this is the case, reason demands that we now turn to a different topic of our subject and confirm the resurrection with divine testimony since it cannot be proved by physical arguments. This is contained in both the Old and New Testaments. We will begin this in chronological order from the Old Testament. The first passage from it is found in Exodus chapter 3: "I am the

---

[56]Gregory the Great *Moralium Libri* (*Exp. in Lib. Job* 5:9) xxxv.15.35 (PL 76, 769).

[57]1 Cor. 1:28; Rom. 13:1–2.

[58]Cf. Augustine on the inaccessibility of reason to contingent, historic truths of Christianity, including resurrection, *De Trin.* IV.16.21 (PL 42, 902), *De vera rel.* 7.13 (PL 34, 128); Gregory Nazianzen, *Orat.* XXVII.4 (*Theol. Prima*, PG 36.15).

[59]Heb. 11:1.

God of Abraham, Isaac, and Jacob." Christ used this passage when the Sadducees tested him.[60] The term for the Sadducees derives from the word צדק, meaning justice. They were men of the law who did not accept any Scriptures except the Law given through Moses. They rigidly followed the letter [τὸ ῥητὸν] and (it seems) did not allow any interpretation. Moreover, because[61] [*219r*] they did not believe in the resurrection of the dead, they also denied that angels existed, as is related in the Acts of the Apostles.[62] Among the Jews of that time (if I may speak parenthetically) there were also the Pharisees, from the word פרש, which means to separate, interpret, and expand. They accepted not just the Law but also the prophets as its interpreters. They also explained and interpreted the divine letters.[63]

Besides them there were the Essenes, who are called after the word עשה, which means to do. They were very upright and worked with their hands to gain a living, also helping the needy; hence we should also call them workers. Without doubt those who think that they are named as if from ὅσιοι, that is "holy ones," are dreaming. The etymology of Hebrew names should not be looked for in Greek words. Among the Jews there were also Gaulonites, named after a certain leader of a faction among the Jews. They agreed completely with the Pharisees except that they thought that tribute should not be paid to foreign nations, since they wanted the sons of Abraham, that is, the people of God, to be completely free. Josephus describes all these things clearly in his *The Jewish Wars* and also in his *Antiquities*.[64]

But to return to the Sadducees. They attributed almost everything to free will, living strict lives and employing sparse and rustic morals. They could be regarded as Hebrew Stoics, except that the Stoics turned almost everything over to God's providence and fate, while the Sadducees regarded such beliefs with no little disdain. Although the Pharisees and Sadducees had factional quarrels among themselves, they agreed in attacking Christ. Therefore in order to mock the resurrection of the dead, the Sadducees said that a woman was present whom seven brothers took as their wife when they passed away without children—according to the command of the Law as found in Deuter-

---

[60]Ex. 3:6; Matt. 22:32.

[61]Reading *quod* for *quia*.

[62]Acts 23:8.

[63]The derivation of the name "Pharisee" remains problematic; see *Abingdon Bible Dictionary* 5:289ff.

[64]Gaulonitis is the land east of the Jordan, mentioned by Josephus as part of the tetrarchy of Philip; its name is probably from Golan, a city of refuge (Deut. 4:43); see Josephus *Antiqu.* 17.8.1, 18.1.1. The three Jewish "sects" are discussed in Josephus *De Bello Judaico* 2.8.2 and *Antiqu.* 13.5.9 etc.

onomy chapter 25. Which of the seven brothers will have her as wife in the resurrection of the dead? The purpose of this question was to deny resurrection since it led to absurd consequences that were opposed to divine Law and could not be made consistent with upholding its integrity. Christ answered: "You are wrong."[65] But we should not believe that the ignorance under which they were laboring revealed their guilt. This is why they were in error: they did not want to understand or hear people who were giving them good advice.

Christ showed them the two main points or sources of their error: first, because they did not understand the Scriptures; second, because they did not take into account divine power. There are many ways of going wrong about the Scriptures: either because people do not have language skills or because literal statements are not distinguished from tropes, or because an obscure passage is not explained through a clearer one.[66] We do not pay attention when at times the things being signified are attributed to the signs, or the reverse, when the properties of the signs are ascribed to the things being signified. Anybody wanting to understand these matters in more detail should look into the useful books *On Christian Doctrine* which Augustine wrote.

There are two errors regarding divine power: first, that all things without exception are handed over to him; second, that very little was granted to him. The Sadducees clung to this second kind of error. For when they heard that the dead would live again after this world, they did not think that any other life was possible from that which we now live, in which we need food, drink, and the procreation of children. Hence by thinking too narrowly about God's power, they did not think that he could transfer those who had already been revived to a heavenly life approaching the condition of the angels. Christ pointed out how they had gone astray, as is found in Luke where he says, "The sons of this age marry and are given in marriage; but in the resurrection from the dead, they shall neither marry nor be given in marriage because they are equal to the angels." In mentioning the angels he was rebuking the Sadducees for denying that angels exist.[67]

21. He assigns a reason why humans will be like that after the resurrection by saying, "For they cannot die any more."[68] Here we should note that the procreation of children was established for a twofold purpose: first, that

---

[65]Deut. 25:5; Matt. 22: 29. On this encounter with the Sadducees, see Matt. 22:23–33; Mark 12:13–17; Luke 20:20–26. Vermigli mixes phrases from the three Gospels.

[66]For Martyr's developed exegetical principles, see *Exhort. ad Iuventes*, LC/CP app.

[67]Luke 20:34–36: "There came to him some Sadducees, those who say that there is no resurrection" (v. 27).

[68]Luke 20:37.

humans might multiply since only two people were created at the beginning; second, so that when they multiplied to a proper number, as many died, others would take their place. Therefore, since there will be a proper number of humans in the resurrection, and death cannot intervene, procreation would be obsolete. The words of the evangelists and of Christ himself should not be understood as if he were teaching that the risen shall be without bodily substance. He did not say they would be angels but would be like the angels, equal to the angels. Nor should we wonder when Luke writes that they will be future children of the resurrection, children of God.[69]

This is not to be understood as denying that the saints in this life are children of God even now—otherwise when they live here how could they call out, "Abba, Father," or pray to our Father who is in heaven?[70] It is sometimes the practice of the sacred writings to say that things will come to exist when they become evident. It is not apparent now that we are the children of God, but it will be clear in the resurrection. For when Christ shall have come, then we too shall appear one with him in glory. Therefore Luke writes that the saints will then be the children of God. I should not omit that what Christ said there relates only to the resurrection of the just. When the unjust will have arisen, even though they shall be immortal, they still will not emerge [*219v*] glorious and impassible like the angels. This is what Christ said about the ignorance of the Sadducees with regard to divine power.

22. It can also be rightly said that they were ignorant of the Scriptures. How could they deny that there were angels when the book of Genesis writes about an angel that prevented Abraham from sacrificing his son Isaac as he planned?[71] It is also stated there that Abraham received three guests, at least two of whom were angels; it says they were with Lot.[72] An angel stood next to Moses near the bush, and took a position between the Egyptians and the camp of the Israelites.[73] The camp of the angels was seen by Jacob at Mahanaim, and he wrestled almost all night with an angel.[74] So Christ was right to say they did not know the Scriptures. He pointed to a passage in the second book of Moses because they did not accept as Scriptures anything except the Law (they did indeed read the prophets and Psalms, just as we read the Fathers, the books of Maccabees, as well as the Wisdom of Solomon and of Sirach), and also because they used Moses in objecting to Christ. Rightly then did he pit Moses against them. In answering them the Lord did not intend to gather all the proof texts in the Old Testament; otherwise, there would have

---

[69]Luke 20:36.
[71]Gen. 22:2, 11.
[73]Ex. 3:2; 14:19.

[70]Rom. 8:15; Matt. 6:9.
[72]Gen. 19:1.
[74]Gen. 32:1, 24.

been no lack of statements from the opinion of the prophets and from other Scriptures.

Although these words, "I am the God of Abraham, of Isaac, and of Jacob," are found in many places of the sacred Scripture, Mark and Luke refer to them explicitly as regards the vision Moses had beside the bush, as is found in the third chapter of Exodus.[75] When Jesus had refuted the Sadducees like this, the crowd was dumbfounded in admiration of Christ's wisdom. But because common folk are sometimes thought to lack judgment, Luke adds that some of the scribes said, "Teacher, you have spoken well."[76] Therefore Christ's argumentation enjoyed the approval not just of ordinary people but also of scholars. And not unjustly. What better interpreter of the divine Law could we wish than the Word [τῷ λόγῳ], by whom it was given from the beginning?

23. The foundations of this argument must be examined more closely so they may appear more clearly. If life was completely over for the dead patriarchs, how can God still be their God? They are indeed dead, by human judgment and according to nature, but not before God. For Luke writes, "For all live to him."[77] The statement that the patriarchs live to God can have two meanings. First, if all this refers to God's foreknowledge and predestination, he has indeed present before him everything that will happen, nor can he be frustrated in what he proposes. Those who are to be raised in a thousand years are said to live to him, while the patriarchs live to him because they reign with him in heavenly glory. Paul employs the same terminology in writing about Christ to the Romans: "The death he died to sin, he died once, but the life he lives he lives to God,"[78] that is, since he is with him in glory and sits at his right hand. But you might have said, "On this basis it is not the saints themselves but their souls that could be said to live with Christ in heaven." This is indeed true, but through synecdoche because it attributes what is a part to the whole. We are not afraid to say that Saint Peter and Saint James are in heaven with Christ, when only their souls dwell there. Paul even said that he wished to be dissolved and be with Christ when he knew that only his soul would be with him up to the last day of judgment.[79] We read in the Gospel account that Lazarus was taken up to the bosom of Abraham and that a cruel rich man was carried down to hellish tortures, when it was nonetheless only their souls which were dispatched to those regions.[80]

[75]Ex. 3:2–6.   [76]Luke 20:39.
[77]Luke 20:38.   [78]Rom. 6:10.   [79]Phil. 1:23.   [80]Luke 16:19–23.

24. A quibble is thrown up against our Lord's argument: God calls himself the God of Abraham, Isaac, and Jacob because he was once their God while they were alive. He helped them and entered a covenant with them. But this objection is in vain, because he is not said to have been their God but by the present tense the statement is made, "I am their God" [ἐγὼ εἰμί]. In the Hebrew the verb "to be" is not inserted, but it is written simply אבכי אלהי.[81] This does not matter because the Holy Spirit through the mouth of the evangelists expresses the verb "to be." They write "I am God" [ἐγὼ εἰμὶ ὁ θεὸς].[82] But if the saints who have passed away were completely deprived of life and were not going to be recalled to it, what enrichment would they expect from him, or how is he their God? A teacher who has some students can say while they are living, "I am their teacher." But when they have passed away, he should not speak like that. So too a wife whose husband has died will not say "I am his wife," but "I was his wife." Or a father whose son is dead will not say "I am his father," but "I was." This indicates that if God says he is their God, life is somehow to be attributed to those patriarchs. For no benefit is bestowed on those who are completely dead.

I do not delay over quibblers who argue that God conferred benefits on the dead patriarchs through their posterity. For we should note in the divine writings that the proposition is copulative, namely that God would be the God of both the patriarchs and of their seed, and therefore this proposition should be true for either group. The force of this argument lies in the fact that we always understand God as benefiting, protecting, and defending those whose [220r] God he is. When the covenant was made between God and mankind, God wanted to be worshipped and honored by them and in turn to recognize them for his people. But who can be a father without children? Who can be a lord without servants? Who can be a king without subjects? Surely no one. Neither can God be their God if they do not exist.

Christ is by no means the first to point out this connection. Habakkuk touches on it in his first chapter when he says, "For you are our God from everlasting; we shall not die," that is, forever.[83] Therefore God does not permit those whose God he is to die completely. He is indeed worshipped and honored by those whose God he is. But the dead neither praise nor worship nor honor God. Hence if Abraham, Isaac, and Jacob have a God, they worship him. If they do this, they are not yet dead.[84] Let us listen to Christ himself, how he strengthens and hands on the argument proposed. When he had said,

---

[81]Ex. 3:6.   [82](Ex. 3:6, LXX); Matt. 22:32; Mark 12:26.
[83]Hab. 1:12.   [84]A good example of Martyr's use of syllogistic reasoning.

"I am the God of Abraham, the God of Isaac and the God of Jacob," it is as if somebody were objecting, "So what?" He added, "God is not the God of the dead but of the living."

Another obstacle to this statement seems to be what is written in Romans: "Christ died and lived again, that he might be Lord of both the living and the dead."[85] Someone might gather from this that it is not absurd for God to be the Lord of the dead. Some may reply that Christ did not say that God is not the Lord of the dead but God of the dead. To tell the truth, this seems to me a very minor shift in debate, for it is well known that "Lord" and "God" are interchangeable in the divine writings. The word *Elohe* [אלהי], which is used in Hebrew, is very frequently translated by the word "Lord." So the knot can be untied a different way, as we say with Christ that God is the God not only of the living—but the living have a twofold division because some of them still have a body joined to them, and some have been freed from it; but all are living. We do not deny that it follows from this that the souls of the departed live with God. Indeed it should be added that God is not the savior of part of them, so that he wishes to save only their soul; just as he is God of both body and soul, so he will save both. It does not suit those who have served God pure and simple to achieve only a halfway salvation. They will indeed have it full, solid, and perfect.

25. Christ's argument scourges the Anabaptists in two ways. First, because they think that the Old Testament has no importance for us. Christ clearly seeks to use its testimony to confirm the resurrection of the dead, as the Apostles frequently did. Second, when they argue with us about baptizing children they want us to produce from Scripture explicit, plain, and clear statements saying that children should be baptized. They do not want to be satisfied with arguments and conclusions drawn from Scripture; but here, about to prove the resurrection of the dead, Christ does not bring forth an explicit statement, but one from which the resurrection may be deduced. In introducing his minor premise he himself adds: he is not the God of the dead but of the living.[86]

There are others of our time, moreover, that think the testimony adduced by Christ was not understood by the ancients in the sense that they thought it referred to the resurrection of the dead. They persuade themselves that the people of old did indeed have salvation through Christ by receiving

---

[85]Rom. 14:9.

[86]Martyr is still discussing the argument of Jesus in Matt. 22:32ff. (see §20 above), in which the major premise is: "The Lord is called the God of Abraham" and the minor premise is: "God is not God of the dead but of the living," with the implied conclusion: "Therefore Abraham is alive."

from him forgiveness of their sins and everlasting happiness, even though they did not understand these things. Similarly, the children of Christians are saved even though they do not yet understand the heavenly and Christian mysteries. They say that God nourished them with earthly and temporal promises, about the land of Canaan and numerous progeny, with victories and riches, and that he preserved them in his worship; but they did not acknowledge Christ as Savior from sin and from eternal death, as author of life and prince of the resurrection and every gift. They urge that Christ was the very first to disclose the full mystery of resurrection, deducing the argument for it in the passage we discussed, whereas the ancients had previously never understood it.

The followers of Servetus today are such persons—they both accept and promote a terrible deception.[87] How dare they say this if they accept the New Testament? Certainly Paul asserts in Galatians that the seed promised to Abraham, in whom all nations of the earth were to be blessed, was Christ.[88] And when Abraham believed and was justified, he certainly did not have this by a faith which was concerned with temporal possessions or a vast progeny, but with Christ the son of God. As Paul writes to the Romans, we are justified the same way that Abraham was justified, namely through faith in Christ.[89] Christ also says about him, "He saw my day and rejoiced."[90] Besides, the prophets very clearly predicted the mysteries of Christ in such a way that they seem not to be prophets but evangelists. Were they saying and writing what they did not understand? That would indeed be the role not of God's prophets but of madmen. Nor is it likely that Christ's argument was unknown; otherwise the Sadducees could have easily answered that the passage was not understood like this by their ancestors nor was it so interpreted about the life of the patriarchs. But the question was so evident that some of the scribes spoke openly: "Teacher, you have spoken well."[91]

As the evangelists recounted, the Pharisees noticed how Christ had forced the Sadducees to be silent, which indicates that this was a public question and that there was no room for evasion. [*220v*] The Pharisees, moreover, affirmed the resurrection of the dead, so there can be no doubt about their proving it from the Scriptures. The history of Josephus sufficiently proves that they went back before Christ's coming; he says they had existed from the time of the Hasmoneans.[92]

---

[87]Servetus was reputed to deny the immortality of the soul, a charge he consistently rejected; it was not among the official reasons for his condemnation; see R. Bainton, *Hunted Heretic: The Life and Death of Michael Servetus 1511–1553* (Gloucester, Mass.: Peter Smith, 1978) 198, 207.

[88]Gal. 3:16.   [89]Rom. 4:23.   [90]John 8:56   [91]Luke 20:39.

[92]The Pharisees emerged as a distinct group shortly after the Hasmonean revolt, about 165 BCE; see Josephus, *Wars* 1.5.2, 2.8.2; *Antiqu.* 12.6.1, 13.5.9.

Therefore Christ was not the first to assert this doctrine, nor did he twist his way of teaching so that he proved it by obscure and uncertain arguments. When he dealt with something from the Scriptures he always brought forward statements that were clear and obvious. When he questioned the Jews on their beliefs about the Messiah and they replied that he would be the son of David, he answered, "How is it then that David, inspired by the Spirit, calls him Lord?" He notes the Psalm in which it is written, "The Lord said to my Lord." He would have gained nothing if everyone did not agree that this Psalm was written about the Messiah.[93] Likewise in dealing with divorce, he cited the passage from the book of Genesis, "Male and female he created them," and what Adam said, "This at last is bone of my bone and flesh of my flesh ... and the two will be in one flesh."[94] This too was not from obscure sources; he wove his argument from clear texts. He worked in a similar fashion regarding the order and dignity of the commandments when he ranked this as the first and greatest command: "You shall love the Lord your God with all your heart, and with all your soul, and with all your strength." And the other is like it: "You shall love your neighbor as yourself."[95] Since he always worked from clear and certain sources, why in this one passage do we want his argument to have been uncertain and obscure and never thought of before?

I will pass over these things and note this: these two vices, namely ignorance of the Scriptures and of God's power, can even today be hurled against all who assert perverse doctrines because they suffer from ignorance of both or at least one of them. Therefore when we come to read the Scriptures we must try to escape both these failings, so that we understand the Scriptures properly, and rightly esteem the power of God. Let this suffice for the text that Christ put forward.

26. Now in keeping with chronological order I will deal with the testimony of Job, found in chapter 19 of his book. But before proposing the words themselves, I would like to touch on what he said earlier. In order that they might think more carefully about what would be said, he caught their attention this way: "Oh that my words were written down not on sheets of paper but in a book, even on lead or on stone with an iron pen so they might be remembered forever!"[96] Laws were once engraved like this on bronze tablets so that the writing would not wear away. It is stated in Jeremiah that the sin of Judah was written with an adamantine stylus so that it would not be erased.[97] So the words that Job wanted so much to mark down were worth

---

[93]Matt. 22:43–44; Ps. 111:1.   [94]Gen. 1:27; 2:23–24.   [95]Matt. 22:37, 39.
[96]Job 19:23.
[97]Jer. 17:1.

being remembered. These are the words: "I know" (not indeed by natural knowledge but by faith) "that my redeemer lives."[98] The statement begins with the letter ד, which is conjunctive ["for"], as if he were saying, "Since other believers believe this, I too with them know and profess that my redeemer lives." He calls him the Redeemer from death, from sin, and from all evils. He also says that he is living, because he is the font of life and makes all things live which have life. He is indeed the Christ, the son of God, aside from whom no other Redeemer is given to human beings. He calls him "The Last" [Extremum][99] because there were a great many partial and imperfect redeemers. But Christ is the final and perfect redeemer, after whom no one else should be expected, although the Hebrew word "at last" [אחרון] may refer to time, as though we were to say "He, my Redeemer, lives and at the last time he shall rise from the dust." Some attribute this to the resurrection of Christ, for he was raised with his own body, which is called dust in scriptural usage. In rising, Christ was the firstfruits of those who sleep.[100] It is said that he had risen in the last time because his resurrection takes place at the beginning of the last age. No other age is to be expected except that in which we are now engaged; that is why John calls it the last hour.[101] This statement can, admittedly, refer very aptly to the resurrection of the dead, since it speaks about that living Redeemer. *At the last time* means at the end of the world: *he will rise* means he will exercise his powers over dust, that is over the bodies of the departed which have been reduced to dust, by raising them up. Then to clarify the question he adds *after*, namely in that time, *my skin* or hide or flesh *which they have gnawed*, pierced or cut—the verb נקפ:[102] signifies this—namely by sufferings, diseases, and worms. It will not be despised or scorned by my redeemer, *but in my flesh I will see God*, that is, existing in the flesh. The Latin version has *I will again be wrapped around by my skin*.[103] Those who translate it that way seem to be attending to the verb כפפ, which means "to wrap around"; in the Nifal conjugation it is נקפו meaning "they have wrapped around," that is, my joints and members—I shall see God in that skin and

[98]Job 19:25.

[99]Martyr does not get this term from the Vulgate (in novissimo die) or LXX (ἀεννάος) but from the Hebrew, taking ואחרון adjectivally; see BDB 31.

[100]1 Cor. 15:20.

[101]1 John 2:18.

[102]Curiously, the text has ב rather than the proper *sofit* form ף. The verb כקפ means "strike off"; see BDB 668.

[103]Vulgate for Job 19:26: "Et rursum circumdabor pelle mea."

covering, and in my flesh.[104] Another sense comes close to resurrection. *I will see him with my eyes*—for myself, not a stranger or outsider. He asserts that he will rise in his own body, not an alien one. As Christ took his own body again, so the bodies that will be given us will not be strange ones but our own. Hence Tertullian says in his *On the Resurrection of the Flesh*: "I will not be another person but another thing."[105] He affirms that there will not be a difference of substance but of conditions, qualities, and properties. Today in the schools, however, they say the opposite, namely another person not another thing.[106] These are different terms, but the reality does not vary. "I will see"— he has י‍ל, that is, [*22Ir*] for myself, for my own profit. Granted that now he is dealing with me severely and seems my enemy, then he will show himself favorable and kind to me. This is the consolation of the saints while they are afflicted in the world, that they look toward their resurrection and find rest therein. When he says, *I will see him with my eyes,* he reveals the twofold nature of Christ, namely the divine and the human, for God is not seen with bodily eyes. These things are so clear they need no greater light. Hence it appears that the ancient patriarchs were not ignorant of Christ the Redeemer and of the resurrection from the dead.

27. Some people want to understand these statements of Job as dealing with his recovery of both health and property in this life, since they do not want to hear that anything was said about the world to come. But that interpretation is strange and inept; two arguments explode it. First, he had despaired of recovering his health as regards this world and was consoling himself, as was said, by the hope of the resurrection. The same chapter 19 makes that clear when he says that God has so utterly cast down his hope that he compares himself to a plant that had been cut down and would not be reborn—this is clear in many chapters of his book. Second, if he was going to speak about this temporal restitution, what was the purpose of such a

---

[104]There is no such verb as י‍ק, but there is a root identical to ﬥ‍ק‍ﬡ ("to strike off") meaning "to go around"; see BDB 668–669. The latter does not occur in nif'al in the Hebrew Bible, but if it did it would mean "be wrapped around" or "wrapped [him]self around." This may be an editor's error, or Martyr (or his source) may be confused by hif'il occurrences of this verb (e.g., Lam. 3:5). Note that the text has ק‍ק‍י instead of ﬧ‍ק‍י, and ﬦ‍ק‍ﬡ‍ﬥ instead of ﬧ‍ﬡ‍ק‍ﬥ. A problem remains about this passage, and so the commentary as such: its editor seems to have little Hebrew, while Martyr's own notes were not always written clearly. John Wolf, who completed the last seventeen chapters, was a Hebraist of note; see Introduction, p. xl above

[105]Tertullian *De Resurrectione carnis* lii (PL 2, 918–919); cf. *De Anima* vi (PL 2.694ff.), repudiating the view of body-soul relationship among the "Academici" (Platonists).

[106]See §7, p. 52–53, above.

grandiose preface in which he hopes that his words would be written in a book and carved in flint or in lead as a perpetual memorial?

When we repent it is usual for calamities to be removed and for God to restore the original situation, and often a better one. Indeed, his friends promised him that would happen if he were to return to the way from which they thought he had strayed. Therefore Job said these things so that all might understand that even in the midst of death he was devoutly taking comfort in the hope of the resurrection, because he wanted to teach his friends and others by his own example.

Hence the interpretation given here is so clear that it seems to be written not in ink but by the rays of the sun. This is why those people looking for trouble where there isn't any are talking utter nonsense. The Jewish exegetes are so obscure about this passage that in reading them, you think you are living with the Cimmerians.[107] They are surely looking for obscurities on purpose. They seem to want to say that because of the effect of the plagues and diseases which he was experiencing as harshly inflicted on him by God, Job knew that the God whom he called his redeemer was alive. To this purpose they drag out his statement that in his flesh he would see God; that is, he experiences and recognizes him in the sufferings which he was bearing and which he himself and nobody else could appreciate. These are trifles, completely beside the point [ἀπροσδιόνυσα]; it is impossible for them to account for all the words in the text. Note also that almost all the Fathers, however ancient, thought this passage was about the resurrection of the dead.

28. Setting Job aside, I will bring in new testimony from David: he sings in Psalm 16, "I keep the Lord always before me."[108] He means by constantly meditating on his law lest I commit some offense against it, or by remembering him in all my thoughts, words, and acts he is always present and near so that I do nothing unworthy of his presence, or by always calling on him in my troubles lest I put my trust in anyone else. He has not failed me but stands at my right hand to protect, uphold, and defend me. "Therefore my heart is glad" with a solid and sincere joy, not an empty, wavering, and worldly joy. "My glory has rejoiced": by the word "glory" many Hebrews meant the soul because it is one's chief part and glory; others argued for the tongue because a person's dignity and excellence was usually thought to lie in speech. The Hebrew word is כבוד, which the Septuagint translates as "tongue." The

---

[107]The Cimmerians were an ancient people in the far north of Europe, first mentioned by Homer *Odyssey* xi.12–19, who described them as living in perpetual darkness. Martyr mentions them also in *Exhort. ad Iuv.*, LC app.

[108]The three phrases quoted are from Ps. 16:8–9.

apostles used it this way in Acts when they were dealing with this passage.[109] Nor is there any lack of examples in which it means the tongue. Psalm 30 says, "My tongue will sing to you and not be silent"; likewise Psalm 108: "I will sing and praise" and adds, "also by my tongue."[110] In Genesis 49, Jacob calls Simeon and Levi "warlike vessels of iniquity, and adds "my soul does not come into their council and my tongue is not joined to their company."[111] This means, "I do not approve of their treacherous plan at all, nor are they being driven to such a serious crime by my tongue, that is, by my command."

Quite rightly among the Hebrews "glory" and "tongue" are signified by this single word, because even granted that human dignity depends on the rational soul, since it is invisible it cannot be better recognized than through speech. Thus many have laid it down that the difference that distinguishes human beings is their being endowed with the ability to speak. Aristotle said that words are the tokens of the passions and affections which are in the soul.[112] Democritus claimed that speech is ῥεῦμα τῷ λόγῳ, that is, a sort of flow of speech, for the thoughts of our reason, which are hidden, flow out and break forth through words.[113]

Therefore David's meaning is that I have conceived so much joy in my soul that my tongue exults in thanking God and proclaiming his benefits. Nor can my joy hold itself in but flows out to the body, for my flesh rests in hope. The word שׁכן means not just to lie down or rest but also to dwell. So some translated it, "he will dwell in confidence." He immediately adds the source which gives rise to this confidence: "Because you will not leave my soul in hell, nor will you give your holy one to see corruption." My flesh rests in hope or dwells confidently because I was hoping that [22rv] I should be raised from the dead to life, and not just to an ordinary life but one truly joyous and eternal. This is why he adds, "You show me the path of life, in your presence there is fullness of joy, in your right hand there are pleasures for evermore."[114]

29. These songs of David are brought before the Israelite people by Peter and Paul in Acts as passages relevant to Christ's resurrection. In examining them we see three things worth noting. First, that the sense of the words may be understood. Second, that we recognize whether they refer to Christ or to

---

[109]Acts 2:26.   [110]Pss. 30:12, 108:3.   [111]Gen. 49:5–6.

[112]Aristotle *De Interp.* 1.16a3: "Spoken words are the symbols of mental experience."

[113]Democritus of Abdera (c. 460–370 BCE), whose atomic theory applied equally to the senses, including speech, as reported and criticized by Theophrastus *De Sensibus* 49ff.; see *Encyclopedia of Philosophy* 4:449; cf. the parallel ῥεῦμα ὀφθαλμῶν; H. Diels and W. Krantz, *Die Fragmente der Vorsokratiker* (Geneva: Weidmann, 1974)2:216.22. Cf. T. Cole, *Democritus and the Sources of Greek Anthropology* (Atlanta, Ga.: Scholars Press, 1990) 60ff., "The Origins of Language."

[114]Ps. 16:10–11

David. Last, how they can be applied to our own resurrection. Above all we must keep in mind the sentence that God laid upon Adam and his posterity, that they should return through death to the earth from which they were taken. They would have remained forever in the earth if Christ had not abrogated and canceled that curse by his death and resurrection. He died and was buried but did not stay in the tomb long enough for his body to putrefy. Like other humans he died and was buried, but unlike them he did not see corruption. Others will not be left in their graves, since they will arise at the end of the world; they could not, however, escape corruption even if their bodies are preserved by the work of doctors or by myrrh or aloes or balsam or other perfumed spices. The flesh is consumed and sticks to the bones after being stripped down and is so rotten and changed that it looks more like skin than flesh. While they live here the saints are not delivered from troubles, vexations, disasters, and diseases; indeed they undergo graver sufferings than others, but nonetheless they are said to rest in peace, not of course in fact but in the hope of the resurrection. In the midst of death they console themselves with that hope. By it the martyrs suffered with constancy and were prodigal with their life and blood, for the name of Christ. The words that follow sufficiently declare how this hope of the resurrection should be understood. "You will not leave my soul in hell, nor will you give your holy one to see corruption." Still, this hope has joined to it groans and sighs, even though it greatly uplifts and strengthens us. Paul writes to the Romans, chapter 8, "We ourselves, who have the firstfruits of the Spirit, groan inwardly as we wait for adoption as sons, and the redemption of our bodies. For in this hope we are saved."[115]

30. This statement also has great importance: "You will not leave me in the grave."[116] In it David prophesies that Christ is going to be buried. We do not leave something anywhere unless it has been first placed there. Hence this passage does not deal with some sort of protecting, guarding, and defending the flesh in this world but with the resurrection of the dead and life everlasting. When cattle and animals die they find rest from both diseases and labors, but not in hope because they have no hope of a blessed and happy resurrection. The Septuagint translators used ὅσιον, that is "holy," for the Hebrew word חסיד. Thus Christ is specially called the Holy One of God.[117] Even the devils called him that, as is found in Mark and Luke.[118] *She'ol* [שׁאוֹל] means both "tomb" and "hell" in Hebrew, from the verb שׁאל meaning to ask, because

---

[115]Rom. 8:23–24.
[116]Ps. 16:10.   [117]Acts 3:14.   [118]Mark 1:24; Luke 4:34.

these things seem to be ever seeking and demanding but are never satisfied. The Septuagint translators and the apostles in Acts said εἰς ἅιδην.[119] שׁחת is derived from the verb meaning to destroy or corrupt. Hence both the grave and the tomb are called שׁחת because it is there that corpses rot and corrupt. So much for terminology.

Our profession of faith states that Christ has died and was buried, but not in a way that he experienced corruption. These words do indeed contain a striking and splendid consolation regarding the flesh since we believe that it is this he raised from the dead.[120] There would be no consolation if our body and flesh were subject to perpetual death. The saints boast about their happiness and firm hope because they do not fear death. They recognize in these words that this is not a question of some short-term deliverance that may be offered them for a time. David was often rescued from various dangers and painful, deadly diseases, and he gave God profuse thanks in the Psalms for these benefits. He kept acknowledging that they had been conferred on him by God's goodness. But here it is a question of eternal life and supreme happiness—as the words that follow show when it is said, "You show me the path of life, in your presence there is fullness of joy, in your right hand are pleasures for evermore." Fasting is a consolation which arises from the hope of deliverance from one or another danger and from one or another sickness when others menace us and we have to die in the end. This is merely to keep on breathing for a time.

I also pass over the fact that we share this benefit with the wicked since their death is often postponed and they recover from various diseases. But the great happiness of the devout is that death is for them turned into rest and the tomb for them is not really corruption. In it they lie gently, now delivered from the troubles and labors of this life. Although the flesh is said to rest in hope, this is not to be understood as if a corpse or dead flesh had hope. If [*222r*] we think about the flesh as separated from the soul, it is something crude and brute which neither hopes nor loses hope. But the meaning is that while the saints live here, they console themselves since they hope that their flesh will rest quietly and be restored to a most blessed life.

If David, who passed his life under the Law and in the old covenant, predicted these things about the resurrection of the dead and about Christ, why do these fools dare to say that the Old Testament patriarchs were ignorant of such matters? Peter warned the Israelites to believe in David because he could

---

[119]Ps. 16:10; Acts 2:27.
[120]Cf. Martyr's exposition of the Creed, §§25–26 in EW 46ff.

foretell them correctly since he was a prophet whose role was to predict future events. Further, the Christ was promised to him with an oath added, not only that he would spring from his stock but also that he would sit upon his throne so that he might rule over and faithfully govern the Israelites.

31. Something else we should not skip over is that David did not write: "I will rest in hope." For he attributed that to his flesh lest he give rise to the suspicion that death also touched the soul. People have not been lacking who thought that the soul dies along with the body: at the resurrection of the dead both parts have to be restored.[121] We have refuted that opinion above by clear scriptural testimonies.

But to make the question even more evident, it should be known that "soul" in this passage is not understood the same way by everyone. Some see it in a strict sense, insofar as it is distinguished from body; then the word *Sheol* [שאל] is not understood as the tomb but as hell, so the meaning becomes, "The soul of Christ would not be deserted in hell but recalled quickly to the body." Most of the Fathers, who want to insist on Christ's descent into hell, use this interpretation. The apostles too did not shrink from this view since they said along with the Septuagint, "You will not leave my soul in hell,"[122] and they do not translate the word *Sheol* as tomb. Others interpret "soul" as signifying the dead person, that is, the corpse itself. They think it means, "You will not leave me as being dead," that is, with my corpse in the tomb, so that the second clause repeats what was said in the first clause. Thus they both mean the same thing, the holy one will not see the grave and the soul will not be left in the tomb. David Kimhi follows this interpretation.[123] The book of Leviticus chapter 21, has the soul signify the dead person when God commands the Israelites not to contaminate or pollute themselves with a soul, that is, with a dead person or with a corpse.[124] But right now I do not want to get into a battle over this.

Still, it is no trouble to point out what pertains to Christ's descent into hell, discussed in our previous exposition. They miss the point who think that

---

[121]Psychopannychism was among the divergent views on survival debated in northern Italy prior to the Lateran Council; see G. H. Williams *The Radical Reformation*, 3d ed., Sixteenth Century Essays and Studies, 15 (Kirksville, Mo.: Sixteenth Century Journal Publishers, 1992) 63ff. Cf. Calvin *Psychopannychia* (1534), attributing the doctrine to Pope John XXII, "but after being laid to sleep for a number of ages, it was lately revived by some of the Anabaptists"; see CR*Opera* viii. 335. Martyr cites John XXII's heterodox view in his "Schism" §15; see EW, 186n41.

[122]Ps. 16:10.

[123]David Kimhi, one of the Rabbinic commentators in the Bomberg Bible that Martyr used for exegesis; see the introduction to this volume, p.xxxix

[124]Lev. 21:11.

Christ's soul descended to the lower hell, where the damned are punished as their deeds deserve, so that there his soul might also bear the pains and torments of the wicked to deliver us from these evils. These are foolish human deceptions which find no support in the divine writings. When Christ was giving up his soul on the cross he said, "It is finished";[125] by dying he had completed his vocation insofar as he was sent to redeem the human race, and had acquired for us salvation by that unique oblation or sacrifice, as is written in Hebrews.[126] Scattered through the divine writings are statements that we have been redeemed by the death, cross, and blood of Christ, but never by the torments and pains of hell which he underwent after death. Then when he was at the point of death he said to the Father, "Into your hands I commit my spirit."[127] Those who are in the hands of God are surely not being tortured by the pains of hell. But enough on this point. By now I think I have proved the meaning that should be drawn from David's words. Now we have to see whether the prophecy was uttered about Christ or about David himself.

32. Jews, and among them Kimhi in particular, are of the opinion that David was talking about himself, that he believed that God would so protect and deliver him that he would not be left in the tomb nor see the grave. But Peter corrects him and others like him, as is found in Acts chapter 2; he says to the Israelites, "I may say to you confidently of the patriarch David that he both died and was buried, and his tomb is with us to this day."[128] By these words he showed that David's corpse was not only left in the tomb but had even rotted and that therefore this prophecy could not be applied to him but had been fulfilled in Christ.

But the Jews mock us: "Truly your Christ died and was buried, as you yourselves claim; how then did he not see the grave?" We answer that we do indeed confess that Christ died, but not in such a way as to be detained by hell or by death. Therefore his corpse was not left in the tomb nor did he see שחת, if by that word we mean corruption, which is a legitimate interpretation of the apostle's teaching.[129] If we grant them that the grave or tomb is signified by that term, we will say that it was predicted about Christ that he would not see the grave, by hyperbole or catachresis [ὑπερβολικῶς vel per κατάχρησιν]. In these figures of speech we say that putrefaction did not exist or did not take place because it existed or endured for a short time or a moment. If this is said about believers, as we find in John, [222ᵛ] "if anyone keeps my word, he will never see death,"[130] even though they will be held by death until the end of the

---

[125]John 19:30.   [126]Heb. 10:10.   [127]Luke 23:46.
[128]Acts 2:29.   [129]See Acts 2:14–36.   [130]John 8:51.

world, how much more and more properly is this pronounced about Christ, who was there for three days, and not even three full days? According to these figures of speech his dying was not dying and his being buried was not being buried. He was indeed dead, but he did not remain with death; he was buried but did not stay in the tomb. As for corruption and putrefaction, he did not experience that at all.

Therefore I answer the question proposed: David said these things in the fond hope of his own future resurrection, but he was speaking so as to direct faith and mind wholly to Christ, knowing that he had been given to the Church as a type of Christ. Therefore he first traced back the resurrection about which he was singing to him through whom resurrection would flow to the rest of us. Paul then rightly called Christ "the firstfruits of those who have fallen asleep."[131] For this reason David said things that completely surpassed and excelled the level and condition of his own revivification. He wanted to point us toward Christ himself. He would not have said these things so fittingly unless he had directed them back to Christ as the author of a most blessed resurrection. So let us recognize as a firm and certain rule that all those dignities and prerogatives that have been attributed to the saints, as we read in the Scriptures, have been first conferred on Christ to the highest degree. Therefore David was not speaking only about Christ but also about himself, but insofar as he was in Christ and included along with his other members.

Perhaps you could have said that the Apostles seem to deny this when they affirm that it was completed only in the Lord. I answer that they did not deny that David's corpse was also left in the tomb, for they affirm that it was left there right down to their times. Nor did they deny that he had seen the grave since it was in the grave to that very day. But again they did not deny he would be taken out of it at the proper time and at some point be raised from corruption. Regarding both David's grave and putrefaction there is agreement on this: neither will be permanent for him. From this it is clear how we should answer the third question, namely how these matters affect us insofar as we are members of Christ along with David. Just as Christ conquered death by dying not only for himself but also for us, so too by rising he came back to life both for himself and for us. Therefore a perfect life and a perpetual and eternal happiness for both soul and body reside in Christ, our head. Drop by drop they flow out and trickle down to his members in a measure analogous and proportionate to them.

---

[131] 1 Cor. 15:20.

Some people question why God lets the corpses of holy men lie so long in the tomb, why they corrupt and rot since they too were the sacred temples of the Holy Spirit (as Paul says).[132] The answer to this is that our flesh is indeed of the same species and nature as the Lord's, but many differences have meanwhile come between them. Christ's flesh was clean and not subject to sin in any part. By contrast, we are surrounded on all sides and all but overwhelmed by sin. Secondly we were conceived in iniquities, as David sang;[133] Christ was conceived of the Holy Spirit. In addition, it is right that the head take precedence over the rest of the members, and it is fitting that all members be perfected together simultaneously. Hence the corpses of the saints await the time until the number of the brethren is filled up.

33. The passages cited so far mention the resurrection of the blessed only, therefore perhaps someone may doubt whether the wicked will be raised from death. I reply that the resurrection applies also to them; since all die in Adam and are involved in the sentence of death, so all will be called back to life in Christ. But there is this difference: the devout will be raised to glory, the wicked to destruction. Thus we find in John, "Those who are in the tombs will hear the voice of the son of God and those who have done good will come forth to the resurrection of life and those who have done evil, to the resurrection of judgment," that is, of condemnation.[134] Hence the sacred writings more often recall the resurrection of believers because that is the resurrection to life; the other, that of the reprobate, can better be called an eternal fall and disaster than life and resurrection. Hence in Isaiah chapter 26 the prophet said, "Your people who have been killed will rise." Earlier he said of the wicked, "They are dead, they will live."[135] We must therefore maintain that through the favor of Christ life will be restored to both good and evil. The devout will be honored with great glory but the wicked will be afflicted with perpetual shame. This is the reason why Scripture more often mentions the resurrection of the saints than of the wicked. The words that David adds, saying, "Show me the path of life, fullness of joy in your presence, and delights at your right hand forever,"[136] indicate that this blessed resurrection applies only to those who have kept Jehovah constantly before their eyes.

34. Today there is no lack of those who say that David did indeed predict these things, but not in such an explicit and open way that others could understand them until they were explained and made plain after the coming of Christ. They keep insisting that in the Old Testament the resurrection was

[132]1 Cor. 3:16.
[133]Ps. 51:5.
[134]Martyr melds John 5:25 and 5:29.
[135]Is. 26:19; 27:14.
[136]Ps. 16:11.

wholly unknown. But we say that the prophecy was clear and fell into obscurity only through the fault of teachers who abandoned the Scriptures and began to chase after the dogmas of the Greeks. They introduced statements of the platitudes of philosophers rather than of the divine letters.[137] This could also [*223r*] have come about through the fault of readers who raced through the predictions of the prophets with more haste than care. Otherwise the prophecies should be clear or at least not so hidden and obscure as to defy understanding. They were given for edification; they could not teach people if they were not understood. And in the church they would be no more worthwhile than a foreign tongue, whose use the Holy Spirit prohibits in the church since its practice does not contribute toward edification.[138] They will throw against us the passage from Ephesians where Paul testifies that the secret or mystery of Christ has been hidden for many centuries from the human race, that the Gentiles were the future coheirs, joint members, and partakers of the promises through the Gospel.[139] But several distinctions must be employed to clarify an understanding of the Apostle's words.

35. First we have to distinguish the Hebrews from pagans, for we readily grant that the mysteries of Christ and spiritual teachings were for the most part unknown to the Gentiles. There was no public profession of them, although there were some who knew these things even among the pagans. But the Hebrews, who had received a divinely given Law and had been granted outstanding prophets, were not ignorant of the mysteries of Christ unless and to the degree that they deliberately held God's word in contempt or, hindered by passions and blinded by hate, were unwilling to listen to those who taught the truth. Those wicked Jews serve as example—when Christ said that Abraham saw my day and was glad, they were so incensed that they wanted to stone him. Even so, nothing was better known among the Hebrews than the fact that Abraham, Isaac, and Jacob and the other patriarchs had known the Messiah and had also predicted him. But their wrath so blinded them that they turned the Lord's words upside down, saying: "You are not yet fifty years old and you have seen Abraham?"[140] Christ did not say that he had seen

---

[137]Martyr's failure to mention 2 Maccabees 7, with its several clear references to the resurrection of the dead, is curious. Admittedly Protestants generally did not accept this book as canonical, but it contains important information about Jewish beliefs in the century before Christ that would have strengthened Martyr's case.

[138]1 Cor. 14:9.

[139]Eph. 3:6–9.

[140]John 8:56–57.

Abraham as regards his humanity or had been with him, but that Abraham himself had seen his day in spirit and faith.

Moreover, distinctions are also needed with regard to the Hebrews themselves because everybody did not know the secrets or mysteries of Christ in the same way. Among them some were Epicureans or even atheists [ἄθεοι], who spurned divine things. These people understood little or nothing about Christ and his mysteries. Others were devout though backward and unlearned, but they still were not ignorant about the main points of religion and what should be believed about the Messiah. There were the learned and those skilled in the sacred writings, who possessed nearly complete knowledge about the Messiah and his mysteries.

36. We grant that considering their era, the Hebrews saw the mysteries of our salvation much more obscurely than do we. Prophecies are perceived much more clearly once they have happened than when not yet complete. But we can see how the ancients knew what pertains to the Messiah from the fact that they all predicted that he would be the son of David. For the common folk, the children and the blind all called Christ the son of David.[141] When Herod asked the scribes and Pharisees where the Christ was to be born they mentioned the town of Bethlehem by name.[142] Isaiah in chapter 53 so splendidly, clearly and explicitly predicted Christ's acts and mysteries that he seems to have played not the prophet but the evangelist. The Lord's death, along with his triumph and glory, are scattered so widely through the Scriptures that the Hebrews created two Messiahs, one from the tribe of Ephraim who would undergo death for the salvation of their nations, and a second from the tribe of Judah and son of David, who would achieve victory and would rule over all the Gentiles.[143] Thus they divided in two what belonged to the one Christ according to his twofold coming. The vocation of the Gentiles is quite clear in the divine writings—the passage already cited by the Apostle in Ephesians deals mainly with this. There we find that all the nations will come to Mount Zion to worship Jehovah, and altars to him will be set up even in Egypt, and all the people will speak the language of Canaan; also the name of the Lord will be glorious from East unto West because of the acceptable and sweet sacrifices offered to him.[144]

37. These matters were certainly well known to the Hebrews, but they were called hidden with reference to how they were experienced and carried out. They believed they would happen sometime but not everyone perceived

[141]Matt. 21:15; 20:30.   [142]Matt. 2:5.
[143] Ephraim: Hosea 12:14; David: Matt. 1:1, Luke 1:27.
[144]Isa. 2:3; 19:19, 21.

clearly how or when, their way and mode. We are more blest than they because we perceived the events and are not ignorant of when and how they have been carried out. Indeed, even the apostles themselves, whom Christ commanded to preach the Gospel to all creatures,[145] for a long time restricted themselves to the Hebrews and did not go out to other peoples because they still did not know the time, manner, and mode for preaching the Gospel to the nations. They were waiting for some kind of sign to be given them—this they finally obtained with the conversion of the centurion Cornelius.[146] The very angels, as the Apostle bears witness in the same letter, learned from the Church a great deal about the various and manifold wisdom of God.[147] I am willing to confess that some passages in Scripture are more hidden, and are not yet completely understood, but I say that they are not necessary for salvation and never have been.

So I maintain that the holy Jews of old possessed in effect the main points of religion and believed the things that sufficed for godliness, and I think the predictions about Christ [223ν] were well known to the devout. If some Jews were ignorant about them, we have to think that this happened through their own fault. Isaiah in chapter 29, when he rebuked the Israelite people, said that they had arrived at that point where all the visions of the prophets were for them like a sealed book, which they would not be able to read if it were put before them. He adds the reason for this, saying, "Because this people ... honor me with their lips while their hearts are far from me."[148]

38. For this reason the fault should not be attributed to the Scriptures but rather to the sloth and neglect of those who prefer darkness to the light; otherwise the divine Scripture is lucid and gives understanding to children. Wherefore those who put off reading the Scriptures on the pretext of their obscurity and difficulty are giving themselves very poor advice. You may find some who say they are ignorant of the hidden mystery of the Father, Son, and Holy Spirit and do not know whether they are one God or whether the one God becomes these three, namely Father, Son, and Holy Spirit. Meanwhile they neglect the diligent reading of the Scriptures, and sometimes allow themselves to be so deceived that they let themselves be forced into worshipping and adoring as God one they regard as a creature. They pretend that they are slow-witted about these mysteries when otherwise they are quite sharp and zealous in defending their own inventions. They lay claim to owning knowledge of the Scriptures and boast that they have the key to them, but they

---

[145]Matt. 28:19.   [146]Acts 10.
[147]Eph 3:10.   [148]Isa. 29:13.

neither enter into them themselves nor allow others to enter.

To return to Kimhi: while agreeing that it is David's, as I noted,[149] he interprets it as meaning that those who rely on God's goodness will hope he will help them in all dangers. He does not take these statements as referring to the blessed resurrection—I would have easily thought him a Sadducee, except that elsewhere he did refer to the resurrection. Still he did not skip over a certain statement of the ancients in the מדרש [*Midrash*] which reads in this way: מתח מלמי שלא שלטו כר אחרח, that is, "He teaches that after death maggot and worm [נמח נתילצח] will not lord it over him."[150] I can see no reason why they are trying to run from the light about this passage except the hatred that they bear toward Christians, which is more than the hatred for Vatinius.[151] Since they were not unaware that the apostles, namely Peter and Paul, had made use of this testimony of David to confirm Christ's resurrection, they have concocted so many conflicting and confused explanations, to avoid agreeing with Christ's apostles. Finally we should note that the prophet taught that the resurrection would take place by divine and not by natural power, since he addresses God directly: "You will not leave my soul in hell, nor give your holy one to see corruption," and even more so in the verses that follow, "You show me the path of life," and so forth.[152]

39. Now that the prophecy of David has been clearly explained, I want to bring forward another proof that is found in Isaiah chapter 26. There the prophet wanted to console the Israelites when they were sorely afflicted and pressed down by very heavy troubles by telling them to expect help from God.[153] I mean the help of eternal life which would come through the resurrection. So turning toward God he says, "Your dead will live,"[154] calling martyrs of God those who have been killed or those whose entire life has been

[149]The passage under discussion is Ps. 16:10 ff. (see §28 above).

[150]R. *David Kimhi On the First Book of Psalms*, trans. R.G. Finch (London: SPCK, 1919) 78, writes: "and in the Haggadic interpretation (*Shoḥer Tob* [Midrash Proverbs] and [Talmud] *Baba Bathra* 17a), the explanation is given: 'After death, when worm and corruption shall have no power over it, (shall my flesh dwell in security).'" Kimhi was the Psalms commentator in the first edition of the Bomberg Bible (1517–1518), but was replaced by Ibn Ezra and Rashi in subsequent editions.

[151]*Vatinius* was the name of a Roman *gens*. Cicero denounced one Vatinius so strongly that the name became proverbial for a bitter enemy and was so used by Pliny and Catullus.

[152]Ps. 16:10–11.   [153]Isa. 26:4.

[154]Isa. 26:19. The MT reads: "Your dead ones will live, my corpse will [pl.] rise." "My corpse" is taken as a collective plural, so that following Hebrew grammar the verb of which it is subject can be plural. Although explicable, the phrase "my corpse will [*pl.*] rise" seemed awkward to Latin translators. Martyr favors Münster's reading, which adds a gratuitous "with": "Your dead ones will live, they will rise with my corpse." Later Martyr mentions the Vulgate's interpretation: "your dead will live; my slain ones will rise." Thus Jerome reads "my corpses" instead of "my corpse": *nivlatai* not *nivlati*, differing only by a vowel point: *patah* rather than *hireq*. Strangely, Martyr does not mention either Rashi or Ibn Ezra, who seek to explain the MT as it stands.

a martyrdom because they have celebrated the glory of God by their good works. (Likewise, Paul calls them "the dead in Christ.")[155] He adds, "together with my corpse," joining and associating himself with the elect of God who are to be awakened. The added particle contributes not a little to his vehement assertion. He shows that he is not talking about or dealing with things that are unknown or irrelevant to himself but about things he has truly felt and whose taste he has already experienced to some degree. We too should imitate this, namely by applying to ourselves whatever God has promised to the saints. Those slain for God shall indeed live by a resurrection that is now underway, since God reveals it to his own people in their afflictions: this will be carried to a solid and perfect completion on the last day in the blessed resurrection. Hence that day is called "The time of the restitution of all" in chapter 3 of the Acts of the Apostles.[156] We should not skip over the fact that if different points are assigned, the Hebrew word נבלתי can be read in the plural.[157] So it would mean "My corpses will arise," as if God were answering the prophet who had said, "Your slain will live," to which God responds, "My corpses will indeed arise." We should also note carefully that the cause of the resurrection is stated, for the slain will arise precisely because they are God's: "God is not the God of the dead but of the living," as Christ himself bears witness.[158]

40. It is said that "you are awakened" or "you are raised up," also because the death of the devout is considered like sleep, as is found rather often in Scripture. [Isaiah] adds, "Rejoice," for this day cannot be for them anything but the happiest. He calls them people dwelling in dust, which is fitting for them partly because they are ground down and troubled in this life, partly because after death they will be reduced to ashes. Then turning to God he says, "Your dew is the dew of the meadow grass."[159] Just as when dried up by winter or the heat of the sun it receives dew from heaven and again flourishes and flowers, so shall the dead return to life by the force of your goodness and power. The elegance of this metaphor lies here: just as these thrive and flower without human cultivation, so shall the dead arise by God's power quite beyond any natural capacity. God has painted in these material things the form and image of the resurrection we await when what was previously dried up will again [224r] germinate, sprout, flower, and bear fruit. Paul also touches on this metaphor in Corinthians.[160] The prophet continues, "The earth shall give up its dead and will uncover their blood, but you my people, enter into your

---

[155]1 Thess. 4:16.   [156]Acts 3:21.

[157]The MT uses the Hebrew idiom of a singular subject requiring a plural verb. In grasping this point Martyr is not following Ibn Ezra or Rashi (or Münster).

[158]Luke 20:38.   [159]Isa. 26:19.   [160]1 Cor. 15:36.

chambers," namely while you await the resurrection.[161] May you bear the cross patiently since you see so much good laid up for you. "For the sufferings of this present time are not worth comparison with the future glory that is to be revealed in us."[162]

In his book *On the Resurrection of the Flesh* Tertullian speaks of store-rooms which are maintained in the house with the purpose of storing meat that can be retrieved for human use. The rooms are called חדרים in Hebrew, translated into the Latin *cubicula*.[163] Just so, he says, are corpses laid in tombs so that they can be retrieved from them. But I return to those cells or chambers or storage lockers in which God commands that believers should be secreted in the meantime, before the blessed life. If the question arises what the saints will do there while being afflicted, my answer is that they are there to weep and wail, to sigh and beg for help and somehow make known their burdens and whatever troubles them in their Father's bosom. It is not the part of the devout to bewail their sufferings on street corners, in taverns and barbershops, or to proclaim their oppression in public. Their task is to hand over their case to the one who judges justly, as the blessed Peter said about Christ in chapter 2 of his First Letter.[164] "Close the door behind you for a little while."[165] The argument for this consolation is deduced from the shortness of time, as Paul wrote to the Corinthians in his Second Letter, "For this slight momentary affliction is preparing for us an eternal weight of glory."[166] The time is called brief which falls between now and the resurrection; that would not be wrong even if the time should be long, since this is to be understood comparatively. If a long drawn-out time is compared to eternity, it is very short. In the same way the souls of those slain for Christ's name who beseech God to avenge their blood are ordered to be quiet and wait a bit.[167] Ibn Ezra, a famous exegete among the Jews, also brings forward as witness for the resurrection of the dead a passage drawn from the prophet Isaiah.[168] And the Chaldean paraphraser[169] says that your God will cast the dead into hell—an event related to the time of the resurrection. I would have had the right to bring up here what the same prophet says in chapter 30 and at the end about

---

[161]Isa. 26:19–20.   [162]Rom. 8:18.

[163]Tertullian, *De Resurrectione carnis* xxvii (PL 2, 881): private rooms or chambers, Isa. 26:20.

[164]1 Pet. 2:23.   [165]Isa. 26:20

[166]2 Cor. 4:17.   [167]Rev. 6:10.

[168]Rabbinic commentator in the Bomberg Bible; see xxxix and p. 41, n. 15, above.

[169]The Targum of Judges, the Aramaic translator, often paraphrastic.

Gehenna, Tophet, unquenchable fire, worms that die not, sulphur, the bellows, and so forth,[170] but I think I should save time, and come to Ezekiel.

41. This prophet writes that he was led by the spirit into a field covered with bones. This happened in two ways. First, he saw them by God's inspiration, not by sense or human imagination. Second, they were shown to him not bodily but spiritually and by a mental vision.[171] It should be acknowledged that at that time the resurrection of the dead enjoyed widespread belief, so the prophet drew his argument from that. He saw the bones as dried out, bare, withered, and worm-eaten in order better to express the difficulty of recovering their former life. For it might perhaps be thought that complete and moist corpses could more easily return to life. God said to the prophet, "Son of man, do you think these bones can live?" He replied, "You know, O Lord." His faith was being tested, but he answered devoutly, unlike a Sadducee or Libertine.

Now if the resurrection of the dead was an article of belief and accepted widely, why did he not say boldly, "They will live"? I answer: Even if he believed that at the end of the world the dead would be brought to life, he was ignorant whether those shown to him then were going to be raised up at that hour. So he entrusted that question to God. We can fittingly and usefully imitate his example if someone who is scrupulous about the teaching of the faith objects to us by referring the matter to God and saying, "He has the knowledge and power." When he has revealed his will to us in Scripture, we believe that what he has demonstrated will take place.

We should know this about the prophet's vision: the city of Jerusalem had been destroyed by the army of Nebuchadnezzar and the temple had been thrown down by Nabuzaradan, who was in charge of life and death.[172] For the Jews living in the Babylonian capital, everything seemed completely over. There was already almost total despair of returning to the land of Canaan. But God confirmed and lifted up their hope by arguing deductively from a greater event to a lesser one.[173] He says, "I am going to restore life to the departed (which is something far greater than redeeming captives); I will also make you return from captivity as I promised—that is something far easier than raising the dead." So that the first premise, that is, the resurrection of the dead, might be more evident and firm, he puts that vision before the eyes of the prophet.

---

[170]See Jer. 7:31–32; 19:6, 11ff., and Isa. 66:24.

[171]Ezek. 37:1ff.

[172]Nebuchadnezzar's army besieged and destroyed Jerusalem in 589–587 B.C.; cf. 2 Kings 24:10–14. On Nabuzaradan, see 2 Kings 25:8–20; Jer. 52:12–30.

[173]I.e., an argument *a fortiori*.

Through the resurrection of the dead, which is something divine and much more difficult, he brings about faith that something temporal and easier is going to be performed. We should use this same sort of argument if we sometimes begin to think that we will lose what is needed for life. Let us say in such a temptation, "Since God will give us an eternal and blessed life in the resurrection, he is certainly not going to take away from us the food needed for this life." The Hebrews were then so minded that they believed in the resurrection of the dead but had despaired of returning to their homeland. Yet [*224v*] God had promised both. The disasters they were enduring at the time preoccupied their minds so much that they either forgot about the divine promises or gave little or no heed to them. God ordered Ezekiel to prophesy and speak to the bones that lay before his eyes, saying in the name of God, "I will put my spirit within you, and you shall live."[174] The prophet was commanded to do something marvelous: to prophesy and speak to bones so crude, brute, and dumb that they could not hear or understand anything. But we must think that all things, however inanimate and without feeling or movement, obey God without delay. Very similar is what Christ said in John, "The hour is coming when they will hear the voice of the Son of God"—those who are in graves, even though the bones and ashes of the departed lying in tombs hear or feel nothing. It is nonetheless said that they are going to rise at the voice of the archangel and the trumpet of God.[175]

42. The prophet gives a very careful account of the order and disposition of the resurrection of the bones. First, after bone was joined to bone, they were bound and knit together by sinews. Then they were filled out by flesh, which was covered with skin lest it remain foul and ugly to look at. When the corpses were now complete, he commanded the prophet to prophesy to the spirit so that he might come and they might thereby be given souls and life. Spirit is mentioned twice, namely souls that give life to bodies, and the divine Spirit who illuminates and sanctifies souls. So the dead are not just said to have been awakened and to stand on their own feet, but it is added that they know that I am God.[176] God is known from the greatness of his works, but this knowledge does not happen without the divine Spirit. A voice was heard, perhaps there was thunder and the earth was made to shake, for such things usually happen in God's special miracles. When the Law was given on Mount Sinai, there were terrifying thunderclaps and earthquakes. Also at the death of the Lord and at his resurrection there were great earthquakes.[177] The spirit

---

[174]Ezek. 37:14.
[176]Ezek. 37:7–10, 14.

[175]John 5:25; 1 Cor. 15:52.
[177]Ex. 19:16–18; Matt. 27:51; 28:2.

came from the four winds, and so forth. The souls shall return to their bodies from their lofty seats in heaven when the saintly dead arise, but by different routes because their ashes and corpses are not heaped together in some set place on the earth. The Scripture includes all the ways and places through the four winds, that is, the east, west, south, and north winds.[178] Or perhaps this denotes the dispersion of captives to the four parts of the earth. In Deuteronomy Moses also promises to repentant Jews this restitution from the four parts of the earth.[179] From this we conclude, moreover, that peoples' souls are not born in them; just as God breathed a soul into Adam and later created a soul for each person, so in the resurrection he will send the souls back to them from outside.[180] This is also an indication that they do not die along with their bodies. When he adds that all these bones are the whole house of Israel, he is thereby making a statement about the resurrection of the faithful, for they are indeed the house of Israel; the prophet, however, saw an enormous army. For the crowd of the faithful is exceedingly large, as we find also in Revelation.[181]

43. "All these bones are the whole house of Israel."[182] Since the premise [πρότασιν] has been taken care of, he adds the conclusion [ἀνταπόδοσιν].[183] Note that the copulative verb *are* means the same as *signify*, for those bones were not really the house of Israel but indicate it, just as the seven thin and blighted ears of grain that Pharaoh dreamed about were seven years of famine. "The Lord said, I will open your tombs." But they should have been open already since those bones were scattered over the field. One might reply to this that the tombs were already open for those bones. If you examine the conclusion, that is, the restitution of the Israelites in the land of Canaan, that still needed to be opened. Some interpret the prophet's statement, "I will bring you home," allegorically, as if the land of the Israelites should be taken as standing for the kingdom of heaven and of eternal happiness. Instead I put allegories aside and consider rather that this passage refutes the vanity of those Jews who think the dead will be awakened only in Judea. For here the prophet asserts a far different future, because a return to the land of promise is predicted for the dead who had already been brought back to life. It is inept sophistry to attach God's power so much to a certain place that he cannot or will not do elsewhere the same thing he performed in one spot. The tombs denote

---

[178]Cf. Ezek. 37:9.   [179]Deut. 30:1–5.

[180]See "Image of God," p. 37 ff. for Martyr's teaching on the origin of the soul.

[181]Ezek. 37:11; Rev. 7:9.

[182]Martyr continues to exegete the Ezekiel passage sentence by sentence: Ezek. 37:11 ff.

[183]In conditional sentences, particularly contradictories, the *protasis* expresses the condition and the *apodosis* the result; Aristotle *De Interp.* 11.20b23–24, and *An. Prior.* I.1, 24a16 ff.

the Babylonian captivity and the miserable bondage under a tyrant from which God promises to deliver the captives. The tomb of the Jews was also that utter despair they incurred when they lost all hope of their return. God promises to unlock this tomb, opening the way for them to return to their fatherland. Regarding help for the devout, the situation is such that when things have become utterly hopeless, the dawn of heavenly help arises. Putting it briefly, this prophecy shows two things: first, the resurrection of the dead; second, the return of the Israelites to their fatherland. One proves the other: the raising of the dry bones to life confirms the restitution of the Jews.

44. Some passionately oppose this sound and true interpretation for two reasons. First, they say that the universal resurrection of all is not in question here since the revivified bones are called the house of Israel. Second, this vision is imaginary and fictional so that nothing solid can be [225r] drawn from it. To these we reply: We admit that the prophet is talking about the resurrection of the just, as we have already said. If it were a vision it makes no difference, nor does that prevent this vision from being of consolation to all, confirming hope in the general resurrection as well as in the restoration of the Jews. It is enough that the argument be taken over and derived from the resurrection of the dead. Hebrew interpreters too do not deny that the resurrection is operative in this passage.

The quibble that some bring up is without force: that an argument *a fortiori* is worthless if what is assigned as the major is more uncertain or equally dubious as what is brought in as the minor.[184] They regard the resurrection of the dead as more uncertain or equally dubious as the restoration of the Jews to their fatherland. But they are making an enormous error because the resurrection of the dead was accepted as better known by the Hebrew faithful, for whom it was certain and obvious, not indeed by nature or sense knowledge but by faith, in whose light things which are dark to sense knowledge and human reason are made solid and bright. That this situation prevailed is confirmed by the fact that the Hebrews, who are on the lookout for any opportunity against the Christians, have never engaged in controversy with them over the resurrection of the dead, which they and their fathers have always accepted. Thus when Christ promised Martha that her brother was going to be raised up, Martha boldly replied, "I know that my brother will be raised up on the last day."[185]

---

[184]In the categorical syllogism, "superior demonstration is that which proceeds from better known and prior premises"; Aristotle *An. Post.* I.25.87a.
[185]John 11:24.

45. To explain the major premise of this cavil, I think that we should examine what the Fathers thought about it. Tertullian in his book *On the Resurrection of the Flesh* proposed this same objection to himself. He answered that unless an object existed earlier, it could not be reshaped metaphorically to something else, and so if the resurrection was not an established article of faith and something that was really coming, he holds that it cannot be applied to the restoration of the Jews. As he says, metaphors don't work in a vacuum, a parable about nothing gets nowhere.[186] Those who want the resurrection of the dead to be inserted here metaphorically should reflect that it is the nature of metaphors to transfer something from its own place to a different one. It must exist before it undergoes transfer—unless laughter and happiness existed in humans, they could not be applied to wheat fields and meadows. Indeed, those metaphors are especially praised which are derived from the obvious, above all from everyday and familiar sources. The same applies to parables. Christ employed the simile of the vineyard, which after being splendidly constructed and cultivated was rented to evil tenant farmers.[187] This parable would not have been obvious nor had any punch unless elegantly laid out vineyards were found in real life, and unless farm owners were often involved with evil sharecroppers. He also brought up the parable of the fig tree which was sterile and bore no fruit.[188] Manure had been applied to it for one or two years, and when it bore no fruit, it was finally cut down. This parable too would have been employed to no avail if fertilizing fig trees and cutting them down were not everyday sights in agriculture and gardening. No one should bring up objections about chimeras and similar monsters. Granted they do not exist in nature, yet clever fellows have designed them to seem natural, for even if no chimeras exist, their parts are seen: they are the lion, the goat, and snakes, which are generally observable.

46. They say that Jerome was criticized for not interpreting the foregoing passage from Ezekiel as applying to the resurrection of the dead.[189] I admit it. But we should recognize that gathering the resurrection of the dead from the words of the prophet is far different from having to prove and confirm it by a sure and evident demonstration. It is the latter that Jerome denied, and he did it with a sound and correct assessment, for it was not the purpose of Ezekiel to prove the resuscitation of the dead. That was well known and, as we have said, the Jews of the time believed in it. So he deduced from it as from

---

[186]Tertullian *De Resurrectione carnis* 30 (PL 2, 883ff.).

[187]Matt. 21:33–41.   [188]Luke 13:6ff.

[189]Jerome *Comm. in Ezekielem* XI.37, 432–433 (PL 25, 346–347): "non in corpore, sed extra corpus."

a known principle and confirmed the restoration of the Jews. That Father did not deny that the resurrection could be gathered from this, especially when Tertullian says that unless the resurrection was established a comparison could not have been based on it, and nobody uses nonexistent things to support what is uncertain.

Just as the life of dried-up bones seems unbelievable but will come about, so the deliverance of the Israelites from captivity, which nobody thought would happen, will find fulfillment in its proper time. What if someone enquires why a metaphor was taken from the resurrection of the dead rather than from something else, as it could have been? I would say that it was done to demonstrate indirectly that this restoration from an earthly captivity would not be a perfect and complete tranquillity and beatitude for them if resurrection went unmentioned. So much for this passage.

47. Now let us proceed to Daniel. In chapter 12 he says, "At that time shall arise Michael, the great prince who has charge of your people. And there shall be a time of trouble, such as never has been since there was a nation until then; but at that time your people shall be delivered, every one whose name shall be found in the book of God. And many of those who sleep in the dust of the earth shall arise, some to everlasting life and some to shame and lasting contempt. And those who are wise shall shine like the brightness of the firmament; and those who turn many to righteousness, like the stars for ever and ever," and so forth.[190] Daniel has explained that four kingdoms in continuous succession were going to dominate the whole world, and the kingdom of Christ would take control at the end. But before he obtains that, the Antichrist must be [225v] destroyed, who was oppressing the devout like a tyrant. By the Antichrist I understand Muhammad, the papacy, and all who oppose the worship of Christ. Daniel writes that there will be greater and heavier troubles and afflictions for the church in that last time than had ever been before. But meanwhile he consoles the faithful because they will have Michael at hand to help them, that is, Christ the Son of God, the Prince of our church. He promised his disciples exactly this when he said, "I am with you always, to the close of the age."[191]

He adds a second comfort, that not all will die on account of those troubles: they will escape who have been predestined to life, that is, marked down in the Book of God. Finally he comforts the church on this score: the resurrection of the dead will take place. He says that many of the dead will be awakened; he does not write "all" because very many will be found alive at the

[190]Dan. 12:1–3.   [191]Matt. 28:20.

advent of the Lord. So Paul says, "We will not all die but all will be changed."[192] Nor does the word "many" mean just a few because as Ezekiel said, "An exceedingly great host stood there,"[193] namely from those bones restored to their previous life. The book of Revelation describes a vast crowd of the saints.[194] In this passage Daniel deals with the general resurrection, for he divides it into a saving and a shameful resurrection.

There is no doubt that Christ was referring to the prophet's words when he said in John, "All who are in the tombs will hear the voice of God's son and come forth, those who have done good, to the resurrection of life, and those who have done evil, to the resurrection of judgment."[195] Regarding the happiness of the saints to be expected after the resurrection, he adds that those who teach others will be extremely glorious, and compares those who justify many to the splendor of the heavenly spheres and the brightness of the stars;[196] for they will teach especially the promises about the Messiah by which those who give assent are justified. The power and ability of conferring justice is not to be attributed to humans since it belongs to God alone. It can be granted to humans only as ministers and instruments of God's word. I think the same applies to what was said above about the firmament of heaven and the brightness of the stars. For it is the practice in the divine writings to repeat in the second part of any verse what was said in the first.

48. Even though Daniel's prediction was plain and very clear, it was still subjected to quibbles by Porphyry, a philosopher of no ordinary repute.[197] He was incensed at Christians and said that Daniel was an illustrious man but the prophecies written in his name had nothing to do with him but were written by an impostor who lived after the times of Antiochus and the Maccabees. He said that his book did not contain prophecies about the future; rather had he woven together enigmatically events that had already taken place, that the events pieced together in this passage concern exclusively the times of Antiochus.[198] The latter did indeed treat the Jews with the greatest cruelty. First he brought under his control the city of Jerusalem and pillaged the temple; then he began to force the Jews to abandon their ancestral ceremonies and the proper worship of God. He forbade circumcision and forced the flesh of pigs on the unwilling, and erected an image of the Olympian Jove for worship in

---

[192]1 Cor. 15:51.   [193]Ezek. 37:10.   [194]Rev. 7:9.

[195]John 5:28–29.   [196]Dan. 12:3.

[197]Only fragments survive from the *Against the Christians* of Porphyry (234–ca. 305), the Neoplatonic philosopher. See Eusebius *Hist. eccl.* iv.19.2.

[198]Antiochus IV Epiphanes (175–164 BCE). Modern scholars term the book "prophecy after the fact," dating it 164 because of the apocalypse in Dan. 10–12.

the temple of God. After doing these things he later got the idea of marching against Persia where he tried to despoil a very wealthy shrine loaded with many donations, but was driven away in utter disgrace. For this reason he nurtured so much anger that he began to grow sick at heart, and thinking to vent all his bile against the Jews, returned to Syria at top speed. But he fell from his chariot and was badly mangled by bodily injuries; he died, partly because of the accident and partly because of the violent seething in his heart. News of the flight of Lysias and his commanders and of his men killed by the Israelites (for on his arrival he had ordered them to treat the Jews with the greatest possible cruelty) contributed to his death. Then, says Porphyry, the Jews who seemed dead were somehow raised up and resurrected. Thus they emerged renowned and glorious, like those who act with constancy and devoutly serve their country, while those who shamefully revolted from true piety are reduced to dishonor and reproach. Such are the poisonous ravings of Porphyry which he vented against this passage.

We who profess Christ cannot, however, accept the first point of his interpretation, namely his contention that the book was not written by Daniel, since Christ not only mentioned it but cited statements which it contained.[199] Regarding the other point, that he wanted those events to be referred to Antiochus, Jerome asked how the afflictions which that tyrant forced the Hebrews to suffer were harsher than any that had previously existed.[200] For in the time of Nebuchadnezzar the city of Jerusalem was overthrown, the temple completely destroyed, and everyone hauled into captivity and held in it for a full seventy years. This was indeed harsher than what Antiochus inflicted on them. The book of Maccabees softens this statement a little, saying that the evils of Antiochus were worse than those that took place in the time when the Jews were without a prophet, that is, from the time of Ezra, who was the prophet Malachi.[201]

But our attention must focus not on what is written in the book of Maccabees but on that which is contained in the volume of Daniel. Besides, we ask why the violators of the Law are said to be raised from the dead after King Antiochus's death since by Porphyry's account, rather than rising up the rebels retreated. For while the tyrant was still living they were held in esteem and administered the priesthoods and the pontificates. The Maccabees, who perhaps he thought had emerged as famous, experienced the cruelest tortures and

---

[199]Matt. 24:15; Mark 13:14.
[200]*Comm. in Danielem*, Prol. (PL 25, 491ff.).
[201]2 Macc. 9:28.

sufferings and were all killed, almost to the last man.[202] Judas fell in battle, Jonathan was captured and killed, and Simon was beheaded at a banquet.[203] [*226r*]

I certainly do not deny that the things that took place under Antiochus were very terrible, but things as bitter and harsh as the Prophet shows will come under the Antichrist. Not only Antiochus but also Demetrius and the other Greek princes preceded the Antichrist as his types and symbols. They afflicted the Hebrews and opposed the worship of God. I also know that there was a certain other Polychronius who dared to claim that this passage of Daniel should not be understood as referring to the resurrection of the dead.[204] But he does not rest on solid arguments and has been refuted by Johannes Oecolampadius, a man of great learning.[205] We also see that in Revelation, John the Apostle relates almost the same events in the same order as those about which Daniel wrote. In chapter 20 we read that thrones were put in place and a tribunal set up; then he adds that those who had endured death for Christ arose.[206] In conclusion we may say what we noted in explaining the passage from Ezekiel, namely if they want to illustrate the state of Jewish people after the death of Antiochus metaphorically by the resurrection of the dead, an understanding of a real resurrection had to exist; otherwise it would be impossible to draw a simile or parable from it.

49. God commanded the prophet to seal up his book until the time.[207] This is not to be twisted into meaning that God did not want these prophecies read or known, for prophecies are given to edify and to teach. But the Holy Spirit was prophesying through Daniel that people's negligence in reading and knowing the word of God would be great, and that the sacred books were thereby going to be sealed up because of their own incredible folly, so that they can understand nothing about things spiritual. He predicts that there will be great unbelief, but anyone who does not believe does not understand the heavenly mysteries. What a huge number of people you will find even today

---

[202]1 Macc. 1:16ff.

[203]1 Macc. 9:18 (Judas); 12:48 (Jonathan); 16:16 (Simon).

[204]Polychronius of Apamea in Syria (fl. 425), an exegete of the Antiochene method opposed to allegory. Fragments remain of his commentaries on Job, Daniel, and Ezekiel. "His interpretation of the book of Daniel was found to have points of agreement with that of the Neoplatonist Porphyry, which evoked later criticism"; see J. Quasten, *Patrology* (Westminster, Md.: Christian Classics, 1986) 3:423–424.

[205]Oecolampadius, *In Danielem Prophetam* (Basel., 1530).

[206]Rev. 20:4.

[207]Dan. 12:4: "But you, Daniel, shut up the words, and seal the book, until the time of the end. Many shall run to and fro, and knowledge shall increase."

who have never read through the Gospels, even though they want to be counted and called Christians! We can also interpret the sealing up of the divine books as applying to our senses and human reason. The unspiritual man does not perceive the things of God—not only are these things sealed up for him, but they seem to be folly.[208] They are open for those for whom the Lamb has opened them. As we read in Revelation, opening the sealed book has been granted to the Lamb alone.[209]

Moreover many are found who read the sacred books, recite them to others, and teach them; but they are sealed up for them because they do not really feel, do not experience, do not taste what they read and pass on. R. L. Ben-Gerzon thought that by this way of speaking God had commanded the prophet not to omit anything from these visions nor add anything to them.[210] It is written at the end: "Many shall run to and fro, and knowledge shall increase." Others make these words suit their fancy; to me this seems a prediction of the time in the New Testament when the apostles were sent to preach the Gospel to the whole world. Thus after they had traveled about through all the nations, the predictions of the prophets were made much clearer than they had been, because the spirit was poured out more abundantly, and also because prophecies are far better understood once they have been fulfilled than earlier when they were revealed. I think that this is enough about this passage.

50. I now come to the prophet Hosea. God predicted more than once that some day he would destroy death. From this we clearly gather that we should believe in the resurrection of the dead because without the resurrection death will reign and cannot be said to be destroyed. Isaiah in chapter 25 says, "I will swallow up death forever, and I will wipe away tears from all faces, and the reproach of my people I will take away forever."[211] These statements are clear, but Hosea in the passage now under consideration says the same things with greater force and effect: "I will free them from the hand of the tomb [sepulchri] and I will redeem them from death; I will be your plague, O Death, and your destruction, O Tomb."[212] Paul employed this passage as an obvious witness in his First Letter to the Corinthians, chapter 15. It should not matter to us that he does not follow the Hebrew truth but the Greek

---

[208]1 Cor 2:14.

[209]Rev. 5:4–9.

[210]Levi Ben-Gershom (Gersonides, pseudonym *Ralbag*; 1288–1344), Talmudist, scientist, and philosopher. His biblical commentaries on Kings were included in the Bomberg Bible.

[211]Isa. 25:8.

[212]Hosea 13:14.

translators: even if he changed the words, he did not depart from the meaning.[213] At that time the version of the Septuagint translators was better known and was in almost everybody's hands. Paul sometimes used it so that even the Gentiles when he preached to them might understand what was found in the divine writings.

This is the situation regarding the prophet's meaning: a little earlier he bitterly attacked Ephraim, that is, the kingdom of the ten tribes,[214] predicting for them ruin and certain destruction because of their idolatry and heinous crimes. He then brought in the consolation, which I recounted, namely that they were going to be snatched and delivered from death and the tomb. But you may say, "Is it not a contradiction to say that they would be utterly wiped out and that they would be delivered?" But we have to distinguish among the Israelites: on the one hand many of them had very hard hearts, clinging to idolatry and the worst sins—the extermination applies to them because they did not repent. On the other hand some good and holy people were found among them, who worshipped the true God; granted that they were going to be caught up with the others in the temporal disasters, but they would be delivered. The consolation discussed earlier rightly belongs to them. Our opponents will insist still more vehemently and will say, "We do not read that the ten tribes were restored or delivered from the tomb of their captivity. Perhaps some of them returned, but they did not come as a group, nor was the Kingdom of Ephraim, that is, of the ten tribes, restored again." This is indeed true, and for this reason in consoling them [*226v*] God does not promise temporal redemption or deliverance in this life but a blessed resurrection with eternal happiness. He says that he will redeem them from the tomb and deliver them from death, that he will be a plague on death and the destruction of the tomb.

This rule should often be used in reading the prophets: to understand that threats will fall upon those who were hardened in their sins and who simply did not want to repent. Promises and consolations are quite true and are going to be fulfilled regarding the repentant. "Sorrow is hid from my eyes";[215] God interjects this statement in order to establish the certainty of the resurrection, as if he were saying, "I will not repent of this decree—it absolutely will happen that way." "Ephraim will increase and multiply among his

---

[213]1 Cor. 15:55. A strange comment: Paul has "death" in both lines, whereas the Hebrew has "She'ol," LXX "Hades," and the Vulgate "death."

[214]Isaiah, Jeremiah, and Ezekiel sometimes use *Ephraim* to designate the ten northern tribes of Israel; Hosea does so almost exclusively.

[215]Hosea 13:14. Martyr has *poenitentia*, Vulg. *consolatio*.

brothers."[216] By the name Ephraim he understands all those who have Christ for their head, who in the resurrection will be heaped with the highest honors and extraordinary distinctions. Then the prophet turns his prediction against the evil Ephraimites and says that they will be utterly wiped out. They were indeed rich, luxurious, and powerful; relying on their possessions they never thought they would face ruin, but God said, "Behold, I will bring in an east wind, that is King Shalmaneser of Assyria,[217] who will dry up the fonts and their spring—that is, not only the waters but also the spring waters, the sources and roots, so that they can never more be repaired—and he will take away their treasure and all their precious vases. This is the interpretation that seems to me rather plain and evident.[218]

51. I will note, however, that David Kimhi changes the future tense into the pluperfect and says: "I would have delivered the kingdom of the ten tribes from the tomb and redeemed them from death, I would have been their plague on death and the destruction for their tomb, if their kingdom had been wise."[219] By wisdom I understand repentance itself, that is, if they had repented and listened to my words. And lest they despair over so unhappy an event, the prophet talks so wonderfully about liberation and redemption and about the plague on death and the destruction of the tomb, as if to say, "Even if they are annihilated and completely cut off, I would deliver them." We gather from this that no human calamity is so great that God is unable to remove or mitigate it. Therefore we should never lose hope but keep before our eyes that it is God's part to redeem from death and to be death's destruction and plague. But if at times deliverance does not come and death is not removed, it happens through no fault of God but through our stubbornness and unbelief, which we do not forego. Paul was very sharp-eyed in unraveling the predictions of the prophets; he confirms the argument for the resurrection of the dead. From that attribute of God he deduced that the victor over death and the redeemer from the tombs was proclaimed in the Scriptures and that the divine properties should sometimes burst forth in action. He noted that the prophet encouraged the kingdom of the ten tribes to repentance by promising that God would be with them, for he is such a powerful and magnificent conqueror over death. This exhortation would certainly have no force if some-

---

[216]The reference is unclear; perhaps Hosea 11:9.

[217]Hosea 13:15; Shalmaneser reigned 727–722 BCE.

[218]The *interpretatio ... plana et perspicua* is the "plain sense" of Scripture that Martyr accepted in his early lectures at Strasbourg, 1543–1547. His commentary on Lamentations (forthcoming in PML) makes this quite clear.

[219]See n. 123 above.

thing were sought from God which would never really happen. Since the apostle was so confident that it would happen, he used those glorious insults against death, saying, "O death, where is your victory, O death, where is your sting"[220] by which you will bury all humans? The implication is: Christ has stripped you of them.

52. It should not seem strange that Christ is called a plague and destruction since this has to be understood in respect to everything evil: new generation always implies the corruption of the preceding object. For when fire is produced in wood, it is necessary for the form and nature of the wood to perish; otherwise the fire will not be produced. As the philosophers or logicians commonly assert, the corruption of evil things counts among the good things.[221] We are used to saying about a noble and happy emperor: "He is a lion, a wolf, a dragon, ferocious, and savage," but we add, "to his enemies," since elsewhere he is merciful, kind, and friendly to citizens. According to the same prophet God made himself like a bear, a leopard, and lioness,[222] but only against the criminal and wicked, since elsewhere he is kind and merciful toward the devout. God measured out his medicine for us from the death and resurrection of Christ so that we might be liberated and death might die. Like a wise doctor, he prepares a draught of medicine for the sick person, which may relieve him and get rid of the fever or sickness. We drink a healthy dose of this healthful medicine when mentioning the Lord's death and resurrection, in our reading or preaching when we embrace them with a lively faith and when we proclaim our faith by the sealing of baptism and the reception of the eucharist. In these holy actions both the death and the resurrection of Christ are celebrated. In treating this passage Paul adds that death is absorbed by victory, that is, the victory of Christ.[223]

[NEW TESTAMENT]

53. These statements are from the passages of the Old Testament. More could be brought forward, but I wanted to introduce these and rest with them. I have explained them at length because there are many today who argue that there is no mention of the resurrection in the Old Testament or that

---

[220]I Cor. 15:55.

[221]See Aristotle, *Meta*. X.4 1055a33ff.: "The primary contrariety is between positive state and privation—not every privation, however (for 'privatio' has several meanings), but that which is complete." Cf. *Meta*. V.12.1019b5ff., V.22, 1022a22ff.; Plotinus *Enneads* I, 8th Tract.; cf. Lombard, *Sent*. dist. 35.10, privatio vel corruptio boni. Aquinas distinguishes "privatum esse" and "privari"; ST Ia.Q48.1 ad 1.

[222]Hosea 13:7–8.   [223]I Cor. 15:54, 57.

if evidence is found there, it was unknown to the fathers of those times. I now come to the witness and assertions of the New Testament. The first comes from John, chapter 5, a passage I have cited rather often: "All who are in the tombs will hear [*227r*] the voice of God's son and those who have done good will come forth to the resurrection of life, but those who have done evil, to the resurrection of judgment." And in chapter 6, "He who believes in me has eternal life, and I shall raise him up on the last day."[224] Matthew 22, Mark 12, Luke 20: "I am the God of Abraham, the God of Isaac, and the God of Jacob. Now he is not the God of the dead, but of the living."[225] Likewise in Luke 14, when Christ was encouraging the bystanders to help the poor and invite them to banquets: "They are unable to repay you," he said, "but you will be repaid in the resurrection of the just."[226] In John, "He who loves his life in this world, loses it, and he who hates his life will keep it for eternal life."[227] By the word "life" he means the life of the body. The person who hoards it closely and does not want to lay it down for the Gospel's sake loses it, because in the resurrection it will be destined to perpetual destruction. But the person who has poured it out will have it safe for life everlasting. Matthew 25: all nations will be gathered to him.[228] In Mark, chapter 13, "He will send out his angels, and gather his elect from the four winds, and from the ends of the earth to the end of heaven."[229] Acts 17: Paul preached this resurrection to the Athenians when there were Stoics and Epicureans present in the street of Mars. When they heard about that teaching, some of them laughed at him, and others said, "We will listen to you on this topic another time," and they called him σπερ-μολόγος, that is, a street hawker and teacher of new doctrine and deities.[230] In the same book, chapter 23, when Paul was standing before the council of the scribes, Pharisees, and Sadducees and saw that they were badly divided, he shouted out, "I am a Pharisee, and a son of a Pharisee; with respect to the hope and the resurrection of the dead I am on trial." And in chapter 24 of that book, when he was pleading his case before the governor Felix he testified that both the just and the unjust would be resurrected. He repeated the same thing when he was before Festus, King Agrippa and his wife Bernice present.[231]

54. Peter too in chapter 1 of his First Letter says, "By God's great mercy we have been born anew to a living hope through the resurrection of Jesus Christ from the dead ... who by God's power are guarded through faith for a

---

[224]John 5:28–29 (see §47 above); 6:40.
[225]Matt. 22:32; Mark 12:26–27; Luke 20:37–38.
[226]Luke 14:12–14. [227]John 12:25. [228]Matt. 25:32.
[229]Mark 13:27. [230]Acts 17:18, 32. [231]Acts 23:6, 24:15, 26:8.

salvation ready to be revealed in the last time." In his second letter, chapter 3, he says that at that time there will be a new heaven and a new earth.[232] John too writes in his First Letter, chapter 3: "When Christ appears we shall be like him."[233] From this we conclude that since Christ has a body and is risen, we too will rise together with bodies. In Revelation 20 we read, "And I saw the dead, great and small, standing" in God's presence and so forth. Likewise in chapter 21: God "will wipe away every tear from their eyes, and death shall be no more." etc. Also in chapter 22: "Blessed are those who keep his commandments that they may have the right to the tree of life."[234] Paul in Romans 8: "If the Spirit of him who raised Jesus Christ from the dead dwells in you, he who raised Jesus Christ from the dead will give life to your mortal bodies." And in chapter 6: "For if we have been united with him in a death like his, we shall certainly be united with him in a resurrection like his." In chapter 14: "For we shall all stand before the judgment seat of Christ."[235] In chapter 15 of First Corinthians he deals with this question explicitly and very carefully; he so confirms the resurrection as to allow no ambiguity about his faith and conviction. I will not quote the words from there because I would have to recite the whole chapter. But I will refer to this from chapter 6 of the same letter: "Our body is not meant for immorality, but for the Lord, and the Lord for the body. And God raised the Lord and will also raise us up by his power."[236] But in chapter 5 of the Second Letter he writes about our house in heaven not made by hands and our desire to put it on, and while in this earthly tent we groan because we do not want to be unclothed but to put it on so that our mortality might be swallowed up in life. He adds that we all must appear before the judgment seat of Christ so that each one be rewarded for the things done in the body according to what one has done, whether good or evil.[237] Ephesians 2: "When you were dead through sins ... he made us alive together with Christ ... and raised us up with him and made us sit with him," and so forth.[238] Philippians 3: "That I may know him and the power of his resurrection, and may share his sufferings, becoming like him in his death, that if possible I may attain the resurrection of the dead."[239] Chapter 2 of Colossians: "You were buried with him in baptism, in which you were also raised with him through faith in the working of God, who raised him from the dead." In chapter 3: "Your life is hidden with Christ in God. When Christ who is our life appears, then you also will appear with him in glory."[240] In 1 Thessalonians chapter 4 he warns them not

---

[232] 1 Peter 1:3, 5; 2 Peter 3:13.
[233] 1 John 3:2.
[234] Rev. 20:12; 21:4; 22:14.
[235] Rom. 6:5; 8:11, 14:10.
[236] 1 Cor. 6:14.
[237] 2 Cor. 5:1–10.
[238] Eph. 2:1, 5–6.
[239] Phil. 4:10–11.
[240] Col. 2:12, 3:3.

to "grieve over those who are asleep, as others do who have no hope. For since we believe that Jesus died and rose again, even so, through Jesus, God will bring with him those who have fallen asleep." He soon adds, "For the Lord himself will descend from heaven with a cry of command, with the archangel's call and with the sound of the trumpet of God. And the dead in Christ will rise first."[241] In Hebrews 2: "That through the power of death he might destroy him who has the power of death." In chapter 11 of the same letter: when at God's command Abraham was about to sacrifice Isaac, in whom he placed the promise of posterity, he thought within himself that God was able to raise him even from the dead, and so figuratively speaking he also did receive him back.[242] In his letter Jude brings in Enoch, who was the seventh from Adam, saying, "Behold, the Lord came with his holy myriads, to execute judgment [*227v*] on all, and to convict all of the ungodly." Then he adds, "Wait for the mercy of our Lord Jesus Christ unto eternal life."[243] These passages are enough citations from the New Testament. Add to them the article from the Apostles' Creed in which we profess that we believe in the resurrection of the flesh.[244] Also, all the passages in which Christ is said to be the judge of the living and the dead apply to this belief.

[CAUSES OF THE RESURRECTION]

55. After seeing the meaning of the name and its definition, and examining whether this resurrection can be proved by natural arguments, we introduced next the testimonies of the Old and New Testaments. It follows now that we should say something about its causes. It is a result of faith and follows justification. So John chapter 6 says, "He who believes in me has eternal life, and I will raise him up at the last day."[245] Therefore God by his power is its efficient cause. Christ told the Sadducees, "You are wrong, because you know neither the Scriptures nor the power of God."[246] Not just the Father but also the Holy Spirit is the cause of the resurrection. As we said earlier, Romans states, "If the Spirit of him who raised Jesus from the dead dwells in you," and so forth.[247] Also the Son, that is, Christ Jesus, is the cause of this resurrection. He said in John, "I will raise him up on the last day." Again, "For as the Father raises the dead and gives them life, so also the Son gives life," etc. Also "all who are in the tombs will hear the voice" of God's Son "and come forth" and so on.[248] John 11: "I am the resurrection and the life."[249] Moreover an argument

---

[241]1 Thess. 4:13–14, 16.   [242]Heb. 2:14, 11:17–19.   [243]Jude 1:14, 21.
[244]See Martyr's commentary on the credal article, EW 72ff.
[245]John 6:40.   [246]Matt. 22:29.   [247]Rom. 8:11
[248]John 5:21; 28–29; 6:40.   [249]John 11:25.

is drawn from the fact that through his death Christ took away sin, which was the cause of death. No one doubts that if the cause is removed the effect is taken away. 1 Corinthians 15: "For as in Adam all die, so also in Christ shall all be made alive"; "And as by a man came death, by a man has come also the resurrection."[250]

The final cause of the resurrection is in order that a whole and complete person may be judged before God's judgment seat and that he may award rewards and punishments according to how one has acted. Even though angels are the ministers of the resurrection, they cannot be its causes. Christ's own resurrection is also counted among the causes of the future resurrection. Paul says in 1 Corinthians 15, "If there is no resurrection of the dead, then Christ has not been raised; and if Christ has not been raised, then our preaching is in vain."[251] But we can also reverse the argument: Christ has arisen, therefore we too will rise. Hence Christ's resurrection seems to be the cause of our own. This must surely be granted, yet not in such a way that the action by which Christ was raised and which has already taken place is an efficient cause that performs something or does something toward producing our resurrection. It is rather because the divine force and power which resides in Christ, since he is God, will also give us life in his good time just as it raised him from the dead. We see this happen in human affairs. A white person gives birth to a white child, not because the color itself procreates, but those principles or causes which make the parent white also make white the child whom the parent procreates. Thus our resurrection will not be dissimilar to Christ's resurrection. We should also note that the divine actions and heavenly benefits which are conferred on human beings, as Damascene said, flow down to us through the flesh of Christ, which would now be nothing unless it had been raised from the dead.[252] On this understanding the resurrection of Christ can also be called our resurrection, because without it we could not achieve our own. Moreover, were we to follow Plato in philosophizing when he lays down the idea for the four kinds of causes,[253] we could say that Christ's resurrection was the exemplary cause of ours. We assign the final cause: that the whole and complete person be judged before God's tribunal to receive rewards or punishments according to how one has acted. So much for the causes.

---

[250]1 Cor. 15:21–22.   [251]1 Cor. 15:14.
[252]John of Damascus [Damascene], *De Fide Orth*. IV.3 (PG 94.1106).
[253]E.g. Plato *Phaedo* 97–98 on final cause; Plato *Tim*. 29A, 68E on secondary cause.

[CONDITION OF THE RESURRECTED]

56. It follows that we should talk about the properties and conditions of risen bodies. The scholastics call these "attributes," and I cannot object to those they enumerate since I see that they are drawn from the divine writings.[254] Still I do not think they have collected all that are there, nor would that even have been possible. For in this life we cannot be experts about the glory of the saints—we shall know it perfectly and completely at the time when we come to that life. The first condition of the blessed which comes up is *immortality*. In the Scriptures whenever there is question of the future life it is called eternal, as something that will not end. Paul says, "This mortal nature must put on immortality and this perishable nature must put on the imperishable."[255] Since punishments and rewards which are to be distributed on the basis of works will be everlasting, it is necessary that the subject or nature which will be affected by them should also be immortal. Moreover, since there is no doubt that Christ has destroyed sin and death, it means that the life of the saints is immortal. We find in Romans 6, "Christ being raised from the dead will never die again; death no longer has dominion over him.[256] Besides that, there is 1 Corinthians 15: "Flesh and blood cannot inherit the kingdom of God."[257] These are not to be understood as meaning the very substance and nature of flesh and blood, for those who are going to arise will surely be endowed with these things. Rather the Apostle is focused on the corruption to which flesh and blood are subject in this life. That is why he adds, "nor does the perishable inherit the imperishable."

57. Another property follows from this one. After the resurrection there is no need for food, drink, and sex since as Christ taught, people will be *like the angels*.[258] On this point Muslims and [228r] Saracens are in serious error in believing that after the resurrection the blessed will be supplied with sufficient food, generous beverages, and a plentiful use of sex. That is what their Koran said. But Avicenna interprets this with some skill in his *Metaphysics* and says these statements are metaphorical because it was thought that the pleasures of an honorable other life could not be expressed, especially to simple folk, except in the terminology of the crass pleasures which are felt in this one.[259] I

---

[254]Cf. Aquinas, ST Supp.; "Resurrectio" QQ79–86, *s.v.* attributes: impassibility (82); subtlety (83); agility (84); clarity (85); also SCG IV:86, *s.v.* brightness, agility, impassibility, and perfection.

[255]1 Cor. 15:53.   [256]Rom. 6:9.

[257]1 Cor. 15:50.   [258]Matt. 22:30.

[259]Avicenna *Metaphysica* IX.7 (Frankfurt a. M.: Minerva, 1960) 609ff., "Das Entstehen der Elemente durch das Einwirken der himmelischen Agenzien."

said that we could well mention these things because even in the divine writings these sorts of allegories or translations are found. We read in Luke 12, "Blessed are those servants whom the master finds awake; truly he will gird himself ... and will come and serve them." In chapter 22 of the same Evangelist we find, "As my Father has appointed a kingdom for me, so do I appoint for you, that you may eat and drink at my table in my kingdom."[260] Many even among our most ancient Fathers thought that after his second coming Christ would reign together with his saints for a thousand years in supreme delights and great enjoyment. These people are called χιλιασά by the Greeks and can be termed millenarians by the Latins. Augustine talked about them at length in his *City of God*, book 20, chapter 20.[261] The occasion that first led them into this error was that Christ ate and drank together with his apostles after his resurrection. Also, the prophets mention these things rather often when they predict the last times. They also twist in that direction Revelation chapter 20 where these thousand years are mentioned.[262] To refute their error, let us say first that Christ ate and drank with the apostles not to satisfy any need but to leave the truth of his human nature fully attested. He had an incorruptible body which suffered from neither thirst nor hunger. Hence the food and drink he used were not converted into the substance and size of his body, but disappeared and were reduced to primary matter. From this we should understand that some of the things Christ did after his resurrection were to witness to the truth of his human body and some were to show his glory.

Indications of his glory were that he vanished suddenly from their sight and while he was standing next to his apostles, that he came to them when the doors were closed, and that at the end he ascended into heaven. By contrast he showed that he was still a true man when he offered himself to be looked at and touched, when he ate and drank together with the apostles, when he was visibly separated from them during his ascension into the heavens. The fact that the sacred Scriptures in both prophets and evangelists make mention of food and drink we explain allegorically, and through metaphors and figurative speech well adapted for teaching. We can show this on the evidence of the book of Proverbs, where wisdom is described as a woman who has mixed wine and set a table.[263] Such things cannot suit wisdom, whose nature is spiritual and dwells in human minds. But by the name of food and drink we understand the knowledge of God, the burning love for things divine, and the

---

[260]Luke 12:37; 22:29–30.
[261]Augustine *De civ. Dei* 20.18–20 (PL 40, 684 ff.). Tertullian *Adv. Marcion* III,24 (PL 2, 384), shares this view.
[262]Rev. 20:5.   [263]Prov. 9:2.

joy that flows out from the divine presence. I say that these will serve the saints like the most delicious food and drink. Thus when Mary was sitting at the feet of the Lord and was wondrously refreshed by his teaching, Christ himself defended her when Martha charged her with neglecting the work of preparing what was necessary for dining. He said, "Mary has chosen the good portion which shall not be taken away from her."[264] We should know regarding the Revelation passage that the resurrection in which the saints will reign with Christ for a thousand years is not the resurrection we are now dealing with but the regeneration by which we are justified. That is why it adds in so many words, "This is the first resurrection." Nor do the thousand years denote a time different from the one we are now enduring under Christ's protection in his kingdom, which is the church.[265] No doubt some fixed number is put down there for an indefinite one. Therefore those words refer not to Christ's second coming but to his first. If those ancient Fathers had referred to this they would not have fallen into error. So in that immortal life there will be no need for bodily nourishment or the procreation of children. These things serve a mortal life, but that life will be immortal. Because there will be no deterioration of our bodily substance, there will be no need for its repair, that comes from food and drink. And since people will not be dying, there is no need for others to replace them through new procreation.

58. The scholastics call another condition or quality *light* or *splendor*. Regarding this, Paul in Philippians says that Christ will change our lowly body to be like his glorious body.[266] Christ gave an example of this sort of condition in his transfiguration when his face shone like the sun.[267] As we heard earlier, Daniel did not omit their splendor or brightness.[268] Paul says in First Corinthians 15, "What is now sown is perishable, what is raised is imperishable." They think that this splendor flows into the bodies of the blessed from their souls which will see God not in a mirror dimly but face to face.[269] They will conceive such happiness and joy from this sight that it will overflow into their bodies. Everyone knows that the soul and spirit make for a smiling face and cause the body to glow.

In addition, *agility* is attributed to the beatified body. The body and its limbs are wholly under the soul's command so that they neither fight nor oppose the soul. Paul said, "Now it is sown in weakness, then it is raised in

---

[264]Luke 10:39–42.
[265]Cf. Martin Bucer, *De Regno Christi* (1550), esp. 1, "Names of the Kingdom of Christ," and 5, "What the Kingdom of Christ Is...."
[266]Phil. 3:21.
[267]Matt. 13:14, 17:2.
[268]Dan. 12:3.
[269]1 Cor. 13:12, 15:42.

power."[270] On the same point we read in the Wisdom of Solomon about the saints, "They will run like sparks through the reeds" or stubble.[271] Paul says to the Thessalonians, "We who are alive, who are left, shall be caught up together with the risen dead in the cloud to meet Christ in the air."[272] This quickness and agility of our bodies will be so great that we can ascend up through the air to Christ. Christ's body certainly possessed this wonderful power since he walked on water and granted Peter the ability to do it, and since Christ himself was lifted up from the earth to the heavens. Such power lies in the fact that the soul has total mastery of the body so that the weight and inertia of the flesh do not prove an obstacle. This property applies to local motion, so it is curious that the Ubiquitists give this attribute to beatified bodies, as they write in their little books. They nonetheless maintain that heaven is everywhere so that they do not want to attribute fixed locations to Christ's body and to ours, as if there were local motion without any location.[273]

59. *Impassibility* is also attributed to the saints after the resurrection. They are not corrupted or weakened by any sufferings, pains, or diseases. On this point the Apostle wrote, "What is now sown perishable is raised imperishable."[274] The affections and passions in bodies are not to be judged in the same way. Some are harmful; they weaken, debilitate, and finally kill the body, for instance hunger, thirst, sickness, pain, and things like that. From such affections the saints are free. Other passions such as sense-knowledge help and perfect rather than harm. The eye is not hurt when it senses beautiful colors nor is hearing endangered by harmony and skillful musical compositions, nor smell by good odors. Our bodies therefore will not be deprived of these passions when they are in the fatherland after the resurrection.

The scholastics also include *subtlety*, which should not be understood as if the bodies of the risen were transformed into spirit and were going to be airy or ethereal objects or like the wind, to penetrate everything. I take this subtlety to be a precise, fine, and acute perception by the senses. I also refer it to the feelings which accompany the body, which will not be gross and full of dregs, nor troubling to the soul. We can apply to this what Paul says, "It is sown a physical body, it is raised a spiritual body."[275] By these words he did not

---

[270]I Cor. 15:42.   [271]Wis. 3:7.   [272]I Thess. 4:17.

[273]Martyr obviously has in mind the growing controversy between the Lutherans and the Reformed over ubiquity and the proper understanding of the communication of idioms between Christ's two natures. His great contribution to this controversy, *Dialogus de utraque in Christo natura* (published 1561) was written while Vermigli was lecturing on Kings. See DIAL, introduction, for background to Vermigli's role in the controversy.

[274]I Cor. 15:42.   [275]I Cor. 15:44.

mean that the body is changed into a spirit but that the human body, within the limits of its nature, will have access to the properties of the spirit as regards knowing and feeling.

The scholastics gathered together and verified from the Scriptures these outstanding properties. But they still did not list them all, for as Paul said, "No eye has seen nor ear heard ... what God has prepared for those who love him."[276] We should not fail to note that the sacred writings or the ancient Fathers or the scholastics never attributed the gift of *ubiquity* or being freed from place, either to Christ's flesh or to the other saints. Hence it is remarkable that certain people of our era are so delighted with this invention. Indeed, the scholastics and especially Thomas Aquinas said, "The fact that the conditions of beatified bodies approach those of celestial beings shows that their habitation after this life is in heaven, indeed is above the heavens."[277]

The scholastics also argued about what age the risen will be, concluding that it will be fully grown, adult, mature, and robust. To this end they twist the statement from Ephesians, "Until we attain to the unity of faith, and the knowledge of the Son of God, to mature manhood, to the measure of the stature of the fullness of Christ."[278] If they allow me to speak, the Apostles' words do not bear on this point. He was dealing there with the restoration of souls and not the reformation of bodies, as the preceding words clearly demonstrate. Yet I do not disagree with them over the age of the risen, but for a different reason. When God created the first humans, he did not make them either infants or decrepit, imperfect or deformed. But since the resurrection is a sort of new creation or reformation, it is fitting that it conform to the first creation. Therefore just as the first things which God created were very good, that is, perfect in their kind, so too the bodies that his power will restore by the resurrection will be perfect as regards their nature.

60. What will we say about the bodily properties and conditions of the *wicked* when they rise? They will have immortality, but will not obtain the other attributes of the godly—indeed they will be deformed by their very contraries and opposites. They will instantly be deprived of light and brightness, for as Christ taught, orders will be given to throw them into outer darkness. They will not be impassible since they will be tortured and afflicted by terrible sufferings. There will be weeping and gnashing of teeth, says the Lord; their worm dies not and their fire is not extinguished. They will not be swift and agile because they are going to be thrown into hell chained hand and foot. Nor will they enjoy subtlety for the reason we have already described: because

---

[276] I Cor. 3:9.   [277] ST III, Supp. 69.a.3.   [278] Eph. 4:13.

they will live amidst tears and weeping and with gross feelings and violent desires, as the Gospel story about the rich man and the pauper suggests. [279] In the items I have noted there is one thing to be kept in mind above all: it is that the substance of our bodies will not be changed because of this change in qualities and conditions. Exactly the same body and the same flesh will be raised up.

We should not listen to Origen, who thinks that only the body is going to be restored, but not the flesh. [280] Instead we should believe Christ, who said when he had risen from the dead, "Handle me and see; for a spirit has not flesh and bones as you see I have." [281] For if the same body will rise, the same flesh and organs will be returned. A location will also be assigned to them, for they cannot exist without location. [282] Paul clearly proved that the subject would be wholly the same when he said to the Corinthians, "For this perishable nature must put on the imperishable, and this mortal nature must put on immortality." [283] By using the pronoun *this* he points out the substance and nature of a truly human body.

But you will say, "The same apostle wrote in the same letter chapter 6, 'Food is meant for the stomach and the stomach for food,' [284] but God will abolish both the one and the other. It is also said that the blessed will be like the angels so that they neither take wives nor do women marry. [285] What gender difference will be retained among the risen saints? For what purpose, for what end?" We answer that in eternal felicity God will indeed take from the risen the use and function of these parts and organs, but not their substance and nature. But when it is asked why the organs will remain when their use and function are removed, we answer that this will take place because those organs pertain to the integrity and perfection of the human body. If all of them were taken away, how much of it would be left? First the throat, the stomach, and all the intestinal organs would have to be pulled out since they produce feces and distill liquid humors. Secondly, it is right that those parts

---

[279]Dives and Lazarus; Luke 16:23–26.

[280]The resurrection body will be "flesh no more," even if features of the earthly body remain in the spiritual. Origen's eschatology is complex and ambiguous, partly because of (Koetschau's) questionable reconstruction of *De Principiis* I.8.4. In III.6 he speaks of a change "in form and species" so that the resurrected body may participate in the "unspeakable glory" of the divine nature. Cf. §62 (p. 113) below, and Chadwick, "Origen, Celsus, and the Resurrection of the Body," 83–102.

[281]Luke 24:39.

[282]Cf. Aristotle *Phys.* IV.1.208b29, and *De Coelo* I.7.275b9; Martyr quotes these statements in DIAL 14, n. 29.

[283]1 Cor. 15:53.   [284]1 Cor. 6:13.   [285]Matt. 22:30.

that we have put to honorable use while we were living here should gain a reward along with us. Since the blessed used their palates, throats, and stomachs in a careful and temperate way and their genitals in a chaste way, why should not these parts be crowned along with them?

61. It is not valid to conclude that certain human parts and organs should be removed just because their use has ceased. That is not the case in nature. A barren old woman who can no longer give birth or nurse is not thereby deprived of her breasts or even the parts that function in procreation. A brave and noble general who performed many splendid deeds in war has mounted around his tomb after his death the weapons he once used, even though he will not be using them in the future. Likewise sailors drag up onto land the ships in which they gained victories at sea in the past, even if they can no longer use them; they want them to be preserved there intact for a lasting memorial of deeds accomplished. Even Christ himself, when he had been raised from the dead, carried back with him the scars from his wounds and said to doubting Thomas, "Put your fingers here ... in my side and in the nail marks, and do not be faithless, but believing."[286] The wounds had already performed their function, for by them the human race was redeemed, but he still had them after he was raised from the dead, that his body might be displayed as the same one which had suffered earlier. When they fasted for forty days Elijah and Moses kept their palates, throats, and stomachs even though they did not use them for a long time.[287]

62. To return to Origen who thought that the body would arise but not the flesh. We profess in the Creed the resurrection of the flesh, not of the body. As can be seen in his book Περὶ Ἀρχῶν, he says that two errors about the resurrection should be noted.[288] He makes our teaching his first error because we think that we will get back the same flesh, blood, bones, and organs when we are raised up. He regards this as absurd and naive and too gross because he takes it to imply that we will eat, drink, and marry wives again. But the weakness of this argument was discussed earlier when we showed that it is proper and fitting that these parts be received in the blessed resurrection, without their use and specific functions. The second error he attributes to certain heretics who completely denied the resurrection of the dead and granted eternal salvation only to souls and those who dared to call Christ's resurrection a phantom, seen only in imaginary visions. After describing these two errors or

---

[286]John 20:27.   [287]Ex. 34:28; 1 Kings 19:8.

[288]Origen *De Principiis* II.10.2 (vs. "heretics") and 3 (vs. "some of our own people") (PG 11, 235–236); cf. Frag. *De Resurrectione* 18 (PG 11.93): rationis illius virtus quae est insita in interioribus ejus medullis.

opposite extremes, he claimed to support a sort of middle way. He says that when the soul was separated from the body, the four principles which make it up return again to their basic elements. Thus the flesh goes back into the earth, breath into the air, blood and the other liquids into water, and warmth into heaven.[289] He asserts that they do not perish when they return there but are so mixed with those elements that they can longer be recognized or extracted from them.

Yet he holds that bodies will rise, and rise in such a way that souls will get their own bodies back, not a different one. As he says, what belongs to Peter will be returned to Peter and what belongs to Paul will be given Paul.[290] For it is not fair that sins should be punished in a strange body and not in the one where they were committed. He describes how this will happen as follows: a certain pattern and power are embedded by God in the seeds of things so that they will attract to themselves all future material and the corporeal substance of the things that had their sources there. The fruit, flowers, leaves, branches, bark, and trunk are not seen in the seed of a tree, yet somewhere in it exists the pattern and power [*229v*] of all these things. He thinks this is true for the ashes and the residual matter from our bodies. He calls this force by the Greek word σπινθήρισμον or ἀντέριον, or as Erasmus construes it in his scholion to his Jerome edition σωτήριον, that is, conservatory or seedbed of the dead.[291] He says that at the time of the last judgment this will germinate or sprout human bodies, but not flesh, bones and blood lest in heaven we should need food and drink, weddings, barbers and handkerchiefs to wipe away mucus.

[289]I.e., the fourth element, or fire.

[290]Origen *Selecta in Psalmos* I.5 (PG 12.1091 ff.). The LXX for Ps. 5:5 has ἀναστήσονται, but the Hebrew is simply "stand."

[291]Origen *Contra Celsum* VII.32: his concept of "seed" resembles Stoic doctrine; e.g. "the tabernacle of the soul, as it is called in the Bible, possesses a seminal principle [λόγον σπέρμαος]"; "as it were a resurrection takes place from that mere grain sown and cast in the earth" (V.18; cf.*In Cant. Cantic.* II.5); "each soul receiving some special property, the saving element in the irrational" (*Sel. in Psalmos* xxv.38); cf. n. 280 above, referring to a passage in which Origen states: "the form which distinguishes the body is the same … the bodily form, which at the resurrection is again thrown around the soul." H. Chadwick, "Origen, Celsus and the Resurrection of the Body," 101, states: "In order to make the idea of a resurrection more intelligible to his pagan contemporaries, and to rationalize Christian doctrine by interpreting it in terms of Greek philosophy, Origen makes use of the Stoic conception of σπερματικὸς λόγος." The two Greek terms are from Jerome, *Liber Contra Johannem Hiersol.* 26 (PL 23, 376–377). Migne has a significant footnote referring to manuscripts. On Erasmus: "Post multum sudorem sic Erasmus restituere conatur, *quam Graeci* σπινθήρισμον *vocant.*" The words mean "emitting sparks" and "resisting," that is, the power that enlivens and endures. Martyr's library included Erasmus' edition of the *Origenis Adam. eximii Script. interp. Opera* (Basel: Froben, 1550); see CSV 213.

In denying that the flesh will return, he misuses Paul's words when he says that those who are in the flesh cannot please God. By *flesh* the Apostle did not mean substance and nature but rather corruption, vices, and depravity. Paul also writes, "You are not in the flesh, you are in the Spirit, if the Spirit of Christ really dwells in you."[292] Accordingly, Origen thought the body of the risen would be homogeneous, that is, of the same pattern. He says that now we see with our eyes, hear with our ears, walk with our feet, but then we will see, hear and walk with our whole body.[293] In addition he misuses Paul's words to the Philippians when he says of Christ μετασχηματίσει, that is, he will transform our lowly body.[294] He takes this as referring to the substance and nature of our body when the only question is making changes in its qualities and conditions. The Greek word "state" [σχῆμα] from which this word is derived pertains to the predicament of quality, not "form" [μορφή], from which "conformed" [σύμμορφον] is derived.[295] If Origen had thought these things through, he would not have stumbled so badly as to say that the bodies of those arising would be airy or ethereal, so that they would not be subject to the eyes or touch but would be invisible and untouchable. But he allows them location, for they are changed depending on different locations. Meanwhile those who profess that true flesh and bones will be restored to us take away their location.[296]

I return to Origen, who teaches that bodies and not flesh will arise. He distinguishes them as genus and species: all flesh is body but not all body is flesh. Flesh is what is made up of blood, both veins and skin, and also bones and sinews. Some bodies are either airy or ethereal, as Plato attributed to certain demons and to our souls, so that as in a sort of vehicle it would be both carried about and joined to an external body, which is more gross and earthy.[297] And he fancied that things of this sort could not be felt or seen. There are also other bodies that can be seen and touched but still do not exist as flesh, for instance a wall and wood, which are sensible bodies but not flesh. Therefore body, which is a genus, through flesh contracts into a certain species, which Paul's words to the Colossians prove: "You who were once estranged from Christ and hostile in mind, doing evil deeds, he has now reconciled in his body of flesh by his death." In the same epistle, "with a circum-

---

[292]Rom. 8:8–9. [293]Reading *corpore* for *tempore*.
[294]Phil. 3:21.
[295]Aristotle, *Meta.* 5.13.1020b2: "the differentia of the essence."
[296]This seems a dig at the Lutherans, who upheld the ubiquity of Christ's body.
[297]Origen *De Principiis* II.10.3 (PG 11, 235–236). Plato, e.g. *Phaedo* 66–67 (pure soul); *Rep.* IX.585ff.

cision made without hands, by putting off the body of flesh."[298] This statement was from Origen's book *On First Principles*, as related by Jerome in a letter against John, the bishop of Jerusalem.[299]

63. Origen made a grave and complex mistake on this subject. First he philosophizes badly on the "seedbed of the dead" that is left behind in the ashes of the departed after death. What need is there to set up the principle of resurrection in the material of our body? The act of awakening from the dead belongs exclusively to God; there are no forces of the body that sprout again. If I may touch on this in passing, some of the ancient Fathers are to be read with great caution because they seem to attribute to the eucharist what Origen assigns to that pattern or power embedded in bodies. These are not snuffed out in the dead. Irenaeus in his fourth book and Justin in his *Apology to Emperor Antoninus* wrote on this point, that when our bodies have received the eucharist they are no longer mortal because the sacrament works to save our bodies for life everlasting.[300] If they understood these teachings in a literal and simplistic way, as it seems at first glance, teaching that Christ's body and blood are changed into true nourishment for the body, and so became in bodies the principle of the resurrection, their statement would be quite absurd.

Real bodily food is prepared, digested, and circulated through the body's parts and turned into the substance and nature of the person who is being nourished. But since the body of Christ is impassible, it cannot be changed into other bodies and therefore is not buried with them. These Fathers nonetheless wrote the truth, provided we take their words in an appropriate sense. Let us realize that the faithful at the Lord's Supper receive bread and wine with the mouth of their body, but in mind and spirit they receive the body and blood of Christ insofar as they were offered on the cross for our salvation. In receiving these things they find justification and regeneration by faith or are strengthened in justice and in a spiritual birth. But justification and regeneration, which are in the soul, make the body itself fit for the resurrection. On this basis we can say that the outward elements we receive bodily are a preparation for the resurrection, since they are instruments of the Holy Spirit through which he stirs up within us the faith which is truly the principle of the resurrection.[301]

[298]Col. 1:21–22, 2:11.

[299]Jerome *Liber contra Iohannen Hiersol.* 27 (PG 23.379).

[300]Irenaeus *Against All Heresies* IV.18.5 (PG 7.1827ff.); Justin Martyr *First Apology* 66 (PG 6.427). Cf. Peter Martyr Vermigli *Disputatio de Euch.* III.2 (Oxford 1549), forthcoming in PML.

[301]Cf. Martyr's teaching in *Epist. ad amicum* (John Sturm), DM 357–358, and texts in VWG 175ff.

64. Origen went astray in this too, that he thinks the body which he acknowledges in the resurrection will be homogeneous—it will see as a whole, hear as a whole, walk as a whole, as if it did not have eyes, ears, and feet distinct from one another. Certainly when Christ gave the apostles an image of beatified bodies in his transfiguration, he was not so changed that he went about in a round shape like [*230r*] the bodies of the sun, moon, and stars.[302] His face remained distinct from the rest of his members, for the evangelist writes that his face glowed like the sun.[303] After the resurrection, when he ate and drank along with them, I wager that he did so with teeth, palate, throat, and stomach, not with his feet and the top of his head. He also spoke with them, undoubtedly with mouth and tongue and not knees and legs. It is also said explicitly that he showed his side pierced on the cross; therefore he possessed it as distinct from the other parts of his body. Accordingly these members were either real or fakes and tricks. If they are true, let those fellows agree that bodies will be restored in the resurrection with different members. But if they were phantoms and inventions, a deceit provides bad proof for the truth of the resurrection. They say these special privileges belonged to Christ because he was not like us. He was conceived by male seed but fashioned in the womb of the Virgin by the work of the Holy Spirit.

I myself welcome the resurrection of Christ as having been the image and model of our resurrection. Hence if specific members were restored to him, they will also be returned to us. But, they reply, the Lord did these things by a certain dispensation with the apostles when he was summoned from the dead and brought back to life. Otherwise he revealed the airy and spiritual condition of his body, as when dealing with the apostles in such a way that they did not recognize him and he vanished from their presence by becoming invisible. Likewise when he came in to them despite closed doors.[304] The apostles did not recognize him not because he was invisible or deprived of flesh and hands but because, as the evangelist says, their eyes were held so that they would not recognize him. Therefore when later they did recognize him, he writes that their eyes were opened; so we understand that the impediment lay in their eyes and was not some difference in the Lord's body. Moreover he

---

[302] As Origen taught, according to the Second Council of Constantinople's Anathema X; see *Origen on First Principles*, ed. G. W. Butterworth (New York: Harper Torchbooks, 1966) 141n5. Justinian charged: "As Origen madly supposes, the body of the Lord was spherical"; see *Alexandrian Christianity*, ed. J. E. L. Oulton & H. Chadwick (London: SCM, 1954: L.C.C. vol II) 191, 232, 381–382. Origen himself seems content to follow Plato e.g. *Tim.* 33B in imagining that "the bodies of heavenly beings are spherical"; see Origen *De Orat.* XXX.3.

[303] Matt. 17:2.   [304] Luke 24:31; John 20:19.

took himself suddenly from under their eyes, nor did they see him again because their eyes were held back lest they see his departure.[305]

Apollonius of Thyana, at a meeting in the presence of Domitian, suddenly disappeared from their midst and was not seen again, not because his body was rendered invisible or that he vanished into air, but because through demonic trickery the eyes of the bystanders were prevented from discerning him either still present or slipping away.[306] Will we then deny to Christ's body, in whom divinity was fully present, what was done by diabolical trickery regarding a profane human body? The argument about the doors is also weak because it could have been that he went in to the apostles through the roof or windows when the doors were locked. Perhaps the doors gave way when he approached and offered him passage. But why so much fuss? When Ezekiel was relating the resurrection of the dead he did not remember any airy or ethereal body; he said the bones came near other bones and each was linked at its joint by sinews covered by flesh and coated with skin and that they stood on their own feet. Therefore the prophet is describing bodies such as he knew they will be in the resurrection. Job says, "From my own flesh I shall see God with my own eyes,"[307] nor shall I be somebody else but substantially the same person I am now. These are so clear that they have no need for light.

65. In the resurrection the body will not be exactly the same as what we have now, but it too will occupy a place and cannot be in several places at once, because the nature of bodies and especially of human bodies will not allow this. Since it is circumscribed and finite in its parts, members, and lineaments, it must be contained in certain locations. Nonetheless today some people are found who are so impudent and immoderate in defending their own opinion, either about ubiquity or about the real and substantial presence of the body and blood of Christ in the holy supper, that they dare to demand from us that we prove to them, and indeed from the Scriptures, that a body cannot be without a place or cannot exist in different places at once. What if we in turn were to ask them to show us from the same sacred writings by an explicit statement that it is written that the body can exist without a place or be in different places at the same time? Unless they wish to use a different canon of books from those which the orthodox church recognizes, they certainly will never show us the slightest evidence. Therefore we must listen to

---

[305]Luke 24:17, 31; Acts 1:9.

[306]Apollonius of Tyana in Cappadocia (b. 4 BCE?), neo-Pythagorean sage and the subject of several "Lives" with much embellishment. The story of his miraculous disappearance was told by Philostratus and Hierocles to counter Christian claims to miracle; see Eusebius *Contra Hieroclem*, chap.1 (PL 4.795ff.). Martyr had used this illustration in his 1549 *Tractatio de Euch.*; DM 254.

[307]Job 19:26.

the voice of nature, which has God himself as its author. Nature has determined that these things are impossible, as both our adversaries and Augustine in his Letter to Dardanus acknowledged; so did Cyril in his dialogue on the Trinity, who wrote that if the divine nature could be divided up, it too would be a quantity and would be complete in one place, and could not avoid being circumscribed.[308]

The teachings of nature [naturae dogmata] are not to be reshaped except when they contradict the word of God. The teachings I presented do not conflict with it. Therefore since these fellows cannot show in the divine writings that things are otherwise, let them stop pushing on us nonscriptural articles of faith, which it is not right to forge from outside God's word. We follow the magisterium of the sacred writings which universally attribute a place to Christ's body whenever they speak about it. They say that he was sometimes in Galilee, then in Jerusalem, occasionally in Bethany, or in the temple, or the house of Simon. They assign him a set place in a way that keeps him from being in another one. For he says himself when he was about to raise Lazarus, "He is dead ... and I am glad I was not there."[309] Thus he testified that he [230v] was en route in such a way that he was not in Bethany at that time. The angel told the women, in order to show them that he had left the tomb, "He has risen, he is not here."[310] Therefore he had gone away from that place so that he was not present. This is the way that Christ speaks and the angel bears witness. Hence the human nature of Christ was tied down to a place and was not elsewhere. But these people will say, "When we ask about what could be, you answer about what is." I say to this that I waste no time about some power that is shown never to have sprung into action.[311] Secondly, I return to my previous demand and ask that they show me that this can be found in the Scriptures, namely that a human body exists outside of place and is in different places at once. Since they cannot do this, let them stop asserting it and proposing it as a necessary article of faith.[312] I know they say that it is written and asserted by Christ regarding the bread and wine of the supper, "This is my

---

[308]Augustine *Epist. ad Dard.* 187.iv.13 (PL 33, 836–837, 839); Cyril of Alexandria *De Sancta et Consubstantiali Trinitate* dial. II (PG 75.713 ff.).

[309]John 2:13–14, 12:1; Matt. 26:6; John 11:15.

[310]Matt. 28:6.

[311]Martyr likes to distinguish divine *velle* from *posse,* important also for his eucharistic doctrine: "We don't deny that God can turn bread into flesh; the whole controversy is whether he wills to do so"; see Martyr, *Tract. de Euch.* 56 (DM 245); cf. COR 11:24. See p. 174–175 on *potentia absoluta et ordinata.*

[312]On the other hand, Martin Bucer criticized both sides in the debate on ubiquity, warning that the idea of Christ's local presence in a heavenly place should not be made into a "necessary doctrine"; VWG 219–220.

body" and "This is my blood."[313] But wiser persons understand and explain these words far differently than they take them. A firm and certain argument is not drawn from a passage that has been interpreted two different ways. Perhaps they will throw up this: "With God nothing will be impossible."[314] I know that it is written so, but that statement should not be admitted without any exception. Paul makes an exception when he writes that God is so truthful that he cannot deny himself.[315] And the Fathers make very many exceptions. It is commonly said in the schools that God cannot do anything that implies a self-contradiction.[316] Moreover, the heretics have abused this saying. When the orthodox reproved them for setting up absurd and contradictory claims, they used to respond that all things are possible with God. Paul of Samosata, who denied the distinction of persons and asserted that the Father is the same as the Son, was hard pressed by our people who insisted that it is impossible for anyone to beget himself. He confessed that it was impossible for us but that for God all things are possible.[317]

66. I return to Scripture, which recognizes such a close connection between the place and the body it encloses that if the place is taken away, it completely denies existence to the object in the place. This argument would not be solid, but completely invalid, if a body could exist outside a place. For it would not be convincing that something did not exist if its place were totally removed. In Job chapter 7, when the prophet wanted to show that a person does not exist after death he says, "His place does not know him any more," that is, he does not exist. In chapter 20 he writes about a wicked person who is taken from life, "His place will no more behold him,"[318] that is, he will not exist. In Psalm 37 David expresses it more clearly, saying that just a little longer and the wicked will not exist: "you will look for his place and will not find him."[319] This then is how Scripture speaks. Hence Augustine, whom they reject with such condescension, is not to be blamed when he wrote about bodies, "If things are nowhere, they do not exist." He did not take that terminology only from Aristotle or from natural philosophy but from statements in

---

[313]Matt. 26:26–28.   [314]Luke 1:37.   [315]I tim. 2:13.

[316]Cf. SCG II.22: "God can do whatever does not imply a contradiction"; SCG II.25, "How the Almighty is said to be unable to do certain things." See also DIAL 17–18.

[317]Paul of Samosata, bishop of Antioch (260–272), deposed and excommunicated by a synod in Antioch in 268 for teaching that Christ differs from prophets only in degree; divine omnipotence secures his functional divinity. His adoptionist Christology survived in Arianism; see Eusebius *Hist. eccl.* V. 28–30.

[318]Job 7:10; 20:9.

[319]Ps. 37:36.

the divine Scripture.[320]

This does not, as they imagine, pertain only to this world and the present life, since the passages also look to eternal happiness in the kingdom of God. Christ told his disciples when informing them of his departure: "I go to prepare a place for you." Again, "I desire that where I am, my servant may be."[321] In Revelation it is taught that the group of the elect follow the Lamb wherever he goes.[322] But local motion cannot exist outside a place.

So well did the Fathers recognize that one body cannot be in several places at once that they did not wish to concede this even to angels. Indeed they proved that the Holy Spirit is God from the fact that he was at one and the same time in many places—something, they argued, which is impossible for any creature. Basil supported this in his treatise on the Holy Spirit; likewise Didymus, Cyril, Theodoret, and many others.[323]

Scripture too preaches the same thing about the body of Christ, for Peter said in Acts that the heavens had to receive him up to the time when, or until, all things are restored.[324] There is great power [ἐνέργεια], and a great and weighty significance in the adverb of time "until" or "up to" [Donec, Quoad], for it is thereby proved that the body of Christ will be in heaven in a way that meantime precludes his presence in our locations. Perhaps other things could be brought up, but I want the things we have discussed so far to suffice for proving the properties in risen bodies.

[ANSWERS TO ARGUMENTS CONTRA][325]

67. Now at the end we must dispel those arguments stated at the beginning that opposed the resurrection of the dead. [1] The first was taken from Porphyry's statement that to achieve supreme happiness which consists in knowing things divine, souls must avoid all bodies because these impede and weigh down the soul so that it does not apply itself to things divine. For this reason he seems to have forsaken Plato, who posited the return of souls to their former bodies. We reply that this philosopher looked on human bodies not as they were constituted from the beginning but as they are presently depraved and full of vices. But God is so good that he would not have given

---

[320]Augustine *Ep.* 187, *ad Dardanum*: quia nusquam erunt, nec erunt (PL 33.839). This letter "served as the classic text in the controversy over the ubiquity of Christ's risen body. Martyr printed it as an appendix to the Zurich, 1552, edition of his *De sacramento eucharistiae ... tractatio*"; DIAL 14, n. 30.

[321]John 14:2; 17:24.   [322]Rev. 14:4.

[323]Basil *De spiritu sancto* IX.22 (PG 32.107ff.).

[324]Acts 3:21.   [325]See §§7–8 above.

people from the beginning anything evil or that could work against their happiness. He saw all that he had made, and it was very good.[326] It is a ridiculous invention, not to say a wicked one, to assert that σῶμα rhymes with σῆμα, "the body is a tomb," because it is like the tomb of our souls.[327] God made man's corporeal nature good so that the body might help him and not be a handicap. If later on this resulted to some degree, it should be ascribed not to God but to sin. Even now while we live in the midst of these calamities the body is not wholly useless if someone by faith uses it rightly. Add to those reasons the fact that the body is going to be restored to us in the blessed resurrection so corrected and enhanced, and so resplendent with excellent conditions and attributes, that the body will not diminish the resurrection we ardently desire but rather increase it.

[2] Another argument was that after death the parts of our body are so dissolved into the elements from which they were taken and so mixed in with them that they could not be distinguished or separated from them. But this is to put too low and base an evaluation on God's power; we are not giving him as much credit as we grant hard workers in this life. If water were to be mixed with wine, people are found who can siphon it off from the wine again. There are also goldsmiths and metallurgists who can dissolve lumps of mixed gold, silver, bronze, and steel into their parts. Also some who can squeeze from anything, however hard and dried out, oil or rich juice. Will God, who is proclaimed almighty and was able to create the world from nothing, be unable once again to draw out human bodies from the ashes? On this point it is written in Revelation chapter 20, "And the sea gave up the dead in it, Death and Hades gave up the dead in them," and so on.[328]

68. [3] They say, "But it can happen that fish or birds may devour human flesh, and later become food for humans and are converted into the flesh of another human." The answer to this is that dust and ashes will be raised up not insofar as they were the substance of fish and birds, but of the person whom they had previously consumed. The second man who ate the fish and birds and converted them into his flesh will not be raised up with the addition or matter of the other man who came before him. The question about cannibals can be answered the same way. So that the subject may be understood more

---

[326]Gen. 1:31.

[327]Socrates states: "there are philosophers who maintain that even in life we are dead and that the body (σῶμα) is the tomb (σῆμα) of the soul"; Plato, *Gorgias* 493. Cf. *Cratylus* 400: Orphic poets invented the name σῶμα because it is "an enclosure or prison in which the soul is incarcerated."

[328]Rev. 20:13.

clearly, we should know that in nature it is not necessary, in order to retain the substance of the same body, that everything that was in the body remain in it forever, since the material of our body is always flowing out. Hair and fingernails are shed or clipped off; many things flow out from the mouth or the nostrils, and there is other excrement. Our natural heat is always drawing on vital fluid, and the substance which flows out is made up for by new food and drink. This happens every single hour, but the bodies do not stop being numerically the same. We see the same thing happening in trees, whose fruit is plucked, whose leaves fall, whose branches are pruned annually, but the trees remain numerically the same for a very long time. But if the whole substance is taken away at one time, that unity is not maintained. When matter goes away bit by bit and new matter drawn from food and drink is added to what existed before, unity is retained, especially when the same form endures and is conserved. It is therefore not necessary for the truth and unity of a body that everything that passed through the body be in it; in the resurrection God can restore to those eaten by cannibals, not the flesh of the cannibals, but other matter that flowed from their bodies at various times. If perhaps something is missing, he can by his power supply it just as additional flesh was given to Adam's rib when Eve was made from it. Suppose someone says that it can happen that cannibals eat no other food than human flesh. We say that this is improbable since they also have animals to eat; they use milk, millet, grains, and other foods of that sort. In some people their substance will be what it was; in others their substance was overly abundant and will be diminished. [4] Another argument is brought: if there is to be a future resurrection, there would be no need for new procreation; but that continues, as we see. God commanded procreation both before the Flood and afterwards. People who argue this way should think about two things. First, procreation lasts until the end of the world, but after that time procreation will no longer take place. Second, when procreation was commanded, the condition that it go on forever was not added. Thus the argument is very weak, for it is based on the nature of present conditions, even while our present status is due in time for drastic change.

69. [5] It was said also that in death the essential principles of a person are corrupted—not just the body but also the lower parts of the soul. The faculties for feeling perish, namely desires and temper, and those faculties that serve for nourishment and procreation. My response is that the use of these faculties is cut off by death, but the faculties themselves are not destroyed but are preserved whole in the soul which is separated from the body, so that when the

body is returned to the soul, their use is also restored except what in this life is designed for either procreation or feeding the body.

[6] Another objection was that the same unity of the body cannot be preserved since its life or duration will be interrupted. For the being which constitutes us is rooted in a certain succession or continuation of life. We see that when a walk is interrupted, if resumed later it is not exactly the same. Another objection was that the same thing happens in our development as to other qualities. Health is interrupted by sickness; when the sick person is restored, health returns but is not identically the same, for both old and new are different conditions. The answer is that this is true [*231v*] and certainly occurs in efficient causes in which the action or actual production is distinguished from the effecting cause, as happens with every created cause. But the resurrection is a work of God, in whom the action is not distinct from the nature and substance of the agent himself.

[7] The last objection brought forward was this: the mass of those things which have flowed out of our bodies is beyond belief. If everything is restored in the resurrection, the size of our bodies will be enormous. On the contrary, if not all is to be restored, what basis can be assigned for some things rather than others? I reply: We have already said that not everything ejected from our bodies will be received back when we rise, but only what contributes to a size that is right and proper. Why this and not that is returned should be left to the judgment of God, who disposes all things with supreme wisdom.

70. It now remains for us to dispose of the passages in the divine writings that seem at first glance to oppose the resurrection.[329] In Psalm 78 it is written, "He remembered that they were but flesh, a wind that passes and comes not again."[330] In explaining this passage, we have primarily to examine its purpose, that God was led to take pity on his people because their weakness was obvious. He had mercy on them because they were frail and feeble, and did not scatter them all with a single blow. The spirit is sometimes contrasted with the flesh because it is called weak while the spirit is strong and robust. Thus Christ told the apostles who fell asleep while he was praying, "The spirit is indeed willing, but the flesh is weak." Isaiah says in chapter 31, describing the Egyptian's weakness, "The Egyptian is flesh, not spirit,"[331] that is, he staggers out of weakness, he does not stand strong and firm. Sometimes flesh and spirit are taken for the same thing, both indicating weakness, as in this passage, where what was said in the first part is repeated in the second. Therefore

---

[329]See §8 above.   [330]Ps. 78:39.
[331]Matt. 26:41; Isa. 31:3: "Aegyptus caro est, non spiritus"; cf. Vulgate: "Aegyptus, homo, et non Deus."

spirit here should not be understood as the human soul or the divine inspiration but as breath, blowing, or wind; when they have passed on they perish and are never restored. When a human life has been played out, we are not sent back to the beginning, nor do we sprout again like pruned trees or cut grass, but we lie in the dust and do not return to our original state. When I say that after death humans are not like grass I am not opposing David, who says in Psalm 103, "For he knows our frame; he remembers that we are dust. As for man, his days are like grass; he flourishes like a flower of the field; for the wind passes over it, and it is gone, and its place knows it no more."[332] The purpose of the comparison is to teach the sudden and unexpected overthrow of a successful person. The comparison hinges on the fact that men do not sprout again like grass and plants. The passage also shows that nothing is found in humans to move God to mercy except their misery. But if the spirit is taken to mean the soul, we say that the prophet is reflecting on human beings and thinks of them according to their nature and powers; he rightly declares that their spirit departs in such a way that it does not return. The blessed resurrection is a miracle and not a work of nature. This scriptural passage does not talk about humans according to the things they receive through the goodness and power of God but according to the faculties and powers they have from nature. The book of Wisdom, chapter 15, also states: "His spirit goes out from him and does not return."[333] No human being takes the powers to rise again with it from the maternal womb or from principles of nature. Our soul does indeed exist after death but does not have of itself the power of returning to its previous body. In fact it would wholly perish if God were to remove from it his conserving power. This is the common and received exegesis of this passage.

A different meaning occurs to me which fits just as well as the two previous ones. When the Israelites were suffering from adversity in the desert and for good reasons were being punished by God, they cried out to him for deliverance. But they did so quite imperfectly, a fact that did not escape God. Nonetheless he took pity on them because they were flesh, that is, their nature was corrupted and because of this they often fell back into the same sins. Likewise their spirit, that is, the impulse to pray and call upon the true God Jehovah, was not steadfast in them but somehow passed through them and did not return since they fell once again into idolatry after achieving their freedom. Therefore they were fly-by-nights, that is, short-term believers, as the parable of the seed in Luke 8 indicates.[334]

---

[332]Ps. 103:15–16.   [333]Wis. 15:8.   [334]Luke 8:13.

71. In Psalm 115 it is written, "The heavens are the Lord's heavens, but the earth he has given to the sons of men."[335] Some people pull out of this that humans are so bound to the earth that heaven has nothing to do with them. But they are most mistaken since this abundantly illustrates the divine goodness, which has no need of earthly crops, nor does it lack worldly goods in any way, and yet it produced the world for human use and convenience. That God does not need these goods is proved from the fact that he dwells in heaven to which such things do not ascend and where they cannot be born. The prophet does not fix God in the heavens in such a way as to deny that he is everywhere, because he is in all places by his essence and power. But he is said to dwell especially in the heavens, for there his presence is recognized as more resplendent, powerful, and efficacious because of [*232r*] the abundant splendor and light, the constant movement of the planets gliding in perfect order, and the changing ebb and flow; also because from their loftiest levels we have winds, clouds, rains, hail, lightning, thunder, and so forth. The prophet does not shut humans out of heaven completely, as if they were never going to get there, for those who have lived holy and devout lives will go there at the appointed time. The Psalmist is speaking about the status of this life as things now stand.

Arrogant people have sometimes misused David's words so that some people think that God allows them to do anything they please on earth, to attack, to ravage everything up and down, as if God paid no attention to these things since he dwells only in heaven, strolling around its axes, and caring not the least about our affairs.[336] Others twist these words in such a wicked way that since God has heaven for himself and has given earth over to the sons of men, there is no reason for us to seek after heaven; rather we should look out so that individuals may claim for themselves, so far as they are able, larger slices of the earth. Those seem to be of this mentality who join field to field, house to house so that they hardly leave a foot of land for others to own.[337] The prophet then continues and says, "The dead do not praise the Lord, nor do any that go down into silence."[338] The intention behind his prayer is that the devout should be spared lest by their dying nobody would be left to praise God.

You will say, however, "If the sense and life of souls are taken away from the spirits of the departed, will there be a lack of those who glorify God?" It is true that they will not be lacking in heaven, but he has arranged things so that he is glorified and praised not only in the other world but also here on earth.

[335] Ps. 115:16.
[336] Cf. Martyr's reference to Epicureans in "Providence" §6 below.
[337] Isa. 5:8. [338] Ps. 115:17.

This won't happen if the wicked destroy the faithful. God was so set on this that for this purpose he produced humans; in other respects he also gave the earth to cattle and lions as well as to snakes, flies, and reptiles. They are all brought forth here and nourished, but not so humans. For we have been placed on the globe to act as God's heralds. The dead cannot perform that role here since they are far distant from this world; therefore he says, "The dead do not praise the Lord," that is, on this earth. Animals and mute cattle do indeed inhabit the earth and on it they graze and are fed, but they were created for the sake of humans. It does not detract from their purpose that they do not have the mental capacity to give thanks, to call on and glorify God's name. We gather from this that the earth was given to humans not to abuse it recklessly and gorge themselves on its goods like beasts, but in order to glorify and praise the name of God, as his benefits constantly encourage them to do. Since this is done only by the devout, if tyrants and scoundrels crush them, who will be left to recite and sing the divine praises? So far are the wicked from praising and proclaiming God's name that they blaspheme it. The repetitive wording, "the heaven of heaven," signifies a certain special region of the heavens in which God and Christ dwell with the saints.

72. Let us turn to Ecclesiastes where chapter 3 reads, "For the fate of the sons of men and the fate of beasts is the same; as one dies, so dies the other. They all have the same spirit…. Who knows whether the spirit of the sons of Adam goes upwards and the spirit of the beasts goes downwards?"[339] A little earlier he said that the successes of the faithful and the wicked are the same.[340] Thus it happens that no one knows from their condition and external events whom God loves or whom he hates.

He compares humans with cattle and says that their conditions and qualities are the same. But we should distinguish these: some are general and others special. As to the special, they are not the same for all. Cattle have four hooves, humans have two feet; they are without speech, humans speak; they are incapable of vices and virtues, humans are resplendent with virtues or defiled by vices. Therefore in this passage Solomon is dealing with the general qualities of both humans and cattle. For just as humans are born and raised, so it happens with cattle. Just as they dissolve into ashes and the elements, so it happens for humans as regards their bodies. Just as they eat food, quench their thirst with drink, and procreate offspring, so also do humans. But the statement that they all have the same spirit should not be applied to the soul, as if Solomon thought that all humans had one soul, as Averroës and some

---

[339]Eccl. 3:19–21.   [340]See Eccl. 1:14–18.

Aristotelians would have it.[341] By "spirit" he understands wind or breath, for beasts and humans breathe the same air. The spirit of humans ascends upwards, and the spirit of cattle downwards, but who knows this? Who will prove it by solid and rational arguments? Solomon does not deny this happens, but says that as regards rational principles [naturalia principia], the knowledge and understanding of these things exists among humans either barely or not at all. According to Jerome's interpretation, when he says "Who knows this?" he is showing its difficulty, not its complete impossibility.[342] Socrates, Plato, and Pythagoras as well as some other philosophers somehow achieved a knowledge of the soul's immortality. But I am not getting into their arguments.[343]

We read in chapter 9 of the same book of Ecclesiastes, "For there is no work or thought or wisdom or knowledge in hell, to which you are going."[344] Saint Jerome says that these pertain to the good works by which the faithful are to approve themselves to God while they live here, because they will have no place in the other world.[345] Here we have to believe in God's word so that we may be justified, here repentance is undertaken, here the sacraments are to be received and alms distributed, for after death no opportunity has been laid up for such acts. Christ too speaks this way in John: "We must work now while it is day; night comes, when no one can work."[346]

Gregory [232v] of Neocaesarea refers the statements we mentioned in the passage from Ecclesiastes to Solomon himself since he wrote these things about himself.[347] For when he gave himself over to pleasures, somehow he felt his soul was becoming brutish and beset with worries that the fate of humans and of cattle is all one, and that after this life no thought or work, no wisdom or knowledge remains in the other world. It does indeed happen that people who are preoccupied with subhuman thoughts of this sort, day by day, again and again, are also afire with the desire for pleasures and become more and more like brutes. Therefore this commentator does not think that Solomon approved of these things; he thought that he was referring to things he had once experienced and from which he had recovered. The Jews also regard this book of Ecclesiastes as Solomon's repentance.

---

[341]See p. 60, n. 43 above.

[342]Jerome *Comm. in Ecclesiasten*, ad. loc. (PL 23.1042).

[343]See introduction, p.xxiii ff. on the philosophical debate on immortality.

[344]Eccl. 9:10: *in inferno*; MT has *She'ol*.

[345]*Comm. in Ecclesiasten*, ad loc. (PL 23.1086).

[346]John 9:4.

[347]Gregory Thaumaturgus, *The Metaphrastes of Ecclesiastes* 8.15ff. (PG 10.1010–11). Migne wrongly ascribed this to Gregory Nazianzen (PG 36.669f).

The sensual and licentious who fortify themselves with their own filth say that humans die like cattle, that nothing survives after this life, so let us gorge ourselves on fleshly and worldly delights. As Paul says, "Let us eat and drink, for tomorrow we die."[348] Olympiodorus, another commentator on the book of Ecclesiastes, says that these things pertain first to bodily life in which, as has been said, humans and cattle share many qualities in common; and second, those who wallow completely in pleasures and delights come closer to the nature of animals.[349] He therefore wants to warn us here to restrain ourselves from these sorts of things lest we degenerate in our morals to the beasts, when we have been made in the image of God and directed to the goal of being some day like angels. Lastly he interprets those to be human who make good use of their reason, while the others who have wholly devoted themselves to the flesh and to their feelings are cattle. He says, "But who knows who they are who belong to the one group and who to the other, since human affairs are completely murky and hidden?" The human heart is inscrutable! Perhaps Solomon talked like this while speaking in the role of pleasure seeker, or as Gregory of Neocaesarea prefers, he was recalling his own role.

73. Job chapter 14 seems to put humans in worse condition than trees that are cut down, or of streams and the ocean.[350] For trees that are chopped down sprout again and return to their original condition. Streams, although emptied of waters by heat, abound in them again later. Even though the sea retreats from land every six hours, it covers it again. But that is not the case with humans when they have been dissolved by death, because they do not return again, nor are they restored to their original condition. Job laments these things, and rightly so if humans are considered in their own nature, that is, outside God's word and without Christ. But if we take into account that those caught up in these affairs have a bath in which they are washed clean, then not only is their youth restored but they return from death to life: we must judge them differently.

We should note, moreover, that Job limits the time in which the dead do not return to life when he writes, "till the heavens are no more." These words indicate the end of the world. Therefore Job does not deny that after the heavens are no more, we will arise. He seems to assert this even more when in the same verse he compares death to sleep and recalls people waking up. Sleep is not permanent; indeed, it is designed to result in wakefulness. He even adds

---

[348]1 Cor. 15:32.

[349]Olympiodorus of Alexandria (6th century?), a Peripatetic in philosophy, who wrote commentaries on Aristotle's *Meteorologica* and on Ecclesiastes.

[350]Job 14:7–12.

in the same passage, "Oh that thou wouldst hide me in She'ol ... until thy wrath be past." By this way of speaking he shows that there will be an end to divine wrath and that death will eventually be terminated. He says even more clearly, "that thou wouldst appoint me a set time, and remember me," and later records that he is awaiting his renovation. He quickly adds, "Thou wouldst call, and I would answer thee," that is, when I rise from the dead, you will reach out your right hand to your work.

Some commentators even explain this passage as a question, as if it were an *a fortiori* argument that says, "Are a cut tree, a stream, and the sea restored to their original state, and this is not allotted to humans? That is unlikely since people far excel those things, nor do you treat them with less care." Certainly Ibn Ezra acknowledges the resurrection in this passage.[351] But there seem to be greater difficulties which are related in chapter 7 of the same book, where Job says, "My eye shall never return to see good things."[352] We should interpret this in terms of the good things that relate to this life. For after the resurrection the dead will not come back so that they can eat, drink, have children, just as they did before while they lived here. Then he says, "The eye of him who sees me will behold me no more." This can only seem to mean that at the end of the world there will be no more bargaining, agreements, and business deals among people as before. After this he adds, "As the cloud fades and vanishes, so he who goes down to She'ol does not come up; he returns no more to his house, nor does his place know him any more."

74. As I noted before, these things are said relative to our natural powers, as if man were considered outside of God and Christ, as he exists in his corrupt and imperfect nature, and as if death and hell were taken into account as they really are: they cannot be conquered or overcome by our natural powers. That is why it is said there is no redemption in hell—because no one through human efforts or the power of nature can be recalled from it. But if we embrace Christ with a firm faith, since he has overcome sin, death, and hell, we have in him thereafter a great redemption. In the book of Samuel we find that it is God who brings us down to hell and up again.[353] Nor should we omit that metaphor employed by Job [*233r*] about the cloud which suddenly disappears, indicating the shortness of life, as James does also in his Letter when he said, "What is your life? For you are a mist that appears for a little time."[354] Later he says it will not return to its home. This is nothing else than after the resurrection we won't receive a second time the conditions of this

---

[351]Ibn Ezra's commentary on Job appears in the Bomberg Bible; see "Image, n. 12 above.
[352]Job 7:7ff.   [353]1 Sam. 2:6.   [354]James 4:14.

life, so that someone will once again be a prince or householder or farmer or townsman or another person of that sort. Ibn Ezra also did not conceal that this passage does not undermine the resurrection of the dead.

Another argument is taken from the words of Daniel because he wrote that many will arise; he did not say all.[355] This gave rise to a suspicion that he was referring to a particular resurrection, not the universal one that is preached. But we have explained this statement of his and said that he could not have written "all" since many will be found alive at the end time. They are surely not going to die but they will be changed.[356] Nonetheless the Prophet touches on the resurrection of both the devout and the wicked when he says that some will rise to shame and others to glory, even everlasting glory. Nor is that opposed by the statement in the Psalm that the wicked shall not rise for judgment; for the passage deals with their case, not their nature and substance. He says that they shall not stand but will lose their case, for they will not be exonerated but condemned before God's judgment seat.[357]

We have made these answers to the objections, and have explained the main headings of this treatise as promised. It is left to us to strive, while living here, for a share in the first resurrection, taking care that our faith is bright; that our charity is ardent and effective, and our hope firm and unwavering; that our actions, both interior and exterior, are Christian, morally upright; and that we smash the evil movements and inclinations of the flesh, conforming our will and soul completely to the Law of God. By accomplishing these things after the first resurrection, we shall attain that second and blessed one.[358]

---

[355]Dan. 12:2.   [356]1 Cor. 15:51.   [357]Ps. 1:5.

[358]Martyr concludes with "Nunc ad historiam revertamur," that is, to the narrative of 2 Kings 4:38 ff.

¶ To the ryght honorable,

my moſt ſinguler good Lord and Maiſter the Lord Robert Duddely, Earle of Leceſter, Baron of Dynghby, Knight of the honorable order of the Garter, one of the Queenes highnes moſt honorable priuy Counſel, and Maiſter of her Maieſties horſſe.

He old opinion (right honorable and my ſinguler good Lord) being no leſſe auncient then true, whiche accomptes hym an ill man, that is good but for him ſelfe (as who ſaye, from whom no goodnes commeth to the help of others)moſt like a Drone in a Bee hiue, ſhrowded there for his owne ſucke, not for the common wealth of Bees, whom therefore they ſuffer not among them, but kill & caſt out, as an vnkinde member, vnnaturall, and not to be endured in their ſtate : hath bene alwayes the rappyng hammer in my head, and the ſpurre to my ſide, to knocke and pricke me forward(that am of my ſelfe lytle able to do)to procure what I can(to my calling at leaſt)for the profit of my vniuerſal country men, by whom & among whom, as a member I lyue.

In reſpeċt whereof, among other it hath pleaſed God, to geue me leaue(by your Lordſhips meane, vnder the liſence of my moſt dread ſoneraigne Lady and Prince)to publiſh and ſet out to the glory of Gods Maieſtie chiefly : I haue taken vpon me to plant and put foorth (lyke ſuch a huſbande, as can not endure the plowe of my profeſſion to ſtande vnoccupied)this notable and right excellent woorke of that famous, graue, and great learned Doċtor, Maiſter Peter Martir(entiteled His Commentary vpon the booke of Iudges) being turned, at the requeſt of the learned, out of that toungue, wherein he wrote it, into our Engliſh phraſe, in which it is moſt meete for vs. As who ſhoulde ſaye, what he publiſhed into one toung priuately, he went(as I take it)ſhoulde be deliuered to all men generally (Chriſtians or other) to whom it maye doo good Whoſe labour tending to ſuche effeċt, cannot, but like a tree that beares many braunches, ſpread it ſelfe abroad, tyll it ſtretche with hys fruit to many countries, nacions, and languages, out of the ſame ſpryng

A.ij.   and

PART THREE

Our Knowledge of God

IN LIBRVM IVDICVM

D. Petri Martyris Vermilij Flo⸗
rentini, Profeſſoris diuinarum lite⸗
rarum in ſchola Tigurina, Com
mentarij doctiſsimi, cum
tractatione perutili re⸗
rum & locorum.

ACCESSERVNT *praeterea Indices duo locupletiſſ. Rerum ſcilicet & uerborum:*
Locorum item ſacrae ſcripturae, qui in hoc libro ſyncerisſimè explicantur.

GALAT. VI.

Abſit mihi gloriari niſi in cruce domini noſtri Ieſu Chriſti:per quem
mihi mundus crucifixus eſt,& ego mundo,

TIGVRI

EXCVDEBAT CHRISTOPH. FROSCHOVERVS.

M. D. LXI.

Clariſſ.mo Viro D. Rodolpho gualtero
Eccleſiae Tigurinae miniſtro fideliſſ.o ac mihi
plurimū uenerando. Pet. Martyr D.D.

Title page of Commentary on the Book of Judges, printed in Zurich by Christoph
Froschauer, 1561, with Peter Martyr's autograph

About the Translation

Our Knowledge of God

THREE OF OUR SELECTIONS, "Visions," "Dreams," and "Miracles," are from Martyr's commentary on the book of Judges, a lecture series given during his second Strasbourg residence, 1553 to 1556, which alternated with his course on Aristotle's *Nicomachean Ethics*. The commentary was prepared for publication by John Jewel. He lived with Martyr at Strasbourg (Lat. *Argentium*), and with other English refugees formed the "Angloargentinenses," who read the Fathers, especially Augustine, with Martyr in private. One of the group was Edwin Sandys, by then bishop of Worcester (Jewel was bishop of Salisbury) to whom the commentary is dedicated. Jewel's biographer recounts the situation: "Peter Martyr lectured on the *Ethics* of Aristotle and the book of Judges; and here, as at Oxford, Jewel was one of his most diligent auditors. He took down the substance of what was said, before dinner conned it over with Martyr, and after dinner made a fair copy, in almost exactly the words in which the commentary upon Judges was afterwards printed."[1]

* * *

[1]John Ayre, "Biographical Memoir," in *The Works of John Jewel* 4:xiii (Cambridge: Cambridge University Press, Parker Society, 1850). Martyr's *In Librum Iudicum … Commentarij doctissimi* was published in 1561 (Zurich: C. Froschauer), with an English translation (London: John Day) in 1564. Further Latin editions were published in 1565, 1571, and 1582 by Froschauer, and 1609 by Lancelot of Heidelberg. See BIB 36–47.

DE VISIONIBUS. This scholium from the commentary on Judges 6:22 concerns Gideon's vision of an angel. It distinguishes (§1) several pairs of opposites: knowledge through the senses or the understanding; by nature or by revelation (through signs); as signs only, or substantial; knowledge in this present life or in the future life. These distinctions may be compared with those of Heinrich Bullinger; he lists some six kinds of knowledge of God, including that "by visions and divine mirrors," through the figure *prosopopeia*, another by the contemplation of God's works in creation, and another "which is gathered upon comparisons." Both he and Calvin repeat the traditional image of human weakness when looking towards the divine, as if we were to gaze directly at the sun.[2] Because of the biblical context Martyr makes constant reference to another alternative: is it a vision of God or of an angel? He consistently distinguishes a *duplex notitia*, the one weak, serving only to render us inexcusable, the other strong and effective, making us partakers [consortes] in the divine nature.[3] As noted above, Martyr's theory of knowledge follows the "moderate realism" of Aquinas. He considers the agent intellect to be constitutive of our grasp of reality. Sense knowledge may be the basis of our knowing process, but it can apprehend objects only if they possess qualities. But the divine transcends every attribution which posits a compound or complex reality. While we may contact God through the signs and symbols he chooses to use in accommodation to our creaturely capacity and weakness, his essence escapes us: objects of belief are not at the same time objects of reason (§1; cf. "Resurrection" §19 above). Thus visions are to be judged according to their place in the divine economy, that is, their role as means of grace that reveal or save. Martyr attempts a middle course in assessing visions, neither dismissing them as Aristotle does nor exalting them as Augustine tends.

*   *   *

DE INSOMNIIS. Like "Visions," "Dreams" occurs in the commentary on Judges, at 7:13–15, fols. 96v–99v (LC/CP 1.5). Gideon hears of a dream and its interpretation, leading Martyr to introduce a scholium on dreams. He has in mind Aristotle's two short treatises, *Dreams* and *Prophesying by Dreams*.[4] Marvin Anderson notes the significance of this treatise in showing Martyr's

---

[2] The *Decades of Henry Bullinger* (Cambridge: Parker Society, 1851) dec. IV, sermon 3, "Of God and the Knowledge of God," 130 ff. Calvin restricts himself to the *duplex cognitio, Inst.* 1.1–5.

[3] E.g. COR 1:21; SAM 7:20; see Thesis 1N6 in EW 92 and n. 4; also CSV 51 ff. This compares with Calvin's *duplex cognitio Dominum* in *Inst.* 1.2.1.

[4] *De Somniis* and *De divinatione per somnium* belong to the "Parva Naturalia," or short physical treatises.

critical attitude to the Philosopher. For instance, Martyr's "preference for Galen and Hippocrates over Vergil or Macrobius" shows his use of this topic "for moral rather than speculative or purely analytical purposes."[5] Macrobius preserved Cicero's famous *Somnium Scipionis*, a literary creation proposing a climax to the mysterious end of Plato's *Republic*. Dreaming was held in high esteem in the classical world, with relations to ecstasy, healing, and prophecy. This attitude was renewed in the Renaissance, particularly in Paracelsus (1493?–1541), whose *Liber de somniis* exploited the manifold significance of dreams.

Martyr rejects Aristotle's view that dreams are not sent by God, but considers seriously the "humoral pathology" in which Aristotle follows Hippocrates and Galen, founders of the medical arts as *paideia* (§2).[6] Dreams are possible instruments of revelation, although they remain indirect in terms of external stimuli. Here Aristotle's faculty psychology is at work, the way images (*imagines, species*) move from external to internal senses, then to intellect. Martyr also sides with Thomas against Scotus as to the primacy of intellect over will: justification comes from faith, which is an intellectual virtue.[7]

The epistemology on view in these loci reflects the typical Reformed theory of the relationship between reason and revelation or nature and grace. We have already met Martyr's concept of twofold knowledge of God, one partial and frustrated by sin, the other complete and healed by grace. The problematic of the human intellect is, formally speaking, the issue of its unity and immortality, as Aristotle recognized. But the material principle of theological epistemology introduces the fact of a fallen nature and its corrupted reason. Both visions and dreams may be used by God in revelation, but like every medium they stand under the final verdict of the healing grace necessary for reason to recover its proper, or "natural," power of discerning the presence of God as mediated through instruments of his gracious will. Like his teaching on sacraments, Martyr's judgment on visions and dreams falls under the basic problematic of how the divine is knowable by created minds limited by sense and spoiled by sin.[8]

---

[5]Marvin W. Anderson, "Peter Martyr Vermigli: Protestant Humanist" in PMIR 72–73.

[6]See Werner Jaeger, *Paideia: The Ideals of Greek Culture* (Oxford: Oxford University Press, 1944) vol. 1, chap. 1, "Greek Medicine as Paideia," 3–45; cf. CHGM 58.

[7]E.g. GEN fols. 35v, 119r, ETH 169, 291; see CSV 85 ff. on "Intellect and Will." Donnelly states: "It might be argued that the intellect is even more pre-eminent for Martyr than for St. Thomas since the Thomistic doctrine of salvation centers on charity, a virtue of the will..." (85).

[8]Cf. T. F. Torrance, *Calvin's Doctrine of Man* (London: Lutterworth, 1949), 128 ff.: "The Mind's Knowledge of God."

Commentary on Judges 6

Visions: How and How Far God May Be Known

1.THE SUBJECT AT HAND affords us opportunity to comment on visions of divine things, just how and how far God can be seen by humans. I will propose certain distinctions which I consider necessary, so that our discussion may not lack method or order.

First, knowledge [notitia] of God is regarded as offered either to the senses or to the understanding; we also think it is given by nature, or else by special sign and revelation that transcends nature itself. Further, knowledge of God's very substance, nature and (so to speak) essence is distinguished from that which consists of tokens, testimonies, arguments, and signs of divine presence. Lastly, we should speak of that knowledge which either conforms to this life of ours, or else is looked for only after this age.[1]

[1]Cf. GEN praef.: "God may be known in three ways. The first is postponed to another life; when Moses wished it, it was said to him, 'No one shall see me and live.' Paul mentions the second to the Romans, 'For the invisible things of God,' etc. Finally, we apprehend him by faith...."

Scholium in *In Librum Iudicum ... Commentarij doctissimi...* (Zurich: C. Froschauer, 1561) 6:22; LC/CP 1.4, from lectures at Strasbourg 1553–1556. The context is Judges 6:11 ff., in which Gideon experiences an angelic presence and message; he receives a sign that it is indeed a heavenly messenger and responds: "I have seen the angel of the Lord face to face" (v.22).

[SENSE KNOWLEDGE]

Let me begin with the senses. As to knowledge through them, I hold that the nature, substance, and essence of God cannot be grasped by the senses. In fact whatever is perceived by the senses has no affinity with God but is far removed from him. In order to be named, qualities that belong to a certain genus and are regarded as accidents arouse sensible knowledge. Since God is completely uncompounded [simplicissimus] he is not subject to such qualities and, therefore, cannot be known by the senses.[2] The truth of this is understood from the obvious experience that everyone has of his own mind. For it is quite certain that no one has perceived him by sense. The Anthropomorphites, however, persuaded themselves that God can be known by the senses, for they attribute a human body to the divine [numini]; but their opinion is quite unacceptable.[3] For Scripture testifies that God is Spirit, and also draws a clear distinction between spirit and body, when our Savior says: "Touch and see, for a spirit has not flesh and bones."[4] Nor does anyone fail to understand that a human body and its members cannot exist without flesh and bones. Their folly shows itself further since no body can be found that is completely pure and simple. Suppose it to be as unified as you like, at the very least it has parts of which it is composed. Even the pagan philosophers discovered that all composition is against the nature of God.[5]

2. Leaving the Anthropomorphites aside, we should speak of some others whom Augustine mentions in his letter to Paulina, *On Seeing God*.[6] They believe that God is quite uncompounded and lacks a body, as the Scriptures testify and orthodox faith confesses; but they deny that in that beatitude which we await he cannot be seen with the eyes of the blessed. Therefore they say we are deceived because we measure the state of the future life entirely by what we see here as normal. Thus they say that although here the dim eyes of our body cannot see either God, angels, or spirits, yet when they are magnified in eternity [foelicitate] they shall see them—not indeed by their own

---

[2]See Aristotle *Meta.* V.14 on "quality" and V.30 on "accident." Only universals are perceived by the mind alone (Plato *Theaetetus* 185), and therefore the object of "science" (Aristotle *Cat.* 5; *Meta.* IX.10). Cf. Aquinas SCG I.18: "That in God there is no composition," and SCG I.23: "that there is no accident in God." For Martyr's view of the role of reason in apprehending *sensa*, see COR 10:4.

[3]Anthropomorphites or Audians were a Christian sect that took Gen. 1:27, "And God created man in his own image ...," literally; they arose in fourth-century Syria and enjoyed a revival in tenth-century Italy.

[4]John 4:24; 20:27.

[5]E.g. Aristotle *Meta.* XII.9.1075a50–1075a51.

[6]Augustine, *De videndo Deo-Ep.* 147 (PL 33.596). See p. 148, n. 42, below.

nature and power, but they will have such keen sight as to see the very essence of God. Perhaps they err less than the Anthropomorphites, but they do err. For no matter how our eyes are strengthened in heaven, they still remain eyes, and bodily eyes at that: therefore they will not exceed the kind and scope of their objects. They will then be quite able to stand stronger and greater light than they can see now, nor will they be hurt by those colors which at present upset them; yet they will not reach the divine essence. For in the blessed resurrection our bodies are not so enhanced as to be made spirit, or cease to be bodies. Not even the body of Christ is reputed to be turned into a spirit after his resurrection—this would have the body not resurrected but abolished. Therefore whoever thinks that our eyes will be so perfected as to behold the substance of God does not honor them but in fact destroys them. The Anthropomorphites sin against the nature of God by clothing it with a body; these others do injury to human nature, persuading themselves that it will not endure in the blessed resurrection. Therefore, our opinion remains and is true not only for this present life, but also for that in the future, for which we await.[7]

[THE BIBLICAL VISION OF GOD]

3. You will ask, however, what did patriarchs and prophets see, to whom God and angels appeared many times, as we read in Scripture? I answer that with regard to outward senses they saw only certain images, likenesses, and forms occasionally offered by God and angels, signifying that they were present with those fathers, spoke with them, heard them, and informed them about matters of salvation. Such things as the presence of God or of angels, as well as words and meanings, are not understood by sense itself, but are taken by reason and the mind from things obtained by the comprehension of the senses. Thus when it is written in Exodus that God came to Mount Sinai, the Chaldean paraphraser[8] states that God did not simply appear in himself, but translates it "the glory of God," as if to say: certain great and exceptional signs were seen there, by which God witnessed that he himself was present. You have the same thing in Isaiah, chapter 6, where he writes, "I saw the Lord sitting on his throne high and exalted."[9] It is easy to gather from Holy Scripture what sort of likenesses and images presented themselves as evidence of the presence of angels or of God. The burning bush that appeared to Moses, the cloud, the pillar of fire and smoke, voices, thunder, light and lightning, the

---

[7] Cf. "Resurrection" §§56 ff. above.
[8] Paraphrastes Chaldaicus, the Targum of *Judges*, an Aramaic translation, often paraphrastic.
[9] Isa. 6:1.

mercy seat, the ark of the covenant, Urim and Thummim, even various human forms who acted or spoke or in some way showed themselves to prophets and others—I claim that they were all signs and tokens of divine and angelic presence. They were given to be perceived by the Fathers whether they were sleeping or awake. Often the divine Spirit and angelic work, following God's command, formed the human phantasy or imagination by this kind of images and figures [similitudinibus et typis]. Accordingly, what God wished to reveal was expressed within the minds of those who understood no less than if it affected the outward senses.[10]

4. Therefore, when interpreting the prophets we are often doubtful whether what happened was external or simply appeared so to the mind of the prophet. Sometimes, because of the circumstances of the case, we are compelled to grant that it was only a vision. So Jerome asserts in regard to the waistcloth or loincloth of Jeremiah, which at the Lord's command he put near a rock by the river Euphrates, allowing it to remain there so long that it became rotten; then he was told to take it and put it on again.[11] But this vision occurred while the city of Jerusalem was closely besieged by the Chaldeans, when the prophet was not free to come and go to the Euphrates. For during that time, when he wished to go to Anathoth where he was born, he was seized when going out the gates and accused of treason.[12] Likewise, Jerome comments on the passage in Ezekiel about bread baked in cow's dung, and how he lay many days on one side, that it happened only in a vision.[13]

We may add the eating of the scroll and so on, which either human nature or the circumstances of those events and times did not allow to happen exactly as recorded. But in regard to preaching or explaining to the people what the prophets had in mind, something seen by phantasy or image was the same and had the same force as if it had been seen externally. Yet there was no need to resort to mental visions when the thing itself could be shown sensibly. Since God can use both modes, he sometimes takes this way and sometimes that, as it pleases him and as he judges fitting and profitable for us. In all these matters it seems to me that the opinion of Ambrose is to be accepted: Addressing the matter of images, he says that they were such as the will

---

[10]On the function of phantasmata, see Aristotle *De Anima* III.7.431b3: "The faculty of thinking then thinks the forms in the images"; 428a6f: "To the thinking soul, images serve as if they were contents of perception"; Aquinas, ST Ia Q 84, a. 7: "Cognition operates through mental images (*phantasmata*) by which the *species intelligibiles* are known."

[11]Jerome *Comm. in Jeremiam Prophetam* III.xiii (PL 24.764).

[12]Jer. 37:11 ff.

[13]Jerome *Comm. in Ezechielem* I.iv (PL 25.44).

chooses and not as nature forms. Doubtless this counts against those who consider prophecy to be natural, as if such images and sights were given to be seen by the prophets' outward senses, or known inwardly by imagination and phantasy, either through heavenly power or a sort of influx of nature or proportion of humors. Ambrose says that the will of God or angel willed those things and chose them over others; they were not formed by natural power.[14]

[WHETHER GOD IS REVEALED, OR ANGELS]

5. There is another doubt that should not be ignored. This is whether at any time God himself was revealed under these images or forms, or whether it was always angels alone that appeared, who acted and spoke with the prophets, sometimes in their own name and sometimes in God's. Some have said that God himself never appeared, and that everything reported as spoken and done in those visions was accomplished by angels in God's name. They contend that they have scriptural testimony to support them. One of these is found in the Acts of the Apostles, where Stephen explicitly calls the one who summoned Moses from the bush an angel, even though in Exodus he is named as God. Moreover, Paul testifies to the Galatians that the law was given in the hand of a Mediator, through the disposition of angels.[15] But no one doubts that in Exodus it is written that the law was given by God. So they conclude that we should understand that God did not appear in person but through angels.

Since the divine essence or nature cannot be removed from the Holy Spirit or the Son (for both are by nature divine) how will they defend their opinion when it is written expressly in the Gospel that the Holy Spirit descended on Christ in the form of a dove?[16] If they say that an angel came and not the Holy Spirit they are charging Scripture with falsehood. But if they admit that the Holy Spirit appeared as one with that dove,[17] what prevents God himself from appearing to the Fathers under other figures and images? There is no escape from this except by denying that the Holy Spirit is God, which I doubt they will do, unless they wish to introduce obvious heresy. My answer concerning the Holy Spirit may be applied to the Son, from Paul's words to Timothy, chapter 3: "Without dispute, great is the mystery, God was manifested in the flesh, vindicated by the Spirit," and so on.[18] For the universal

---

[14]Perhaps *De Spiritu Sancto* I: prol. 18 (PL 16.708–709).
[15]Acts 7:30 (Ex. 3:4); Gal. 3:19.
[16]Matt. 3:16.
[17]*Una cum ea columba*; reading "spiritum" for "spiritu."
[18]I Tim. 3:16.

church and orthodox faith acknowledge the Word who appeared under human flesh to be the true God. If he did so, as in good faith and without deceit he did, why may we not say that he did the same in the Old Testament under various forms and many images? Indeed what he has bestowed on us in the latter age is greater: but we have not the least doubt that he who has given the greater can surely also give what is less.

6. Perhaps they will object that the sacred writings propose for belief things that happened later, whereas what was done at that time is never told. But if we listen closely, the Scriptures teach us this as well. For the Evangelist calls the Son of God word or *logos*, to be believed not as if spoken idly, but so that when Scripture says he spoke it might be understood that God spoke through him. Thus as often as we read that the word of the Lord came to this one or that, I conclude that it is to be attributed to the Son of God, Christ our Lord, through whom God spoke to Fathers and prophets.[19] Lest I seem to speak in vain, I will bring two witnesses for this opinion. The first is found in John chapter one: No one has ever seen God. In anticipation he adds at once: "The Son who is in the bosom of the Father, he has revealed him."[20] For one may ask, if no one has ever seen God, who appeared to the Fathers when divine things were shown them? Who talked and acted with them when various forms and images appeared to them in the name of God? The answer comes immediately: "The Son who is in the bosom of the Father, he has revealed him"; he was the truest interpreter of the Father among mankind. In another place in the same Gospel, chapter twelve, it is quoted directly: "Therefore they could not believe. For Isaiah again said: 'He has blinded their eyes and hardened their heart, lest they should see with their eyes and perceive with their heart, and turn for me to heal them.' Isaiah said this when he saw his glory and spoke of him."[21] These two pronouns, "his" and "him," quite clearly refer to Christ. For just before, the Evangelist had said that although he, namely Christ, had done so many signs among them, they still did not believe in him, that the saying of Isaiah might be fulfilled which he spoke, and so on. Chrysostom, Jerome, Cyril, and Augustine concur in this opinion, which is authentic. Moreover, the words of Hosea the prophet, twelfth chapter, are to be weighed carefully. There the Lord says: "I spoke to the prophets; it was I who multiplied visions, and through the prophets gave parables," and so on.[22] We see from this that not only were analogies given to the prophets from the

---

[19]Cf. Prop. 31P1 (in EW 129), on Ex. 3: "When in the Old Testament (as often happened) the name of Angel is joined with the name of God, it means the second person of the Trinity"; see VWG chap. 2, "Christ and the Old Testament Signs."

[20]John 1:18.   [21]John 12:39 ff.   [22]Hos. 12:10.

beginning, but also that God himself spoke to them.

7. Now we must confirm, through the clearest examples, that appearances of God are quite distinct from visions of angels. First, the book of Genesis tells us: Jacob saw a ladder, which reached from earth to heaven, and by it angels ascended and descended.[23] At the top of the ladder, that is in heaven, stood the Lord, from whom Jacob heard great and wonderful promises. Unless we remain blind, we conclude from this that angels showed themselves in one kind of image while God himself appeared in another form. The same may be seen in Isaiah, when he saw the Lord sitting on his throne, and with him two seraphs that cried to one another, "Holy, Holy, Holy."[24] They worshipped God, who was between them,

with such great reverence that they covered their face with their two upper wings and their feet with the lower. Who cannot see here the great difference between God and the angels who appeared? I pass over Ezekiel, who saw angels in animal form—an ox, an eagle, and a lion—by which wheels were turned; but God himself sat in the highest part in the form of the Son of Man. Daniel also saw the ancient of days; the Son of Man came to him.[25] He adds that thrones were placed there, books opened, and a special form of judgment appointed. Then he mentions angels, of whom ten thousand and ten hundred thousand were present, ministering to God. From this we hear what great difference there is between God and ministering angels.

There is a very clear passage in Exodus, when God was angry with the people and refused to accompany them further through the desert, lest he should be provoked by their sins and destroy them once for all.[26] But he promised to send his angel, a promise that did not satisfy Moses, who said he would never go with the people unless God himself went along. Sure enough, by praying and holding to his opinion he won in the end, and had God as guide for their journey, as he wished. How then can they say that God himself was present under those forms, although only angels were seen in such images? Remember also (as is written in the same book of Exodus) that Moses entreated God to see the divine face. Since God loved him so much he could not entirely refuse this request, yet would not grant him everything. So he replied, "You cannot see my face, for no one shall see me and live; but you shall look upon my back."[27] What evidence is clearer than this? Surely in plain words God promises to appear to Moses in human form [sub humana specie], of which form or image Moses was to see not the face but the back. And he did

[23]Gen. 28:10 ff.   [24]Isa. 6:1 ff.   [25]Ezek. 1:4ff.; Dan. 7:9 ff.
[26]Ex. 32:34–33:17.   [27]Ex. 33:17 ff.

so in good faith: for as God passed by, Moses saw the back of his image close by the rock and heard the great and noble names of God declared with clearest voice. When he saw this he fell prostrate on the ground and worshipped; it cannot be doubted that he offered him that adoration due to the one God alone. For since he believed that God was present as he had promised, it is not debatable whether he worshipped him as truly present. Without doubt, since he commanded them to call on him and worship him there, God would have plunged the Israelites into idolatry if he had not revealed himself to be truly present at the ark and the mercy seat, but had angels alone answer those who came to seek counsel.

We may add the history written in the book of Kings concerning the prophet Micaiah, who prophesied before King Ahab of Israel, saying that he saw God present with a host of angels, and heard the Lord ask, "Which of them will snare Ahab?" And one offered himself as a lying spirit in the mouth of the prophets of King Ahab.[28] From this vision also we understand that there was some clear difference between God and the angels who appeared together to the prophet. Thus the bounty of God shown to the fathers must not be diminished or lessened; it should be admitted that he was indeed present when he appeared, since we read that this is how it happened, and that there is nothing to prevent it, so far as can be gathered from the sacred writings. Nor does the divine nature itself count against its being done. It is not prudent to attribute to angels everything that we read in Scripture concerning such visions: if so we might easily slip so far as to believe that the world was not created by God in person but by angels at his bidding. Therefore whenever we hear it witnessed and declared by Scripture, let us acknowledge that God was truly present and revealed himself under various images.

8. Now we should respond to the passages cited above.[29] Regarding the letter to the Galatians, I agree that angels were used in the giving of the law. In fact they stood beside God when he spoke, they supplied darkness, thunder, light, and lightning, they prepared the tablets of stone, and in various ways ministered to God who was present and speaking. Nor do the Apostle's words deny that God himself spoke and gave the law, as the words of Scripture state. There are even some who interpret the phrase "by the hand of a mediator" not as referring to Moses himself but to the Son of God; whether this is correct or not, there is no leisure at present to discuss. We do not need many words to answer what the blessed Stephen said, as written in the Acts of

---

[28]1 Kings 22:19 ff.
[29]Gal. 3:19; Acts 7:30; see §5 above.

the Apostles, that an angel appeared to Moses in the bush and talked with him. For if by angel we understand the Son of God, as I have often suggested, no hesitation will remain.[30]

[Patristic Evidence]

9. It seems good to confirm my proposals on the subject by some testimonies of the Fathers, so that they may be understood more clearly and firmly. Chrysostom, Homily 14 on John, says:[31] "What the ancient fathers saw was all that could be permitted; yet they did not see the pure and simple substance of God." And he adds: "If they had seen that they would not have seen any distinction of parts, for it is pure, simple, and indescribable; thus it does not stand or lie down or sit, as was sometimes revealed to those prophets." To this he adds: "Before the son came in the flesh, God taught the fathers through those visions and images." He also writes what we have already proposed, that we cannot see created spirits such as our souls and angels with bodily eyes. Therefore much less may we believe that we know God by the senses. And lest one think that it is appropriate for God the Father alone to be invisible and not the Son, he cites Paul to the effect that he is the image of the invisible God.[32] The nature [ratio] of an image would certainly be deficient if he were not invisible, as is the one whom the image represents.

Augustine also, in his third treatise on John, says of Moses: "Although it is said that he talked with God face to face, yet when he asked to see the face of God, that is his very substance, he could not obtain it." In the same place he adds: "He saw the cloud and the fire, which were figures [typi]." And a little later: "If they say that the Son was visible before he was incarnate, they talk nonsense." Augustine has collected much more of the same opinion in his letter to Fortunatianus, from Nazianzen, Jerome, and other fathers, too lengthy to repeat here.[33]

10. I bring two arguments commonly brought against this view. From the beginning we have said that the essence of God cannot be comprehended by the senses, since his nature is not bodily. But not all the old Fathers seem to have believed so. Tertullian writes against Praxeas that God is a body, and affirms this many times elsewhere. In his little book *On the Soul* he even teaches that our souls are bodily. Stranger still, he strives to confirm it by

---

[30]"Without doubt Christ was that angel who defended the Jews and fought on their side" (IUD 4:15); see n. 19, p. 143, above.

[31]Martyr is paraphrasing *Hom.* XV.1 (al. XIV) (PG 59.97–98).

[32]Col. 1:15.

[33]Augustine *Tract.* III.17; *Ep.* 148.II (6) ff. (PL 33.624 ff.).

numerous arguments.[34] The book *On Ecclesiastical Doctrine,* chapter 2, states that all creatures including angels are bodies, since nothing fills all things as God does. Everything is limited to definite places, as is clear with the soul which is enclosed in its body. In his Letter to Quodvultdeus, Augustine excuses Tertullian on the grounds that by body he understood the substance and what truly exists; as if he wrote that God is a body lest he seem to deny his existence, especially as the common people think that what is not a body is nothing at all. Yet Augustine reproves him in his book *The Literal Meaning of Genesis,* because sometimes he acknowledged the truth, saying that every body is passible; to avoid making God passible he should have denied that he is bodily.[35] Nor did he need to bend himself so far to the capacity of the people as to utter a falsehood about God. For Christians should not be taught to think, like the ignorant, that nothing exists without a body (something even Aristotle criticized); rather, when thinking of God, they should be taught to claim nothing unless there are rules from Scripture. As for the book *On Ecclesiastical Doctrine*, we should not defer to it too much, since it is ascribed to Augustine but the learned do not believe that it is his.[36]

11. Another objection introduced by the Anthropomorphites is not really an argument. They contend that we should not believe God to be bodiless because Scripture testifies that man was made in the image of God, which is quite inappropriate unless he has a body as we have. For the image would lack the likeness of that to which it refers. They also think that Scripture supports them since it often attributes human members to God. But Jerome (as Augustine mentions to Fortunatianus) derides their argument with irony and vigor.[37] If we favor this reasoning, he says, we can easily prove that man has wings, because Scripture at times attributes them to God, in whose image man is obviously created. They should rather have considered that the image of God consists in holiness, righteousness, and truth, as Paul taught. If they had grasped this they would not only have removed body from God but also have raised their minds from lower thoughts. Why do they not add that God is even a bear, a lion, or a fire, since Amos, Moses, and the letter to the Hebrews call him so? In Psalm 94 it is written: "He that made the eye, shall he

---

[34]Tertullian *De Anima,* 5 ff.: "the soul is a spiritual essence ... yet ... a corporal substance" (PL 2.693 ff.). Cf. Tertullian *De Res. Car.* xvii, *Adv. Prax.* 7; also "Resurrection" §11 above.

[35]Augustine *De haeresibus ad Quodvultdeum,* cap. 86 (PL 42.47); Quodvultdeus was a deacon at Carthage, who supplied Augustine with a compend of heresies in 428; Augustine *De Genesi ad litteram* 10.25.41 (PL 34.427).

[36]See *Scripta Dubia* 77 (PL 47.40).

[37]*Ep.* 148.7 (PL 33.625). Bullinger develops his argument from Augustine against the Anthropomorphites in similar fashion, *Decades* IV.3.

not see? And he that made the ear, shall he not hear?"[38] Jerome observes that what should have been said there is: He that made the ear, does he not have an ear? And he that made the eye, does he not have an eye? But it is not put like this, in case you should be deceived when thinking about God, and imagine him as having those parts.[39]

When Scripture ascribes parts to God it is for this reason alone, to help our weakness, because of which we cannot comprehend the essence of God in itself; yet we are still able to understand a little through certain symbols and masks [symbolis et involucris]. Thus by a most profitable metaphor members are attributed to God, that by careful consideration of his properties we may exercise our minds both piously and faithfully.[40] Even the Anthropomorphites might have been excused and not condemned if they had ascribed members to God as Scripture proposes them, to assist our weak understanding. But they insisted that the nature of God was so in fact; therefore they are accused justly and properly. But what shall we answer Paul? About the nature of God to be seen in heaven he states: "We shall see face to face."[41] He seems thereby to acknowledge a perception [intuitum] of God by our eyes and face, and in one sense ascribes a face to God himself. Augustine replies that there is also a face of the mind, when Paul says that now with face uncovered we behold divine things and not with a veil between, as the Jews required when they talked with Moses.[42]

[OTHER KINDS OF KNOWLEDGE OF GOD]

12. Now that we have brought these matters to a conclusion, let us deal in few words with other kinds of knowledge of God. In eternal life the essence of God will be known by the blessed, not of course by the senses but by the soul or mind; as John says: "When he appears we shall see him as he is." Paul affirms the same thing: "Now we see him through a glass darkly, but then face to face."[43] It is conveyed by the words of Christ, "Their angels always behold

---

[38]Ps. 94:9.

[39]*Breviarum in Psalmos* XCIII.9 (PL 26.1108): adversus ... Anthropomorphitae ... qui dicunt Deum habere membra, quae etiam nos habemus.

[40]See *Tractatio de Eucharistia* on the concept of accommodation; DM 167–168, 246, 262. Cf. Calvin, *Inst.* I.13.1: "such forms of expression do not clearly explain the nature of God, but accommodate the knowledge of him to our narrow capacity."

[41]1 Cor. 13:12.

[42]2 Cor. 3:15. Augustine, *De videndo Deo, Ep.* 147 *ad Paulinam* (PL 33.596 ff.) is in Martyr's mind in this treatise, e.g. xi.26–27; xiii.33; xxiii.52. Also *De Genesi ad litt.* xxvi.54 (per speciem) and xxvi.50 ff. (superiority of intellectual over spiritual vision) PL 34.476 ff.

[43]1 John 3:2; 1 Cor. 13:12.

the face of the Father"; elsewhere he taught, "In the blessed resurrection the just will be like the angels of God."[44] Therefore, it follows that we shall see God in the same way as angels do; if they see his face we too will gaze upon it. Another witness is taken from Paul to the Corinthians: "Then shall I know even as also I am known."[45] No one doubts that God sees us absolutely and essentially. But we should not persuade ourselves by this that the blessed will know the nature and substance of God completely and in all respects, but only according to our capacity. For the finite cannot fully receive what is infinite.[46] Nor is the creature able to comprehend its creator totally and perfectly. Thus Chrysostom's fourteenth Homily on John, Ambrose in the first book on Luke chapter 1, and also Jerome, as Augustine states in the place noted above, all deny that angels see God. When instead they are said by Christ to see the face of the Father who is in heaven, this cannot be understood simply and absolutely. Therefore it follows that it must be understood concerning the whole and perfect knowledge of his nature and substance. So is it written in John chapter 6: "No one has seen God except he that is of God, he has seen the Father." Again: "As the Father knows me, so I know the Father."[47] Thus is it given only to Christ, who is God, to know the essence of God perfectly and fully. Others will also see it, but only according to their capacity. What if you ask: Will it all be the same? To this I will not respond just now. For opportunity will be given elsewhere to speak of the diversity or equality of rewards in heaven.[48]

13. What shall we say about the condition of the present life? While we live here, will our mind be capable of knowing God in his essence? Not at all, for it is written, "No one will see me and live." "No one has seen God at any time." Paul adds: "He cannot be seen, because he dwells in inaccessible light."[49] Now this should not be understood regarding all knowledge; even while we live here it is given us to know God in a certain way. So these sayings are to be understood about substantial and essential knowledge, as the schoolmen say.[50] Nor does what is written weigh against it, that Moses saw God face to face, as was said of Jacob before him; nor what is written in another place about Moses, that God talked with him as friend with friend.[51] For this is not

---

[44]Matt. 18:10; 22:30.

[45]2 Cor. 13:12.

[46]non enim finitae res, quod infinitum est prorsus capiunt; cf. DIAL 27 (19v): quia quod finitum ac terminatum est, infinita non capit.

[47]John 6:46; 10:15.

[48]See COR 14:41, LC 3.17.8–14.

[49]Ex. 33:20; John 1:18; 1 Tim. 6:16.

[50]E.g. Aquinas, SCG III.47: "that in this life we cannot see God in his essence."

[51]Ex. 33:11; Gen. 28:10 ff.

said absolutely but in comparison with others, because those excellent men knew in a preeminent way what was revealed about God at that time. God chose to show himself to them in a distinct and extraordinary way, which he did not to others. Such is the sense of the text, from which Augustine and Chrysostom conclude that later when Moses wished to see the face of God he was refused.

14. It remains for us to discuss the knowledge of God that we may obtain while we live here. First there is natural knowledge, as we said, quite tenuous and obscure. This was familiar to Simonides, who (as Cicero writes in his book *The Nature of the Gods*) was asked by Hieron, tyrant of Sicily, what God is; he kept postponing his answer because the more he thought about it the more obscure it seemed to him.[52] In *Stromata* 5, Clement of Alexandria gives reasons why knowledge of God is so difficult and says: It is neither genus nor difference nor accident nor subject of accidents, therefore it cannot be understood by us who comprehend only such things in mind or reason.[53] The effects by which philosophers come to know God through reason are not equal to his dignity, power, and faculties. So they distinguished only some light and common aspects. But we ascribe to him attributes or properties, namely good, just, beautiful, wise, and others of that kind, since we have nothing greater, nor names more excellent that could be applied or could suit him. Even so, such things are not in him exactly as we say, for he is absolute [simplex], far otherwise good, just, and wise than men are or are said to be.[54]

[KNOWLEDGE THROUGH FAITH]

15. Beside this natural knowledge of God another is offered to us, one that consists of faith and is revealed to us through the Word of God. Faith does not come from ourselves but is the gift of God, as is said to the Ephesians; Christ also says: "No one can come to me except the Father draw him."[55] Therefore faith obtains knowledge of God abundantly from Scripture, so far as it makes for salvation and as much as our present life is able to receive. Yet, as Paul declares, this knowledge too is imperfect: "For now we know through a glass darkly, and in part."[56] Even though we advance in this knowledge while we live here, still we cannot achieve a perception of the essence of God. I

---

[52]Cicero *De Nat. Deorum* I.22; and Barth, *Church Dogmatics,* I.i.185, recounts the same anecdote.

[53]Clement of Alexandria *Strom.* v.XII (PG 9, 122).

[54]For Martyr's important concept of analogical predication, cf. ETH I.6.135 ff., II.6.321 ff.; DEF obj. 135 (403 ff.); VWG 79 ff., 172 ff.

[55]Eph. 2:8; John 6:44.

[56]I Cor. 13:12.

know that Augustine thought that at times both Paul and Moses, while on earth, saw the substance of God in their minds. But I cannot easily assent to that because I judge those passages of John, of the Law, and of Paul that I noted above to be quite clear. We could add what is written in the sixth chapter of John: "Not that anyone has seen the Father; he who is from God, he sees the Father."[57] Nor should it be passed over that what is spoken here of the Father is also true of the Son in respect of his divine nature; as I have declared above from Chrysostom and Augustine, the Son's nature as well as the Father's is invisible. It is no answer to say, as does Augustine, that they saw the nature and substance of God not by using outward sense but in a kind of ecstasy or rapture, or alien to this ordinary life.[58] Such things are not taken from Scripture; on the contrary, we have heard that Moses was denied the sight of God's face. Therefore by the knowledge of faith we discover God and his good will toward us, as much as is sufficient for our true and certain salvation.

Among all those ways in Scripture through which we know God, none is more excellent than Christ himself. Hence, Paul rightly said, "Without doubt, great is the mystery, God is manifest in flesh," and so on. The Lord said: "Philip, he who sees me also sees the Father." Paul also said that he knew nothing else except Jesus Christ and him crucified.[59] There is no doubt that in Christ God may be said to be made visible, because he was joined together with man in the same person [hypostasis]. So those who saw Christ could say that they had seen God. And whoever beholds and perceives him by faith sees much more than if he should see the burning bush of Moses. Hence it is written to the Colossians that in him are placed all the treasures of the wisdom and knowledge of God.[60]

16. Further, you will notice that whenever the ancient Fathers saw God or angels they were in the greatest fear, so frightened to death that they expected to die at once. Little wonder, for they were not ignorant of God's reply to Moses when he desired to see his face, "No one shall see me and live." Also John the Baptist, according to John 1, says: "No one has ever seen God." Paul to Timothy confirms this, writing: "No one has seen God, nor is able to

[57]John 6:46.

[58]Augustine *De Genesi ad litt.* XII.19, "The causes of visions." Bodily states are caused "sometimes by the body, sometimes by the soul," bodily humors in the first case, but affective disturbance in the second. When "sound and healthy people are transported" in spirit, authentic visions result.

[59]1 Tim. 3:15; John 14:9; 1 Cor. 2:2.

[60]Col. 2:3.

see; for he is invisible, since he dwells in light inaccessible."[61] Both Gideon and Manoah, the father of Samson, were witness to it. Also Jacob, after his nocturnal wrestling, which he thought was with a man; seeing that it was an angel, he marveled how he had escaped safe and sound. "I saw the Lord," he said, "face to face, yet was my life spared," as though he could hardly believe it to be true.[62] When the Lord descended on Mount Sinai to give the law, the Hebrews were so seized with fear and trembling that they said to Moses, "We implore you to deal with God, lest if he continues to speak to us in person [coram nobis] we will die." Support for these passages is given in the same book of Exodus, when the covenant had been instituted between God and his people. Moses had proclaimed the pact and sprinkled the people with the sacrifical blood, and led the elders to the mountain where they saw God sitting on a throne in great glory and majesty. After describing this vision it adds, "Yet God did not lay his hand on them."[63] This shows that it was a novel and uncommon sight for men to see God and stay alive both safe and sound. Therefore it is told as if it had been given through a special omen. Jerome states that Isaiah was killed by the Jews on this pretext, that he claimed to have seen God sitting on his throne, as is written in chapter 6 of his book.[64] Ironically, they charged that it was a lie, since God cannot be seen by men who survive. Therefore they condemned him falsely, as if by prophesying he taught the people his own inventions and not what God had revealed. They devised this against the innocent prophet when they had no other cause against him.

17. Similar examples are not lacking from the New Testament. When our Lord revealed a kind of example of his majesty and glory to his apostles on Mount Tabor, he was completely changed before them and shone with an awesome brightness and light; Moses and Elijah were present and the voice of God sounded from heaven. Since these matters far surpassed the power of human sight, the eyes of the apostles could not endure them, so that they fell on the earth as if dead.[65] Again, when Peter fished at Christ's bidding he made an incredibly large catch (for before Christ's command he had toiled in vain); he marveled at the new event and saw that God was in Christ, growing so afraid that he said to him: Lord, depart from me for I am a sinful man and cannot abide the divine presence without peril.[66] Paul wished to relate how he had been caught up into the third heaven where he learned such divine things as could not be explained to men in words, and wrote: "Whether in the body

[61]Ex. 33:20; John 1:18; 1 Tim. 6:16.
[62]Gen. 32:30.   [63]Ex. 20:19, 24:11.
[64]Jerome *Comm. in Isaiam Prophetam* I.cap. 1 (PL 24.33).
[65]Matt. 17:1–8.   [66]Luke 5:1–11.

or out of the body, I do not know."[67] Surely he did not dare affirm that those things happened to him while he made use of the body and senses of this life. Therefore it is clear that Gideon was not amazed without reason.[68]

18. Now it seems good to show the reason why the sight of God or angels appears to bring sudden destruction to men. Perhaps it happens because of the burden of the body which is, as the Platonists say, like a dark and shadowy prison to us; we are so impeded by it that we cannot perceive divine reality.[69] If by chance we sometimes see it, it soon comes to mind that the union of soul and body is now to be severed and that we will die on the spot, so that the sight of divinity is granted us because of the imminent divorce of soul and body. Further, in his *Metaphysics* Aristotle holds that the power of our understanding is so little able to perceive divine things which are so clear in their own nature, that it may well be compared with the eyes of owls or bats which cannot look at the brightness of the sun in daylight.[70] Those who speak like this speak well, yet not well enough for a clear explanation of the matter.

19. From its original creation the body was not given us to be a hindrance in knowing God, nor to shut up our souls in a sort of blind and dark prison. In that case the goodness of God would be found guilty for making human nature bodily. That this is so is proved by the history of Genesis, which shows that God was intimate with our first parents, despite their having bodies. For he led them into the Paradise he had planted, showed them the plants which they could eat, making a law that they should not touch others; he placed all the animals before Adam so that he might call them by whatever name he chose. The body was not an impediment but the means by which the first humans enjoyed no little familiarity with God. In fact it was sin that removed the sight of God from us. From it obscurity, darkness, blindness, and ignorance about the divine came upon us. For this cause are we transformed into moles, bats, and owls. Otherwise, unless the stain of sin intervenes, God is in his own nature clear, in fact light itself.

Perhaps you will say that enough has been shown of our blindness as the result of sin. But it has not been proved why men become so fearful at the sight of God. The whole matter turns on this, for when men are overcome by

---

[67]2 Cor. 12:2.

[68]The context for this scholium is Gideon's wonder at the angelic miracle; Jud. 6:19–22.

[69]Plato *Rep*. VII.514A ff. Cf. "Resurrection" §67, above, on the *sōma sēma* gnome.

[70]Aristotle *Meta*. II.1.993b9: "as the eyes of bats are to the blaze of day, so is the reason in our soul to the things which are by nature most evident of all." Cf. Bonaventura, *Itinerarium Mentis in Deum* V.4.

the divine light on account of their darkness and bad conscience, they fly from the judge who is as mighty as he is just. For they conceive that deity as bearing in his presence nothing unclean or evil, because of his purity and justice. So they consider having God present as nothing less than receiving the punishment prepared and the penalty deserved. For this reason the first parents concealed themselves as soon as they had sinned and were struck by the voice of God, so that they decided to hide among the trees of paradise. This surely came from a troubled conscience, since in his own nature God exists as the giver of life and author of every comfort. So it is quite clear that these terrors and disasters happen not through any defect of his but by our very own fault. John, therefore, provides salutary advice in the third chapter of his First Letter, that whoever hopes to see God as he is should prepare himself for it by purifying himself, as God is pure and perfect.[71]

---

[71]1 John 3:3.

Commentary on Judges 7:13

Dreams

1. [*96v*] Since we intend to speak at length about dreams, we will first see what may be said of them by natural reason, then what should be attributed to them by the Word of God. Concerning the first, Aristotle, Hippocrates, Galen, and other famous philosophers have written much. Among them Aristotle in his little book "On Prophesying by Dreams" (if it is his, although it is without doubt both learned and scholarly)[1] first said that this kind of prophesying should not be completely rejected, because much is widely attributed to it, and such things as are received by all are never totally false. He adds that there are many dreams for which an appropriate and apt reason may be advanced; experience teaches that they are not useless but prove to be correct. Therefore it is unwise to condemn every sort of prophecy [divinationis genus] through dreams. Nevertheless we should be careful in accepting them, since it is difficult to show their causes; in this regard nature works most obscurely.

[1]*De divinatione per somnium* is no longer doubtful as Aristotle's work. The reference is to 462b13 ff.

De insomniis is a scholium from *In Librum Iudicum … Commentarij doctissimi*, from the Strasbourg lectures of 1554–1556 (Zurich: C. Froschauer, 1561) fols. 96v–99v; LC/CP 1.5. See BIB 36 ff. The passage in Judges 7:13–15 narrates how Gideon received divine advice on attacking the Midianites by hearing about a dream and its interpretation.

Aristotle does not think that dreams are sent by God. He says that if they were sent by him, he would give them to the good and the wise; but in fact it happens otherwise, for the foolish and evil often excel in this faculty.[2] Moreover, animals dream, but who will claim that prophecy is given them by God? Nor is it true of visions that accompany the phantasy of sleepers, as if in this way they should foretell the future. Besides, if God did send such visions he would do it rather during the day, so that men might study them more diligently. It is not easy to see why he has chosen nighttime for such a purpose. To conclude: Since God is not the least jealous, he would not so vaguely warn those whom he wished to instruct about things to come, but would show those matters clearly and plainly. Dreams are so obscure that for their interpretation we must turn to prophets and interpreters [coniectores]. These things are gathered generally from Aristotle, in which he transferred the whole matter from God to nature, as if the causes of dreams are to be drawn from there. I will deal with them later, when I come to theological doctrine. Now I will show what he has on this subject.

2. "Dreams," he says, "are either signs, or cause, or else they are referred to things contingently or by chance."[3] Each of these three kinds is explained as follows. He said that dreams are sometimes signs of the states of body or mind since they often reveal humors that prevail, abound, and offend in the body. For signs and images of things occur according to the quality of nature and the proportion [temperamentum] of humors that predominate in the body.[4] Where choler [flava bilis] abounds, flames, fire, coals, lightning, brawls, and so on are seen. If melancholy [bilis atra] prevails then smoke, deep darkness, everything black and base, corpses, and such like present themselves. But phlegm [pituita] excites images of showers, rains, floods, waters, hail, ice, and

[2]Aristotle *De div. per somnium* 462b23: "those to whom he sends them are not the best and wisest, but merely commonplace persons."

[3]Aristotle *De div. per somnium* 462b27: "either as *causes*, or as *tokens*, of the events, or else as *coincidences*...."

[4]The "humoral pathology" deriving from the Greeks, notably Hippocrates and Galen, survived until the eighteenth century, although Vesalius, *De Humanis Corporis Fabrica* (Padua, 1543), countered Galen's authority with his experimental science, while Paracelsus had burned Galen's works publicly at Basel in 1527. Four bodily humors (blood, phlegm, yellow bile, black bile) were supposed to determine health and sickness by their proportion and mutual relation. Cf. Aristotle *De Somniis* 461a15 ff. on the "spiritous" affections; Augustine *De Gen. ad litt.* XII.19.41 on the causes of visions. W. Jaeger, *Paideia*, vol. 3 (Oxford: Oxford University Press, 1944), 294, n. 18, indicates that Galen regarded the humoral thesis as "the mark of Hippocrates' own work." See Hippocrates, *Humours* (Περὶ Χυμῶν) Loeb Classical Library, 4 (London: Heinemann, 1931). Marvin Anderson, "Peter Martyr Vermigli: Protestant Humanist," in PMIR, 72–73, comments on this scholium; he identifies Martyr's source as Galen on Hippocrates'*Aphorism* I.5.

that which has much moisture joined with coldness. Excellent sights are stirred up by blood—clear, white, fragrant, and what resembles common purity and the normal form or face of things. Nor are such matters neglected by physicians. As Galen and Hippocrates report, they examine their patients diligently concerning them, because in this way they can find out [*97r*] the proportion of those humors which lie hidden within the body.

The reason why we perceive the nature of these motions by vision, when asleep and not attentive, is this: because at first they are small and their sensation vanishes as soon as we awake. Outward things that capture our eyes draw us to other and stronger passions, but when we are at rest from outward activity we are quiet and free from the baser things that occupied our senses.[5] Therefore, the sights and images that humors always arouse are apprehended by the phantasy while we are asleep rather than awake. We perceive small things far better when sleeping than waking, as is shown in that we judge every noise, however small, to be loud thunder. If a little sweet phlegm happens to remain on the tongue or palate we think that we taste honey, sugar, sweet wine, and rich treats, or sometimes we eat and drink abundantly. Therefore those small feelings of humors appear during sleep as if they were huge; physicians may learn from them the beginnings of many diseases.

Dreams are also like signs of mental affections, such as desire, hope, joy, and mirth as well as qualities [*habituum*].[6] Thus the timid see different things than the bold, covetous men, other things than those who trust, and the learned have quite different dreams from peasants or laborers. For even when we sleep the mind is occupied with what we continually or usually do. Something else should be considered, as Galen rightly reminds us:[7] That certain kinds of food that are naturally choleric, melancholic, or phlegmatic arouse the phantasy of sleepers because of their quality, the shapes and forms of things corresponding to such humors, even though their bodily temperament does not itself offend through those humors. A physician should observe this about dreams, namely to see what kind of food the patient had. As Aristotle teaches, when wine is taken immoderately, it produces many deformed images during sleep.[8]

When a dream is a sign it is referred to the cause, namely those abundant

---

[5]For this material, cf. Aristotle *De div. per somnium*, 463a10 ff.; *De Somniis* 460b27 ff.

[6]Aristotle *De Som.* 460b5 ff.

[7]Galen of Pergamos (ca. 121–200), physician, anatomist, and philosopher: *On the Natural Faculties* II.viii, Loeb classical Library, trans. by A. J. Brock (London: Heinemann, 1916): "Whether this humor has its genesis in the human body, or is contained in the food."

[8]Aristotle *De Som.* 461a24.

humors which it indicates. It may also be called a sign of some future event, since either health or sickness may be derived from the same cause, that is the humors which are signified. Thus since a dream is a sign of a humor it provides evidence of the effect that will follow. For the disease as well as the dream arises from the same cause, namely the humor. Yet they do not in turn refer to one another, because sickness and health are not signs of dreams.

[ARE DREAMS CAUSAL?]

3. Now let us see how dreams may sometimes be called causes. That happens when one is led by a dream to do or attempt something, as when someone is cured of an affliction of the spleen because he bled on the back of his hand, as it appeared in his dream. Sometimes it happens that scholars discover things about which they expressed doubt in their books, where they saw themselves in a dream finding and reading them.

Let us consider the third part of the distinction we advanced, namely when dreams by chance or accident refer to things that happen later. That takes place in matters where the cause is not in ourselves but rather distant and far removed, as if one saw a victory or stratagem taking place in the field at a distance, or someone absent advanced to the highest honor. As the Peripatetics say, these things are joined by chance [per accidens] and cannot be compared as causes or signs. Just as when talking of someone who happens to arrive just then we say, "Talk about the wolf!"[9] yet mention of him was neither cause nor sign of his coming. Therefore these things are said to be joined by chance, because they are accidental and occur infrequently. For this is the nature of chance events, to happen rarely.[10]

4. Aristotle teaches who they are that know many things in advance of others through dreams. He ascribes this chiefly to such as are lazy and talkative, then to melancholic and frenetic persons, alienated from both the senses and the mind.[11] He also seems to attribute something to relatives and friends. Indeed such kinds of people have many dreams in their sleep. The talkative and the idle are completely given to their own thoughts, filling them inwardly with fantasies and apparitions. The melancholy also, through the strength and nature of black bile, dream of many things; moreover, they are quite given to cogitation. And the frenetic sort, whose mind is empty of both the knowledge of outward senses and the use of reason, are thereby completely given up to

[9]Lupus est in fabula; a proverb found in Terence and Cicero.

[10]*De div. per som.* 463b8: "neither token nor cause … but a mere coincidence."

[11]*De div. per som.* 464a27: "they have an especially keen perception of the alien movements" of their minds.

imagination. Lastly, friends see much about each other in their dreams, because they are full of thought and care for them.[12] All these just described commonly predict many things by their dreams, [*97v*] because in such various and even infinite sorts of vision it is likely that some things should happen to be true. Those who exercise themselves all day long in archery hit the mark more often than others who practice rarely. Those who spend the whole day playing at dice or tables cast many more lucky throws than those who amuse themselves in that kind of game but seldom or little.[13]

It should be understood that those signs attributed to dreams of the first kind discussed above are not necessary, since they may be prevented; yet this does not mean that they may not be signs. For this occurs also in clouds, which are sure signs of rain, when they continue to be driven by the wind before it rains. Also urine has signs of both sickness and health, yet the effect may be prevented by stronger causes; the same happens with the pulse. Even decisions that we have resolved on and determined with much deliberation often fail because of things that intervene, through which we cannot proceed further. Therefore it is no wonder if the same happens in dreams, since they are signs of things not quite complete but rather just begun; also the weak and feeble motions of humors may easily be hindered by many other causes.

5. Democritus expounds those dreams that refer to chance and distant occurrences as follows.[14] He said that there is always a flowing from real objects, carried to the bodies of sleepers, and affecting them with the quality and likeness they bring with them; he gives two reasons why this is more easily perceived in sleep than in waking. First, because air is more easily moved at night, as we see happen in water when struck with a stone: many circles are made with that blow and driven out a long way, unless some contrary motion prevents it. But at night the air is quieter than in the day, because it is not driven in various ways by creatures in constant motion. Another cause is that every light movement is easily perceived by those who are asleep. To conclude, this author also does not refer the causes of dreams to God.

---

[12]*De div. per som.*, 463b1 ff. (the garrulous and excitable); 464a34 (the atrabilious); 464a27 (friends).

[13]*De div. per som.*, 463b21: "the gambler's maxim: 'If you make many throws your luck must change,' holds good in their case also."

[14]Martyr follows Aristotle's critique here (Aristotle *De div. per somnium* 464a4ff.), referring to atomism, a theoretical explanation of physical and mental activity. Democritus of Abdera (ca. 460–360), an early systematizer and materialist; few writings survive. Plutarch mentions his interest in dreams, as does Cicero: Democritus "strongly affirmed his belief in a presentiment of things to come" (*De divinatione*, I.iii.5); see W. Capelle, *Die Vorsokratiker* (Leipzig: A. Kröner, 1935) 425–426.

In the little book he wrote about prophesying by dreams, Galen explains this better than others.[15] When we see things in dreams that we neither did nor thought of while awake, they are not to be referred either to arts or habits, or to the practice of such things as happened while we were conscious, but to humors. This rule seems to mean that we may understand what kind of things dreams signify. He grants that they are known better by night than by day, because then the soul approaches its inmost part, where it perceives more easily what is there. He tells of a certain person who while asleep imagined that his leg became a stone; many thought that it referred to his servant, but within a few days the same leg became paralyzed. Another seemed to himself to be sunk up to the neck in a cistern full of blood, from which he could not escape. That showed that his blood was abundant and that he should have it lessened. He mentioned also another, who on a day of crisis saw himself in a dream in the plentiful water of a bathhouse; soon after he fell into a great sweat. "Moreover," he said, "when asleep, people sometimes imagine themselves to have so great a burden on them that they cannot bear its weight, but at other times they are so light and nimble as if they were running and almost flying. All these things indicate either the excess or the lack of humors."

Hippocrates writes about these matters in the same vein, namely that during the day the mind distributes its powers to the senses and other faculties, but at night draws them into itself and so knows them better.[16] Yet there is a kind of divine dream by which calamities are predicted of cities or peoples and certain great figures. To expound such dreams some profess certain arts, to which Hippocrates seems to attribute very little. When it is observed from dreams that humors afflict us, he says they are to be helped by trying diet, exercise, and medicines. And whether the dreams are good or bad, he would have us pray. "When health is signified," he said, "we must pray to Sol, to heavenly Jove, to Jove the possessor, to Minerva, rich Mercury, and Apollo. But if they are unlucky dreams, pray to the gods who turn evils from men, the gods of the earth, and the Heroes," etc. Thus Hippocrates was either superstitious or appears so. But for my part, as to genuine piety I do not deny—I

---

[15]Galen *De Presagiis insomniorum.* Cf. A. J. Brock, *Greek Medicine ... from Hippocrates to Galen* (London: Dent & Sons, 1929; New York: AMS Reprint, 1972) 31: "It is noteworthy that Galen was a believer in dreams....While holding that most dreams are purely physiological, being caused by excess of one or other of the bodily humors, he also recognized a class of dreams that were 'prophetical'—were indeed of the nature of divine revelations."

[16]Hippocrates *Dreams* (*On Regimen in Health* IV.86): "When the body is at rest, the soul, being set in motion and awake, administers her own household." Cf. Jaeger, *Paideia*, 30 ff., commenting on the pseudo-Hippocratic *On Diet*, in which dreams are treated in light of "the Orphic conception that the soul is most free when the body sleeps."

rather recommend—that if we are ever troubled with disturbing and fearful dreams, we should pray to God to turn away those evils that may threaten us. [*98r*].

6. Another kind of dream proceeds from an outward cause, namely the power or (as is commonly said) "influence" of heaven, which changes the air. On touching our bodies it gives them a new quality, from which various appearances and visions arise in those who sleep. Thus many effects come from heaven, some produced in the phantasy and in the power or faculty of imagination, and others in the objects themselves. This is easily shown by an example. Rain is surely in the air or clouds; before rain falls there is such a change in the imagination of a crow that it begins to call. Even so, the effects in the phantasy of dreamers and in reality surely come from the same cause, but they are far different because of the subjects in which they occur. There is doubtless some small and obscure likeness between these effects, but it is hard to see the reason behind this proportion or analogy. If we agree that the cause of such effects or affections lies in the stars, who can refer these signs to their proper cause, that is, to some stars rather than others? I think there must be very few, if not to say nobody can. Besides, if they are referred to their proper stars, what can we expect to happen through them, especially regarding contingencies, since astrology was always held in the courts to be quite uncertain?[17]

To sum up: The images and likenesses said to portend future events are so doubtful, uncertain, and ambiguous that nothing can be determined through them with any confidence. Add to this that dreams may come not from one but many causes (as has been explained), so that we will easily fall into error if we embrace any one among those many causes. Consequently we should suspend our assent and not lightly predict anything from dreams, since rather than events being inferred from them, they may more easily be judged after the event. What remains from dreams is only a kind of suggestion, which must also be slight.

Those two most famous poets, I mean Homer and Vergil, suggested two gateways of dreams, one of horn and the other of ivory. They attribute the horn to true dreams, but the ivory to false: more dreams, they said, pass through the ivory gate than through the horn.[18] Therefore in judging natural

---

[17]Astrologia iudiciaria: "judicial astrology" studied the influence of the stars on human destiny, while "natural astrology" predicted the motions of heavenly bodies, eclipses, etc. The former might well be called "astromancy."

[18]Homer *Odyssey* xix.562; Vergil *Aeneid* vi.893–896. Tertullian, *De Anima* 46, remarks that horn is the gate of truth, being transparent, whereas ivory is opaque, creating error and delusion; cf. Anderson, "Peter Martyr Vermigli: Protestant Humanist," PMIR, 72.

dreams, let us not either exceed the measure of doubt [suspicionis modum] or cling too much to visions. It is not the part of Christians to lean too closely towards dangerous and uncertain conjectures. While preoccupied about these, they omit things of greater moment, and the devil often mixes them on purpose, either to divert us from good actions or to drive us to evil.

[DIVINE AND DEMONIC DREAMS]

7. Now let us consider what to say about dreams put into us either by God or by the devil. When something is foreseen in dreams with the help of God or his angels, two things are required. The first is that certain marks or images of the revelation should impress some form in our phantasy or imagination. Second, judgment should be added, by which we can come to know what they imply. As to the first, we should understand that such marks and apparitions are often impressed on our senses because of what God causes to appear outwardly, as when Belshazzar, the successor of Nebuchadnezzar, saw the fingers of a hand writing on the wall, as we have in Daniel.[19] Sometimes images and likenesses are described in the imagination or phantasy itself without any external sight. This happens in two ways. Either the forms or likenesses present in the mind are applied to such use as God wills, as when a seething pot turned toward the north was revealed to Jeremiah.[20] Or else new forms never known to the senses before are displayed, as when the forms and likenesses of colors are revealed to someone blind from birth.

In this kind of prediction the images or forms stand for letters. Oracles are given in various ways as they are ordered and disposed, just as by changing various letters our speeches and sentences are changed. Teachers who instruct students may by their zeal and industry in teaching impress many images in the minds of their hearers, although they cannot give them judgment and right understanding. But God supplies both, though not always at the same time. He imparts only forms to some, as he did to Pharaoh, his butler, and his baker, as well as the king of Babylon; all of them required interpreters such as Joseph and Daniel to explain their dreams.[21] People like this, to whom only images of the future are shown, are not truly taken for prophets; for they have only a certain beginning and trace of prophecy, just as Caiaphas the high priest is not to be taken as a prophet, since he did not understand what he said.[22]

8. As to why God would sometimes disclose the future to kings and princes through dreams, [*98v*] at present I think there are two reasons. The

---

[19]Dan. 5:5.
[21]Gen. 40:5 ff.; Dan. 5:13 ff.
[20]Jer. 1:13.
[22]John 11:49 ff.

first is that he had regard to the people and nations they governed. For if the approaching shortage had not been announced to Pharaoh, Egypt would have utterly perished through famine. Second, by the interpretation of these dreams it was the Lord's intention to make those hidden prophets and holy men known to the world, which the Scriptures tell us happened with Joseph and Daniel. Secular histories also write many things about the dreams which princes sometimes experienced. Tertullian mentions some of these in his book *On the Soul*,[23] about Astiages concerning his daughter Mandane, likewise about Philip of Macedon, and Julius Octavius, whom M. Cicero saw in a dream while he was still a child; after awakening he knew him when they met. Other things like this are recited by him.

[SCRIPTURAL TESTIMONY]

9. But these things aside, let us confirm by the witness of Holy Scripture (which is easily done) that some dreams are sent by God. Matthew testifies that Joseph, the husband of Mary, was warned three times by the angel. Pilate's wife also understood through a dream and made sure that her husband was told not to condemn the innocent Christ. And in Acts 16 a man of Macedonia appeared to Paul and persuaded him to go into Macedonia. Moreover, in a dream the Lord ordered him not to leave Corinth, because he had many people in that city.[24] I could recite many more places from the Old and New Testaments, but time will not permit. Philo Judaeus, as Jerome in his book *On Illustrious Men* testifies, wrote five books on dreams sent by God.[25] Cyprian also reported that in his time certain matters were shown during sleep, which made for the edification of the congregation: he granted them not a little but a great deal of credit.[26]

Augustine in *On the Literal Meaning of Genesis,* book 12 chapter 3 said there are three kinds of visions.[27] The first relates to the outward senses, which he called corporeal; another kind he called spiritual, consisting of images and found in the phantasy or power of imagination. The last he named intellectual, because they are comprehended only by reason and mental judgment. He shows that the imaginative or middle kind do not make prophets (as we

---

[23]Tertullian *De Anima* 46 (PL 2, 771 ff.).

[24]Matt. 1:20; 2:13, 19; 27:19; Acts 16:9; 18:19.

[25]Jerome, *De Viris Illus.* XI: Quod somnia mittantur a Deo libri quinque (PL 23.849, 627). Philo, *De Somniis* (Peri Tou Theopemptous Einai Tous Oneirous, 2 lib.).

[26]Unknown reference; Cyprian did not write a *De Insomniis*, nor did anyone else in his name.

[27]Augustine is commenting on Paul's "third heaven" (2 Cor. 12:2–4); see Augustine *De Genesi ad litteram,* 12.3 ff.; Visionum genera tria, 6.1 (PL 34.455 ff.).

too declared a little earlier), stating that Joseph was a far truer prophet than Pharaoh. We may say the same about the soldier who in Gideon's hearing interpreted the dream of his fellow soldier, that he was the prophet rather than the one who had the vision.[28] In this order or degree of prophets, Daniel exceeded all others. For not only did he interpret the king's visions, but even when the king had forgotten what he had seen in his sleep, he could recall it to his memory. Moreover, he not only interpreted the visions of others but was also instructed by God about things he himself had seen.

10. Sometimes dreams are also sent by the devil. In his book noted before, *On the Literal Meaning of Genesis*, Augustine tells of one possessed with a devil who by a vision told the very hour that the priest should come to him and through what places he passed.[29] Nor are we ignorant that there were oracles among the pagans, where men passed the night to obtain visions and dreams: such were Amphiaras, Amphilocus, Trophonius, and Aesculapius.[30] While sleeping in those places an evil spirit showed them medicines and remedies to heal the sick; they also gave answers to other matters. To obtain such dreams and visions, those who came to inquire of anything were urged to use certain foods, to dwell apart, and to observe some days of purifying. The Pythagoreans are said to have abstained from eating beans because they bred confusing dreams.[31] In order to declare himself free from such things, our God showed Daniel the king's dream, after he and his fellows had implored him for it by prayer. No doubt the devil can insert himself into dreams, since by his help there have been and still are many false prophets. In chapter 19 of the book cited, Augustine said: "If an evil spirit possesses men, he makes them either demonic, or out of their minds, or else false prophets. On the contrary, a good spirit makes faithful prophets, uttering mysteries for others' benefit."[32] In the eleventh chapter of the same book he asks how we can tell the difference between revelations of good and evil spirits. He answers that this cannot be

---

[28]Jud. 7:13 ff., the passage occasioning this scholium.

[29]Augustine *De Genesi ad litteram*, 12.17.35 (PL 34.468). cf. Tertullian *De Anima* 47: dreams are "inflicted on us mainly by demons, although sometimes they turn out true and favorable to us."

[30]Amphiara(us), seer of Argos, whose sanctuary at Oropus was famous for healing springs and dream interpretation; Amphilocus, legendary seer and cofounder of the oracle of Mallos in Cilicia; Trophonius, builder of the temple at Delphi; Aesculapius, legendary physician, later hero and god of healing. He was reputed to prescribe remedies in dreams, thus developed the practice of sleeping in his temples.

[31]The first Pythagorean rule of life was "to abstain from beans"; J. Burnet, *Early Greek Philosophy* (London: A. & C. Black, 1908) 195 ff. Cf. Tertullian *De Anima* 48 (PL 2, 777): Pythagoreans "reject the bean as an aliment which would load the stomach, and produce indigestion,."

[32]Augustine *De Genesi ad litteram* 12.19.41 (PL 34.470).

done without the gift of discerning the spirits.[33] But he adds that in the end an evil spirit always leads men to evil opinions and perverse actions, even though at first the difference cannot be perceived without the gift of the Holy Spirit. In the hundredth Letter to Euodius who had asked the same question he replied: "Would that I could distinguish between visions which are given to deceive me and those which make for salvation."[34] Nonetheless we must be of good cheer, because God at times allows his children to be tempted, but not to perish. [*99r*]

[RATIO I][35]

11. But what shall we reply to Aristotle, who denied that dreams come from God, particularly on the grounds that he would then give the power of prophecy to the wise and good and not to the foolish and wicked?[36] We may answer that for the most part true prophets enlightened by God in dreams and visions are both good and godly. But lest we think that divine power is tied to human wisdom and ways, God will sometimes use the works of evil men in such matters, so that the great and wonderful strength of his providence may be revealed, which can use all kinds of means. Further, as Tertullian writes in his book *On the Soul*, since he distributes his sun and rain to both just and unjust, it should be no marvel if he also imparts these gifts—especially those that enlarge human learning—to the bad as well as to the good.[37] To prevent our remaining ignorant of his practice, sacred history declares that pagans were often warned and corrected by God in their sleep. So Pharaoh, king of Egypt, was ordered to restore Abraham's wife again, and Abimelech, king of Gerar, was likewise admonished.[38] Tertullian added that God instructs the wicked in their dreams to make them good, while on the contrary the devil invades the godly while they sleep to seduce them from the way of righteousness in their dreams. Aristotle thought that in distributing his gifts, God should have special regard to the wise and to philosophers, whereas Christ taught the contrary, saying: "I thank you, heavenly Father, that you have hidden these things from the prudent and wise, you have revealed them to little ones," etc. Paul said that the calling of God pertains chiefly to the poor, the unlearned, and the weak.[39]

---

[33]Charisma discretionis; Augustine *De Genesi ad litteram*12.11.23–24, on Daniel and Peter (PL 34.462); cf. 1 Cor. 12:10.

[34]Augustine *Ep.* CLIX (alias 100) (PL 33.699).

[35][Marginalia]. Martyr returns to the question of cause by submitting three "reasons" or proofs; see §1 above.

[36]Aristotle *De div. per somnium*, 463b12.

[37]Tertullian *De Anima* 47 (PL 2.776).

[38]Gen. 12:17; 20:3 (the former passage does not mention dreaming).

[39]Matt. 11:25; 1 Cor. 1:26 ff.

[RATIO II]

Another argument was that animals dream in their sleep, yet no one will say that their dreams are initiated or arranged by God.[40] That philosopher is deceived in thinking that if God sent some dreams to men he must therefore be the author of all; clearly this is far from our meaning. We do not refer all natural things to God himself, as particular effects by which he instructed men immediately (as the schoolmen say) of things to come. We have already shown sufficiently the reasons why dreams arise in animals. To speak logically [dialectice], from the personal or particular proposition to the universal, is not a cogent argument.[41] Therefore, if God suggests some dream we should not conclude that all dreams either in animals or in men come from him. Otherwise we would have the following: animals have the power of hearing, nor do they lack ears, yet God does not send prophets to speak to them and reveal the future; therefore God never sends any of his saints to men, to admonish and instruct them.

[RATIO III]

12. [Aristotle] said moreover that if God were the author of dreams it seems that he should work them in the daytime no less than at night.[42] But I say that God is free to use whichever time he wishes, since he is Lord of the day as well as the night and of sleeping as well as waking. In fact the Scriptures testify that he showed visions to the prophets sometime sleeping and sometimes awake, as seemed most appropriate to him.

Further, how absurd is it to use the opportunity of night and rest, since philosophers themselves as well as physicians grant that at that time we are very apt to discern the lightest movement? Does such an opportunity allow the physician to detect bodily humors and not serve God for the saving of souls? In the book of Job chapter 33 there is an excellent passage of relevance to this point: When sleep has fallen on men so that they are at rest in their beds, then God opens the ear and warns of punishment.[43]

Lastly, it was objected that if God wished to admonish men he would do it openly and clearly, not covertly through enigmas.[44] I answer: True prophets and those inspired by God well understood what God said to them in their sleep; therefore they had no need of soothsayers. If at any time such a thing

---

[40]Aristotle *De div. per somnium*, 463b12.
[41]I.e., arguing from a minor premise; cf. *An. Prior.* 26a30.
[42]Aristotle *De div. per somnium*, 464a5 ff.
[43]Job 33:15 ff.
[44]Aristotle *De div. per somnium*, 464a21–22.

happened to pagan princes (as it did to Pharaoh and Nebuchadnezzar) it was God who did it, so that his hidden prophets, in this case Joseph and Daniel, might be made famous. In general, he blessed his prophets with judgment and clear understanding of the visions he granted them. Aristotle was deceived on this point because he looked only to impostors who claimed to prophesy and who deluded the people, as though they were able to expound all sorts of dreams, and to show what they predicted. But we cannot apply what is claimed here to all kinds of dreams or all sorts of prophets. For they refer only to those truly sent by God, and so do not include the conjectures of impostors and soothsayers.

In any case, the authority of so great a philosopher should not affect us greatly, even though Epicurus agrees with him—to free his gods from troubling themselves about dreams he affirmed that, like everything else, they come through [*99v*] fortune and chance.[45] Plato, on the contrary, ascribed much to dreams sent from God, while the Stoics taught that nocturnal dreams are a sort of familiar and household oracle by which mankind is cared for by God.[46] I will add that Augustine in the place now cited, *On the Literal Meaning of Genesis*, book 12, chapter 15, asked whether the soul by its own nature has the power to know the future. He said that it does not seem so to him, because in that case it would use that power, since everyone greatly desires to know the future. Thus the visions and dreams of prophets derive their truth not from nature but from God.[47]

13. If dreams are suggested by God and his angels, let us see the reason why we are forbidden to consider them. For if this is the case, dreams are not to be condemned but observed with care. I answer: not every way of regarding dreams is forbidden, but only what is procured by evil and vain arts and associated with the worship of demons. Otherwise nothing prevents us from judging humors through dreams, or following them if they are from God and understood to come from him. Moreover, it is forbidden to extend natural dreams beyond what nature allows. This is done by those who match their dreams to chance events about which they have no knowledge, either of the cause or of the effect.

---

[45]For Epicurus, the gods dwell impassibly in the *intermundia*; all human experience results from natural causes (e.g. *Diog.* 78), so that no divine intervention is required (*Diog.* 87); cf. Calvin, Inst. 1.2.2: Epicurus' God, "discarding all concern about the world, indulges himself in perpetual inactivity."

[46]Cf. Plato, *Rep.* 9.572; for the Stoics the universal Pneuma guides human activity; revelation and prophecy are sometimes manifested during sleep (Cicero, *De Div.*i.50 ff.).

[47]Augustine *De Genesi ad litt.* 12.xxvi.53 [*sic*] (PL 34.476).

This superstitious prediction through dreams is not only condemned by Christians but was also rejected [confossa] by Roman law. In book nine of the code *De Maledicis et Mathematicis*, the law *Et si excepta* decrees that such prophets should be punished severely; even if they were in some high office, including Caesar's own court, they could be punished, something otherwise unlawful for nobles to endure. They are expressed by these words: "Or any secret art of divination, for the interpretation of dreams," etc.[48] The difference assigned for lawful and unlawful observance of dreams is well described in Jeremiah 23, where God detested vain and foolish dreams but commended those that are true and divine.[49] In Deuteronomy 18, all observers of dreams seem to be reproved in general, but we should understand that according to the true Hebrew text no mention is made of them. Other superstitions and idolatries are indeed condemned there, but nothing is said of dreams although elsewhere their wicked observance is reproved.[50] Therefore, a good and lawful attention to dreams is not to be forbidden; the godly are permitted to pray that they may be instructed even in their dreams, especially about those things they consider beneficial, and which they cannot untangle themselves. Wishing that her son should marry in order to avoid fornication, Monica the mother of Augustine asked God to reveal something to her on the subject even in sleep; she stated that she obtained from God some taste [nescio quo sapore] by which she discerned the matter that she herself saw in sleep, from those things revealed by divine inspiration: So Augustine writes in his *Confessions*, book 6, chapter 13.[51] We know with certainty that Daniel prayed for the understanding of Nebuchadnezzar's dream.[52] It cannot be denied that the devout should pray to God that even while we sleep we may be preserved chaste and pure in both body and spirit. Augustine himself prayed like this in *Confessions* book 10, chapter 30.[53] For those nocturnal visions by which the mind is troubled or the body defiled are punishments for sin, especially for that drawn from our first creation. It would not have been so in paradise, if Adam had persisted in that truth in which he was made, as Augustine wrote in book 5, chapter 8 against Julian.[54]

---

[48]*Corpus Iuris Civ.* C.9.18.7.

[49]Jer. 23:25 ff.

[50]Deut. 18:10. The Vulgate has "et observet somnia atque auguria," but MT had only "anyone who practices divination, a soothsayer, or an augur..." (RSV).

[51]Augustine *Conf.* 6.13.23 (PL 32.730–731).

[52]Dan. 2:17 ff.

[53]Augustine *Conf.* 10.30.41 (PL 32, 796).

[54]Augustine *Contra Iulianum Pelagianum* 5.8.31 (PL 44.803–804). After the scholium Martyr returns to the text (Judges 7:16) with the words "Now let us return to the history once more."

PART FOUR

Providence, Miracles, and Responsibility

IN PRIMVM LIBRVM

MOSIS, QVI VVLGO GE-
NESIS DICITVR, COMMENTARII
doctissimi D. Petri Martyris Vermilii Florentini, professoris diuinarum literarum in
schola Tigurina, nunc denuo
in lucem editi.

Addita est initio operis vita eiusdem à IOSIA SIM-
LERO *Tigurino descripta.*

ACCISSERVNT *praeterea in hac editione, octo postrema ca-*
pin huius libri, LVDOVICO LAVATERO *inter-*
prete: Item que Indices locupletissimi Rerum &
verborum, atq, Locorum communium.

Absit mihi gloriari nisi in cruce Domini nostri IESV CHRISTI
per quem mihi mundus crucifixus est & ego mundo.

TIGVRI

EXCVDEBAT CHRISTOPHORVS
FROSCHOVERVS M. D LXXIX.

Title page of Commentary on Genesis, printed in Zurich
by Christoph Froschauer, 1579

About the Translation

Providence, Miracles, and Responsibility

DE PROVIDENTIA. This is an early scholium from the lectures on Genesis given at Strasbourg between about 1545 and 1546.[1] Can fate coexist with freedom? The debates on this question had raged over centuries and countries: Padua was heir to their fruit, in Pietro Pomponazzi especially.[2] The divine will is paramount for Martyr's theology, a total governance over human acts and apparently accidental occasions. It is more than "pro-vision," for *willing* is always involved: Martyr rejects the definition of Ambrose because it limits providence to foreknowledge.[3] Such a case is saved from fatalism by the complex causality learned from Aristotle. One might say that the problem of *causation* informs Martyr's thought at every turn. In this he resembles Ulrich Zwingli, for whom providence represented "un théorème, à partir ... de l'idée de souverain bien (et non plus d'Etre)," functioning much like the concept of grace for Luther.[4]

---

[1] Peter Martyr Vermigli, *In primum librum Mosis, qui vulgo Genesis dicitur Commentarii doctissimi ...* (Zurich: C. Froschauer, 1569), fols. 115r–117v (Gen. 28:16), included in LC 1.13, CP 1.16. Martyr's treatise may be compared with Calvin's treatment of the topic in *Inst* 1.16–18. The second scholium is from Peter Martyr Vermigli, *In Libros Samuelis Prophetae ... Commentarii doctissimi ...* (Zurich: C. Froschauer, 1564), fols. 56v–59r, beginning with §5.

[2] See CHRP 653ff., and "Providence," n. 44, p. 186 below.

[3] GEN fols. 109v–110r; see CSV 69.

[4] J. V. Pollet, *Huldrych Zwingli et le Zwinglianisme* (Paris: J. Vrin, 1988) 45. See Zwingli, *De Providentia Dei* (1530), esp. 39–52 (CR 93.3).

The first part of the topic (§§1–4), from the lectures on Genesis, provides a brief overview, including the question of "whether providence implies change in God."[5] Almost two decades after the lectures on Genesis, Martyr was still wrestling with the problem of divine and human willing, while lecturing on the books of Samuel at Zurich. Here he uses Aristotelian logical categories to argue that as pure act, God's action is required to move all things, and he is even "the first efficient cause." But since divine concurrence relates directly to human moral decision, Martyr is able to develop a theology of personal grace despite the burden of the *concursus divinus* noted above. The second part (§§5–16) does not much differ from the earlier, but it is more developed and better organized. Besides the analysis of necessity and contingency, it gives closer attention to the complex causality required to justify the supremacy of the divine will. As noted before, the topic relates to the debate on predestination, since it concludes: "In this question we have in a sense established the roots and foundations of predestination."

We have already discussed the thorny problem of how providence and predestination are related.[6] We saw that for the "Reformed" tradition the former should form part of the doctrine of creation and the latter of the doctrine of God. We challenged this view by arguing that Peter Martyr does not fit easily within such a schema, and indeed that even a strong proponent like Karl Barth concludes the issue with a dialectical relationship similar to Martyr's. For our Reformer it appears that the more crucial question is not how predestination relates to providence, but rather how the emphasis of both on the supreme divine willing can escape the charge that God is responsible even for human sin. This is a test case that reveals Martyr's practical and pastoral intent. It does indeed show awareness of the often esoteric debate among Christian theologians of his day, but its chief concern is with the live issues of belief and unbelief, of how the Gospel is to be preached and heard, and the divine command obeyed in daily human existence.

*   *   *

---

[5]Bullinger rewrote his draft of this personal confession during 1562, when he expected to die of the plague; it was Martyr's final year and he embraced it warmly. See P. Jacobs, "Die Lehre von der Erwählung in ihrem Zusammenhang mit der Providenzlehre und der Anthropologie im Zweiten Helvetischen Bekenntnis," in J. Staedtke, ed. *Glauben und Bekennen: 400 Jahre Confessio Helvetica Posterior* (Zurich: Zwingli Verlag, 1966) 258–77.

[6]See "Providence and Predestination," pp. xxxiiiff.; see also introduction to "Free Will and Predestination," pp. 265ff. below

DE MIRACULIS. The treatise on providence prepares us for the shorter scholium on miracles, from the lectures given on Judges during his second Strasbourg period, 1553 to 1556.[7] Like the former, the locus on miracles shows its historical context of "classical theism," the dominant theology of Catholic and Protestant alike in the sixteenth century insofar as omnipotence is assumed to be the chief divine attribute: divine governance implies power to suspend the natural order. It is curious that in this scholium Martyr is not so explicit on the logical ambiguity of "omnipotence" as he is in the treatise on resurrection. There he qualifies omnipotence as Aquinas does, with the caveat that God's will cannot order "things impossible in themselves."[8] In the present case, he favors the dual definition of Augustine that a miracle is something both "astonishing" and "outside the usual order assigned to things."[9] This is disappointing for a logician of Martyr's stature. As our various selections show, he knows well scholastic distinctions that would help, e.g. between *potentia absoluta* and *potentia relativa*; the former is an abstraction, the latter a power related to wisdom and goodness. There is also a distinction of necessities: one through which something follows (*necessitas consequentiae*, applicable to divine willing) and one that is merely deduced from the result (*necessitas consequentis*). The Thomist thesis recognizes that you cannot separate God's power from his will: "There is no application to God of the concept of trying but failing"; omnipotence is "not a position consistently maintainable."[10] So the little treatise reads more like a homily than a reflection on a theological dilemma. Like his Augustinian predecessors, he also argues questions of whether angels or devils work miracles (§§7–10), and how miracles, like sacraments, confirm faith by a sealing office (§§11–13).

*   *   *

---

[7]Peter Martyr Vermigli *In Librum Iudicum ... commentarij doctissimi* (Zurich: Froschauer, 1561), fol. 208. The scholium appears on fols. 90v–94v, chap. 6 fin. and is included in LC 1.8 (CP 1.9). See BIB VI.1–6.

[8]See "Resurrection" §13 (p. 56) and §65 (p. 118), above; Aquinas in ST Ia.Q 25.3c; cf. SCG I.84 (impossibilium secundum se); *Disp. 1 de potentia* 3: "Whatever implies contradiction does not fall within the scope of omnipotence."

[9]See F. Van der Meer, *Augustine the Bishop* (New York: Harper, 1961) chap. 19: "Belief in Miracles," 527ff.

[10]P. Geach, *Providence and Evil* (Cambridge: Cambridge University Press, 1977) 5, 13. Geach's chapter "Omnipotence" (3ff.) surveys four main historical and modern ideas of divine power; in his judgment, they all break down.

AN DEUS SIT AUTHOR PECCATI. A major theological problem emerges from the material on providence and miracle as well as Martyr's stress on predestination: If divine oversight is so complete, must not God be held responsible for human sin? The sense of unease created by this dilemma drives him to ponder the question of *Whether God is the author of sin* several times throughout his writing career. He handles it on Romans (while at Oxford), on Judges (at Strasbourg), and twice in his final years at Zurich: one on Samuel, translated here,[11] and a final locus on Kings. The problem is endemic to Augustinians, for "the logic of the Reformed doctrine of election left theologians with the obligation to show that God did not cause the fall."[12] For Martyr the resolution involves an appeal to two sorts of argument. First, in causal terms sin entails only a "deficient" cause, so that God is not an efficient cause but simply the necessary final cause. Second, the divine will embraces all human actions, but differently when these are evil rather than good.

As we saw in "Providence," for Martyr the divine will encompasses everything, both necessities and contingencies. Now he formulates the classic dilemma boldly: "That God is not *per se* and properly the cause of sin; second, nothing happens in the world, not even sins themselves, outside his will and choice or providence" (§6). Like John Calvin, Martyr rejects the distinction between positive will and mere permission, for permission is "not completely without God's will."[13] Once again Martyr insists on an *effective* divine will, distinguishing the *posse* from the *velle*. One option for the Reformers was to adopt the Nominalist distinction between the divine *potentia absoluta* and *potentia ordinata*—what God could have done and what in fact he has chosen to do.[14] The distinction was strongly rejected by Calvin.[15] Martyr agrees,

[11]Peter Martyr Vermigli, *An Deus Sit Author Peccati*, scholium on 2 Sam. 16:5–23; *In duos Libros Samuelis Prophetae … Commentarii doctissimi* (Zurich: C. Froschauer, 1564) fols. 275r–285r (LC 1.14/CP 1:17.1–37). There is a brief scholium of the same title earlier in the commentary, fols. 19v–22v, part of which (20r–22v) is included in Marten's English translation (CP 1.17.38–42). See CSV 116–123, for this material.

[12]J. H. Leith and W. S. Johnson, *Reformed Reader: A Sourcebook in Christian Theology* (Louisville: Westminster/John Knox, 1993) 187.

[13]§24; cf. CSV 120–121, and Calvin, *Inst.* III.23.8: "We should contemplate the evident cause of condemnation in the corrupt nature of humanity—which is closer to us—rather than seek a hidden and utterly incomprehensible cause in God's predestination."

[14]See H. A. Oberman, *The Harvest of Medieval Theology* (Grand Rapids: Eerdmans, 1967) 30ff. Donnelly, CSV 204, shows that Martyr's "scholasticism" is closer to Thomism than to Nominalism: "The thesis that Occam is the foster father of Protestantism needs revision in the light of Peter Martyr's theology." In Karl Barth's treatment of "the foundation of the doctrine" of election, he gives a typically strong opinion on this point: "To distinguish between a *voluntas Dei ordinata* and *absoluta* is a blasphemy from which we can only recoil in horror"; see Barth, CD II.2.23.

[15]E.g. Calvin, *Inst.* 3.23.2, *Comm. in Isa.* 23:9: a device of "the sophists under the Papacy," as implying *potentia inordinata*, a disorderly power. See D. C. Steinmetz, "Calvin and the Absolute Power of God," *Journal of Medieval and Renaissance Studies* 18, no. 1 (Spring 1988): 65–79.

particularly as it involves both Lutheran and Roman appeal to an absolute and hidden will, as seen in his arguments against ubiquity and transubstantiation.[16] In the present case of responsibility for sin, he presses the distinction between primary and secondary causes to acknowledge the final will behind all creation, while absolving it of guilt *per se et proprie*; proximate second causes constitute sufficient reason to account for human sin, without accusing God of their authorship.[17]

These texts consider the divine goodwill in its universal implications. In his preface to "the golden history of the Judges" Martyr states: "In those mighty acts, the incredible power and wisdom of God's providence shines forth everywhere abundantly and brightly.... God does not neglect human affairs. He has consideration and regard for both believers and unbelievers, giving joy and pleasure to the one and at the last punishing the other severely" (*IUD* Praef.). Like Augustine, Martyr's concept of the divine willing is not so much a philosophy of history as a theological perspective on human affairs and their ultimate outcome. As his constant biblical references show, what governs this perspective is not the formal logic of events but the modality of Christian hope.

---

[16]On ubiquity see "Resurrection" §65 (p. 118 above), and CSV 167; on sacraments see the 1549 Oxford *Tract. de Sac, Euch.* (DM 254–255; 284, n. 42). Donnelly states: "he raises this distinction only to reject considerations resting on the *potentia absoluta*"; see CSV 27.

[17]Calvin, *Inst.* III.23.8–9, agrees.

Commentaries on Genesis and Samuel

Providence

[INTRODUCTION[1]]

Now since it is said that [the promise] will certainly come true, we can see that all events, even the smallest, as well as our own decisions, depend on divine providence and are guided and arranged by God, although to us they often seem to have occurred by mere chance. But a large and difficult question arises: if all our acts and experiences are so certain, how is it possible that they can also be contingent? And since we are often faced with this problem in the sacred writings, I decided that it might be worthwhile to comment on it at some point.

---

[1]This passage introduces the original scholium in GEN but is omitted in LC/CP. The scriptural context is the story of Jacob's ladder and the divine promise to care for the patriarch.

Two scholia from biblical commentaries compose this topic in the *Loci Communes*. Sections 1–4 are *De Providentia* on Genesis 28:16; *In primum librum Mosis*.... (Zurich: C. Froschauer, 1569); fols. 115r–117v. §§5–16 are *De Providentia Dei* on 1 Samuel 10:2 (*In Duos Libros Samuelis Prophetae*.... [Zurich: Froschauer, 1564]) fols. 56v–59r. The Genesis lectures are from the first Strasbourg period, 1543–1547, the Samuel from Zurich, 1556–1562. Our section numbering follows LC 1.13/CP 1.16; the subheadings are from marginalia.

[DEFINITION]

1. [*115r*] The Greeks call providence πρόνοια or πρόνοος. The Hebrews call it הֹשְׁגָחָה, which they derive from the verb הִשְׁגִּיחַ (hif'il), which means to see precisely and distinctly.[2] So far as its definition is concerned, Cicero has this to say in his book *On Invention*: "It is that by which anything future is seen before it happens."[3] But if we apply this definition to divine providence it does not express the matter completely since it shows only knowledge of the future and the power to know it beforehand, whereas divine providence includes not only the knowledge of the divine mind but also his will and election, by which future things are arranged and determined in one way rather than another.[4] It also includes a power and faculty of directing and governing those things it is said to foresee; for there is not only their substance and nature but also the order according to which they are related to one another. One thing strives for another in order to support it or to be perfected by it. Everything is well ordered in both ways: each in particular is said to be good in itself, and all generally are very good as to order. We may prove that this order is in all things by the very nature of order itself. It is defined by Augustine as "the disposition of things both like and unlike, giving to each one that which belongs to it."[5] Everyone knows that the parts of the world are diverse and unlike when compared with one another.

Both experience and Scripture teach how well God allots everything its own proper place and standing. It is said that God set bounds for the seas and their waters, nor may they pass their prescribed limits; again, that he measures the heavens with his hand, and so on.[6] Since so great a benefit should be

---

[2]Following the original in GEN; the LC text is incomplete, reading merely "The Hebrews derive it from the verb...."

[3]Cicero *De Inventione* §2: "Providentia, per quam futurum aliquid videtur antequam factum est." Cicero is a primary source for Martyr on this subject; cf. p. 183, n. 30, below.

[4]The crucial point for Martyr that divine *willing* unites with divine *knowing* contradicts the "theology" of Aristotle, *Phys.* VIII and *Meta.* XII.6ff., which posits the famous "unmoved Mover" of pure thought: "Therefore, it must be of itself that the divine thought thinks (since it is the most excellent of things), and its thinking is a thinking on thinking"; see *Meta.* 1074b33. W. D. Ross, *Aristotle* (London: Methuen & Co., 1923), 183, states: "What Aristotle ascribes to God is knowledge which has only itself as its object," although Alexander Aphrodisias argued for a recognition of divine providence. Such "provision" is strictly *modo obliquo* however, as Aquinas, *In Met.* xii, lect xi, acknowledged in positing indirect knowledge of things: "Intelligendo se intelliget omnia alia," based partly on Aristotle's own critique of Empedocles, who denied a knowledge of "strife" to God in Aristotle (*De An.* 410b4, and *Meta.* IV.4.1000a25ff.). Aquinas also tackles the related question of whether God "knows future contingent singulars"; see SCG I.67. Cf. CHGM 119–120.

[5]Augustine's strong doctrine of *ordo* sees *caritas* as an "ordered love" that observes the "orders of nature"; see, e.g., Augustine *De doct. christ.* I.xxvii.28, and *De vera rel.* 48.93.

[6]Jer. 5:22; Isa. 40:12.

attributed to him by reason of his providence, we may define it as follows: It is the measure [ratio] which God uses in directing things to their proper ends. This definition includes not only the knowledge, but also the will and power to effect it. In the first chapter to the Ephesians, Paul brilliantly sums up what we are discussing when he says: "Who works all things according to the counsel of his will."[7] In his oration for Milo, Cicero taught the signs by which this providence may be known by natural reason. He writes, "Surely no one may judge otherwise, unless one who thinks there is no heavenly power or divinity [numen divinum], and who is not moved by the sun or motions of the heavens and their signs, nor even by the order and changes of things," etc.[8] Paul demonstrates the very same in the first chapter to the Romans. And Job, chapter 12, states: "Ask the cattle, and the birds of the air, the fish of the sea, and the plants of the earth, and they will tell you." Also in Psalm 19: "The heavens declare the power of God." Job again, in chapter 31, regarding goats, deer, horses, Leviathan, and Behemoth.[9]

[QUESTION: WHETHER ALL THINGS ARE RULED BY GOD'S PROVIDENCE]

2. Let the subject be arranged as follows: The order of things declares that what is created is not made blindly or by chance, for God works according to his purpose; all things are subject to his providence, as to the universal and highest art, nor can anything be found that escapes it. Yet some dare to deny it, ascribing only the greatest and principal things to divine care and attributing the rest, if they are of little account, to natural causes, while greater matters they leave for angels or demons to accomplish. This may be seen in the *Protagoras* of Plato, where creation is described as giving some things to Epimetheus to make, and some to Prometheus.[10] The only thing said to be done by the gods is to make good provision for humankind. But in the Gospel we are taught differently by Christ: "All the hairs of your head are numbered" and "Not one of two sparrows falls to the ground without the will of your heavenly Father." Again, "The Lord himself has looked down from heaven on all the children of men."[11] If they understand the matter like this, as if providence does not extend to everything in the same way as to humans, we agree: not because providence, which in itself is one, can be said to be composite, but because the effects directed by it are various and different, so that it itself

---

[7]Eph. 1:11.
[8]Cicero *Oratio ad Mil.*; cf. *De div.* I.1, *De nat. Deorum* 1.8, 2.29 on Pronoia.
[9]Rom. 1:18–20; Job 12:7; Ps. 19:1; Job 39–40 (*sic*).
[10]Plato *Prot.* 320ff.   [11]Matt. 10:29–30; Ps. 14:2.

seems to have a variety of elements. Thus we grant that providence is so much greater over godly men, that the Lord says to the lost and foolish virgins, "I know you not";[12] it will also be greater for humans than for irrational creatures.

By a lively faith in this providence we reap many benefits, especially consolation in adversity, knowing that those things do not happen to us blindly but by the will and deliberation of God our Father. Also we are more disposed to good things when we understand that God both knows and sees our actions, who at the last will judge them fairly. Besides this, the gifts which we enjoy are much more acceptable to us in that they are offered us by God in his providence. Further, in providence we see predestination, which brings so great a comfort to the godly as to strengthen them greatly.[13]

[WHETHER PROVIDENCE IMPLIES CHANGE IN GOD][14]

3. We should not be afraid that there might be mutability in God because of his providence. Through parents we are brought into the world without knowledge, and cannot develop knowledge without changing; but we should not imagine the same thing in regard to God, since he has possessed his knowledge from eternity. Moreover, we deduce it from the nature of things, but he has it through himself. So James wrote truly that with him there is no variation or shade of turning.[15] Nor does it ever happen that God's knowledge is altered by the change in things. Moreover, this highest knowledge is securely placed in God, since there is no danger that he might abuse it like those of whom Jeremiah writes, in chapter 4: "They are wise only in order to do evil."[16] God is most excellent and knows what is best; whoever has this cannot misuse other things. Plato taught this in his second *Alcibiades*, where it is proved that without such knowledge it is better to be ignorant of many things.[17] It had been much better for Orestes if he had not recognized his mother when he met her, after he decided to kill her.[18]

---

[12]Matt. 25:12.

[13]For the problem of the relation between providence and predestination, see "Introduction" pp. xxxiiiff., and "Summary on Providence and Predestination," pp. 328ff.

[14]For the subject of possible mutability in God, see also LC 1.11, "When God's Anger is Mentioned"; LC 1.14, "How it may be said that God repents or is tempted," LC 1.14, "Whether God is Author of Sin"; and the Summary of "Whether God is the Author of Sin," pp. 333ff.

[15]Jas. 1:17.

[16]Jer. 4:22.

[17]The Pseudo-Platonic *Alcib. II*, 142.

[18]Orestes, son of Agamemnon and Clytemnestra, avenged his father's murder by killing his mother and her lover Aegisthus.

God does not lose his calm felicity or contemplation of better things on account of this care over all. Sometimes it happens that humans are distracted from serious and nobler occupations through dealing in superficialities. Thus not without reason did Paul condemn vain and curious questions.[19] This arises through the limitation of our understanding, which cannot embrace a number of things. But God is infinite in respect of all his acts and so can easily comprehend everything that is, that shall be, and that ever has been. Nor is God provoked to evil by this knowledge of things; that happens to us because we have corrupt passions.

Solomon said: "Look not on the wine when it sparkles in the glass," etc. Psalm 119 says: "Turn my eyes away lest they behold vanity." And Job 14 says that he made a covenant with his eyes, lest he should think about a maiden.[20] But God, the principal rule of all justice and goodness, cannot be swayed towards evil. Now Averroës said: "His understanding would at least be affected if he were to look at and perceive all these weak things."[21] But we disagree, for it does not follow, since he acquires this knowledge not from things but from himself. We see that a mirror is not stained because it shows the images of vile things, nor is the sun defiled when it shines on what is foul and base. The labor of understanding does not affect God at all, since in this act he uses no bodily instrument—unlike humans, for whom the process of understanding comes from effort, causing the body to suffer much distress and weariness. Solomon aptly called this studious labor a torture and affliction of spirit. Knowledge at times fosters disquiet, for the more people understand, the more they see that annoys and upsets them. It is not unfairly said: "He that increases knowledge increases sorrow."[22] For we do not easily endure things that happen without being fulfilled. But God, who has the capacity to foresee the end of all things, is not subject to these human affections; even if things are undeserving he still directs them and knows that they tend to his own glory.

[WHETHER PROVIDENCE DESTROYS CHANCE AND FORTUNE]

4. It has not been hard to remove from divine providence those objections we have just dealt with; a plain and easy method presented itself to refute them. But other and harder things remain to be explained. The first is

---

[19] 1 Tim. 2:23; Titus 3:9.

[20] Prov. 23:31; Ps. 119:37; Job. 31:1 (*sic*)

[21] Averroës or Ibn-Rushd (1126–1198), Spanish-Arabic philosopher, "*the* Commentator" on Aristotle, who taught (*In Meta.* IV.2.2, etc.) an Unmoved Mover and single Active Intellect impassible to human emotions. See "Introduction," p. xxiii, and "Resurrection," p. 63, n. 49.

[22] Eccl. 1:18.

that if we attribute to God the providence of all things, chance and fortune seem to be taken away from nature. For nothing is more against chance and fortune than reason. Fortune is a cause that works outside purpose when something not planned or appointed or chosen takes us unaware, against our expectations. We reject this argument as follows: Fortune and chance are not taken from us by the providence of God. Why should it not be true that nothing is done by chance in relation to God, while as for ourselves much is done blindly and by fortune? An apt illustration may be offered: Suppose a master sends his servant to the market to stay until nine o'clock; before the hour is past he sends another of his servants there. For him it will not happen by accident or chance that the two servants meet, since he expected it when he sent them to the same place, but to them it does not happen on purpose, since the one knew nothing of the other's coming. Similarly, many things done by God's foresight and knowledge happen by chance according to our dull and weak understanding.[23]

They say, however, that if, as we believe, all things are directed by God and happen by his counsel, where will their contingency be? For everything will fall out by necessity. Some think this argument against divine providence so strong that the freedom of our will can hardly be defended. Now the same kind of answer that we used a little before regarding contingencies is relevant to this reasoning. For it may be (if you examine proximate causes), those things that happen are, and are rightly called, contingencies; for it is not contrary to the cause to bring forth one effect as well as its opposite. In respect of my own will, it can happen that I may sit or not. If those effects are referred to that cause they will be contingencies, since they could have been different; but since they are subject to the providence of God we must not deny that they are necessary. Thus a double necessity obtains, namely one absolute and the other hypothetical [duplex necessitas, sc. absoluta et ex hypothesi]. It may be, however, that if things necessary by supposition are taken without the hypothesis, they are contingents and not necessary.[24]

In chapter 14, Isaiah talks about the destruction of the kingdom of Babylon. This was but chance in terms of worldly causes (for there was no reason

[23]Cf. Plato *Laws* IV.790: "That God governs all things, and that chance and opportunity cooperate with him in the government of human affairs."

[24]Aristotle, *Phys.* II.9: the necessity involved in material things, e.g. building a wall, depends on the whole process and its end. "What is necessary then, is necessary *on a hypothesis;* it is not a result necessarily determined by its antecedents. Necessity is in the matter, while 'that for the sake of which' is in the definition" or absolutely; see Aristotle *Phys.* II.9, 200a12ff. These distinctions are crucial to the lecture on Free Will below (e.g. §5); see also *De Praed.* (LC 3.1.50). Cf. Calvin, *Inst.* II.16.17.

why it should not be otherwise), yet wishing to show that this is sure to happen, the prophet points out the divine purpose and says, "God has planned it so, and who will annul it? The Lord's hand is stretched out, and who will turn it back?"[25] And so for this reason it was necessary. In Psalm 37 we read: "The counsel of the Lord stands forever, and the thoughts of his heart to all generations."[26] Yet they still insist on the contrary, that necessity seems to hinder divine providence. For we do not deliberate about what cannot be otherwise: Since many things in the world seem to be necessary, their kind seems to exclude divine providence. Here we must remark that all things are necessary insofar as they are done and decreed in relation to the decision and purpose of God, but for God himself, who appoints and decides the act, all things are contingent, nothing in the world being of such necessity that it may not be otherwise. We are not speaking here of the definitions of things, or of necessary propositions or conclusions, since these matters are not governed by divine providence; they are expressions of eternal truth and divine nature.[27] There are also some who think that no evil should exist in the world if it is governed by God through his providence. For no one dealing providentially in his actions would allow evil to occur. They may be easily answered, that no evil will be found which would not be useful for the saints as conducing to salvation: nor is there evil which would not promote universal order and its preservation, by declaring the justice and mercy of God.[28]

[METHOD OF THE DOCTRINE OF PROVIDENCE][29][56v]

5. Since events are said to be so certain, surely we can see that even the smallest works, as well as our own decisions, depend on the providence of God and are guided and arranged by him, although to us they often seem to be mere chance. But the question is large and difficult: If all our acts and experiences are thus certain, how can they also be contingent? For it often happens in the sacred writings that the value of events is judged by something that is said at the time.

---

[25]Isa. 14:27.

[26]Ps. 33:11 (*sic*).

[27]Cf. Aristotle *NE* VI.3.1139b23: "Things that are of necessity in the unqualified sense are all eternal."

[28]This completes the GEN scholium (116r). For a fuller treatment of the problem of evil, see "Whether God is the Author of Sin," pp. 215ff.

[29]This paragraph introduces the major scholium *De Providentia Dei* in the commentary on 1 Samuel. It is omitted in the LC, which does not indicate that a different scholium is now commencing; Marten's English translation mentions somewhat ambiguously "The same place is expounded in 1 Samuel 10, verse 2"; see CP 1.16.5.169b.

To follow some method, let us first inquire whether providence exists; second, what it is; third, whether all things are subject to it; fourth, whether it can be changed; finally, whether it allows any contingency in things. But before I come to the matter itself let us discuss the signification of its names.

[*56v*] Among the Greeks a contingency is called "possibility" [ἐνδεχόμε-νον], meaning it may or may not be; whether it exists or not there is no absurdity, either against human reason or the word of God.[30] It is distinguished into three parts; the first is called by the Greeks "from which of the two" [ὁπο-τερέτυχεν], that is, it inclines equally in either direction. Another is "for the most part" [ὁς ἐπὶ τὸ πολὺ], which usually falls one way or the other but may happen differently. The third is called "the least" [ὡς ἐλάχιστον] because it occurs rarely.[31] Philosophers identify two grounds [duplex fundamentum] in contingencies: matter, which assumes one form or another as it acquires one effective cause or another; and the will, by which our actions are governed. The will considers the matter as directed and compelled by the intellect. In his *Eighty-three Questions*, question 31, Augustine says that philosophers divide knowing [prudentia] into three parts, namely, understanding, memory, and providence.[32] Memory is referred to what is past, understanding to things present, while a provident person can determine from the past and the present what will occur later. But God not only understands and sees what will happen, but brings his will to it as well. For we affirm not only a bare understanding in God but an effectual will also, by which he rules and directs all things. This is called by the Greeks Πρόνοια. In *The Nature of the Gods*, Cicero calls it an old prophetess of the Stoics. She was held in such esteem among the ancients that in Delos she was worshipped as a goddess, because she helped Latona at childbirth.[33] But that fable means nothing other than that second causes may have some power in themselves yet effect nothing without the providence of God. For Latona is nature, and Providence the midwife. Unless

[30]For the following discussion of Greek teaching on chance or the logic of contingency, see Cicero *De Fato*, esp. 6–12. In opposition to Stoic fatalism, Alexander Aphrodisias, "following Aristotle, asserted the possibility of contingency, that is ἐνδεχόμενον"; CHRP 641. Latin Averroism revived ancient determinism, linked with astrological theories of influence. Pietro Pomponazzi, *De fato, de libero arbitrio et de praedestinatione* (1520) countered philosophical freedom with the sort of theological fatalism espoused by Luther; see CHRP 653ff.

[31]Arguing against Chrysippus' rejection of conditional propositions, Cicero *De Fato* 10, cites the Epicurean recourse to the atomic "swerve" popularized by Democritus: "Epicurus, however, thinks that the necessity of fate is avoided by his fortuitous concourse of atoms. ... Epicurus calls it *elachistos* or infinitesimal," See p. 187, n. 52.

[32]Augustine *De div. quaestionibus LXXXIII* 31 (PL 40.20), referring to Cicero *De Invent.* 2.

[33]Cicero *De Natura Deorum* III.18. Cf. Ovid *Met.* vi.165–381, "The Story of Latona."

the latter is present and plays the midwife, as it were, the other brings forth nothing.

[WHETHER PROVIDENCE EXISTS]

6. Now I turn to those five points[34] that I planned to treat individually. To begin, I propose that there is a providence, which may be proved by many of the soundest arguments. First, God is author and creator of all and can do nothing without deliberation; he has his own certain and firm reasons in himself; therefore, necessarily providence exists. If there were no maker—but who would not see the reasons and aims of his works and the ways he maintains by which to bring them to their intended goal? It would be insane not to attribute it to God, the chief artisan, whom the divine writings take for the creator of all things, as well as a kind of potter. Chrysostom says, in the 19th homily on Ephesians,[35] "If a ship, no matter how sound and well rigged, cannot withstand the seas without a navigator, how much less can the round of the universe be maintained without God's care and rule?" If a master builder will not begin construction before he has prepared in his mind all the parts, figures, and forms of the building, are we to think that God has made everything in creation rashly, without counsel or reason? Clearly the heavenly spheres, the stars, the firmament, air, water, heat, cold—so many forms and changes of things contrary and hostile to one another—would fall in ruins unless sustained by some ruler. Without care and providence our body could not be defended from the inclement heavens. We consider provident those who, with balanced mind and judgment, keep all parts of their body in their proper function; now God occupies the same place in the world as does the mind in man. Moreover, Scripture ascribes to him the fall of kingdoms as well as prophecies and miracles, which surpass the reach of our nature, and finally, the Judgment by which one day he will render to all according to their works. Therefore, led by these and many more reasons, we conclude that providence exists. We reject the Epicureans, who say the following:

Clearly the labor of heaven is a care that robs them of peace.

And this:

---

[34]See §5, p. 182, above.
[35]Chrysostom *Ad Eph.* chap. V, homily XIX.3 (PG 62.131).

God walks on the poles of heaven and has no regard for human affairs.[36]

They have produced these monstrosities partly because they are poor in imagination and cannot perceive higher things, and partly because they lead a gross and shameful life; they wanted to invent this consolation so that they should not be continually tormented by the fear of punishment. For whoever does evil hates the light.[37] When children have done something wrong they do not want their father to be at home or their teacher present in school.

Regarding the first part, this should be enough for Christians who are persuaded not by reason but by the word of God alone, that providence exists.

[WHAT PROVIDENCE IS]

7. What providence is may be quickly understood from its definition. It is the power or faculty of God by which he directs all things and brings them to their ends. In this definition, the genus is power or faculty. God is completely single-minded [*simplicissimus*]; yet for the sake of our capacity we say that there are two faculties in him, Understanding and Willing [*Intelligendi et Volendi*]. God understands and sees everything; not only that, but he also wills everything. At this point I bring no needless discussion whether the will of God precedes the understanding, or the understanding the will. Any who wish to know such things I send to Scotus and Thomas.[38] This power and faculty of which I speak refers to quality, since it is a natural power. The difference[39] is that [*57r*] by this power God directs all things that are or will be. Even more, he also leads them to their ends. To which ends? Whatever is appropriate [*ad congruos*]. They are appropriate which his purpose determines. The cause is the power or faculty; the effect is that things are brought to their proper ends. Here we include all the kinds of causes that can be assigned in this matter.[40] I say this because there can be no efficient cause of divine

---

[36]E.g. Epicurus *Principal Doctrines* 1: "The blessed and immortal nature knows no trouble itself nor causes trouble to any other"; Lucretius, *De Rerum Nat.* V.70: "Godheads lead a long life free of care" (cf. III.18ff.); Cicero *De Natura Deorum* I.37, describes the "inactive" Deity of Epicurus; Plato *Laws* X.886, condemns the view that the gods "have no care at all of human affairs." The Epicurean gods dwelt in *intermundia*, the tranquil void between worlds—where, according to the Epicurean Philodemus, they held philosophical discussions in Greek. See H. Chadwick, "Origen, Celsus, and the Resurrection of the Body," 91ff.

[37]John 3:20.

[38]Thomas Aquinas taught the precedence of reason over will, Duns Scotus that of will over reason. See "Introduction" p. xxvi, n 36 above.

[39]See Aristotle *Meta* V.14.1020a33: "'Quality' means the differentia of the essence...."

[40]For the Aristotelian fourfold causality see "Philosophy and Theology," p. 7, n. 4.

providence. The formal cause is the power of God. The material to which it applies is every kind of existing thing, for we exempt nothing. The final cause is that everything may attain its own end and redound to the glory of God. We see by this definition that the providence of God is not only mere knowledge [nudam cognitionem] but has certain effects. As Paul says: "In him we live and move and have our being." Again: "Of him and in him and through him all things exist."[41] And as Solomon says: "Man may prepare his heart, but God governs the tongue."[42] For we cannot move the tongue, the slightest part of the body, without the providence of God. Christ states that "a sparrow does not fall to the ground without the will of your father: and all the hairs of our heads are numbered."[43] Some imagine that God made all these things and afterwards cast them aside. Likewise carpenters are content to stop building a house after having built it. But if the world were governed in this way, it would soon come to ruin. For a house weakens and falls unless it is regularly repaired and strengthened. If the soul is severed from the body, what remains for the body but to decay and perish?

We should not heed those who say that while it is true that God rules all things, it is nothing else but supplying that common influence [*communem influxum*] which everything draws into itself. This makes God the ruler and governor of the universe not in reality but in name only. If everything bends and applies that common influence of God in its own way, then God follows the nature of created things; whereas, on the contrary, everything created should follow after God. But they say that just as someone who throws a stone or shoots an arrow is content with that first impulse even though not pursuing it further, so it was enough for God to have endowed all things with their power, without continuing to govern them. But these are not the same, for an arrow or stone falls to the ground once it is launched, because in creatures impetus cannot endure. If God did not follow initial impulse with his everlasting care and providence, the nature of things could not persist. When the Peripatetics saw that all these inferior things are constantly troubled, they established the providence of God beyond the moon, as if it should not be concerned with such lesser beings, except for the common influence supplied to all.[44] But these are lies, for Scripture teaches that what seems to us to

---

[41]Acts 17:28; Rom. 11:36.
[42]Prov. 16:1.   [43]Matt. 10:19.
[44]E.g. "it is impossible for the infinite to be acted upon by the finite or to act upon it"; see Aristotle *De Caelo* I.7.274b34. For Aristotle, "the realm of celestial bodies is ruled by *heimarmené*, the sublunar realm by *physis*, the human realm by *phronēsis*, *pronoia*, and *psychē*"; see Ross, *Aristotle*, 74. The sublunary realm was considered by his successors as the proper sphere of divine care. Cf. Augustine's critique in *De Genesi et litteram* 5.21. Pomponazzi, whose influence remained at Padua during Martyr's years there, had noted the contradiction between Aristotle's views of motion in the *Physics* and of contingency and freedom in the *Ethics*; see CHRP 656–657.

happen by sheer chance is still governed by God's providence. In Deuteronomy, if an axe flies from the hands of a woodcutter to strike and kill a passerby, "It is I," says the Lord, "that delivers it into the hand of the manslayer."[45] In the 14th chapter of Job it is said of God: "You have appointed his bounds which he cannot pass."[46] Also, in the book of Wisdom, which contains much that is good and godly even though it is not in the canon, it is written in chapter 8: "Wisdom strongly [εὐρωστῶς] reaches from end to end and disposes all things usefully [χρηστῶς]"; it says that it extends *eurōstōs*, that is, with strength and might. Also it disposes things usefully, for so *chrēstōs* means, and not "pleasantly" [suaviter], as the old translation has it.[47] Although we do not always perceive it, such usefulness is of the kind that tends to the glory of God.

[WHETHER ALL THINGS ARE SUBJECT TO PROVIDENCE]

8. It is a matter of debate whether all things are subject to divine providence. Some say they are and others say not. But as we observed before, if God has made all things, nothing can be outside his providence; for if it were outside his providence it would be outside creation too. It is written in the letter to the Hebrews: "He upholds all things by the word of his power."[48] This is a Hebrew phrase: "word of power," stands for "mighty word." The passage agrees with what we cited from the book of Wisdom. Ezekiel calls God "the Lord of all flesh"; and in the book of Numbers, Moses calls him "the Lord of spirits." Paul says to the Ephesians: "Who accomplishes all things according to the counsel of his will."[49] Even Hesiod, the pagan poet, says, "In this life we can nowhere escape from the mind of Zeus."[50] Yet some wish to exempt from the providence of God's name both free will and what is either necessary or contingent. Cicero says in *On Fate* that the most ancient philosophers such as Empedocles and Heraclitus affirmed that all things stand under necessity. For the Peripatetics, however, many things are contingent.[51] As an honorary arbiter, Chrysippus taught that all other things are necessary, although the human will enjoys freedom as to its original choice. Therefore, Eusebius, in *Preparation for the Gospel*, quipped that Democritus made men slaves while Chrysippus made them only half slaves.[52]

---

[45]Deut. 19:4–6.   [46]Job 14:5.
[47]Wis. of Sol. 8:1 (Vulgate): et disponit omnia suaviter.
[48]Heb. 1:3.   [49]Ezek. 18:4; Num. 11:29; Eph. 1:11.
[50]Hesiod *Works and Days* 3.   [51]Cicero *De Fato* 4 ff.
[52]Eusebius *De Praeparatione Evangelica* 7 (PG 21.438.257). The atomists Leucippus and Democritus (ca. 460–362 BCE) were materialists. Chrysippus (ca. 279–206 BCE) had written a work entitled *De providentia*, which is not extant; he taught a strict determinism coexisting uneasily with human responsibility. Martyr *De Praedestinatione* (LC 3.1.54) uses this same material. See p. 183, n. 31, above.

Cicero also, in his second book, *On Divination*,[53] would rather exclude all providence than say that men are not free. Augustine derides this supposition in his fifth book, *On the City of God*, chapter 10, saying: "To make men free he made them sacrilegious."[54] So we see that some do not think that all things are subject to providence. They explicitly except mankind, God's highest creation, [57v] which seems especially insulting to God. If artisans disparage lesser works of no ultimate value, but embellish and take special care for the more excellent, who will imagine that God could despise that work he had chosen above all others? And if it were so, where would we be? What refuge would we have in adversity? David says: "Cast your burden on God, and he will sustain you." And Peter says: "He cares for you." Zechariah also: "Whoever touches you touches the apple of my eye." The Lord says: "I am your shield and your strong wall." David says: "The Lord is my helper, and I fear not what man can do against me. Though they pitch camp against me, my heart will not be afraid."[55]

[ἀπορία.[56] IF PROVIDENCE RULES EVERYTHING, WHY IS THERE SUCH CONFUSION?]

9. You may say that in regard to lesser things, much happens without order or else against it. We often see the faithful oppressed while the wicked flourish. Granted; yet is there no providence just because we do not see a cause? If you happen to be in a blacksmith shop and see many tools, some hooked or bent, some saw-toothed or curved, would you at once condemn them all because they do not look straight and handsome? I think not; rather you would admit that you did not understand their uses. Such honor must be attributed to God that when you see the prosperity of tyrants and evil men, you can say that they are instruments of divine providence, even though you cannot grasp what God intends to do with them. Augustine says that God is "so good that he can even draw some good out of evil."[57] Further, if there were no tyrants, what would become of the virtue or patience of martyrs? God wants his goodness to triumph in this way: He wants others too on whom he may exercise his might and power. But you might say, is it not enough that

---

[53]Cicero *De divin.* II.7. See Martyr, *De Praed.* for the same use of Cicero (LC 3.1.54–55).

[54]Augustine *De civitate Dei* chap. 9: "and so instead of making men free, makes them blasphemous."

[55]Ps. 55:22; 1 Pet. 5:7; Zech. 2:8; Gen. 15:1; Ps. 27:1, 3.

[56]Like Aristotle (and Plato) Martyr views the task of philosophy as problem solving (aporetics) rather than system building. While he occasionally uses the label *problemata*, this may be his only use of the Greek term *aporia*.

[57]Probably Augustine *Ep.* 166.V.15 (PL 33.727).

some become martyrs through preparing their souls? There are indeed noble virtues hidden in the souls of the devout, yet often this does not satisfy God; he would bring them out into action that they may be seen. Thus our eyes should be lifted up, so that we think not of the unfaithful, but of God. Even so did the prophets call Nebuchadnezzar, Pharaoh, and Sennacherib axes, hammers, saws, and swords in God's hand.[58] When Job lost all his possessions, he did not look to the Chaldeans or the devil, but said: "The Lord gave, and the Lord has taken away."[59] We count him a wise physician who can draw to the surface corrupt humors that lie hidden within the body. We shrink from inflammation and sores, but the physician says that the patient begins to recover after such things come out. So God brings to light what lay hidden in our souls by his medicine and the fires of persecution. Let the wicked do what they will, they can do nothing beyond the will of God. So said Peter in Acts about Pilate and Herod: "They agreed together that they would do whatever your hand and counsel had resolved to take place."[60]

[WHETHER NECESSITIES ARE UNDER PROVIDENCE]

10. You may say: Some things are necessary which cannot be other than they are;[61] do they fall under the providence of God? Nothing whatever is created with such necessity that it has not the nature of contingency in relation to God. For as we said, God reaches from end to end and orders all things. What is more necessary than the course of the sun? Yet Joshua made the sun stand still.[62] What is more necessary than that fire should burn, if fuel is supplied? So goes the old saying: If active things are applied to passive, the effect follows of necessity.[63] Nevertheless, God brought it about that those three youths remained unharmed in the fiery furnace.[64] What is more necessary than for shadows to follow the sun's shining? Yet God caused the shadow to go backward when the sun shone.[65] Yet it seems as if man is created and left to his own counsel. "You shall keep those things," says Ecclesiasticus, "and they shall keep you."[66] I grant that in respect to inward causes man was originally so made that nothing could be necessary for him. Yet we do not therefore exclude the grace and providence of God. Let us hear Holy Scripture on this point. (Ecclesiasticus is not counted in the canon). Solomon says: "The heart of the

---

[58]Isa. 10: 5, 15.   [59]Job 1:21.   [60]Acts 4:28.

[61]Aristotle *Meta*. V.5.1015a324: "We say that that which cannot be otherwise is necessarily as it is. And from this sense of 'necessary' all the others are somehow derived". Cf. p. 181, n. 24.

[62]Josh. 10:13.

[63]Cf. Aristotle *De Gen et Corr*. I.8–9 for discussion of action/passion, with fire as example.

[64]Dan. 3:25.   [65]Isa. 38:8.   [66]Ecclus. 11:17.

king is in the hand of God."[67] God said: "I have given them precepts," but then adds: "I will cause you to walk in my precepts"; and again, "I will give you a new heart and a new spirit."[68] Therefore, man is not to be excluded from the providence of God.

[WHAT SEEM TO BE ACCIDENTS ARE UNDER GOD'S PROVIDENCE]

11. Much less should we exclude those things that seem to happen by chance. For although we cannot perceive the reason for second causes, God does. Indeed, the philosophers teach us that every cause which they call *per accidens* must be referred to that which is a cause *per se*; what is accidental cannot be a true cause. Thus in his little book *On Good Fortune,* Aristotle asks why some were fortunate and some not, answering that it happens by a kind of impetus and impulse, the reason of which is unclear to anyone subject to it.[69] Thus some emerge as fortunate and some not. He states further that if this event is referred to our will and knowledge, it happens by chance. For an impetus is a cause in itself. But the question is not yet settled. For how does it happen that this fortune is given to one and denied another? Astrologers wished to supply what they thought Aristotle lacked. In his book *Apoteles-matōn* Ptolemy refers it to the stars—he claims that those born at different times are moved by them in various ways, some to prosperity and others to adversity.[70] Some call this a divinity, some [*58r*] a constellation, and others some particular destiny; Socrates called it a "daemon." But why it happens to one more than to another, or more at one time than another, the only cause to be assigned is the providence of God. This is so that everything might be referred to the glory of God.

Joseph said to his brothers, "It is not you that sold me into Egypt, but God sent me ahead." God said also that he sent Saul to Samuel, even though it seemed that he had turned out of his way to meet him by chance. Christ said to his apostles: "One will meet you carrying a jar of water."[71] These matters were inevitable for divine foresight, although to human eyes they may seem accidental. But you will ask: Are there then no second causes? Does God do

---

[67]Prov. 16:1.   [68]Ezek. 20:11, 36:26–27.

[69]For Aristotle's distinction *per se/per accidens* see *Meta.* V.6–7.1015b ff. Martyr uses it often, e.g. *Dialogue* 18v (DIAL 36), ROM 1:16, DEF 722–723. The book *On Good Fortune* is not listed among Aristotle's works, although there is a fragment *De Bono.*

[70]According to Ptolemy's *Apotelesmatikōn,* astrological influences contribute to human destiny.

[71]Gen. 45:8; 1 Sam. 9:15ff.; Mark 14:13.

nothing through angels? We do not remove second causes, but we regard them as instruments of the providence of God. For angels are ministering spirits; David says, "who do his will." Even though God sends angels, he himself is present and head over all things. "If I ascend into heaven," says David, "you are there; if I descend to the underworld, you are there."[72] He does not give his angels charge so that he himself might be absent. The poets imagine this about Apollo, that he placed Phaethon in his chariot, and so during his absence all the heavens were set on fire.[73] But some will say that sins do not depend on providence. How sins are governed by God will be discussed later.[74] The cause of sin undoubtedly comes from us; but at what time and against whom it is to be directed, is in the power of God. Nebuchadnezzar determined completely on his own to subdue certain people, but it was God who ordained that he should oppress the Jews more than others.

[WHETHER PROVIDENCE IS IMMUTABLE]

12. The next question is whether such providence is immutable. Why not? It is the rule for everything that happens.[75] It is written in Malachi 3: "I am the Lord, and do not change." In the first of James, "With him is no variableness, nor shadow of turning." And in Proverbs 19: "Many are the plans in the heart of man, but the purpose of the Lord will endure." In the 46th of Isaiah: "It is I who speak, and my will abides, and I do whatsoever I purpose."[76] Seeing that providence is the will and knowledge of God relating to the divine essence, it cannot be changed unless at the same time God himself is changed. Second causes sometimes hinder one another because of their diversity—we see this happening in the influences of heaven, that some are impeded by others; but no power can hinder God's will. In ancient times God ordained the ceremonies of the Jews, and later he would have them abolished. How then is God's providence not changeable? I answer: there is one and the same will in God, although from the beginning he foresaw what is appropriate to different times. Augustine said to Marcellinus that the farmer sows at one time and reaps at another, fertilizing the soil in between; but we cannot therefore say that the rural art is inconsistent.[77] He said that Vinditian, who was a

---

[72]Ps. 139:8.

[73]Ovid *Metamorph.* end of I and beginning of II.

[74]See "Whether God is the Author of Sin, " pp. 215ff.

[75]Theodore Beza quoted the following material, to the third sentence in §14, in "An Evident Display of Popish Practices, or Patched Pelagianism" trans. W. H.[opkinson], London, 1578; see M.W. Anderson, "Peter Martyr Vermigli: Protestant Humanist" in PMIR, 77ff.

[76]Mal. 3:6; Jas. 1:17; Prov. 19:21; Isa. 46:10–11.

[77]Augustine *Epist.* 138 I.3 (PL 33.526–527).

physician, administered medicine to a sick man and healed him. After many years the man fell ill of the same disease and took the same remedy without consulting the physician. When he grew worse he came to the doctor to show him the problem, and began to complain of the medicine. Then Vinditian said, "Small wonder, since I did not prescribe it for you." Some wondered at this and were of the opinion that he used to employ some sort of magic. He replied, "Not at all, for he is now a different age and has other complaints than when I gave him that medicine." Yet is the art of medicine inconsistent because of this? Just so God foresees all things, but has not decreed that all things happen at the same time.

[DOES PROVIDENCE ALLOW ANY CONTINGENCY IN THINGS?]

13. Now let us come to contingency: If the providence of God is so certain, can it allow any chance? First I will make use of two distinctions and then respond. There is one necessity that is absolute and another that is conditional [simplex, ex hypothesi].[78] When we say that God is wise or just, we understand it to be a simple and absolute necessity. Other things are conditionally necessary, such as this subject of debate in the schools: Whatever is, is necessary while it exists.[79] Christ and the prophets predicted that the city of Jerusalem would be overthrown; therefore, of necessity it will be overthrown. Not that such necessity belongs to the nature of the city, but because Christ and the prophets foretold it, and they could not be deceived. Paul says: "There must be heresies," and Christ: "It is necessary that offenses come."[80] Once the causes are established—the corruption of human nature and the devil's hatred toward humankind—and the end is fixed, that the elect should be tested, it is hypothetically necessary that it should happen.

Moreover, things may be considered in two ways, first as they are in actuality, in which case they have the nature of necessity since they are no longer indefinite. For instance, to write or not to write is hypothetical. But if you are now in the act of writing, it is no longer contingent but necessary. Hence we say that sensory knowledge is certain, because the objects themselves cannot be otherwise. Secondly, things may be considered as they lie hidden in their causes; but since causes may sometimes produce effects and sometimes not, there is no necessary power of acting in them. But if they are referred to God, the reason is quite different. "For he calls those things that are not as if they were."[81] He encompasses all of time, and has neither begin-

---

[78]See p. 181, n. 24.
[79]"Necessaria ex hypothesi... Quicquid est, dum est, necessarium est."
[80]I Cor. 11:19; Matt. 18:7.   [81]Rom. 4:17.

ning nor ending, and even everything future in infinity is present to him.[82] The will of God also comes in here, for we must not ascribe to him bare knowledge, but practical [πρακτική].[83] In this way I hold that things themselves possess necessity. Augustine, *On the Literal Meaning of Genesis*, book 6, chapter 15: "There are many ways by which man and other things might have been made by God, and those ways had the form of possibility and not necessity. But this is by the will of God, [*58v*] whose will is the necessity of things."[84] Although such matters are necessary when referred to God, yet they must be weighed by us according to their inward and proper causes and be termed contingents. For it is not necessary for the effect to resemble the efficient cause.

14. If you inquire why there are these two kinds of cause in the nature of things, so that some are limited and necessary, others indefinite and contingent, there can be no other answer than that God has laid these conditions on all. God brings forth all things, setting limits and bounds to all, yet in such a way that he neither perverts nor destroys their nature. In his *Topics*, Boethius says, "destiny [εἱμαρμένη] is named from 'to bind and to loose appropriately' [ἀπό τῶ εἵρειν καί χωρεῖν ἀκολουθῶς]."[85] For God draws all things together, but moves in such a way as to disturb nothing. Likewise, things may in their own nature incline equally to both sides, yet God bends them more to one. By its own nature, the will of Saul was not more determined to go than to stay.[86] But when God wished him to go to Samuel, that will began to turn to one side. Therefore, God put his father's wishes into his mind, and made it effectively move and influence his resolve, subduing all other desires of leisure and ease, if there were any, that might keep him at home. So it happened that Saul's will yielded to the providence of God. Meanwhile, the nature of things

---

[82]Martyr's practical intent makes him disinterested in the traditional problematics of how God can know "future contingencies," the debate associated with Ockham's *Tractatus de praedestinatione et de prescientia Dei ei de futuris contingentibus*. See M. M. Adams and N. Kretzmann, *William Ockham: Predestination, God's Foreknowledge, and Future Contingents* (New York: Appleton-Century-Crofts, 1969). Cf. Aquinas in SCG I.67: "That God knows future contingent singulars." If future contingencies are true/false only indeterminately, i.e. becoming so on the realization or non-realization of the predicted event, then the divine will is present in indeterminate mode.

[83]See p. 177, n. 4, for this decisive point.

[84]Paraphrase of Augustine *De Genesi ad litteram*, 6:15 (26): "It was determined in the causes that man could be created in such a way, not that he must necessarily be created in such a way"; (PL 34.349–350).

[85]Boethius *Top.* 4.6. Martyr gives the popular etymology following Boethius; in fact *heimarmenē* derives from μείγομαι, to apportion. The passage misquotes ἀκολούθος for ἀκολύτος. Ps-Aristotle *De mundo* 401b.

[86]I Sam. 9.

was not violated, for Saul's own will was equally free towards either side. This shows how necessary the grace of God is to us. Since our own will is completely corrupted, it turns everything to the worse part. Many things dull and blind our understanding so that the will cannot easily follow. Therefore, God sets the good before our mind; afterwards he kindles faith and arouses the will, that we might choose it effectively.

[Why What God Determines Is Called Contingent]

15. You might ask: Why is anything said to be contingent, since God has already in one sense determined it so that it becomes a necessity? I answer: Everything is contingent from its properties and principles. But the providence that bestows necessity is an external cause whose name should not be applied to things. I know there are many who hold that what cannot be done by human power is brought by God to this point where our will may either choose or refuse it, and that God's providence sticks there, going no further. Even if God foresees what everyone will choose and refuse, his foreknowledge is not an obstacle. Yet these statements do not agree sufficiently with the Scriptures. For they teach that God does not look to things in order to abandon them, but as was said, to lead them to their ends. Those ends, moreover, serve divine providence. Paul states that God has made all things according to the purpose of his will. So says God himself in Isaiah: "All things that I will, I do." And Christ said: "Even a little sparrow does not fall to the ground without the will of our father."[87] I know that when Origen, Cyril, Chrysostom, and other Fathers are baffled by straightforward passages of Scripture, such as "It is necessary for the Christ to die; it is necessary for Scripture to be fulfilled,"[88] they interpret them as follows: Such matters do not happen because God foresaw them, but rather God foresaw them as they were to happen. If these statements refer to simple perception, they can hardly be refuted. For someone does not write because I see him writing; but because he writes, I see him writing. Yet we cannot postulate bare knowledge in God; for the will is added, by which he directs and ordains all things. Nevertheless, what they say will be true if understood from the effect or, as they say, *a posteriori*. For from the fact that something is done we understand that it was the divine counsel that it should be done. Otherwise, the Scriptures speak clearly, that Christ had to die, that Scripture had to be fulfilled. But how was it necessary? Conditionally, since God foresaw it, and not because such necessity was in the nature of the thing.

---

[87]Eph. 1:11; Isa. 46:10; Matt. 10:29.   [88]Luke 21:22; 24:26.

[How Causes Are Infinite]

16. Perhaps you will say that causality as such may be considered infinite, since I am not taking perfect and complete causes;[89] for then the providence of God should have been included. I answer: I take only the inward and proper causes of everything whose effects are contingents, since they might or might not be produced by them. I do not add providence because it would be an exterior cause. If it were added we could not avoid having some necessity follow conditionally. For example, Saul met men carrying kids, bread, and wine.[90] In its very nature their choice was unlimited, whether to give something to him or not. But by his providence, God limited that will to one choice. They were going to Bethel to sacrifice; they met Saul, weary upon his way and almost dead with hunger, so it seemed a kindness to refresh him. God put this in their minds, and restrained whatever might have hindered this will. Our debate is about human wills only. In general, in other things that are contingent, I know that God uses unlimited means. We have another example of this matter in chapter 12 of Ezekiel.[91] Nebuchadnezzar marched into Syria; on his way he came to a crossroads and began to deliberate whether it was better for him to direct his strength against the Jews or against Rabbah, the Ammonite capital. He decided to draw lots on it, which God so arranged as to lead him to Jerusalem. The nature of the thing itself was contingent, but when determined by God it became necessary. Joseph was sold and carried into Egypt, so that in the nature of the case it could happen that he would always live in bondage, or else at some time be released. [591] God sent dreams to the baker and butler, which Joseph interpreted; afterwards a vision was given to Pharaoh, which none of the diviners could explain; the butler told him about Joseph. So it happened that Joseph was released from prison.[92] It must be concluded that, as we have often said, all things are necessary in relation to the providence of God, while in their own nature they are contingent.

But you will ask whether the effects when taken absolutely should be called contingents, or rather necessities. Some will have them called necessary for the sake of the dignity of providence; but I would rather call them contingent according to their own nature. Yet I will not argue much if the necessity is understood only as conditional. The Greeks rightly called providence "fate" [πεπρωμένη] from "being finite," which pervades everything; others call it

---

[89]Cf. Cicero *De Fato* XIV–XV on infinite series of causes, as in Carneades' determinism.
[90]I Sam. 10:3. This is the scriptural passage immediately following the scholium.
[91]Ezek. 21:18ff. (*sic*).
[92]Gen. 39ff.

Nemesis [Αδράστεια] because nothing escapes it.[93] Some will say that we are reviving the opinion of the Stoics concerning fate; that is false. They defined their fate as the necessity of the connection of causes, and said that it overruled even God himself.[94] We teach that God governs all things and uses them to his glory. But if they hold that fate is nothing else than divine providence, the question concerns the term only and not the essence, as Augustine taught somewhere. Finally, you will say that by this device there will be no place for counsel, warning, or reproof, since the future is completely as God wills. The same objection was raised against Augustine, so that he wrote the book *On Rebuke and Grace*.[95] Even though God has decreed that something should be done, he still uses means to bring it about. He wishes to change the wicked will of men; he uses admonition, preaching, and censure. For these are organs and instruments of God's providence, and it is far from providence to exclude them.

In this question we have in a sense established the roots and foundations of predestination; but we will speak about that another time as opportunity affords.[96]

---

[93]ἀπὸ τῶ πεπερατῶσθαι; another quotation from Ps-Aristotle *De Mundo* 401b, omitting *panta*: "fate so-called because all things are finite." Adrasteia was the Ionian name for Nemesis. The same passage defines Adrasteia as "ἀναποδράστος αἰτία" a cause whose nature is to be inescapable."

[94]I.e., a logical determinism; cf. Cicero *De Nat. Deorum* I.14, on Zeno; he himself presents a modified Stoic doctrine of providence in II.30–31.

[95]Augustine *De correptione et gratia*; See Augustine *Retractiones* II.67: "I wrote ... 'On Rebuke and Grace' because I had been told that someone there [the convent of Adrumetum] had said that no man ought to be rebuked for not doing God's commandment...." (PL 32.656).

[96]A strange comment for these lectures on Samuel of 1556–1558, since Martyr had included the treatise *De Praedestinatione* in ROM (chap. 9 fin., published 1558). He did not include a scholium on predestination in this series or in his final lectures on Kings. Perhaps his public lecture on free will (translated below, pp. 265ff.) fulfilled this promise since it was part of the predestinarian controversy associated with Theodore Bibliander. More important is the significance of this sentence for the question whether predestination is for Martyr *pars providentiae*; see this section's Introduction above, pp. 171ff..

Commentary on Judges

Miracles

1. Two CHIEF DISTINCTIONS should be examined. First, what miracles are. Second, whether and how far it is permitted to ask for them.

[DEFINITION]

Regarding the first, the Hebrew word is אלף or אלפ, that is, "it was difficult or wonderful"; from this the nouns נפלא or מפלאות are derived, denoting matters hidden from others on account of their greatness and excellence; I mean exceptional and astonishing.[1] The Greeks call it *thauma* [θαῦμα], from the verb *thaumazein* [θαυμάζειν], which means "to marvel." The Latins call them *miracula*, because they are worthy of admiration. They also say *prodigia*, *monstra,* and *portenta*, from which we understand that through them God meant to show that something beyond the common order of things would

---

[1]The verb פלא does not occur in the Hebrew Bible in the qal, so Martyr gives the nif'al form (נפלא). Strictly speaking, נפלאות is a substantive (Ex. 3:20 etc.). מפלאות occurs only once (Job 37:16). See BDB 810–811.

De Miraculis is a scholium from *In Librum Iudicum … Commentarij doctissimi …* (Zurich: C. Froschauer, 1561), fols. 90v–94v, chap. 6 fin. (LC I.8, CP I.9). John Day published an English translation (London, 1564). The lectures on Judges were presented at Strasbourg 1554–1556; the immediate context is the story of Gideon's request for a miracle (a wet fleece on the dry threshing floor) to prove God's promise to deliver Israel.

happen or be done, above hope or expectation. Therefore, since miracles are performed beyond the nature of things [praeter naturam rerum], they cause admiration. To be sure, many miracles are made famous by writers, such as the temple of Diana in Ephesus, the tomb of Artemis Queen of Caria, the Colossus of the Sun at Rhodes, the walls of Babylon, and many others like them. In his 16th chapter against the Manichean letter, Augustine wrote wisely: "I call a miracle whatever appears difficult and unusual, above the expectation or reach of the wonderer."[2] From these words we may gather a broad description of miracles. And since a miracle is said to "appear," we may rightly accuse those who fabricate transubstantiation and hold it to be a miracle: It should not be called a miracle because it cannot be confirmed by the Holy Scriptures, and it neither appears nor is seen.

2. After this general and broad description, let us add that some miracles are true and some false. False miracles are said to be those which are either not what they seem to be, or if so, are not accomplished by any power above nature, but by their own power, even if secret. Angels, whether good or bad, may do this in three ways. Sometimes they apply the powers of nature, which are quite familiar, to some material; effects follow from such joining of matter with efficient causes; this happens so suddenly that onlookers cannot help but wonder. Demons know that frogs, worms, and certain kinds of serpents proceed from what is putrid, as heat is added by degrees. Since it is not hard for them to join these things together, they sometimes do so in order to deceive people. Augustine thought, as he wrote in *On the Trinity*, book 3, that this was how the sorcerers of Pharaoh did the same things as Moses.[3] Moreover, any disorder of spirits, blood, and humors greatly disturbs human bodies.[4] Specters, images, and the likenesses of things contained in them are brought before the phantasy or imagination, according to that reason and order in which the troubler of the spirit casts them. Many different visions arise from them, as we sometimes see in those who are delirious. Things may proceed so far that the shapes and images kept within are passed to the outward senses. Thus someone who experiences them thinks that he sees and feels those things which affect his imagination or fancy and senses, whereas in fact no such thing occurs

---

[2]Augustine *Contra Faustum Manichaeum* XXVI.(*sic*) 3: "Whatever God does contrary to [the common course of nature], we call a prodigy, or a miracle" (PL 42.480). Cf. Augustine *De civitate Dei* xxl.8: "A portent, therefore, is not against nature, but against the most common order of nature" (PL 41.721).

[3]Augustine *De Trinitate* 3.7–12 (PL 42.875).

[4]See "Dreams," p. 156, n. 4, for humoral pathology.

outwardly. This kind of miracle should be referred to as illusion rather than as the miraculous. [*911*]

It also happens that by their power these spirits fashion certain bodies, sometimes of air or other elements, so that they seem just like human bodies, and through them appear to anyone they wish. So they came at times to Abraham, Lot, and other Fathers. If we speak properly and plainly, such things are not genuine miracles, but according to our reason and judgment nothing prevents calling them so. Certainly jugglers are commonly said to do miracles, even though they perform only by sleight of hand, or else they present wonders to the spectators through some power of nature.

3. Here is the definition of true miracles: *A miracle is a difficult and unusual work of divine power, surpassing every capacity of created nature, made public in order to fill those who perceive it with wonder, and to confirm faith in the words of God.*[5] Therefore, the matter of miracles is works; the form is their being difficult and unusual; the efficient cause is the power of God, which surpasses created nature; and their end is both admiration and the confirmation of faith.[6]

So that we will have no doubts about the efficient cause, I think it best to add that the power of God, which completely transcends natural powers, is to be understood as sometimes through God himself and sometimes what he does through angels or humans, in such a way as will be shown later. I add the saying of Augustine in the place already noted against the Manichean letter, chapter 26: "Miracles would not move us unless they were wonderful, and they would not be wonderful if they were familiar."[7] They say that Philosophy arose from wonder, which Plato thought of as Iris, and, therefore, the daughter of Thaumas.[8] Even so, we may believe that faith, which comes from the word of God, is confirmed by miracles, even though it does not derive from them completely. Therefore, in his twelfth book of confessions, the 21st chapter, Augustine says: "Ignorance is the mother of wonder at signs: This is the entrance of faith for the children of Adam, who had forgotten you."[9] By this sentence he teaches that, having forgotten God, men have an entrance or way into faith by their wonder at miracles. This is quite true. For the will of God is

---

[5]Italics added.

[6]The four Aristotelian causes: material, formal, efficient, and final. See "Philosophy and Theology," p. 7, n. 4.

[7]Augustine *Contra Faustum Man.* XXVI.3 (PL 42.481).

[8]Iris, messenger of gods to men and daughter of Thaumas ["wonder"] and Electra. See Plato *Theaet.* 155D; cf. *Crat.* 408B: "Iris also appears to have been called from the verb 'to tell' (*eirein*), because she was a messenger."

[9]Augustine *Confessions* 13.xxi (30) (PL 32.857): "Ignorance, the mother of admiration."

hidden from us, but since he is good, God has revealed it to his Prophets and Apostles. And so that they could declare it to mankind with greater profit, he gave them the gift of his word. But because he knew that mortals are strangers and enemies of his word, he granted power to perform miracles, so that what drove messengers to speak for our benefit could be more easily believed. At the end of his Gospel, Mark testifies that the confirming of faith comes by miracles: "And they went out and preached everywhere, while the Lord worked with them and confirmed the message by the signs that followed."[10] It is clear how apt this corroboration is. The promises of God depend on nothing else than his will and power. And the signs of which we now speak witness to the divine power, because in every respect they exceed the order of nature and create confidence in his will; for they are grasped through the invocation of his name, and through his grace and Spirit. Hence in the place noted above against the Manichean letter, Augustine writes that miracles win authority for the word of God. For when God acted in such a way he seems to have given a kind of guarantee [arram] of his promises. We should not overlook what Augustine has in the 24th treatise on John: "Miracles do not consist in the greatness of works; for otherwise it is a greater work to govern this entire structure of the world, than to restore to a blind man the sight which he lacks."[11]

[DISTINCTIONS WITHIN MIRACLES]

4. After these explanations, it remains for us to divide miracles into their parts by suitable distinctions. Some of them are wonders because of the event itself, since they appear to be so great and uncanny that their like cannot be found in the nature of things. Such was staying the sun in Joshua's time, and turning the shadow in Hezekiah's, the conception and childbirth by a virgin, the food of manna in the wilderness, and such like.[12] But some are miracles not in regard to the nature and greatness of what is done, but by reason of the way and the means [modum rationemque] used to produce them. Among these were the clouds and rain of Elijah, the budding of flowers and fruit in Aaron's rod, the thunder of Samuel, the turning of water into wine, and similar things.[13] For they may be done naturally, yet they were miracles because of the way in which they were done; that is, not by natural causes but by the will and commandment of saints.

---

[10]Mark 16:20.
[11]Augustine *In Ioann. Ev.* Tract. 24.1 (PL 35.1592–1593).
[12]Josh. 10:13; Isa. 38:8, 7:14; Ex. 16:13–14.
[13]1 Kings 18:45; Num. 17:8; 1 Sam. 12:18; John 2:9.

Another distinction in miracles is that some of them merely arouse admiration, as did the lightnings and thunders on Mount Sinai, the turning of the sun's shadow in Hezekiah's time, the transfiguration of the Lord on the mountain.[14] Others, besides wonder, bring an actual benefit to humans, as when water was given from the rock by means of the staff or of manna from heaven, and when the sick were healed by the Lord and his Apostles.[15] Sometimes miracles bring punishment and harm to those that offend: Ananias and Sapphira died at the words of Peter, Elymas the conjurer was struck blind by Paul, while he delivered others to Satan to be tormented.[16]

Miracles also differ in that some are obtained by prayers. In this manner Elijah [*91v*] and Elisha restored their dead to life through prayer. By making intercession for Pharaoh, Moses delivered him from frogs and various other plagues.[17] Other miracles are effected by command and authority: Joshua ordered the sun to stay its course; the Lord Jesus commanded the winds; Peter said to the lame man, "In the name of Jesus Christ rise up and walk."[18] Still other miracles are made neither by prayer nor command, but come on their own, while believers themselves are otherwise occupied. Thus Peter's shadow healed the sick as he walked, and cloths or handkerchiefs that came from Paul cured the ailing.[19]

5. Lastly, here is how Augustine distinguished miracles in his book of 83 questions, question 79:[20] Some are done through public order, that is, by the stable and firm will of God, which counts in the world as civil law. Through it God wishes his ministers, that is Apostles and Prophets, to perform miracles by preaching. Others are accomplished by the signs of this justice, as when the wicked work any miracles in the name of God and of Jesus Christ, something allowed only in respect of the honor and reverence of the divine name that they use; not that God or nature or any creature wishes to indulge them. If someone has secretly stolen a public seal or writing and through it has extorted from countrymen or citizens across the land, the goods are given only to the seal, which they acknowledge as the magistrates or princes; even so, one who does not follow Christ casts out devils in his name. Thirdly, they count as miracles that are done by some private contract, by which sorcerers

[14]Ex. 19:18; Isa. 38:8; Matt. 17:2.
[15]Ex. 17:6, 16:13; Mark 16:18.
[16]Acts 5:5–6., 13:11; 1 Cor. 5:5.
[17]1 Kings 17:22; 2 Kings 4:34; Ex. 8:12, 30–31.
[18]Josh. 10:13; Matt. 8:26; Acts 3:6.
[19]Acts 5:15, 19:12.
[20]Augustine *De div. quaest. LXXXIII* 79.1 (PL 40.90–91); *partim privati ... partim universitatis legibus....*

bind themselves to the devil and the devil to them. But they are not accomplished through public justice or its signs, but only by some private arrangement. We should note that miracles of the second and third kind are not firm, nor do they happen necessarily. For we read in the 19th chapter of Acts that the children of Sceva would have cast forth devils in the name of Jesus, whom Paul preached; but the devil said to them, "Jesus indeed I know, and Paul I know, but not you."[21] After saying this he set upon them. As for the third kind, the act of Cyprian before his conversion confirms my saying. For he attempted to bewitch a godly young woman to incline to his impure desire; at length the devil told him that he could not bring this about for him.[22]

[TRUE AND FALSE MIRACLES]

6. We should note that miracles worked through private contract are not true miracles, but belong to the kind I mentioned before the definition.[23] For although sometimes they are indeed what they seem to be, they are not genuine miracles. Who doubts that it was in fact fire that consumed Job's cattle, and in truth a stormy wind that tore down his houses and destroyed his children?[24] Augustine states that the serpents that the Magi produced were not illusions, but true serpents. For the sacred history reports that when they came to the third miracle, the wise men said: "This is the finger of God," and confessed their failure, that they could no longer do what Moses did by the power of God.[25] Surely this shows that they had not worked by illusions before, and that until then the Magi struggled with Moses in reality and not pretense. But some will ask: If things produced by the devil and the magician are sometimes exactly as they seem to be, why is it written to the Thessalonians about Antichrist that many would be deceived by him through his false signs and wonders?[26] It should be said that the falsehood lies not in what is done but in calling it a miracle. For although sometimes later events seem to be so, yet they were not the miracles they appeared to be. Augustine answers: "Signs and wonders are called lies either because they will appear to be but are not, or because they lead men into lies. For by such signs Antichrist seeks nothing else but to deceive, and drive men to believe errors."[27] Nor is this anything new or

---

[21]Acts 19:13ff.

[22]From an apocryphal story from one of the lives of Cyprian, but not the most famous, the *Vita Cyprianis* by Pontius.

[23]See §2, p. 198 above.

[24]Job 1:16, 19.

[25]Ex. 8:19; Augustine *Quaest. in Heptat.* 2.25 (PL 34.604).

[26]2 Thess. 2:9ff.

[27]Augustine *De Antichristo* (PL 40.1132); see *Scripta deperdita* 55 (PL 47.38).

strange, that a cause should take either the name or property [ἐπίθετον] of its effect. The fact that things are not what they seem may be taken in two ways: Either when some counterfeit are mixed with true items, or because they are called miracles when they are not miracles.

7. Another doubt to be resolved is why the power of God, which surpasses nature, uses angels or people, whether good or evil, to do miracles. Whatever the means used, a miracle sometimes happens at their desire, request, and order, without any outward labor of theirs. Sometimes he has them exert their work or function. For Moses struck the sea and rock with his rod; Christ touched the lepers and anointed the eyes of the blind.[28] But it must be understood that there are two kinds of instruments. Some are prepared in such a way that while not the chief efficient causes, together they are enough to produce the effect: such as iron to cut hard objects and medicines to heal a disease, when they are still only workers' tools. But God uses other kinds of instruments in doing miracles, which in their own nature have no strength to produce results. For what [*92r*] power had the rod to divide the sea? or the shadow of Peter to heal the sick? Nothing at all if you consider their nature itself. Therefore, in themselves the means used by God add nothing to these miracles, or may even impede them, as with looking at the bronze serpent, the salt of Elisha, the water Elijah poured on the burnt offering, the clay that Christ put on the eyes of the blind.[29] Accordingly, when miracles occur through means like this, which do not help but rather hinder, the power and might of God is revealed more clearly.

To teach us that natural powers can do no more, Christ said to his mother at the wedding: "Woman, what have I to do with you?"[30] Not that he meant thereby to lessen the authority of his mother, but to show that the nature which he had taken from her was not in itself able to make him work miracles. Therefore, seeing that God uses both men and angels, good and bad, to do miracles, and that they are sometimes benefits and sometimes punishments by which people are either punished or helped, we need not doubt whether God punishes anyone through his good angels or not. For it is clear enough that Sodom was destroyed by angels; by an angel, the host of Sennacherib was slain; David saw the angel who was the agent of the plague against Israel.[31]

---

[28]Ex. 14:16; 17:6; Matt. 8:3; John 9:6.
[29]Num. 21:9; 2 Kings 2:21; 1 Kings 18:33ff.; John 9:6.
[30]John 2:4.
[31]Gen. 19:1–2.; 2 Kings 19:35; 2 Sam. 24:17.

8. Augustine, on Psalm 78, doubts whether through evil angels God has performed miracles by which people have received immediate benefit, and says that he has not read it in the Holy Scriptures.[32] Neither have I, unless we say that Paul benefited from being tormented by the angel of Satan. Or that he delivered some to Satan, so that their souls might be saved in the day of the Lord.[33] Yet Augustine's question does not refer to this, but to whether genuine and obvious benefits, such as gifts of healing, prophesying, tongues, food, freedom, and so on, are sometimes miraculously bestowed on the faithful by God through the devil. I think, like Augustine, that the Scriptures nowhere affirm any such thing. Yet it is apparent that the godly as well as the ungodly are tempted, punished, and molested by evil angels, but in various ways. For as Augustine says in the same place, there are in a sense two flocks of people, the bad and the good: the good are the flock of God, just as the wicked are the flock of the devil. The latter deals more freely against the wicked, as his own, harassing them, deluding and mistreating them, in his own right. But he cannot go beyond the prescribed measure allowed him by God. Against the flock of God he dare do nothing, except that God himself sometimes for various purposes gives him leave, as we see from Job. Otherwise, God allows the devout to be grievously afflicted by the devil, so that his grace should be more conspicuously extended towards them.

When Augustine expounds the words of the Psalm, "visitations through destroying angels,"[34] he doubts whether the plagues of the Egyptians were inflicted through a good angel or through the devil. At length he shows that the plague and destruction of the firstborn may be ascribed to the work of the devil, and that all the other plagues must be attributed to good angels, so that the words of the book of Exodus and of the Psalm may stand as they are. But concerning that plague of the firstborn, it is written in Exodus under the name of God: "In that night I will pass through Egypt, and will smite," etc.[35] These words seem to attribute that destruction either to God or to a good angel, not to the devil. But that does not impress me, for even if it were done by the ministry of the devil, yet the punishment can be ascribed to God. For when he was bereft of all his goods and children, Job said: "The Lord has given, and the Lord has taken away,"[36] and what was accomplished by the devil he said was done by God. Some will object that if we assign these things to the devil, he

---

[32] *Enarratio* in Ps. 77 (PL 36.1002).

[33] 2 Cor. 12:7; 1 Cor. 5:5.

[34] Ps. 78:49, "immissiones per angelos malos" (Vulgate); "a company of destroying angels" (RSV).

[35] Ex. 12:12.   [36] Job 1:21.

may seem to have fought against himself. For by the devil's help, the magicians withstood Moses when they did the same things as he. But if the plagues were sent against the Egyptians by evil angels and yet the sorcerers withstood them, then Satan seemed to resist Satan; nor could the sorcerers have truly said that they failed, and testified that it was the finger of God at work. In my judgment these things have no good ground because what the sorcerers did was accomplished by the power of Satan, which is natural for him. Through it he is able to apply the seeds of things and active causes to matter already prepared, and to work marvelous things so far as human sight is concerned. But those things by which God afflicted the Egyptians were done by his own supreme power, through the instrument of the devil. So it is no wonder if the sorcerers failed, and perceived the most excellent power of God's finger.

The book of Wisdom, chapter 18, seems to ascribe these plagues completely to God, where it says: "While everything was held in silence, and your almighty word," and so forth. And in the 17th chapter it is written that in the midst of those plagues, especially when they were oppressed with darkness, the Egyptians were greatly troubled with frightening mental images and terrible sights, as if the most fearful ghosts had been always before their eyes and within their phantasy; this could well happen at the instigation of evil angels, as the Psalm mentions.[37] Moreover, their heart was hardened, and every day their mind was more and more obstinate against the Israelites. That seems to refer to sendings by evil angels. So these two places can easily be reconciled [92r] by ascribing the plagues spoken of in Exodus to good angels, and the awesome sights and hardening of the heart to the sending of evil angels, which the Psalm in question mentions.

9. We have shown that God uses both good and evil angels as well as humans to work miracles; therefore, the faithful should not be offended because this power is not often given them. They are not for this reason any worse than others to whom the working of miracles is granted. The Lord said to his disciples when they returned from their mission: "Do not rejoice in this, that spirits are subject to you; but rejoice that your names are written in heaven."[38] There are some whose desire for these things in order to work signs is so great that they are not afraid even to use the help of the devil, and excuse themselves under the pretense that God himself uses Satan to work signs. In imitating God they say they do well, so far are they from confessing themselves guilty of any offense. Further, they say that Paul handed some people

---

[37]Wis. 17:2ff., 18:14–15, referring to Psalm 78:49.
[38]Luke 10:20.

over to be harassed by the devil and so they also may use his help.[39] But what sort are they, I ask you, who think it right to do as much as is proper for God? God is the author of all creatures and it is no wonder if he uses them all. But we are forbidden from doing so by the divine law. The imitation of God is commended to us, so long as we are forbidden the contrary by his law. Otherwise, he himself will revenge his wrongs. Who will say that it is lawful for ordinary people to do what God does? He used for his own sacrifice an animal intended for Baal, as we have heard, and took over for his own holocaust the wood dedicated to the same idol;[40] shall we all therefore eat things dedicated to idols? The rule of our life is the word of God. Therefore, to imitate him we must be led only so far as the law allows. He made that law not for himself but for men, that they should fashion their life according to it. Thus it was lawful for him to ask Abraham to sacrifice his son,[41] something none of us is allowed to require of a friend. Paul and other apostles had evil spirits subject to them, and through them they were sometimes permitted to punish the guilty for the sake of their salvation;[42] therefore, those to whom such a gift is not granted should abstain from its practice.

10. The use of the power of evil spirits is of two kinds: One is with authority, and that belongs chiefly to God; it also belonged to the Apostles and saints of the primitive church. The other consists of agreement and obedience, which is utterly forbidden to men. "For what fellowship can there be of light with darkness, and God with Belial?"[43] For this reason, Magi and whoever gives credence to them cannot be excused; rather, the Law condemns them as guilty of superstition and idolatry. We should know that God has forbidden these things for reasons of the highest justice and of the greatest benefit to us. He took care that we should not be deceived and in these ways run headlong to destruction. This is where pacts with Satan lead. For the devil is a liar, and the father of lies; and he is also a murderer, even from the beginning, as Christ has taught.[44] Therefore, let this be a sure saying, as it appears also in the Scholastics, in the second book of *Sentences*, distinction eight, and confirmed among them, especially Thomas and the ancient Fathers: That if we seek anything that transcends human power, we must ask it from God alone; those who do not, fall away as apostates from the faith, worshipping creatures instead of God.[45] I wish that both the old Fathers and the Scholastics had stuck with this—afterward forgetting themselves I know not how, they have now consented to the invocation of dead saints, and have instituted a sort of

[39]1 Cor. 5:4–5.   [40]Jud. 6:25.   [41]Gen. 22:1–2.
[42]1 Cor. 5:5.   [43]2 Cor. 6:14–15.   [44]John 8:44.
[45]Peter Lombard *Sent.* II.8.5 (PL 192.669).

exorcism for the bodies and relics of the dead. They enjoy no special gift of miracles, but command demons with the gravest threats and as much power as they can muster, begging the saints already dead to drive out evil spirits from those possessed as they are ordered; but demons do it not against their will, but pretend obedience in order to establish idolatry. It is no less pleasing for them to possess souls than to torment bodies. In *The City of God*, book 10, chapter 11, Augustine shows how Porphyry wrote to Anebos that certain sorcerers were so used to terrifying demons with threats that they said "If they would not do what they were ordered, they would crush heaven and earth together," to force them.[46] Who does not see here the devil's wiles, who pretends to be afraid of foolish incantations, so to speak? But we have dealt enough with these matters.

[MIRACLES AND FAITH]

11. It is best to return to the examination of the last part of our definition, in which it was said that miracles are performed for the confirmation of faith. It may seem a strong objection to this point that we should not believe miracles easily, since they may give occasion for error. From this we could draw a sure kind of argument, but quite dangerous; this is proved by many places. First, the Lord said in Matthew 24: "False prophets will in the latter days deceive men through signs so as to lead astray, if it were possible, even the elect." This sentence was handled more broadly by Paul to the Thessalonians.[47] Also we learn from the book of Exodus that we should not give credit to signs: For some time Pharaoh's magicians performed the very same things as Moses.[48] In Deuteronomy also, it is commanded that even though he works signs we should not believe a prophet if he draws people to idolatry.[49] Therefore, since miracles may be performed for the defence of false doctrine as well as true, they must not be judged proper [*93r*] to confirm our faith. In book 10, chapter 16, of *The City of God* Augustine wrote: "If angels require sacrifices to be made to them and work signs, and on the contrary if others declare that we must sacrifice to God alone yet work no miracles, we must believe these, and not the other." The same Augustine against Faustus, concerning the Manichees: "You work no signs that we should believe you, and if you were to do so, we still would not believe you."[50] So we should understand clearly that miracles are not sufficient to confirm faith. Above all, we must test

---

[46]Augustine *De civitate Dei* X.11.2 (PL 41.290): coelum se collidere comminatur.

[47]Matt. 24:24; 2 Thess. 2:9–10.

[48]Ex. 7:11. [49]Deut. 13:1–2.

[50]Augustine *De civitate Dei* X.16.1 (PL 41.294) and *Contra Faustum Man.* XXXII.8 (PL 42.507).

that doctrine which is brought forth by the witness of Holy Scripture; if it agrees, we must believe it even without signs. But if miracles are added, believers are confirmed the more, while those who have not yet believed are at least made more attentive, and the way is prepared for them to believe.

12. Miracles are also somewhat like sacraments; for both are added to promises like seals.[51] And just as miracles do not profit unless there is first a regard for doctrine, so likewise the sacraments bring no advantage but much harm unless they are received with sincere faith. Both serve to confirm faith, but neither is sufficient by itself. Doubtless those are blessed and surely to be honored, who believe without the help of miracles. Our Lord said: "Blessed are those who have not seen and yet believe."[52] Even so, confirmation by signs should not be denied. Perhaps you will ask: If they are so helpful in confirming faith, why did the Lord in Matthew, chapters 9 and 11 and other places, charge that they should not be made public?[53] There were many reasons: He wished his doctrine to be preached first, and miracles to follow afterward. But if he had permitted some whom he healed to proclaim what he had done right away, teaching would not have been joined with that announcement of the miracle, since they were not yet instructed in godliness. He did this also lest he seem to be gripped with a vain desire of worldly glory. By his own example he wished to drive us away from that very thing. Moreover, none knew better than he who they were that he healed. He would not let everyone publish and preach his deeds, and so he forbade many to do so. Further, he saw that the mere report of his miracles would not assure that the fickle and unsteady multitude would be led to accept a sincere faith; they would rather accord him worldly honors and advancement, which he himself had not sought. This is proved in John 6, where it is written that because the people had received loaves from him, they would have made him king.[54] Lastly, he would not stir up against himself the rage and envy of the high priests, the scribes and Pharisees, more than the time would bear. In Luke 9, when he had shown his Apostles a demonstration of his glory in the transfiguration, he commanded them not to make public at that time what they had seen. Asking what was thought about him, he obtained the truth from Peter, who declared him to be the son of God, and he charged that they should not tell others that Jesus was Messiah. For they were not yet well enough grounded to spread such things around, and be able to confirm it in argument by fitting testimonies. He

---

[51]Miracles and sacraments are related also in ROM 10:17: "Sacraments also are believed, but they are nothing else than the visible word of God, which is heard...." (LC 3.3.8). Cf. Martyr,*Tract. de Euch.* §§60ff. (DM 251ff.), for an attack on miracle as an argument for transubstantiation.

[52]John 20:29.   [53]Matt. 9:30, 11:25.   [54]John 6:25–26.

thought it best for them to wait until they were fully instructed. He did not wish the truth to be completely silenced, but chose the right time to begin. Thus from the fact that Christ sometimes forbade them to be published, it is not a proper conclusion that miracles are useless to confirm faith, since that commandment of the Lord referred only to choosing better occasions, not to perpetual silence.

13. Lastly, something else seems to qualify that part of the definition. It seems that faith cannot be confirmed by miracles, since they require faith and presuppose it. In Matthew 13, it is written that, because of the incredulity of his own people, Christ performed almost no miracles; Mark adds that he could not.[55] Therefore, it seems we should say rather that miracles are determined and established by faith, since if faith is not present, as the evangelists say, miracles cannot be done. I answer: Those who wish to obtain miracles by prayers must in the usual and proper manner be endowed with faith; for prayers that do not rest on faith are counted worthless. But if a miracle is given, nothing prevents the initial faith from being stirred up and confirmed. Moreover, we can be sure of this, that there is nothing to prevent God from giving miracles to unbelievers; indeed, he has often done so. Undoubtedly Pharaoh and the Egyptians were unbelievers—who does not know that many miracles were done to them by Moses? Likewise, Christ showed the miracle of his resurrection when everyone in a sense despaired of his doctrine and truth. Therefore, nothing prevents faith from being confirmed by miracles.

The reason just noted is why those who labor through prayer to obtain signs struggle in vain unless they have believed; for prayers without faith are of no value with God, as Christ plainly taught in Matthew 17.[56] When his disciples could not heal the disturbed child and he was asked for the reason, he said that it happened because of their unbelief.[57] This answer clearly shows how we are to judge these exorcists who endeavor to drive away devils at the sepulchres of the saints and their relics. Everything there is done falsely. The dead are called upon without faith and the devil makes alliance with idolaters, [93v] feigning to believe in order to maintain a deadly worship; this is obvious, because those exorcists, while quite impure, do all these things without faith.

Origen writes very well against this abuse, on Matthew 17. "If at any time," he says, "we are required to help such people, let us not converse with the spirit by exorcism or demand, as if he heard us; but let us simply persevere by giving ourselves to prayers and fastings."[58] He spoke these words when the

---

[55]Matt. 13:58, Mark 6:5.
[57]Mark 9:19, 29.

[56]Matt. 17:21.
[58]*Comm. in Matt.* XIII.7 (PG 13, 1111).

invocation of the dead and worship of relics were not practiced in the church—what would he say today if he could see the madness of our age? But to return to the chief point in doubt, I think that faith precedes miracles in those who effect them by prayers, but not those who stand by and have not yet believed the preaching which they have heard.[59]

14. Let us see how miracles may sometimes be done by evil men. For there are some who will say in the latter time: "Lord, have we not cast forth devils in thy name; have we not prophesied?" and so on. They will be answered: "Truly I say to you, I do not know you."[60] In working miracles, it seems clear that they used prayers, but lacking faith, were not justified, nor did they belong to the kingdom of God. So it does not seem a sure argument that prayers offered without faith are not heard. But we must note that evil men who have obtained miracles by prayers were not totally without faith. For we find that there are three kinds of faith.[61] The first is a faith that consists of human opinion and persuasion, by which those things written in the Holy Scriptures are believed to be no less true than the histories of Livy, Suetonius, and what is now written about new islands. On many points this kind of faith is common to both Turks and Jews.[62] There is another faith, through which we are inspired from heaven to assent to the promise of God's mercy actively and effectually. Our justification stands on this faith. Finally, the third is called the faith of miracles, by which we are neither changed nor made one hair better. For it is an impulse of the divine Spirit by which men are roused to look for miracles, believing implicitly that it is God's will that they should happen and that their search should be successful. While they hold to this faith, they sometimes obtain their request; I say this because they do not always do so, nor are they always enlightened by that inspiration.

If you ask how this kind of faith can be proved, let Chrysostom answer, who mentions it on Matthew 17. There Christ said, "If you have faith as a grain of mustard seed, you will say to this mountain, throw yourself into the sea, and it will be done."[63] In exposition this Father says: "Since these things do not happen in the church today, shall we therefore say that Christians are

---

[59]Cf. ROM 10:17: "Miracles are like witnesses by which men are more easily led to believe."
[60]Matt. 7:21–22.
[61]Cf. ROM 3:22 on kinds of faith (LC 3.3.1).
[62]Cf. COR 13:3: "Many Turks acknowledge many things that we believe, such as the creation of the world, the resurrection of the dead, and that Christ was born of the virgin Mary. Nevertheless, we will never count them to be endowed with true faith"; LC 3.3.26. Martyr is harsher toward Jewish religion: they maintain the Scriptures but read them in an unspiritual way, so that only in "an earthly and carnal manner" are they to be considered within the covenant; LC 2.4.46ff.
[63]A blending of Matt. 17:20 and 21:21.

without faith? God forbid that we should judge the people of God so harshly. Justifying faith is present, but what is called faith in miracles has already ceased."[64] This kind of faith is also shown by the words of the Apostle, in first Corinthians: "If I have all faith, so as to remove mountains, but have not love, I am nothing." It should not trouble us that he says "all," for its scope is to be applied to faith in miracles. This is clearly seen in the twelfth chapter of the same letter, where the Apostle refers to free and acceptable gifts, saying, "To one is given the utterance of wisdom, to another that of knowledge, to another the power of healing, to another the gift of faith by the same spirit," and so on.[65] In this passage, faith cannot be understood to be the same as that by which we are justified. For it is not counted among the gifts that are privately distributed to some, but is common to all Christians. Now I think it is clear how those who are not yet justified might sometimes obtain miracles by their prayers, namely, because they do not lack every kind of faith. This should be sufficient on the first question.

[WHETHER MIRACLES ARE TO BE SOUGHT]

15. Now let us see whether it is proper for the faithful to desire miracles. This is asserted for reasons that may seem to count against it. First, that by it God would be tempted, something the divine law utterly forbids. Moreover, our Savior responded to the devil with this answer: "You shall not tempt the Lord your God."[66] The Hebrews are blamed for the fact that they tempted God in the desert. When the Pharisees said: "Master, we wish to see a sign from you," the Son of God said, "An evil and adulterous generation seeks for a sign, but no sign shall be given to it," etc.[67] Also Ahaz, otherwise an evil king, pretended a display of righteousness, saying that he would not tempt God, and therefore deferred asking for a sign.[68] My answer to the question is that in one sense it is proper to seek a sign, and in another it is not. The first part of the sentence is thus proved: The faithful seek greater assurance of the will of God concerning some new vocation, but are afraid of being deceived, finding nothing positive about it in Holy Scriptures. For them, neither men nor angels are to be believed hastily, since evil angels often transform themselves into angels of light. In this perplexity, with the will prepared and anxious to obey the commandment of God, the faithful cannot be accused either of tempting God or of rashness if they wish to be confirmed by some sign. For in such cases whoever seeks things that God usually offers does no wrong.

[64]A paraphrase of *In Matt. Hom.* LVII–LVIII.3 (PG 58, 562).
[65]1 Cor. 13:2, 12:8–9.   [66]Matt. 4:7.
[67]Matt. 16:1–2.   [68]Isa. 7:10ff.

Everyone knows that Ahaz was offered a sign by Isaiah so that [*94r*] he might be assured of the promises made to him. Therefore, to seek what God himself sometimes gives and freely offers should not be prohibited. There is no shortage of examples: Whenever Moses needed God's help in the wilderness, he often obtained miracles for the people of God. To confirm the truth of the doctrine, both Elijah and Elisha petitioned God that life might be restored to the children of their hosts.[69] To the same end Christ said: "But that you may know that the Son of man has power to forgive sins," he turned to the paralytic and said, "Rise, take up your bed and walk."[70] Thus miracles are rightly desired by the devout so that they may be made more certain of their vocation, or else some great and urgent need may be met, or a testimony of sound doctrine given. Whenever they seek miracles for these purposes it is not from any creatures, but God alone; and in asking they use a standard, for they declare that they choose or desire nothing except what is agreeable to the will of God.

16. On the other side, let us consider how signs are sought unworthily and unjustly. First, some want miracles because they are not truly persuaded of God's power, goodness, and providence; they wish only to experiment with those things. Nor do they rest on scriptural doctrine, which plainly and clearly teaches us all things. They are rightly rebuked, since they are more ready to give credit to miracles than to the word of God. The rich man was tormented in the flames of fire and wanted Lazarus sent to his brothers lest they too should be cast into the same punishment; he was answered by Abraham: "They have Moses and the prophets."[71] These words plainly declared that we should believe the Holy Scriptures rather than miracles. There are others who desire miracles so that they can enjoy the flesh more sweetly and satisfy their lusts. The Hebrews are accused of this fault, because when an abundance of manna was served them in the desert, they wanted meat so that they might live more comfortably in that wilderness. Finally, some want miracles to satisfy empty curiosity. For as Pliny says, "Human nature is greediest over novelties."[72] Therefore, it seems that they wished to use signs as pastimes for their amusement. In this way Herod expected miracles from Christ.[73] For when he was brought to him, Herod desired to feed and delight his curiosity with strange signs. Now I hope it is clear what kind of signs is forbidden, and that it is sometimes lawful to seek them.

[69]1 Kings 17:17ff.; 2 Kings 4:18ff.   [70]Matt. 9:6.

[71]Luke 16:19–20.

[72]*Natura hominum avidissima novitatis*; Pliny the Elder *Naturalis Historia* bk. 12.11.6: *natura hominum novitatis avida*.

[73]Luke 23:8.

17. Here we should explain those matters that seemed to refute us. Those who seek miracles according to the manner and form [modo et ratione] we have described do not tempt God in any way, because to tempt God is nothing else than to make trial of his will and his power with a rash and unbelieving heart. This vice is rightly and worthily condemned in Holy Scripture. Not without reason did the Lord Jesus Christ repel the devil, who tried to persuade him to throw himself down from the temple to gain greater assurance of God's favor toward him, when human reason could easily perceive another way of descending. Again, quite rightly did the Son of God condemn the Jews as an evil and adulterous generation, who were denied a sign.[74] For they had already seen many and yet scoffed at them all, mocking Christ, not wishing just any miracle but one from heaven, as though they would not have derided signs from heaven as well. Their intention sought no other end than to alienate God's people from the Lord, although he had accomplished great miracles. But as for Ahaz, the evil king, not much needs to be said. For when called by the prophet, he pretended to believe most faithfully, as if he required no miracle at all, even though he was quite skeptical. This is plainly shown in the second book of Kings; he sent to Tiglathpileser, king of the Assyrians, to deliver him from the siege, so far was he from trusting in the Lord.[75] And when God, who was not ignorant of his disease, offered him the remedy of a miracle and gave him a choice, he refused through hypocrisy. If Ahaz had truly believed God, he would not have refused to obey, since obedience is counted among the chief fruits of faith.

I ask you to compare this evil king with his son Hezekiah, a most godly prince. He did not act in this way: To be more assured of recovering his health, he modestly required a sign. When Isaiah offered him the option whether he would have the shadow of the sun advanced or turned backward, he chose as he thought good, not rashly refusing the miracle offered him by God, as his father did.[76] But the evil Ahaz added hypocrisy to his unbelief. He saw that miracles are denied for two reasons, either because someone openly believes in God and does not need the help of miracles, or else because he detests God totally and wants nothing that is based on his work. He wished to hide the latter sickness from which he suffered, namely contempt of God. He pretended to have the virtue which he entirely lacked, a solid faith, as though he dare not tempt God. But since God knows our hearts and minds thoroughly, [94v] he punished him by the prophet as he deserved. What else is

[74]Matt. 16:4.
[75]2 Kings 16:7; see §15, p. 194, above.
[76]2 Kings 20:8ff.; Isa. 38:7–8.

it to refuse a miracle offered by God but to reject what would help our spiritual infirmity? Someone near starvation who refuses bread is to be accused; even so was he to be reproved who rejected the medicine God offered him, since God knows far better than ourselves what each of us needs. This is now enough on those matters from the beginning of this question that seemed to forbid asking for any miracles.

18. I know there are some who think that miracles should not be sought in any way, only that they should not be refused when God offers them. They support Augustine, who agrees with them in book 4 of *The Consent of the Evangelists*, and in question 63 on Genesis, where he seems to affirm this.[77] But if one objects that many faithful and righteous men have done so, especially our Gideon, they answer that they were moved by the Spirit of God to seek miracles, so it was the same as if God had offered them signs as something extra, and they obeyed and received the miracles offered. But these things should not trouble us because in the places cited Augustine does not flatly and absolutely forbid desire for miracles, unless they are sought either to tempt God or for some other evil cause. In question 63 on Genesis, he says: "When this is not done rightly, it amounts to tempting God." Let us rather hear what he says in book 10 of *The Confessions*, chapter 35. "In religion also it is tempting God when signs and miracles are sought in order to make a test."[78] I also issued this warning earlier. I freely grant that the righteous sought miracles not by impulse of the flesh or human reason, for then their prayers would have been vain and fruitless, since as Paul testifies it is necessary for the Spirit to pray for us with inexpressible sighing.[79] But now I think that enough has been said on the questions proposed.[80]

---

[77]Augustine *De consensu Evang.* IV.5.6 (PL 34.1219), and *Quaest. in Hept.* I.63 (PL 34.564).
[78]*Conf.* 10.xxxv (55) (PL 32.802).
[79]ROM 8:26.
[80]This ends the scholium in IUD (fol. 94v); Masson's LC adds two further sections from ROM 15:18.

Commentary on 2 Samuel 16

Whether God Is the Author of Sin

1. *[275r]* Now it remains to consider the question whether God is the author of sin. Both the cursing of Shimei and the defiling of David's concubines[1] may seem at first glance to come from God. David himself said that the curse came from God, while the adultery of David's concubines was proclaimed by Nathan in the person of God.[2] Therefore, we may well raise the question whether God can be the cause of sin. There are indeed many valid arguments for both sides. I will review a good part of them, to which all others may be referred.[3]

[1] 2 Sam. 16:5–14, 20–23, the passages interpreted just before the scholium. David has fled Jerusalem after Absalom's revolt; Shimei curses him, but David says: "Let him alone, and let him curse; for the Lord has bidden him" (v. 11). It is said of Ahithophel, who urged Absalom to take David's concubines for himself: "Now in those days the counsel which Ahithophel gave was as if one consulted the oracle of God" (v. 23).

[2] 2 Sam. 12:11.

[3] Marginal numbers identify twenty-five arguments in defense of the thesis that God is not the author or cause of sin (§§1–2); §§3–4 identify opposing arguments; the first set are repeated with commentary in §§25–27, the second in §§28–34. There is some inconsistency in the numbering and some discrepancy between LC and CP; I have footnoted my rearrangement below. Other marginalia are used to mark chief divisions of the treatise.

The scholium *An Deus Sit Author Peccati* is from *In duos Libros Samuelis Prophetae …Commentarii doctissimi. …* (Zurich: C. Froschauer, 1564), 2 Sam. 16:22, fols. 275r–285r; LC 1:14, CP 1.17,1–37.

[ARGUMENTS THAT GOD IS NOT THE CAUSE OF SIN]

God cannot truly and rightly be said to be the cause of sin. [1] Augustine's sentence in his book of eighty-three questions is excellent: "God is not the author of anything by which a man becomes worse; but no one doubts that men are worse through sin; therefore, God cannot properly be called the author of sin."[4] It is unlikely that God will deform man; artists seek to adorn their works. [2] Further, God always declares himself a punisher of sins. If he is punisher he is not author, for then he would punish his own. If he were truly the cause of sin, he should condemn what he has made, which is absurd. [3] Thirdly, it is said that he loves those things which he made, and hates nothing that he has made.[5] But he acknowledges that he hates sin, therefore he does not encourage sinning. To hate and to love are contrary; both cannot be spoken of something at the same time. If he hates sin then he does not love it; but if it came from God it should be loved, for God loves the things he has made. [4] If God were the cause of sin, he would sin in producing sins. Whoever steals is a thief; whoever commits murder is a murderer. But far be it from God that he should be said to sin or to be a sinner: what else is sin but to stray from the right end? But God is infinite, and cannot be diverted from his purpose by some other greater force. Nor is he ignorant, so that he can stray from the goal, for he is most wise. That he himself should cause others to sin seems absurd.

[5] Let us consider what happens among these natural things created by God. There are many efficient causes; it seems that every efficient cause seeks to make the object of its work like itself. If fire takes hold of wood, it works so that what it works on becomes like itself; man gives birth to man. So agents work in things created—why shouldn't we say that in God's doings, his aim is to make them resemble himself? Therefore he does not sin. The Holy Scriptures teach us the same: they bring in laws that stir up good works, but never sins. [6] If God were to incite to sin, or will it to be done, he would look like a hypocrite; he would do in a hidden and secret way something other than he pretends openly. [7] Jeremiah spoke of false prophets: "I did not send the prophets, yet they ran; I did not speak to them, yet they prophesied," that they should say this word.[6] [8] Hosea said: "Your salvation, O Israel, comes from me, your ruin from yourself."[7] But everyone knows that sin is the cause of

---

[4]Augustine *De diversis quaestionibus LXXXIII*, Q. 1.III (PL 40.11).

[5]Cf. Aquinas SCG I.96, "That God Hates Nothing…"; *Book of Common Prayer*, Ash Wednesday Collect: "Almighty and everlasting God, who hatest nothing that thou hast made…." Calvin *Inst.* III.24.17, agrees, but "I maintain still … that the reprobate are hated by God."

[6]Jer. 23:21.   [7]Hosea 13:9, 14:1 ff.

damnation. If ruin comes from Israel, then sin also. But salvation, along with whatever goes before it, comes from God. If the effects of salvation and damnation are distinguished like this, so must the causes, one from God and the other from man. Sin will proceed from men *[275v]* and virtues from God. [9] What is written in John 8 is even clearer, where Christ spoke of the devil. "When he lies, he speaks according to his own nature";[8] if it is on his own, he does not need to be stirred up by another. [10] Again, "This is the judgment, that the light has come into the world, and men loved darkness rather than light."[9] [11] James asserts that God tempts no one.[10] Through temptation men are provoked to sin; if God were the cause of sin, we could not say that he tempts no one. It is lust [concupiscentia] that tempts us, and that is not from God, but from the world.

2.[12] In the last chapter of 2 Chronicles there is a specific place where the cause of the destruction of Jerusalem is given, and ascribed to the sins of the people. God is denied to be the author of sin so much that he declares that he wished that things were different. Hence the cause must not be ascribed to God. "He sent his prophets to them persistently," it says, "but they hardened their heart."[11] [13] Christ wept over the city of Jerusalem; he was sorry for its overthrow.[12] If the effect displeased him, much more the cause; he wept because they sinned and so deserved utter destruction. If Christ mourned, being not only human but also truly divine, he was displeased with its sins; therefore God is not the author of sin. [14] We cannot affirm that God is the cause of sin unless we charge him with tyranny, in that he condemns people for their sins because they have done evil, whom in one sense he has led into evil. It is common for tyrants to enact laws and then devise ways for their subjects to break them, so that they may punish them. [15] Scripture attributes to God judgment over all flesh; how can he judge the world of sin, if he himself were its author? In chapter 3 to the Romans: If our wickedness reflects the divine purpose, is God unjust for being angry?[13] We can see how absurd it is that our sins should witness to the glory of God. For if so, why does he condemn them? If this is good reasoning, this passage makes it even stronger: if God is the cause of sin, how will he judge the world? [16] It will also seem that he has two wills in mutual contradiction. But in God there is only one will. If there were more they would fight each other on every point, so that he would have us do and not do the same things. We ask: why are there so many exhortations, appeals and callings to do well in the Holy Scriptures? They all seem

---

[8]John 8:44.   [9]John 3:19.   [10]James 1:13.
[11]2 Chron. 36:15ff.   [12]Matt. 23:37.   [13]Rom. 3:5.

to be vain. Why did Christ warn Judas, if he wished to be betrayed by him? These sayings would seem to be done in a sort of game; but in his dealings with men God is serious and earnest. [18] A great absurdity would follow, for the differences between good and evil and between virtue and sin would be removed. God would be appointed author of both; whereas being the highest good [summum bonum] nothing but goodness can come from him. If one detests murder, adultery, and incest, he would say it is a good work. Things would come to such a state that good would be called evil and evil good; there would be in fact no difference whatever between them. For through the will of God, by which he forbids and commands any thing, we judge between good and evil; but in this case we would lose all judgment [κριτήριον].

[19] Similarly, the judgments of our consciences would be removed. We read in Romans that we have thoughts that defend and accuse one another in the judgment day of the Lord.[14] If this other opinion were true, we should not accuse ourselves but God the author. [20] There is no end of excuse for the wicked. They will say: why should I repent of this, seeing its author is God himself? [21] Repentance will be taken away and a window opened to great evils. [22] Why should we give thanks to God for delivering us from our sins? Sin was good; we could well have stayed in sin. We will not lament over sins, but rather rejoice, for it is the work of God. [23] It is fitting to celebrate the works of God. If God himself is the author of sin, praise and rejoicing will follow, not sorrow. [24] Much will be drawn away from the honor of God, if he should be hailed as author of sin. [25] They introduce a saying that might also be brought forth, namely that God would have all men to be saved.[15] If he will have them to be saved, he uses good means; he does not encourage men to sin, for sins lead to perdition. Many more reasons might be brought, but meanwhile we rest content with these.

[OPPOSING ARGUMENTS: THAT GOD IS THE CAUSE OF SIN]

3. Let us see on the other side what might claim that God is the cause of sin. [1] In Romans 1 it is written: "Those idolaters who knew God and did not honor him as God, he gave over to a depraved sense and to shameful passions."[16] If he gave them, he provoked and moved them. [2] It is written in Exodus that God had hardened and dulled Pharaoh's heart, so that he would not listen when Moses commanded him in God's name to let the people depart.[17] [3] In Isaiah 6 he is said to blind the people, that they should not

---

[14]Rom. 2:15–16.   [15]1 Tim. 2:4.
[16]Rom. 1:21–26.   [17]Exod. 9:13.

see.[18] [4] When we pour out our prayers before God, we ask, "Lead us not into temptation, but deliver us from evil."[19] Why pray like this if such things never occur? No one asks for something unless it can happen or hangs over his head, or he fears it will come about. They hold that God does and wills these things, not as sins, but insofar as they are punishments to chasten the sinner. Now it is hard to count punishment and fault to be identical, since the nature of punishment and fault is different [diversa ratio poenae et culpae]. Fault arises from the will, punishment is laid upon us against our will. If taken on voluntarily it is not punishment. Affirming something to be both voluntary and involuntary can hardly be reconciled.[20] [5] The cause of a cause may also be called the cause of its effect. No one doubts that God gives us a will, inclinations, qualities, and effects by which we are provoked to sin. If God is said to be the cause of these things, why do we shrink from saying that he is the cause of sins? [6] Whatever removes obstacles will be called the cause, if the event occurs afterwards or the effect follows.[21] What chiefly prevents sins? Grace and the good Spirit of God: unless they restrain us, we will rush headlong into the worst crimes. Who can remove grace or take away the Spirit except God alone who gave them? If he removes obstacles, he is surely a kind of cause of sins. [7] Also, someone who assists [subministrat] anything by chance seems to be its author. Even if not the leading cause, if he gives opportunity he will not fail to be called author. God knew the hardness of Pharaoh's heart, that unless helped by the Spirit he would be provoked to sin. So the law is said to increase sin, unless it is proposed to the regenerate.[22] We always incline to what is forbidden and covet what is denied. God commands him to let the people go; what is this but to offer occasion to become more hardened? We cannot deny that God assists us on occasion. [8] Not only does he give opportunity; we can also show commandments by which he orders sin. In the history of Kings we have it that Ahab was evil; God decided to punish him in battle. He would have him brought to this by the flatteries and false encouragement of pseudo-prophets. God is introduced talking with spirits: "Who will entice Ahab?" An evil spirit came forward, saying "I will be a lying spirit in the mouth of the false prophets." God approved and ordered it: "Do so." He gave encouragement: "It will be so."[23]

---

[18]Isa. 6:10.   [19]Matt. 6:13.

[20]Cf. Martyr, ETH III.1 (LC 2.2.41).

[21]On *causa removens prohibens*, see CSV 119–120; Donnelly provides an excellent commentary on the whole treatise, CSV 116–23. Cf. ST Ia.Q.19.12 co: removens prohibens dicitur movens per accidens.

[22]Rom. 7:1ff.   [23]1 Kings 22:19–23.

[9] Further, we cannot deny that sin is a kind of human action; every act as act depends on the first principle of all things. God is *primus actus*, as the philosophers acknowledge.[24] Unless he sustains it there can be no act; therefore sin depends on God as upon the efficient cause. Sins are mostly motions; motions have an order, the inferior depending on the superior; therefore the cause of sin, so far as it is a motion, is directed to its own mover. [10] Augustine has certain teachings on this point, and also confirms it by some scriptural passages. In his book *On Grace and Free Will* chapter 21, he says that God truly works in men's minds making their wills incline either to good according to his mercy or to evil according to their merits, by his judgment which is sometimes open, sometimes secret, but always just.[25] In the beginning of that chapter he says: "Who does not tremble at these horrible judgments of God, by which he works what he will in the hearts of the wicked, rendering to each according to his merits?" And he adds, "Truly he works in the hearts of men the motions of their will, and through them does what he wishes to do, who nevertheless cannot will any thing unjustly." He proves this by the Scriptures. [11] In 1 Kings we have the history of Rehoboam, who did not heed the counsel of the elders that he should deal gently with the people. It is said that this refusal was from the Lord, that he might confirm the saying of Ahijah the Shilonite.[26] As Augustine interprets it, that evil will came from the Lord. He notes another place, from 2 Chronicles 21. God stirred up the Philistines and Arabs against Jehoram, who pursued idolatry; God wished to punish him.[27] Certainly the minds of the Philistines and Arabians intended evil against Jehoram; they invaded other countries and behaved cruelly; yet God is said to have stirred them up. In the same history of Kings, Amaziah is dealt with, who provoked the king of Israel to battle.[28] Jehoash himself, as well as the prophets of the Lord, tried to dissuade him from his purpose. But because of his ambition he did not heed the righteous admonitions even though they came from God, who wished him to be delivered into his hands because he followed the idols of Edom.

4. [12] In Ezekiel 14 we read: "If the prophet is deceived, I have deceived him; and I will stretch out my hand and strike him."[29] He treats of false proph-

---

[24] Aristotle *Meta.* XII.6.1071b20, XII.7.1072b27.
[25] Augustine *De gratia et libero arbitrio* 43 (xxi) (PL 44.909). This treatise is a major source for Martyr's scholium. Augustine deals specifically with the Samuel passage in chapter 41 (xx).
[26] 1 Kings 11:29, 12:15.
[27] 2 Chron. 21:16–17; Augustine *De gratia et libero arbitrio* 42 (xxi).
[28] 2 Kings 14:8–10; cf. 2 Chron. 25:17–19.
[29] Ezek. 14:9.

ets, who constantly duped the people. [13] Jeremiah 4 says that the Lord deceived his people.[30] [14] In Isaiah 63 the prophet complains: "Why has God made the people to err and withdrawn himself, that they should depart from him?"[31] [15] Solomon says in his Proverbs: "The king's heart is a stream of water in the hand of God."[32] Pharaoh was indeed a king, and so turned his heart wherever he wished. Nebuchadnezzar was a king; therefore, he inclined his will in whatever direction he chose. [16] Psalm 104 says of the Egyptians that God bent their hearts so that they hated the children of Israel.[33] Before that they seemed to love the Israelites. In 2 Thessalonians 2: "Because men refused to love the truth, God sent them a strong delusion, to make them believe what is false."[34] [17] It is written in Joshua 11 that among all the nations of the Canaanites none made peace with the children of Israel except the Gibeonites. For God strengthened them to fight against the Israelites; the aim was to destroy them. They were encouraged to desire war and not peace.[35]

[18] We see that whoever has a purpose wills whatever promotes it; the same will chooses those means that seek the goal. Wishing to heal a sick man, the doctor sees that cutting or cauterizing, or else a bitter potion is in order, and uses them for healing. When God wished for a witness to the truth to be given by the martyrs, and that Christ should die, he chose those things that would produce this end, namely the affliction of the saints and the cruelty of kings and people. For it was fitting to attain that end by such means. [19] In the prophets, especially Isaiah, kings are said to be in the hand of God like rods, hammers, and axes;[36] these analogies do not hold unless it is understood that God moves the hearts, for they are not moved unless they are driven. [20] When God was angry with the people of Israel, as became clear later, he directed the heart of David to number that people by census, which was wrong. It matters little if you say that according to Chronicles, Satan provoked him, for Satan can do no more than God allows.[37] Whether God did it by himself or through Satan, you see that David was aroused by the will of God to what was unlawful. The usual excuse is that God permits but does not help. We say this is not enough, for the offense remains in our minds. [21] God still seems to will sin in some sense; he knows that men cannot stand by themselves. Suppose a blind man walks in front of us, and we see him about to stumble on a stone or fall into the ditch—we are there and could help him, but we choose not to, we allow him to go on; when he falls, won't we be counted in some way guilty of his fall? For you chose to have him fall if you did not pre-

---

[30]Jer. 4:10.   [31]Isa. 63:17.   [32]Prov. 21:1.
[33]Ps. 105:25.   [34]2 Thess. 2:10–11.   [35]Josh. 11:19–20.
[36]Isa. 10:5, 15.   [37]2 Sam. 24:1; 1 Chron. 21:1.

vent him when you could. What is still more serious: if an old and helpless man were leaning on his stick in order to proceed, and if someone removed the stick on which he leaned, even though he did not make him fall, wouldn't he in a sense be called author of the fall? God takes his Spirit away from the weak, who without it cannot continue; does he not in some way seem to be the cause of their fall? So they offer a weak defense when they say that God forsakes men. While we seem to be excusing God, we are charging him with more serious matters, namely that he is not more fully God; and while we avoid the smoke we fall into the fire. If anything happens outside God's will, against his will, if it has any effects of which he is not the cause, then he is not the universal cause of all, nor is he God. Yet he compels no one to fall; the excuse will not do.

[22] Imagine a father whose family behaves itself badly: if he is reproved he will excuse himself, saying, "I did not order them." Such an excuse cannot be considered sufficient, for he should not permit something he could have prevented. Often the father cannot prevent crimes; but the power of God is invincible. There are no wills so evil and corrupt that he cannot make good. [23] In his book *The Fall of the Devil*, chapter 91, Anselm asks: why do we count it absurd that God does particular actions through an evil will, since we know that he makes some things that are produced through dishonest action? As when a child is procreated by adultery: no one doubts that adultery is evil, yet the child is a creature of God.[38] [24] This seems to be affirmed twice in the Acts of the Apostles. In chapter 2 Peter says of Jesus the Son of God, that the Jews had taken him and delivered him to be killed by the deliberate will and counsel of God. Afterward in chapter 4, when the church gave thanks to God, it prayed in this way: Pilate, Herod, Gentiles, and the people of Israel gathered themselves together against your holy son Jesus, to do those things your hand and counsel had determined to be done.[39] I will be content for now with these arguments, to which others could be added.

[THE QUESTION AT ISSUE]

5. After setting down the reasons for each part, we should expound the question itself. I find three opinions. The first is detestable, namely that of the Libertines, who say that God is completely the cause of sin.[40] They affirm that

---

[38]Anselm *De Casu Diaboli* chap. XX [sic] (PL 158.351–352).

[39]Acts 2:23, 4:27ff.

[40]Cf. Calvin, *Contre la secte phantastique et furieuse des Libertins qui se nomment Spirituelz* (1545) 14ff. on the "consequences that follow from saying that God does everything"; B.W. Farley, trans. and ed., *Treatises against the Anabaptists and against the Libertines* (Grand Rapids: Baker Book House, 1982).

all sins are excusable and not to be reproved, because they are the works of
God. If there is any fault they charge it to God. They seek one thing, to
remove the feeling of sin from everyone. If anyone has committed murder,
they say that it is not he that has done it, but God. And unless one thinks like
this, they claim he is imperfect and cannot accept the divine works. Can anything more profane be imagined? The devil could not have discovered an
easier road to hell. Since we cannot correct them, let us commit them to the
worst: let us pray to God to remove these pests from the church. The second
opinion comes from some learned men, who do not reject that sense which
the Scriptures appear to have at first glance. They say that God hardens, that
he punishes sins with sins; in the end they concede that he is the cause of sin.
But they add that since these acts proceed from corrupt human nature, insofar
as they are from God they have to do with justice—men are not excused
because they are inclined to them; they do not blame God, who does his part
rightly. They observe that if we cannot comprehend by reason how he does
justly and we unjustly, we must rest in the judgment of Scripture. There are
many other things that human reason cannot know, which we yet believe. The
third opinion is of those who interpret all these places of Scripture by the
words: he allowed or permitted, or as the Greek puts it, "did not prevent it"
[ἔασε, ἀρίν], and so on. In this way they think all dangers are avoided.

6. I am willing to declare my own opinion; afterward you may judge for
yourself. It is worth examining the matter more deeply, so that it may be
better understood. I will say something about evil, the genus under which sin
is included. Evil is a lack [privatio], I mean of goodness; not of all goodness
but of such a good as is required for the perfection of the creature, which I say
belongs to the perfection of the subject that is corrupted.[41] If we take sight
away from a stone, it receives no injury, for that quality of nature does not
apply. As a privation, evil cannot exist without good, for it must have a subject. Since a subject is a substance [natura], it is good; so evil can exist only in
some good—blindness is a deprivation of sight; it does not hang in the air, but
stays in the eye. This may be shown by many other examples. But not to
depart from the matter in hand: sin itself deprives human action of honor and
obedience towards the word of God. This should be an activity, but when we
sin, action is robbed of that good. Seeing that action is a certain substance, it
is in its own nature good; therefore, evil cannot exist except in the good.

---

[41]ad rei absolutionem quae spoliatur. Privation is the lack of a quality or form, a change that
is incidental or *per accidens*. Aristotle introduced the concept in *Physica* 192a3; cf. *Categoria* 12a26 ff.,
and the commentary of Aquinas in *i Phys.* 13.3–4; Lombard *Sent.* II, dist. 35.10: privatio vel corruptio boni.

Moreover, evil is not desired for itself, but men sin in relation to the good; for unless there appeared some likeness of good, they would not run from goodness.[42] So great is the power of the good, that evil can exist only in the good and tending towards it. Accordingly, the wise have said something which we accept, that there is a highest good, but we could not assert a highest evil that would completely deny goodness. For in that case it would destroy itself: it would have no subject in which to exist, nor any image [species] to be desired. [*277r*]

Turning to the subject of evil: It is distinguished into punishment and fault. Fault is called that which we commit against the law of God; punishment is that which afflicts us on account of sin, involving the absence of former goodness. When God sends sickness it is a loss of health and occurs in the body of a living creature. He sends famine and sterility, which is the lack of fertility and is in the earth itself; I say that this belongs to punishment. But sin takes place in the mind only; punishments doubtless may be in both mind and body. A third item is added, namely punishment of such a kind that it is also sin. There is original sin, and so a natural corruption remains after baptism.

Now that these matters are concluded, I present an assertion or proposition to be proved, in two parts. The first is, *that God is not by himself and properly [per se et proprie] the cause of sin*; second, *nothing happens in the world, not even sins themselves, without his will and choice or providence*.[43]

7. To prove the question, we must confirm it in regard to both parts. Let us speak of the first: that by himself God is not the cause of sin. The arguments of the previous section serve this purpose. But I add: when good and evil are opposed, as property and its absence, the property by itself never leads to absence. Light by itself always illuminates, it never causes darkness. Therefore if we put good and evil as opposing privations, evil will not come from good. God is the highest good; let us then put him as the property; thus by himself and properly he makes no privation. But I said that he is not the cause of sin by himself and properly. I have added these words because, if we speak less properly, he may be said in some sense to be either the beginning or the cause of sin; not indeed the proper cause, but what philosophers term removing or prohibiting.[44] Let me explain by similes. The sun is completely light; its proper effect is to illuminate, yet in one sense it may be said to darken, not

---

[42]Aristotle *NE* 1.1.1094a2: everything "aims at some good." Cf. Aquinas *SCG* I.81: "the good understood is the proper object of the will"; and §24 below.

[43]Italics added.

[44]See p. 219, n. 21.

insofar as it shines but as it is moved and travels from one place to another. For bodies are round, so that as it moves it cannot by its motion continue to supply light to that place from which it goes, but shadows enter; so then in a way it is said to make things dark by its departure, since bodies are so disposed and it is itself moved.

Something similar happens with a ruined house that is propped up; someone comes and removes the support, and the stones and building fall down from the top through their own weight. They have the causes of their falling in themselves; yet whoever takes the prop away is said to cause the fall in some way, because he removes the support that prevented the ruin. So in his own nature God is good, but insofar as he is just, he will punish sinners, he removes grace, and in a sense may be called the cause of those things which afterward may be termed evil. Not the true cause — that proper cause is inward, that is their evil will. But a reason may be given why he sometimes takes his Spirit from men. He removes his grace from sinners not only as a punishment, but so that the greatness of his favor may be known, and we may understand that what God gives, he gives freely, it is not from nature. For if we always possessed it in the same way, as if God would never let go his power, we would credit our own strength with the good things that we do. This is the case so that we may acknowledge our weakness and pray more earnestly for the continuance and increase of the heavenly gift. When divine grace and favor are rightfully removed from us, sin naturally follows; we need no other efficient cause; I mean, no other cause is required apart from our infected and corrupt affections.

This is seen in the similes we brought. If the sun is removed, darkness follows, not through any efficient cause but by itself. If a property is removed, privation is immediately present on its own. If one hurts his eye so that the sight is lost, blindness follows at once. You need not look for some other agent. Since the Manichees did not grasp the point, they went most shamefully astray. They would not attribute the cause of evil to the good God, but seeing that there are many evils, and judging that evils could not exist without a genuine cause, they posited two first principles. They saw great power in both evil and good, introducing two gods, one good, the other bad. We read at length of these in Augustine.[45] But the evil which is sin arises when the Spirit of God is removed, for then man is left to himself. But is he left so that God no longer does anything about him or his sin? To understand this I will outline three kinds of action that we see in God towards his creatures; not that

---

[45]Augustine *Contra Faustum Manichaeum* XXI.2 (PL 42.387–388).

other works of his cannot be identified, but because these three serve best for the matter in hand.

8. Some acts of God are general, since by his providence he nurtures, sustains, and governs all things in their conditions, qualities, and tendencies, as they stood at the beginning when they were created. So the order of nature is upheld, an excellent point to be known. We see that heaven retains its own nature; surely it has much to be marveled at. We see that the nature of fire is intense, of air is pleasant, that water flows; we see also metals, trees, the works of artists—surely such things are wonders. All are governed by God; if he should withdraw his hand from them, they would fall to nothing. It is quite clear that reflection on his divine government is of benefit. God often exhorts us in the Psalms to praise him for these works. In Romans 1 it is written that the Gentiles knew God through these creatures, something of his eternal power, activity, governance, and godhead.[46] As Aratus said, "We are indeed the offspring of God."[47] We have an excellent example of this work in ourselves. The invisible soul is indivisible, yet it moves [*277v*] and quickens the whole body. Even so do all creatures retain their purposes and properties.

9. Second, there is another work of God by which everything is not only preserved and ruled, but submits to the divine will as well. For God uses the actions of all things, including men, even if they are evil; he uses them to establish his purposes. When he favors his own, he gives them abundant increase of fruit; the rain falls early and late. But if in his justice he wishes to punish the wicked, nothing turns out well; we receive a heaven of brass and an earth of iron; if fruit ripens, it perishes in a single night. Such things should not be ascribed to fortune. When we do not know the cause, we take it to be chance, of which the poet says:

> The goddess Fortune we call you,
> And place you in highest heaven.[48]

Accordingly, we should not busy ourselves only with the general consideration of worldly things, but must weigh their use, through which they serve the providence of God. Sin comes from its own causes, I mean from our own fallen will and corrupt affections, yet they also serve God. Here is a simile: there are many poisons in the world, with many dangerous qualities, yet the

---

[46]Rom. 1:20.

[47]Acts 17:28; Martyr quotes the Greek, from the *Phaenomena*. Aratus (b.?315 BCE) was a Greek didactic poet.

[48]*Te facimus fortuna deam coeloque locamus;* perhaps paraphrasing Horace *Ode* i.35 "To Fortune": "O goddess ... / Ready to raise mere mortals / To the heights...."

physician sanctions them, and the magistrate uses them lawfully. The doctor mixes the drugs to heal the sick; the Athenian magistrate gave poison to remove the guilty. So was Socrates compelled to drink hemlock. Although poisons are evil, the magistrate and the physician may use them well for the health of the commonwealth and of the sick. Just so God overrules sins, whose proper causes are corrupt, to accomplish and activate his counsels. I might use another simile also: those things in life we seem to do by chance, serve the providence of God most of all. The Lord says in the law, Exodus 21 and Deuteronomy 19: if two go together into the forest to cut wood, and the axe flies out of one of their hands and his neighbor is struck by it and killed, he shall not be guilty of death because he acted unintentionally.[49] God delivered him, for just causes and some purpose; we do not understand it, but he knows it. Even so those who commit sin do as they choose, they have decided by themselves what they will do, yet God uses these actions. Therefore through the curse of Shimei God wished the patience of David to be thoroughly known to all, and his judgments against his adultery and murder to be revealed; but he himself meant to show his enmity for David. God does what he will regarding those crimes which men committed with a different purpose; not so that they might obey the will of God, but their own corrupt lusts.

To return to the evidence before us. Whoever cuts wood does it on purpose, but the axe hits someone else, and the blow serves the will of God. Jerome on the twelfth of Jeremiah writes: "Nothing, whether good or evil, happens by chance and without providence, but all things happen by the judgment of God."[50] Creatures are thus like instruments in the hand of God; he uses them according to his own purpose. Yet these agents are not all of one kind; some have no knowledge or feeling or will, yet they render service to God. But there are others who feel and understand and choose what they do, yet not always with the purpose of serving God; rather they often unwillingly and unintentionally do what God ordains. So we say that living creatures as well as the inanimate, both sensible and insensible, good and bad angels, and all creatures together, are instruments of God, which he uses according to his providential care. He used the Assyrians, Chaldeans, Persians, Greeks, and Romans to punish the erring Hebrews; he also used the devil against Saul and against Job. But we should note further that when God uses creatures, especially rational, and evil creatures such as evil men and devils, he does not employ them as if they themselves did nothing; they fulfill their own corrup-

---

[49]Exod. 21:13; Deut. 19:6.
[50]Jerome *Commentariorum in Jeremiam* III.12.4 (PL 24.759).

tion, but God puts it to use. God does not deal with them as with stones that lack all feeling; they choose, they know, they have senses; when evil men and the devil act wickedly and are moved by their own lust, they serve the providence of God. They perceive and will, not that their mind is such as to wish to serve God, for they seek their own good. Nor are they so moved by the superior cause as not to make use of their own evil.

10. You will object that if as highest cause God concurs with these actions in this way, and that as proximate causes evil men do so, it would all be one work—of God, the devil, and the wicked. Certainly this should not be denied; yet this work comes quite differently from the superior good cause than from the proximate cause which is corrupt. Insofar as this work is of the devil and of sinners it is evil. It is infected by the depravity of the devil and of evil men, who are evil trees and cannot bring forth good fruit. As God, the supreme and best cause, concurs with these actions, he does them with righteousness and order. Both God and the devil wished to have Jerusalem destroyed, but for different reasons: God, that he might punish the obstinate; the devil, that he might satisfy his cruel hatred against mankind. Christ was to be given up to the cross, and it was done; as this deed proceeds from the hatred and malice of the Jews it was evil; but since God would have mercy upon mankind through that most holy event, it was good. Therefore it is said in the Acts of the Apostles that "they did those things against the Son of God, which his counsel and hand had decreed."[51] Yet what they did against Christ must be called evil as such; because they take both their name and nature from the proximate cause, even though God used them with justice according to his own providence. The devil and God trouble Job in far different ways; the Sabeans and other robbers ravaged his substance to satisfy their own hatred; so did the devil. But God did it to prove his patience, and to reveal his good will towards the godly, by a happy outcome. Therefore the works were the same but the purposes different. So when Job said: "The Lord has given, and the Lord has taken away," he praises God as the highest cause, without whose providence these things were not done, and whose providence used them all for a good purpose; yet he does not praise thieves and the devil.[52] David behaved in the same way; he did not commend Shimei, he did not say that those cursings were good in themselves, but turned to the providence of God. The work was evil, yet in one respect it may be called the work of God, because he ruled it and used it. Also it is said in the prophet: "Cursed is he who does the work of the Lord with slackness";[53] he calls the Lord's work an

---

[51]Acts 4:27–28.   [52]Job 1:9ff., 15, 21.   [53]Jer. 48:10.

affliction of the people, by which the wicked oppressed them. So the wicked cannot excuse their sins on account of this divine use; they have the cause in themselves. Just as God's good use of these things does not excuse sinners, so on the other hand the wickedness of sinners does not taint the good use and providence of God, who can employ evils for the best.

In his *Manual for Laurence* chapter 101, Augustine shows that God and man may will the same thing, and that by so willing God acts rightly while man sins, even if he chooses the same things as God.[54] He brings an example. The father of a wicked son sickens; it is God's will by a righteous judgment that he should die from the illness: the ungrateful child also wishes it, but so that he may sooner come into the inheritance and be free from his father's power. God wills with justice, but the son from evil. On the other side, he says that someone might will what God would not, yet he as well as God wills rightly. Suppose the father who is sick has a good son. God would have the father die; the child through an honest affection would not, for he wants his father to live; their wills are different and yet both are just. It consists strictly in the judgment of the will [in consilio voluntatis]; for both goodness and corruption often depend on that. But I have some hesitation. If the same work depends on both God and man—drawing evil from human depravity, it must possess some good insofar as God uses it (since nothing escapes God or his providence)—why does Zechariah 1 complain: "I was angry only a little with my people, but they furthered the disaster,"[55] that is, they exceeded their limits? Their sin seems to exceed the providence of God, so that they did more than God had decreed. We answer: it must not be understood as if they did more than what might serve the use of God's providence; for nothing at all can be done outside the will of God and his decrees, which are most firm. In the same *Manual for Laurence*, chapter 102, Augustine says that the will of God is invincible.[56] How then are they said to have gone too far? Not as to the bounds of the eternal decree, but to the just measure of victory. There are certain allowable limits and laws which should be observed by victors. They exceeded what was fitting, but we cannot agree that they could do more than providence would use.

11. What is suitable for saints we call the third kind of God's works; for through it he effects many things for them in his mercy. He reigns, he lives and works in us both to will and to perform.[57] Apart from this we are by nature

---

[54] Augustine *Enchiridion ad Laurentium* 101 (PL 40.279).
[55] Zech. 1:15.
[56] Augustine *Enchiridion ad Laurentium* 102 (PL 40.280).
[57] Phil. 2:13.

merely barren trees, we are blind, we do not perform the good. Judgment is spoiled, the will and choice is corrupt in that filth of original sin; but by his Spirit, God renews his elect. From the beginning we are granted a nature according to the likeness of God, to which willing and choosing, doing this matter and that, should correspond. Insofar as we can do no good by ourselves, it comes from corruption; but as we choose the right and serve God by an initial obedience, it comes from the supernatural grace of God. So the first kind of divine works attending universal providence does not help the present question. The second and third kinds of work do.

12. Even though God rules over sins and evils, he may not be said strictly to be their efficient cause. In *The City of God*, twelfth book and seventh chapter, Augustine speaks very well about the corrupt will: "An evil thing does not have an efficient cause, but a deficient one. And if anyone inquires into this efficient cause, it is as if he would see the darkness with his eyes, or apprehend silence with his ears. Since they are privations, they do not need efficient causes."[58] Still, they are known to us; for contraries involve the same sense. Sight sees only bright objects, the ear hears only noises, yet by these senses we do know them—not by their use, but only by their absence. God uses a corrupt will for his own purpose; not because he is unable to obtain what he wills except through such means, but because it pleased him to declare his wisdom and power in this way, showing himself able to do something either mediated or immediate, as they say;[59] nor does it matter to him whether the means he uses are good or bad. Therefore let us seek out the deficient cause of evil actions; among others, wicked affections and inclinations may be found. Since they abandon the word of God and right reason, it is no wonder if defects proceed from them. These are the inward causes of sin, but they are rather deficient than efficient causes.[60]

The devil also is said to be the cause of sin. We read in the book of Wisdom, "Death entered the world through the devil,"[61] therefore sin also, for death is an effect of sin. The devil, however, cannot be called the proper and absolute cause of our sin. The reason is that such is the nature of a proper and perfect cause that when it occurs, the effect follows from necessity. It is not so with the devil. No matter how much evil he heaps on the faithful, sin does not always follow, for many saints resist him. When sin does not result, he cannot

[58]Augustine *De civitate Dei* 12.7 (PL 41.355).

[59]I.e., both sorts of human knowledge are attributable to divine illumination: mediate or discursive, immediate or intuitive. See Aquinas, ST Ia.Q 12.5 ad 2; ST IIaIIae.Q 174.3 sed c.

[60]On *causa secunda deficiens*, cf. Aquinas, ST Ia.Q4, and §16, p. 234; §19, p. 237, etc. below.

[61]Wis. 2:24: "Death came into the world through the Devil's enmity."

be called its single and perfect cause. He did indeed provoke men, yet not so far that sin follows necessarily.

I could bring another reason. Let us imagine that the devil had not revolted from God, and that after mankind was created he could still have sinned by his own nature, having its cause in himself. Since he was not yet alienated from God, the cause could not have been the devil's temptation. The devil cannot lead the will to sin necessarily; therefore he is an imperfect and not the complete cause of sin, but one who persuades and entices. So we have declared where sin gets its deficient cause, namely from our own corruption. Nevertheless God does govern and rule sin itself; he does not observe idly, but plays the part of judge and governor; nor does he leave all things without guidance. But how is he said to govern sin? As regards time, mode, form, and matter, that it is turned sometimes this way and sometimes the other. Our corruptions lie hidden within us, but God does not always allow them to prowl about, nor for as long as the wicked would like; he curbs sins and sometimes obstructs them. Further, he makes our wickedness lean to one side rather than another. So was the rage of Shimei bent against David more than anyone else.[62] And the providence of God is shown at one time rather than another; God directed the power of Nebuchadnezzar against the Hebrews rather than their neighbors.[63]

13. Something else should be considered about sins when they result in action. God himself suggests some things to us that in themselves are good; but because they are shown to the wicked, they are taken wrongly and become occasions for sinning. So sins that previously lay hidden break out. Yet these suggestions, whether inward or outward, cannot properly be termed the causes of sin, since those causes are within us; but they may be called occasions. Some occasions are given and some taken. It resembles the definition of scandal: a scandal taken is an occasion of offense.[64] Not on behalf of the one who gives it, for he does what benefits himself, but a wicked individual interprets it in an evil way; that is, offense is taken. Christ says of the Scribes and Pharisees: "Let them alone; they are blind, and leaders of the blind."[65] The apostle taught that men ought to act rightly; if others are offended, the fault did not cling to them. But an offense occurs when we do those things we should not. It is the same with God: he suggests things that are naturally good, which fall into an evil nature and become occasions for sinning.

---

[62] 2 Sam. 16:13.   [63] Ezek. 21:18ff.

[64] scandalum acceptum est occasio offensionis. Cf. Aquinas, ST IIaIIae.Q 43, art. 1, corpus: "'Dictum vel factum minus rectum praebens occasionem ruinae' sit scandalum."

[65] Matt. 15:14.

14. The subject should be explored by examples. Some godly person sees someone sin; he comes to him and warns him earnestly to take heed. The advice is good but falls on an evil mind, which begins to break out more and more into a hatred of virtue, and to grow fierce against the faithful. The admonition was an occasion for him to leap into action. Through the man of faith God suggested what is itself good, and so is said to act rightly, for he plays his proper role. But to evil men good things become occasions of sinning, and of even more harmful sinning than if perhaps they had not happened. Hence the difference between God and us: while we suggest good things, we do not know whether the party will become worse, but God is not unaware. For example, God sent Moses and Aaron to Pharaoh, ordering him to let his people go; this suggestion in itself was good, but Pharaoh took it the wrong way and began to act more cruelly. If the advice had come to a godly person he would have said: it is right for me to obey God, and because his will is that I let the people go, I will certainly do it; for I have no authority over them greater than his own will. But when Pharaoh heard these words, he began to blaspheme, saying "Who is this God?" And he exploded with cruelty.[66]

The same will is shown by other examples and testimonies of the Scriptures. That warning given to Pharaoh by Moses and Aaron is good, and is applied outwardly by God, while he who was evil used it wrongly. We have the same thing in Romans 7: The law is holy and spiritual, but it works lust and death in me.[67] The divine command by itself makes for life, but sin seizes on the suggestion as an occasion. Nor does this happen only externally— sometimes also God accomplishes it inwardly through good thoughts; for we should always regard good thoughts as from God. The Pharaoh who came after the death of Joseph began to think: we must take care that the commonwealth come to no harm. This idea was good, and derived from God, but it came to an evil mind and was twisted against the Hebrews. He said: "The Hebrew people will increase, and given the chance will overcome us; therefore let them be destroyed."[68] He issued an edict that all sons of the Hebrews should be thrown into the river. The first notion was good, but through his sin turned into evil. Nebuchadnezzar said that it is not the part of a good prince to be idle; he should exercise what power he possesses. This was a good idea, but he turned towards foreign nations, and failed to strengthen his power against his own people's crimes as he should. The same prince, as we read in Daniel, was in his hall contemplating the victories he had won, and the

[66]Ex. 5:2.
[67]Paraphrase of Rom. 7:12ff.
[68]Ex. 1:9–10.

wide rule he had established. These thoughts were good, for we should acknowledge the benefits of God. But they fell on an evil mind; straightway he thought to himself that he had established the kingdom by his own powers; here he sinned [*279r*] against God.[69] The sons of Jacob also thought to themselves that Joseph's parents loved him, and that divine dreams were granted him by God;[70] this was a good thought, for we must observe the works of God in others, even more than in ourselves. If they had used that idea properly they would have thanked God, but they turned it to evil, scheming how to carry him off and sell him. These positive ideas were suggested by God, who certainly knows of their doing, and does not prevent their becoming occasions for evils but allows them to be done; for he is present with his providence and oversees them. Accordingly, he wished to be glorified by Pharaoh, he would punish the Israelites through Nebuchadnezzar, and would have Joseph honored in Egypt with great advantages, and feed the household of Jacob, all through his brothers' selling him. Shimei saw that David would be deposed and the kingdom given to Absalom; he said these are the judgments of God. The reasoning was good, but it came to a fallen mind, he abused it and slandered David, pursuing his own wrath and vengeance. After getting the kingdom, Absalom had in mind to heed the counsel of the wise, namely that many eyes see more than one.[71] The notion was good but struck an evil mind; he judged that counsels should be accepted if they prove profitable, even though in their own way they are wicked and dishonest. He used the first suggestion, the good one, badly; God allowed it, he would place no hindrance, he overruled it so that David's sin might be punished and God's hatred of sin might be shown. Now I think that the matter is clear.

15. Here is the question: why does God suggest such inward and outward notions, knowing that the wicked will abuse them, even though they are good? He knows the reasons for his own judgment; two are offered us. The first is that his justice may appear the greater, for we are blind when it comes to seeing divine justice. Yet it may be known by making comparisons; one is from injustice, where none can be seen in God, although we see it in devils and the corrupt. Another is that men's boldness may be restrained. For many would say: if God puts good thoughts into our mind, we should have the will and the power to do good. See what good notions are given—when they fall into a corrupt nature that is left without restraint, sin will arise through our own fault, even concerning the best things; I mean of occasions taken, not given. In this way I understand what Augustine says in his book *On Grace and*

---

[69]See Dan. 4.   [70]Gen. 37:8.   [71]2 Sam. 16:20.

Free-will: God sometimes bends our will either to good or to evil. If the things he suggests come to good men they incline to good, but if to the wicked, they tend to evil.[72] So do I understand what he writes against Julian, book 5 chapter 3, that God works not only in our bodies but in our minds.[73] So likewise I understand what Zwingli—a learned and steadfast man of holy memory— once wrote, that by God's providence men are at times provoked to sin; and that the same act comes from both God and the wicked, with justice from him, and unjustly from them.[74] So do I understand those Scriptural passages which say that God gave them up to a base sense, he aroused them.[75]

16. Clearly there is permission, but something greater is shown by these telling passages. We acknowledge the permission, for if God wanted to resist, they would not be done; therefore, he allows it. We should note, however, that consent belongs to the genus of willing: not the efficient will, but still a kind of will. As Augustine says in his *Manual for Laurence*, God permits either willingly or unwillingly; certainly not unwillingly, for that would mean with regret, so that there would be a power greater than himself. If he consents with his will, permission is a kind of will.[76] But you ask: if he wills at all, why does he forbid it? On the other hand I would inquire: if he did not desire it, how does it happen? For the will of God is invincible. Paul says: "Who can resist his will?"[77] God wills, and what he chooses is according to justice. Those who sin choose unjustly what they will. That Julian against whom Augustine argues claimed that there was a bare permission in such things, therefore we could take it that God does nothing at all; he stated that God rather endures it, and that this relates to his patience. Augustine replies: Not only to his patience but also to his power, because he rules sin, and works what he will with it. He brings a passage to the Romans: "If God, desiring to show his wrath and make known his power, has endured with much patience the vessels of wrath";[78] we see here that he endures, but his power is also mentioned. In 1 Peter chapter 4 it is written: "Therefore let those who suffer according to God's will"[79]—so he attributes the afflictions of Christians to the divine will. But they cannot suffer unless there is some agent. If he desires suffering, he desires the act as well; for suffering proceeds from someone who acts. This will is a permission, but yet of a kind that belongs to the will.

[72]Augustine *De gratia et libero arbitrio* XXI.43 (PL 44.909).
[73]Augustine *Contra Julianum* III.8 (PL 44.786–787).
[74]Ulrich Zwingli *De Providentia* chap. 6 (CR 93.3, SW VI.3) 152–153.
[75]Rom. 1:28.
[76]Augustine *Enchiridion ad Laurentium* 100 (PL 40.279).
[77]Rom. 9:19.   [78]Rom. 9:22.   [79]1 Pet. 4:19.

Augustine showed this in his *Manual for Laurence*, chapter 100, handling that place of the Psalm: "Great are the works of God, studied on all their wills." He follows the Greek translation; the Hebrew has: "Towards all their wills."[80] He writes, "So far as belonged to them (he is writing about sinners) they did what God did not desire. They could by no means bring this about with regard to his power. For even in what they did against his will, it was working on them; therefore great are the works of the Lord." He adds, "By means both marvelous and inexpressible, even what is done against his will is not done without it; for it would not happen unless he allowed it. He does not permit it [*279v*] unwillingly, but willingly; nor would he, being good, permit evil to be done, but being almighty, he can bring good out of that evil."[81] The will of God concurs with both the good and the bad, but in different ways. Indirectly with the bad: he allows them to be done. He suggests good things, but because they happen to evil men, sins follow. As for good things, he not only suggests but fulfills them. Yet he rules and governs sin also, that it may not attack everyone, whether at all times or beyond measure. Those evils lurk within us, but when they break forth, they cannot escape the providence of God. But as I have said, he not only does not prevent good, but accomplishes it, working together with us and gently bending our will, that we may enjoy doing those things we dislike.

Providence operates generally in one way, in another when it uses even evil things, and still another in respect to what God works in us who are regenerate. So I understand that Pharaoh was hardened by God, and that he also hardened himself; for he had within him the cause of obstinacy.[82] But we say that God hardened because he suggests and governs, and also because he ruled over sin and used it to his own glory. Paul says that he raised him up to display his power—I take this as the vessels of wrath to be prepared for destruction.[83] How? In themselves, in their own wickedness and corrupt nature, they are prone to sin. Similarly, they could in one sense be said to be prepared by God because evil arises through his good suggestions, while it appears it is still in God's hand to direct it as he wishes, one way or another. For God works with a good will what we do with bad intentions. Permission is a kind of willing, not absolutely, for God's will is properly the cause of things: not like the human will, where we attempt many things that we do not accomplish. Why then doesn't God will sin? Because sin belongs to those things that do not need an efficient cause, but a deficient. Therefore sin does

---

[80]Ps. 111:2: exquisita in omnes voluntates eijs (LXX); ad omnem voluntatem eorum (MT).
[81]Augustine *Enchiridion ad Laurentium* 100 (PL 40.279).
[82]Ex. 8:15, 9:12.   [83]Rom. 9:17.

not properly fall under the divine will. If God is put as the cause, not efficient but deficient, shall we say that God fails in himself? No, he is said to fail because he does not hinder, nor resist, nor soften. What kind of will is this? A will not to hinder, a will not to relent, a will not to illuminate.

17. For all this, God does not compel the will, either by some suggestion or by abstaining from hindrance; nor can the devil. For if the will doesn't work of its own accord, it is not will but unwillingness. It is as wrong to ascribe compulsion to the will as to say that fire is not hot. So corrupt is our nature and will that if God's favor is withdrawn, it inclines to evil solely on its own. Yet it was not evil from its beginning; because it is produced out of nothing, if what sustains it is withdrawn, it will at once become worse on its own. Now if the human will is not forced into evil nor is evil because of its creation but is said to sin by corruption, what shall we say about the sin of the first man? Nature was good at that point, grace and divine assistance were not lacking, and still he sinned. In this regard we say that we must make one judgment about the first man, and another about the corrupt nature that we now possess. God bestowed many gifts on him, but he made him in such a way that just as he could stand he could also fall. If he had chosen, God could have made him so perfect that he was not able to sin.[84] The state of the blessed illustrates this; the holy spirits in heaven, like ourselves when we will be there, will be so strengthened as to be able not to sin anymore. Otherwise it would not be perfect happiness, but would be joined with the fear of falling. He did not do this to Adam; aware by his foreknowledge that he would fall, he might have prevented him but would not; he allowed him to fall, and by his eternal decree appointed Christ to be the remedy for his fall. We cannot explain other things concerning that state in greater detail because we lack perfect knowledge. Let us return to our own state. Before being renewed through Christ we could not will the good, but of necessity remained in sins, and could not lift ourselves. We could not stand upright any more than was the first Adam given this power.

Though God is not properly the cause of sin, as we said, yet must he not be dethroned; he also rules sins, and offers remedy for them. We may be sure of this, that nothing can be done either by us or any creature, outside God's will. But do not let this excuse our sins, as if we seek to obey the will of God through sinning. We should accuse ourselves, seeing we have the origin of sin within us. Concerning the will of God, we must follow what Scripture teaches, and must not depart from his Law. When we do desert him, we must

---

[84]*ut posse stare, posset item labi / peccare non posset.* See "Free Will, " p. 279, n. 38.

acknowledge that the motion of turning away from God and inclining to worldly lures is something proper to our will now corrupted, and not as it was instituted by God. Therefore there are deficient causes of this motion, but we must not ask for an efficient cause which God has worked together with us. We note in the book of Genesis that darkness is not said to be made by God: "Darkness was upon the face of the deep."[85] Nevertheless, God so arranged things that the night should continue, it was a lack [of light]. Therefore since this motion of turning away from God fails, and deprives human acts of their rightful good, it has a cause, but it is deficient.

[THREE SPECIAL POINTS]

18. With these matters complete, we must consider three items. First is the guilt of sins, the punishment that is due; second is the subject of deformation and privation, that is, the act itself of the human will; [*280r*] the third is acknowledged by all, that sin is the punishment of sin. May we say for these three reasons that sin depends on God? For the first, we should understand that a degraded and evil act is in some respect the basis for the punishment that is due. The Apostle says: "The wages of sin is death."[86] When we sin, a debt is born through which we must endure punishment for the evil committed. Such guilt is said to arise through divine justice, since he gives to each what belongs to each. Obligation arises only when sin is past or present; by sinning we give a just occasion to the necessity of punishment. Therefore if we understand by sin the guilt and its necessity, we admit that these things are from God as efficient cause. Yet they should not properly be called sin, since they relate to justice. Sometimes they are called so, as when we say that God remits, blots out, and forgives sins. He does not cause them to disappear; certainly there are evil inclinations in us, but the obligation of suffering punishment for past evil is removed. As we have said, this belongs to justice, and is something good.

19. Secondly, let us consider the subject itself, in which the deformity of sin inheres. Speaking of this, we will not hesitate to say that God is the cause, since this action is a natural fact. Whatever exists, insofar as it exists, is produced not by creatures alone, but by God; for "All things were made by him," Scripture says.[87] This universal particle includes all things, no matter what they are and by what means, or how far they reach. In his book *The Morals of the Manichees*, near the beginning, Augustine says that the catholic church

---

[85]Gen. 1:2.
[86]Rom. 6:23.   [87]Gen. 1:3.

believes that God is the author of all natures and substances.[88] A little before
he stated what he understands by nature as follows: nature is nothing else than
what is understood to be something specific of its kind. So we perceive that by
a new name, from *esse*, we have *essentia*, which we often call *substantia*. The
ancient Fathers, who did not have those names, called it "nature" instead of
essence and substance. Since therefore our mental motions are specific things,
clearly in this sense they depend on God. God operates as the highest cause,
and creatures cooperate with him. In his book *The Fall of the Devil* Anselm
wrote that even the evil will of the devil depends on God insofar as it is a
choice: the thing itself is not wicked, except that he wills it in his own evil
way.[89] The same act is a fact, as is shown because it is in the genus or predicament of action; since it is something, it is from God and is a creature.[90]
Augustine, *The Trinity*, book 9 chapter 10, said that the qualities of the mind
surpass those of the body, on account of the nobility of the subject.[91] Because
the form or appearance is in the mind, it far excels what is found outwardly in
the body. And the soul itself, as soul, no matter how bad it is, is still more
noble than any body. Therefore insofar as they are real, the mental acts in
which privation remains afterwards through our own fault, are not effected
without God. In the place cited above Anselm says that God himself is the
producer of entities, not only substantial things but also accidental, universal
and particular things, including the subtle motions of the will, even when evil;
the power of God is infinite. Therefore there is nothing he brought forth,
whatever it may be, that is not subject to his act. For if anything could escape
it, it would not be infinite, nor would it fill all things; our wills could not issue
in action, unless that supreme will acts along with us. Augustine writes, *On
True Religion* chapter 34: "However small it may be, it is good, for the highest
possible is the highest good."[92] A little later: "The highest being [summa spe-
cies] is the highest good, the least is the lowest good, yet still good." Therefore
if the act we are speaking of pertains in any way to being, it has some good.
When we discuss sin we must distinguish it and see what it has that is positive,
as they say in the schools.[93] First the subject itself is to be considered, and on

---

[88]Augustine *De moribus Manichaeorum* chap. 3.5 (PL 32.1316–1317).

[89]Anselm *De Casu Diaboli*, chap. 2 (PL 158, 352–353). Martyr, SAM 168r–v, deals with this
item further when commenting on 1 Samuel: *An Liceat consulere Diabolum, et eius opera uti: Deus
enim, utitur opera diabolorum*; cf. SAM 162v–168r, *An Diabolus Possit … Scire futura*.

[90]Aristotle's predicables in *Categories* 4.2aff.

[91]*species mentis*; see Augustine *De Trinitate* IX.10 (PL 42, 997).

[92]Augustine *De Vera Religione* xxxiv.63 (PL 40.150)

[93]The scholastic distinction between *peccata positiva et privativa*, the one requiring *causa effi-
cacia*, the other *causa deficacia*: Aquinas, ST Ia-IIae.Q 86.

the other hand to see what defect and privation is present. Since we see a defect in this privation, we must seek its deficient, not efficient, cause. But what is found to be positive needs an efficient cause, and the sum of all efficient causes is God.

20. A serious doubt arises just here. Certain sins are called sins of omission; they do not seem to be grounded on the act or work of the will, where defect or privation is possible; whatever is present seems to be privation. Someone is said to omit his duty because he does not do what he should. For example, if someone does not love his neighbor, or come to the holy gathering to hear the word of the Lord and to share in the sacraments, there seems in such a sin only a privation, without any particular action on which it could be founded. Some answer that even in this instance we should look for a nature or act, a work or something that provides the ground for privation; and they say that it is the will that causes the defect. For the will that sins is sustained in its order by God, since it is a nature, but not inasmuch as it sins. This opinion may be accepted, but in searching the matter more closely, it seems otherwise to me. I see an action in those sins of omission. For the same omission of duty is sometimes done through contempt; then that corrupt person wills not to love his neighbor, or go to the holy assembly.[94]

So we see that the act of will, and the action that is natural, depends on God, while deformity and privation do not. But [*280r*] sometimes they are omitted because one does not think of them, out of contempt I mean. I hold that although no such act is evident in this case, yet there is another that opposes right behavior. He is not mindful of the holy gathering, because he wants to take a walk or amuse himself, and such doings are enemies of right action. Or if at that moment there is no act, there was just before. For example, he would gorge himself at night, and afterward could not rise early enough to be present in church. Therefore we do find action in sins of omission, either proper to its kind or some other that preceded or continues to be present, struggling with a good motion of the will.

21. Thus is God the cause of all things: inferior things receive the impulse of the first cause according to their own nature; if sin is acquired it comes through the nature of second causes. I will illustrate by a similitude. In living creatures we have the power that is called local motion.[95] It impels animals to walk or to run; they are moved as they receive their impulse from that

---

[94]Cf. Aquinas, ST IaIIae.Q 76.2 ad 3: *ipsa omissio, inquantum est aliqualiter voluntaria.*
[95]Aristotle *Phys.* III.1, 201a14: one distinction in classifying motion is "of what can be carried along, *locomotion.*"

local motion. But if a leg is defective, out of joint or crooked,[96] limping is added to the forward motion. The limp derives from the moving power of the soul, since it is a motion; insofar as it is defective and lame, it depends on the fault in the leg that was broken. So it happens with that continual moving by which God impels his creatures. There is indeed a common influence, and it is received in things according to their quality; the subject of deformity or privation derives from God, and the divine moving sometimes passes through the corrupt mind, so that the fault of the action is not with God, but is drawn from the secondary cause. What God does there and how he governs that deformity was explained above; here we are dealing with the act which proceeds from our will. It is rightly said that the privation of righteousness does not follow the work of our will and its motion, insofar as it exists in a kind of nature, but rather as it is in the kind of moving.[97]

Augustine writes in *The City of God,* book seven chapter 30: God governs his creatures so as to permit them to exercise and work with him their own proper motions.[98] For God does not act alone, but as already noted, the wicked and the devil also use their malice in their deeds. When we say that the act itself, which later through our own fault is evil, is produced by the supreme cause, that is, God, and by us, that is, our will, how should we understand it? is it completely through God, or through ourselves? is it partly from him and partly from us? Just now we will limit this work to our will's act itself. We answer: if the consideration of the whole is referred to the cause we must speak in one way, if to the effect in another. If we refer the whole to the cause so that we understand our will to be the entire cause of the action, that it is able by itself to work without God, it is not true. For unless God gives assent it cannot produce action. So although by God's absolute power he could perform the work himself, yet as the course of things stands he will not act alone, but will have creatures work with him. By this means neither the will nor even God is said to be the whole cause. If it is referred to the effect, God and the will are the full cause. For God and the will constitute the entire effect, although joined together in action. I will show this by an example. To produce an action we have the will and understanding, and our will makes it complete. But one is near, the other more remote. So is it concerning the will and God: our will does all, and God does all, but one is the first cause and the other secondary.

---

[96]Reading *curvus* for *curus.*
[97]*in genere naturae ... in genere motus.*
[98]Augustine *De civitate Dei* VII.30 (PL 41.219f).

22. On the third point, the sin that follows is sometimes said to be a punishment for previous sin; so is God said to punish sins with sins. If the sins that follow are weighed so as to be punishments, in one sense they are attributed to God; not that God instills new evil, or drives men directly into sin, but when he has withdrawn his gifts sin follows, by which the mind is destroyed. Insofar as those destructions and mental wounds are punishments, they fall on us by just desert. We read of this in the first chapter to the Romans: "God gave them up to a base mind," as we explained before.[99] It is clear that sin has an aspect of punishment because it corrupts nature. Augustine said what is often repeated: "You have commanded, Lord, and truly it is so, that every sin is the punishment of him that sins."[100] The heathen also acknowledge this; Horace says:

> No Sicilian tyrant could invent
> a fiercer torment
> Than envy.[101]

Those evil affections dry up the bones, rob us of strength, and afflict our minds, yet this happens according to justice. For God is just and righteous in all his ways; if we are deprived of grace, we have deserved the sins.

23. We conclude our question by stating that to speak properly and plainly, God is not the cause of sin; neither would he sin himself. Yet we do not say that God is less perfect or powerful because he cannot make sin; for that is not imperfection and impotence, but perfection.[102] God is unable to do such things because he is the highest good and perfection. Rather does he legislate against sins, he cries out against them and punishes them. Do not wonder when I say that God cannot properly will sin, for if so he could turn men away from himself, he would deny that he is God. Paul says to Timothy: [*280v*] "God cannot deny himself."[103] For this reason Bernard was moved to say in his little book *On Precept and Dispensation* that God can soften a little the precepts of the second table, but not of the first.[104] He did remit the second to some degree—as when he wills Abraham to kill his son, also when he

---

[99]Rom. 1:28. See §15.

[100]Augustine *De gratia et libero arbitrio* 41 (xx) (PL 44.906): "We find that some sins are even the chastisement of other sins." Cf. Augustine *De natura et gratia* LXVII.8 (PL 44.287); "Free Will" p. 278, n. 26, and *De libero arbitrio*, scholium on Rom. 7:25 LC/CP 2.21–30, §27.

[101]Horace *Epistles* I.2, trans. Burton Raffel, *The Essential Horace* (New York: SUNY Press, 1974) 204.

[102]On the dialectic of omnipotence/impotence see the introduction to this section, p. 173.

[103] 2 Tim. 2:13.

[104]Bernard of Clairvaux, *De Praecepto et Dispensatione* 3 (PL 182.864–865).

ordered the children of Israel to carry away the goods of others.[105] But commands of the first table cannot be compromised. If God is not to be loved and worshipped, he would deny his very being. If he is the highest good, should we not love and worship him? Some reason that the goods belonging to our neighbors are particular, and God can remove any private good and replace it with a greater, whereas those things that relate to his worship have regard to universal good, and therefore cannot be taken away. In the book entitled *Catholic Refutation*, falsely ascribed to Augustine, the third chapter says, "Whatever is condemned in anyone is foreign to the author of nature." In the same place: "the opinion that holds God to be the author of any evil deed or will is to be condemned."[106]

[THE CAUSE OF SIN]

24. We have shown in general the proper causes of sin, but if we are to treat them particularly, we identify the cause of sin as the human will, the understanding, depraved sense, base appetite, and what offers itself under pretense of good (for nothing is desired by us unless it relates to some good).[107] The fumes of original sin appear, continually emitting evil desire as if from a sewer. Our own infirmity and ignorance is also a cause, along with insinuations of the devil and of evil men, although they cannot prevail further than God allows. There are examples of evil, sin itself causing sin: a wastrel steals to satisfy his craving. Since there are so many actual causes of sins, we must not make God into the author in order to excuse ourselves. So it may seem that the evil opinion of the Libertines must be condemned, who excuse every kind of sins.[108] Those who make God the cause of evil, even though not so as to excuse ourselves, do not appear to expound this question well. It is the same with those who allow only minimal consent [promissionem].

To bring everything together in few words: we have said that God is not properly the author of sin. Next, that when he wills, it is with justice he withdraws from us the grace that would prevent sin. We hold that God governs sins by his providence in such a way that they will not range any further than he permits, and not otherwise than may suit his providence. We have said that at times God suggests, both inwardly and outwardly, such things as are good in their own nature; but if they fall on the corrupt, they become occasions taken and not given of sins. Also that God does not prevent, but permits sins,

---

[105]See *Theses for Debate*, Propositions on Exodus 31.N.9 and 31.P.6 in EW 129.
[106]Prosper of Aquitaine *Resp. ad Cap. obj. Vincentianarum* (PL 45.1845).
[107]*sub ratione boni*; see n. 42, p. 224, above.
[108]See p. 222, n. 40, above.

this permission being not completely without God's will. Further, that since sin is a defect and privation, it does not need an efficient, but a deficient cause. Then, that our motion of turning away from God is proper to our will insofar as it is corrupted and not as it was instituted by God. We said also that guilt depends on God; that the action which is the subject of deformity comes from God as well as from us, as to the kind of cause. We showed that sins are punished with sins. Last of all, we summarized the true causes of sins.

[Arguments of the First Part]

25. Now we will examine the arguments noted above.[109] Those who, like us, denied God to be the cause of sin, used these reasons. [Ad 1] First, Augustine said, in the book of 83 questions, question 3: "A man is not made worse by having a wise man as author; nor is he therefore worse if God is author." I agree, for man did not become worse when God gave the Law, for he did not command evil by his law. Nor has man become worse regarding the natural act which God brings forth. One becomes worse through failure, for which we have deficient causes in ourselves. So the devil, evil men, our own sensuality, and especially a corrupt will, make us worse; we agree that we are not made worse by God or by man. [Ad 2] Second: Fulgentius says that God does not avenge things of which he is himself the author.[110] We grant the argument: God does not avenge an act insofar as it is natural and depends on him; nor does he avenge his own governance which he uses, but rather the depravity that depends on us, that comes from us. [Ad 3] The third reason: God does not hate those things that he makes, but he hates sin. The reason is firm, yet a doubt remains: if he truly hates sin, why does he not forbid it, since he can? Human reason can scarcely discern God's perfect hatred for sin, since he does not remove it completely. Without doubt it is obscure. Yet often it happens that something hateful is not removed for a good purpose; there are many examples in the human condition. Someone has an illness that attacks the body so that disease breaks out, and a serious wound develops in some member. Even though this brings great trouble, yet because he knows that it will be to his benefit, he endures the pain and does not stop the sore. Weeds spring up among the wheat: it is a worry, but they are not destroyed completely because men are afraid that the wheat might be pulled up. So we could say

---

[109]The original twenty-five arguments described in §§1–2. I will not repeat earlier footnote references.

[110]Fulgentius of Ruspe (467–533), African bishop and theologian, dubbed *Augustinus abbreviatus*; see F. Cayré, *Manual of Patrology* (Paris: Desclée, 1930, English trans. 1940) 2: 196. The quotation is probably from Fulgentius *De Remissione Peccatorum* I.12 (PL 65.637).

that God has his purposes, to proclaim his goodness and righteousness. He hates sins, yet not in such a way that he will not accomplish through them the goal he has in view.

[Ad 4, 5] Other arguments: if God created sin he would be a sinner, and if he were to lead us to sin he would act against his own nature; for by their efforts natural things seek to make the result like themselves, etc. These arguments are solid. Divine action and creaturely cooperation, that is, the human will, are not affirmed as if we ourselves [*281r*] did not supply our own sinfulness. [Ad 6] God might seem to act deceitfully if on the one hand he were to command good and on the other wish for sin. I answer that the argument would be cogent if we could say that God introduced new wickedness; but since he overrules sin he does nothing against his law. Moreover, in regard to the divine will we must distinguish how it bears on the commandments, and on humanity. We take the written commandments to be the will of God, for they express his nature and attributes; but if we examine how the divine will bears on humanity, claiming that God wants to encourage all equally to keep his commandments and gives his grace equally to all, we cannot accept it. God has his elect, and has others as well whom by his just judgment he passes over and leaves to sin and destruction. The Lord says: "I will have mercy on whom I will have mercy."[111] That is, I will have mercy on whomever I choose. But they say that men have free will through which they can keep the divine law if they wish, and that there is no distinction in the divine help and grace, as if it were not given to all in the same way. I assert free will in God—he is free in his election, and in distributing his graces, but his freedom does not depend on us, who will truly be free if the Son makes us free.[112] Thus in the law or commandments, God shows what his nature is, and what he judges to be right. As to the favor with which he overrules individuals to keep those commandments, that is another question.

[Ad 12][113] It was said in 2 Chronicles: "God rose up early and sent them his prophets"; therefore he is not the cause of sin. That God did so is certainly true, yet suggestions which are good in themselves fell on those evil in nature, who through their own wickedness were made worse by those orders; they were aroused to sin by their own fault. God gave notice in order to spare his people, and the warnings were of a kind to grant pardon when received. Yet we should not say that it was God's decision [*decretum Dei*] to save them

[111]Ex. 33:19, Rom. 9:15.
[112]John 8:36.
[113]The order of arguments being answered is inconsistent; after 1–6, Martyr responds to 12, 13, 8, 9, 7, 10, etc.

completely at that time. For he withdrew his grace from them with just cause, and by themselves they neither could nor would obey the prophetic warnings. [Ad 13] The Son of God wept for the destruction of Jerusalem,[114] and this happened on account of sin, not that God willed there to be sins. I agree that, strictly speaking, sins are not performed by the divine will. Then why did he weep? He was now one of us [proximus] and the evils of his fellows could not help but make him sad; also he knew that sin was against the will of God, even if he was aware that it could not be done without that will.

26. [Ad 8] It is written in the prophet Hosea: "Your perdition comes from you, O Israel, but your salvation from me."[115] The statement is true; since sins proceed from ourselves as the proper causes, perdition also is from us. The guilt or obligation to bear punishment may be said to come from God, but as we said before, that is not properly called sin, but relates to justice. [Ad 9] In John 8: "When the devil speaks a lie, he speaks according to his own nature." That is quite true; God does not instill malice into him, yet he usually employs his falsehood, just as he does other things. [Ad 7] We read in Jeremiah: "They ran and I sent them not." That passage does not deal with divine providence, but with the wicked affairs of false prophets, who pretended to have received a word from God, while their own conscience bore witness that God did not speak to them. They said they had dreamed, and babbled that God had given them revelations, yet they lied and knew they did. Therefore no reproaches should be made against God on this matter, as though it were unlawful for him to use their lies through his providence.

[Ad 10] "This is their condemnation, that light came into the world, but men loved darkness rather than light"; so God is not the cause, but those who loved darkness. We accept the argument: by its own proper malice, mankind has within it the motion of turning away from light to darkness. [Ad 11] It was said that "God tempts no man," but if he were the cause of sin, he would tempt us. You should understand that passage like this. Every kind of temptation is not intended, otherwise the statement would not be true. At times God tests his own, not in order to add to his knowledge, but that men may know him, and that others may see what great deeds God has performed among them and what grace he has bestowed on them. There is one kind of testing to be desired, as David says in the psalm: "Prove me, examine my mind and my heart."[116] Nor should we forget our own reasoning: sometimes God suggests inwardly and outwardly things that are good in themselves and are received according to human nature; such kinds of temptation need not be separated

---

[114]Luke 19:41.   [115]Hos. 13:9.   [116]Ps. 26:2.

from God. But James speaks of inward lust by which evils are specifically insinuated, provoking us to act contrary to the divine law.[117] Such desire does not depend on God except that he does not resist it, just as he does not always hinder the devil.

[Ad 14] They added that God might seem to deal tyrannically. We answer that he does not actually incite to sin, but uses the sins of the wicked, and also guides them lest they progress beyond their limits. [Ad 15] Again: how could he judge the world? For if he were the author of sin he should judge himself. We say that God will judge the world justly, for the evil that men commit against the law of God is done willingly and of their own accord, not by constraint. "The spirit of God will reprove the world of judgment, of sin," and so on.[118] [Ad 16] It was inferred that for this reason it would follow that there are wills in God which oppose one another. We answer that there is one will in the divine being, absolute and single, which is the essence and nature of God. Yet if we consider also its various objects, it may be called manifold. In regard to the commandments it is just, good, and single, but in regard to men it promotes some while depriving others quite rightly of his favor. They are not opposing wills because they [282r] do not concern the same matters. Things that are opposite must refer to one subject. A father has two sons: his will is that the one should devote himself to learning, and not the other. Are there two wills of the father? No. It is single; therefore he acts properly and with good reason.

In chapter 4 James says: "You say, we will go into such a city; you ought rather to say, 'If God will.'"[119] So the will of God is not only about the law and commandments, but everyday human affairs as well; that will does not belong to the commandments, for such matters are not contained in the Decalogue, and are in one sense things indifferent. Augustine wrote very well in his *Manual for Laurence*, chapter 102: "The omnipotent God, whether through his mercy he has pity on whom he will, or through judgment condemns whomever he will, does nothing unjustly; he does nothing without his will."[120] [Ad 17] Afterward it was held that if he were the cause of sin, why are there so many of his warnings and entreaties through the Son of God, the prophets and apostles? We say that they are not done in vain, but are beneficial. Those who admonish, rebuke, and exhort, obey the commandments of the God who would have this done. But you will ask, will it profit me? The event must be committed to God. Further, they benefit the saints, the predes-

---

[117]*cupiditas*; see James 1:14.
[118]John 16:8.   [119]James 4:15.
[120]Augustine *Enchiridion ad Laurentium* 102 (PL 40.280).

tinate. Although it does not appear at present, sometimes they already have their fruit; they make the ungodly less excusable. You can read about this matter in Augustine's book *Rebuke and Grace*, since they were also objected against him.[121]

27.[Ad 18] It was argued that if matters remain like this, all difference between good and evil falls; everything without exception would be God's work, as the Libertines say. We grant that if God were truly the cause of sins, the Libertines would speak correctly, but their opinion is detestable. [AD RELIQUA ARGUMENTA: 19–24] The judgment of consciences would be removed along with inward accusations and repentance, a window opened to evil, thanksgiving would be withdrawn, for we would delight in sin, and much of the regard for God would be lost. All these things are true, yet they do not count against us, since we do not say that God is truly the cause of sin. [Ad 25] It was argued lastly that God wants everyone to be saved. If this is his will, he uses means that are good, not evil; therefore he is not the cause of sin. We declare plainly that God is not properly the cause of sin; but here I hold with Augustine in his *Manual*, chapter 103, that the sentence must not be taken so absolutely as if there were not some whom God did not wish to be saved.[122] He takes this sentence to mean that God has his elect among every sort and condition of men; in this respect he does not accept the person. He calls kings and citizens, slave and free, men and women. This interpretation squares with the place of Paul. He had commanded praying for princes; some might think their condition such that salvation would be foreign to it. Not at all, he says: God has his elect among every kind of people. He brings a similar reason from Matthew 23: "You tithe mint, rue, and every herb,"[123] that is, all kinds of herbs that exist among you, not those in India and Europe, for how could they tithe all the worlds's herbs?

This opinion was supported by the author of the book *The Call of the Nations* attributed to Ambrose.[124] He says that God has his own perfection. He considers this universal proposition to be restrained, as if to say that God would have those saved who belong to his flock and number, like the saying, "All will be taught of God [Θεοδίδακτος]," "all flesh will see the salvation of God."[125] Augustine interprets this passage another way in the same place: we understand that none will be saved except those that God wishes to be saved.

---

[121]Augustine *De correptione et gratia* VII (11) (PL 44.923)

[122]Augustine, *Enchiridion ad Laurentium* 103 (PL 40.280).

[123]Matt. 23:23; Luke 11:42.

[124]Ambrose *De Vocatione Gentium* I.9 (PL 17.1101).

[125]Isa. 54:13; Luke 3:6; Ambrose has *dociles Dei*.

As if we said: there is a grammarian in Zurich who teaches grammar to all. He does not say "all the citizens," but that there is no one who is taught grammar whom he does not teach.

Augustine understands similarly that passage, "He lightens every one that comes into this world,"[126] that is, however many are lightened, are illuminated by this word. He denies that God wants absolutely everyone saved. For in Matthew 11 it is written: "Woe to you, Chorazin! woe to you, Bethsaida! for if the mighty works that were done in Tyre and Sidon had been done in you, they would have repented of their sins long ago in sackcloth and ashes."[127] Christ would not display the power of miracles among those who, he said, would have repented if they had been shown. And [Augustine] adds: whichever way you expound it, we are not compelled to believe that God the omnipotent would will something to be done that is not done, when the truth says "All things, whatever he would have done in heaven and earth, he has done,"[128] and surely what he did not will would not exist. So much on arguments made to the first part.

[REBUTTAL OF ARGUMENTS OF THE SECOND PART][129]

28. [Ad 1] Now let us take their arguments who say that God is the cause of evil. In Romans 11 it is said, "God gave them up to a reprobate sense." The interpretation is easy: he gave them up to the desires of their own hearts, which were therefore evil first, as [Paul] expounds it later himself. What did God do? He allowed them to obey their own evil desires; he did not do evil, but by leaving them destitute of his grace, wicked desires arose in them (privation itself followed); God used their evil desires to perform his justice, namely by punishing them. [Ad 2] On the hardening of Pharaoh's heart, we have spoken enough above. [Ad 3] In Isaiah 6, when God says through the prophet: "Blind their hearts that hearing they may not hear, and seeing may not understand" etc. This may be expounded two ways. To interpret these words, Jerome takes a place out of Romans 11 where it is said of Gentiles and Jews: "The Gentiles were in times past unbelievers, while you believed, but now they have obtained mercy through your unbelief."[130] While the Gentiles did not believe, the Jews seemed to have the true worship, and on the other side, when preaching was offered them later they did not believe. The apostles forsook them and turned to the Gentiles; they were to become unbelievers, that the Gentiles might be admitted into grace. So God used the unbelief of

[126]John 1:9.   [127]Matt. 11:21.   [128]Ps. 135:6.
[129]See the twenty-four arguments in §§3–4; earlier footnote references are not repeated.
[130]Jerome *Comm. in Isaiam Prophetam* III.vii (PL 24.99–100).

the Jews, adding "God shut up all under unbelief, that he might have mercy on all."[131] Therefore that same blinding of unbelievers was to do service to divine providence, as the prophet foretold.

A better interpretation is possible. God wished to send Isaiah to preach, but predicts what was going to happen in order to keep him from subsequent discouragement when he would see their obstinacy and their offense at the word. The word of God by itself does not do this, but he withdrew his spirit and grace from them with good reason. "Your word," he says, "will be an occasion taken through which they will become more blind and be turned away from me." This must be understood regarding the majority, for some good people were among them. For this reason the future is announced, so that by perishing they might manifest the righteousness of God, who would use their blindness for his service, through his just judgment. We are to understand that the blindness came from God externally, for he offered them his word through Isaiah.

29. [Ad 4] Another place: "Lead us not into temptation." This is said as if God does lead some into temptation and so is the cause of sin. In his little book *On Nature and Grace* chapter 58, Augustine interprets this saying of the Lord: "We pray that we may resist the devil, that he may fly from us when we say 'lead us not into temptation.' So are we warned, like a general exhorting his troops, saying 'Watch and pray, that you may not enter into temptation.'"[132] Augustine refers it to the temptation of the devil who can effect nothing unless God allows. In chapter 67 of the same book he adds: "We provide two ways against the diseases of the body, either that they may not happen at all, or else if they do come, that we may quickly be delivered from them. Thus when we say 'lead us not into temptation,' we desire that God may turn away sin from happening; but if we have fallen and committed sin, we pray him to remit and forgive it."[133] The same author against the two letters of Pelagius, book 4 chapter 9, cites the opinion of Cyprian: "When it is said, 'lead us not into temptation,' we are warned of our infirmity and weakness. For it is said by the Lord: 'Watch and pray, lest you enter into temptation'; the reason is added: 'For the spirit is willing, but the flesh is weak.'[134] Let us not be puffed up with vanity."[135] Here temptation is ascribed to the flesh and to weakness, therefore God is excluded as author.

---

[131]Rom. 11:30.
[132]Augustine *De natura et gratia* LVIII (68) (PL 44.281).
[133]Augustine *De natura et gratia* LXVII (80) (PL 44.287).
[134]Matt. 26:41.
[135]Augustine *Contra duas Ep. Pelag.* 4:25 (ix) (PL 44.626–627).

In his book *The Gift of Perseverance*, chapter 6, Augustine says that Cyprian introduces that clause with these words: Do not allow us to be led into temptation, for he sees that the devil can do no more than God has permitted him.[136] Regarding his own people, God brings it about that the devil will not prevail; but as for the evil one, if he has the upper hand we cannot blame God unless we hold him responsible because he does not hinder, and rules evils by using them according to his providence. We have objected that it can hardly be that punishment and fault are the same. For it is called sin because it is voluntary, whereas punishment is always imposed against the will; how could voluntary and involuntary be the same? We answer that we may regard our will in terms of sin in two ways. One is that since sin proceeds from the will and is made effective through it, in that respect it is called voluntary. In the other way, sin is considered as being in the mind or will and deforms it, and in this sense cannot be voluntary; for no evil person wishes his mind polluted, wounded, or destroyed. Therefore since sin is produced from the will as the essential cause it is voluntary, but when it brings pollution it is against the will. For we all wish to be perfect. [Ad 5] It was added: God is the cause of the cause of sin, therefore also the cause of sin.[137] By what means do we sin? Through the will and affections which God has brought forth; therefore he is also the cause of the last effect. We answer that sin does not depend on the will and affections as they were created by God, but as they are now corrupted; I gave an example of lameness before.

30. [Ad 6] We said that God removes his grace and spirit, which deter sins and therefore, etc. We accept, but add that it is with just cause that he removes his spirit. Removing an impediment is a cause, but not the proper cause; for inward causes of evil remain in us. [Ad 7] He gives occasions, it is true, suggestions both outward and inward, yet these are good things that men abuse through their own evil. [Ad 8] Not only does he provide occasions; he also issued his commandments. He said to the devil, "Go forth, do this." I will mention a few things on this subject. By the figure *prosopopoeia* the prophet introduces God, as it were, sitting on a seat like a judge;[138] he would have Ahab killed, and looks for someone to deceive him. Where does this line of question lead? It suggests that we should look elsewhere, because it is not in the divine nature to deceive. The purpose is supplied by his justice; he wills that Ahab should die. Various ways are devised: this spirit showed one way

---

[136]Augustine *De dono perseverantiae* 12 (vi) (PL 45.1000).

[137]causa causae peccati, ergo causa peccati; see Aquinas, ST Ia-IIae.Q 75.a 4: Utrum peccatum sit causa peccati; cf. Lombard *Sent.* II, dist. 36 a.1, 42 qu. 2, a 1,3.

[138]Heinrich Bullinger *Decades* IV.3.138, also uses *prosopopoeia* (personification).

and that spirit another, so that we may understand that divine providence has countless ways by which he can punish. Those ways were proposed but not put into effect because providence did not wish to use them. A spirit stepped forth who said, "I will deceive him." We gather that demons are ready to deceive, and when they do it is their own act. Meanwhile we are taught that those spirits can do no more than God allows; so far as he makes use of them, they are [*283r*] his executors. Therefore God said, "Go forth"; this is the imperative mood. If we consider the purpose, it was to slay and punish Ahab; leave was given so that the devil should exercise his evil will and deceive. God used the sin of the devil and would not prevent his work, nor Ahab from believing the false prophets. In his book of 83 questions, question 53, Augustine makes three points: first that what God did against Ahab was by his discretion; second, he did it through an angel and not by himself; third, he says not any sort of angel but an evil angel, ready in his own nature to deceive.[139]

[Ad 9] It was said that sin is a motion and a kind of action. The first mover is God. Nothing happens unless the subject of sin, that is, the act itself, has the will as its nearest cause, and insofar as it is something natural, also God himself. [Ad 10] The saying of Augustine in *Of Grace and Free-will*, chapter 21, interprets one inclination to good in itself and another to evil indirectly [per se ... oblique]. The doings of Rehoboam, the incitement of the Philistines, Amaziah's refusal to listen to the warnings of the king of Israel's prophet—these have to do with divine justice: God wished to punish them. [Ad 11] As to the words of Ahijah the Silonite, that he might fulfill: these things were not done because they were foretold, but were foretold because God foresaw that they should be. And that they might so be, he made them punishments for the wicked, knowing how he would use them; such reasons are proper to God. [Ad 12] It is written in Ezekiel 14: "If the prophet is deceived," etc. Put simply, this means the sin of the false prophet may be taken two ways. Since it originates from the will of an evil prophet it displeases God, and so he said he would punish him. But if we consider its later use, that God wished to punish the people through this deception, then he withdrew his grace from them rightly; further, he used that seduction which in itself and properly may not strictly be ascribed to God.

31. [Ad 15][140] A passage from Proverbs 21 was introduced, where it is said: "The king's heart is in the hand of God, and he turns it wherever he will." The proposition is general—he inclines whichever way he wills without

---

[139]Augustine *De div. quaestiones* LXXXIII.q 53.2 (PL 40.36).
[140]The arguments are out of sequence: 12, 15, 16, 14, 13, 17, etc.

exception, to good as well as evil. In Job 12 we have: "God takes away their hearts who are rulers of the earth, and makes them stagger like drunken men."[141] I have explained how this subject of turning the will is to be understood. So I take this sentence of Solomon in the same way as Augustine's words in his book *Grace and Free-will*, that he inclines our wills toward good or evil, according to his good pleasure.[142] [Ad 16] There was another argument from Psalm 104 where it is said: "God turned their hearts, to hate his people."[143] Augustine teaches very well about the sort of change God made in their hearts, in the same place: "It was not a good heart that he made evil, but such is God's goodness that he uses both angels and men; when they are evil, he draws the good from them." He increased the Israelites with children and with wealth, things that were good. Therefore by blessing the Hebrews, God turned the others' heart to envy, for envy arises through hating the happiness of others. So God turned hearts to hatred against the Hebrews that had chosen to be evil; he did not make their heart evil. You can see that I was not mistaken when I said that God promotes inwardly or outwardly such things as are good by nature, but through our fault occasions of sinning arise, yet occasions taken and not given. The opportunities he provides are not the most remote causes, like the fir tree felled on Mount Pelion,[144] but immediate occasions that stir up our desires, just as the Hebrews' happiness was the direct reason why the Egyptians sinned.

[Ad 14] Isaiah 63: "Why have you led us astray, Lord?" Jerome interprets this as God's lovingkindness.[145] God did not punish their sin immediately, so they began to condemn his judgments. God extended his mercy to them, which was good, but through their fault it was twisted into contempt. They could also be the words of the wicked casting the cause of their sins on God. Or else when believers think they are abandoned by God's grace through his just judgment, but afterward acknowledge their sins and speak like this—clearly they are not blaming God but marveling at his judgments. But no matter how you take it, God is exempted from the fault. [Ad 13] It is written in Jeremiah 4: "You have seduced your people." Jerome answered that what is said here seemed to the prophet to oppose the other words said before in the third chapter, where God revealed to the prophet "that Jerusalem would be

---

[141]Job 12:24–25.
[142]Augustine *De gratia et libero arbitrio* 43 (xxi) (PL 44.909).
[143]Ps. 105:25.
[144]A wooded mountain in Thessaly, prominent in Greek mythology as home to the Centaurs; the giants were said "to pile [Mt.] Ossa on Pelion" to scale Olympus; Vergil, *Georgica* i.281.
[145]Jerome *Comm. in Isaiam Prophetam* XII.xliii, vv. 15 ff. (PL 24.617–618).

called the throne of God and all nations gather to it. But now God said that the heart of king and princes would quake, the priests and people would be astonished."[146] Therefore the prophet cried, "You said there would be peace, but behold a sword."[147] Jerome says that we should distinguish the times; what was told first was to be fulfilled after the Babylonian captivity, while the calamity revealed afterward was already at the gates.

32. [Ad 17] Joshua says that God hardened the hearts of those nations of the Canaanites, that they should not make peace with Israel because God wished to cast them out;[148] therefore he seems to be the cause of sin. We answer with Augustine, from *Grace and Predestination,* chapter 8; it is also written in the book *On the Will of God*: "What is it to harden? that he will not soften. What is to blind? that he will not illuminate. What is it to draw or reject? that he will not call."[149] He does not speak of general calling, but of effectual. God does not induce fresh hardness not already within the heart. Thus it may be said that God hardened those nations because he would not make them relent, and so made peace with the Hebrews; nevertheless they were bound to be lost because of their own sins. It is further objected that no creature is destined to perdition. God did not create man in order to cast him off. Jerome is summoned, on the prophet Habakkuk chapter 2: "Although on account of its corruption the soul is made a habitat [*283r*] for Chaldeans, yet by nature it is the tabernacle of God, and no rational creature is made to give a home to demons."[150] To respond: he did say this, but if you take it in an absolute sense, he is against Scripture, which speaks otherwise. It says that the potter has power to make the same lump a vessel of honor or another of dishonor, and said of Pharaoh: "I have raised you up for the purpose of showing forth my power."[151] God endures vessels prepared for destruction in order to make his power manifest. It is said through Solomon in Proverbs 16 that "the wicked are made for the day of trouble."[152] The epistle of Jude mentions certain men who were designated earlier for this judgment or condemnation.[153]

The truth is that before this divine decree is put into effect, it has just cause for condemning someone. For meanwhile sins are committed for which those who will be condemned are judged. Yet it is God's decree not to call them effectually, and surely that decree is just. As to Jerome himself, I answer that the rational creature is not made for the purpose of being compelled; he

[146]Jerome *Comm. in Jeremiam Prophetam* I.iv, v. 10 (PL 24.708).
[147]Jer. 3:17.   [148]Josh. 11:20.
[149]Perhaps *De praedestinatione et gratia,* a spurious work (PL 45.1670).
[150]Jerome *Comm. in Abacuc Prophetam* I, chap. 1 [sic] (PL25.1280).
[151]Rom. 9:17, 21.   [152]Prov. 16:4.   [153]Jude 4.

sins through his own fault, yet it is in the decree of God not to hinder his fault. I answer further with Zwingli in his little book *The Providence of God*, chapter 6, that it would follow that God oversees theft and other things. He says, go further and you will say that this is done to declare his justice.[154] We see for what purpose the rational creature is made, to declare on the one hand the goodness of God, and on the other his severity. Who is wise that would appoint something to a goal he knew could not be reached? God foreknows all things; he knows that the wicked will be damned; accordingly, it is not to be said that he saves those who are to be condemned.

[Ad 18] Another argument was that if God wills the end, he also wills the means to that end. I agree: he willed the patience of martyrs, and therefore persecutions. Certainly he did so, but not in the same way, for what is good he willed for its own sake. The persecutions inflicted by tyrants he willed in another sense, namely because he wishes to permit and not obstruct; he wants to use them. If I say "in a sense" it must not be inferred that this is sophistry or falsehood. John says, "No one born of God commits sin,"[155] that is to say, against the Holy Spirit and without repentance. Since he sins in some way, it must not be inferred that he does so sophistically. That does not follow, for he sins truly, not in a manner misleading or false. The law is holy in a certain sense, yet causes wrath and damnation, but not falsely or sophistically. Paul himself speaks like this, and it is the truth. It does not follow that since God wills in some way, he willed it in falsehood and deceit. If God willed those things which aim at a goal, and sins in one sense because he has determined not to hinder them and wishes to use them, then an inevitable necessity follows, since his will is immutable. I answer: there will be necessity but no constraint [coactio]. If our will is deserted by the grace of God, it is through the necessity of sinning.

In terms of God's decrees, his providence is like iron, hard as steel. Zechariah, regarding the chariots and empires that would come after him: "They went," he says, "through mountains of iron."[156] The decrees of God are most firm. Christ said: "Those whom my father has given me, no one can snatch from my hands."[157] Yet something may seem to challenge this saying. Psalm 68 has: "May they be blotted out of the book of life."[158] If they are erased who were written in before, the will seems to be fickle. Read Augustine

---

[154]Zwingli *De providentia* VI: "But do not stop when you have said, 'Providence influenced the robber.' Go on, and say, 'He influenced the robber, but he also influenced and roused the judge against the robber.'" (CR XCIII.3; SW VI.3) 155.

[155]1 John 3:9.   [156]Zech. 6:1: "mountains of bronze."
[157]John 10:28.   [158]Psalm 69:28.

on that place: "We say, 'What I have written, I have written,' and will God wipe out what he has written? Then how are they said to be blotted out? The kind of speech mirrors their hope: in fact they were not written down but thought they were."[159] Some refer blinding and hardening to foreknowledge alone. But there is not a bare foreknowledge of these things, but the sort of divine will by which God cannot foreknow future things unless they are such as will happen. And those things that will or will not be cannot happen or exist unless God wills them to happen with some kind of will. Therefore there is a will of God that precedes foreknowledge; he has a will not to obstruct, but to use them according to his predestined counsels.

33. [Ad 19] Another argument: These tyrants Nebuchadnezzar, Sennacherib and others were in the hand of God as a staff and rod; therefore God seems to be the cause of sin. It is true that they were like a rod, and after they had fulfilled their office were thrown into the fire; yet they were not without sense, but were driven by their own evil will, and so are punished justly. There are two kinds of means, as I explained above. Yet this is no charade, as if God wished to use these evil things while warning against doing them. They act from an evil will; God uses their malice. Men also can make good use of the wrong acts of their enemies, and often do so without any deceit, in order to care for themselves and to show patience. Sometimes God uses sins to punish the sinners themselves; indeed this is ever the case, because sin is always a punishment of the sinner; at other times he uses them for the punishment of others.

[Ad 20] There was another argument, that God put it into David's heart to number the people. Scripture does speak like this: we don't hear these kinds of speech in the poets, but in the word of God. Plato might banish poets from his republic, but we may not reject Scriptures that speak like this.[160] I explained above how they are to be understood. God withdrew his help from David, not hindering him; he would use that work to punish the people. But it is objected that if God withdraws his grace, he does it justly. I agree; nevertheless he withdrew it. He even uses the devil. In Chronicles it is said that the devil drove David; therefore God also did it, since he gave the devil permission. But against that they object something we have often remarked, that when grace is removed from us, sin creeps in on its own, since [*284v*] by itself our own will inclines to it, as darkness naturally comes after light has gone. They say that God is like the sun, because his light shines everywhere, but

---

[159]Augustine *Enarratio in Psalmum* 68:29, cap. 13 (PL 36.862).
[160]Plato *Republic* II.377A–B and III.398A.

there are men who get into corners, and if his illumination is everywhere, what corners can men find where that light is not present? The divine Scripture says something else: it says of him that abused the talent, take it from him. David prayed: "Take not your spirit from me."[161] So God meant to use David's sin to punish the people. Some accuse the tragic poet Aeschylus unjustly for saying that if God will destroy and do away with someone, he provides causes and occasions.[162] Scripture says the same thing; it can speak against the laws of Plato, but not against the laws of God. It says that the sons of Eli did not listen to their father, because it was God's will to destroy them; Rehoboam would not heed the elders, because his overthrow came from God.[163]

It was said that if this is the way things stand, then if God is not the cause of sins he would not be the cause of all. That does not follow, for although God is not the cause of sin, he governs sins that are committed, he uses them and supplies their basis [substratum], insofar as it is something physical. But sin ought to be voluntary: this is true of actual sins but not of original sin. Moreover, the initial motions that are sins are not voluntary. In his treatise *On Free-will* Bernard notes certain degrees of men. Those who are blessed in heaven cannot sin. Adam was able not to sin. After sinning we are unable not to sin.[164] So are the damned, also the reprobate and wicked. But the godly and regenerate are able to resist sin, and make sure that sin will not reign in them completely; they receive this from the Spirit of God. By this distinction it seems that the sin of the damned is necessary, yet is it still sin. Even though it is from necessity, it is chosen; but not chosen in such a way that we have the strength by ourselves to choose the opposing side; we cannot choose the other except through the same Spirit of God. Sins are rightly punished, but without regard to whether you are able or not, only whether what you do is against the law of God or not.

[Ad 21] God does injury to no one. Therefore this objection does not hold in relation to him. If you see a blind man falling and don't stretch out your hand to help him or set him on his feet again, it looks like cruelty. God sees someone ready to fall but does not extend a hand; it looks like cruelty. In

---

[161]Matt. 25:28; Ps. 51:11.

[162]E.g., Prometheus is punished by divine decree and agents; the trilogy traces the transition from the rule of Force to that of Justice. Cf. Aeschylus *Suppliants* 88 ff., 533 ff.: humans depend on Zeus the "all-seeing" and "all-powerful father."

[163]1 Sam. 2:25; 1 Kings 12:15.

[164]Bernard of Clairvaux *De gratia et libero arbitrio* III: Triplicem esse libertatem, Naturae, Gratiae, Gloriae (PL 182.1004–1005). Cf. Augustine *De Genesi ad litteram* III.xxiii.37: posse non peccare/non posse non peccare/non posse peccare.

whom? In men, because the law is prescribed for them, but God is not subject to these laws. Zwingli responds in his books *On Providence* and *On True and False Religion*, where he deals with merit.[165] While God does not bestow such great gifts on the reprobate as on others, he gives them many things. The preaching of the Gospel is offered them, many other things are given to all, although he does not have saving mercy on all. God may do what he wills with his own. These, you say, reject his mercy. Here is Jerome on Jonah: God is by nature merciful and compassionate, ready to save by mercy those he cannot by justice, but we cast away his mercy that is offered us.[166] I accept it, as offered us by general preaching. Yet God does not change their wills; who denies that he can do this? If he does not choose, it is with justice he does not. Augustine in *On the Gift of Perseverance* chapter 4, says "In the same thing we see a difference of God's judgment, and in various things we see the same judgment."[167] There were twins in Rebecca's womb: before they had done either good or evil it is said, "Jacob I loved but Esau I hated." Some labored in the vineyard the whole day, others only one hour, yet all received the same reward.[168]

[Ad 22] As for the instance of the father of the house whose sons and servants sin, he claims that he does not compel them: he is rightly accused, because he has a prescribed law, but God has no law prescribed for him, he has prescribed for himself that he will do nothing unjustly; his will is the chief rule of justice. God forsakes the reprobates and is forsaken by them, and he acts rightly. Abandoning those who leave him is corroborated in 2 Chronicles, chapter 25. The prophet Azariah, son of Oded, says to King Amaziah: "When you forsake him, he will forsake you."[169] God is everywhere through his essence and power, but he is with his own by favor, grace, and assistance. In the first two ways he does not leave the wicked, only in the third. [Ad 23] The statement of Anselm in *On the Fall of the Devil* was introduced: "If God through an evil deed such as adultery brings forth a child, why cannot that will produce it through an evil will, since it is something natural?" We grant that a subject may be produced by God, but the defect must be considered in itself.

34. [Ad 24] We read in the Acts that they came together against Christ to do whatever the hand and counsel of God had decreed, and that Christ was delivered by the deliberate intention of God. As to the death of Christ, the divine will has another intention for Christ than for the Jews. God would have

---

[165]Zwingli *De providentia* VI (CR 93.3, SW VI.3) 184ff.; *De falsa et vera religione* 24 (CR 90.3, SW III) 842ff.

[166]Jerome *Comm. in Jonam Prophetam* III.6ff. (PL 25.1142).

[167]Augustine *De dono perseverantiae* VIII, 17 (PL 45, 1002–1003).

[168]Rom. 9:13; Matt. 20.   [169]2 Chron. 15:2; 25:7–8.

Christ bear the cross out of obedience and love; because he is our redemption, the divine nature made it possible for him to bear it. God allowed the Jews to act so cruelly, but in that permission lay a will not to hinder their evil choice, that he might use it and that redemption might follow. This shows that he could have prevented it if he had wished: "Could not my father," said Jesus, "give me eleven legions of angels to fight for me?"[170] He used that sin to redeem us. God offered many good things to the Jews: he used preachings, miracles, and warnings, but through their fault they took them the wrong way. Therefore they are left to the necessity of sinning.

Where will free will be now? It is lost. Augustine in chapter 30 of his *Manual for Laurence* says: "When man had sinned, he lost both himself and his free will."[171] He says so twice in that chapter and elsewhere. We have it in book 2 of the *Sentences,* distinction 25.[172] Bernard, however, says that it is not lost. They do not disagree when rightly understood. Augustine takes free will as the faculty of choosing opposites, this or that. While we are unregenerate, we cannot truly perform acts acceptable to God, unless we are restored by the Son of God, because free will does not remain in us in regard to such matters. When Bernard says that free will remains, what does he mean? Although men sin, they are not compelled, they consent and are willing, and this kind of free will remains. He explains himself when he distinguishes three kinds of liberty. He lists freedom from compulsion, from sin when one is regenerate, and from misery when one dwells in heaven. We have no freedom from misery in this life, but we do from necessity; by necessity he means compulsion. This appears in Bernard.[173] He places freedom of the will in God; he is necessarily good, yet this does not destroy his freedom. Angels and saints in the heavenly country cannot sin, yet they have free will. Also he grants a freedom to the devil and the damned, yet they are unable to be good. They willfully choose evil of their own accord, not that they can do the opposite. The same author says: "It is grace that preserves and choice [arbitrium] that is preserved. How? It accepts healing, that is it assents or consents," but he does not say that it consents by itself; rather he refers to the place of Paul that "We cannot by ourselves think anything good, much less consent," and "God works in us both to will and to perform."[174] Apart from us, he says, "God precedes us by convey-

---

[170]Matt. 26:53 [sic: *undecium*].

[171]Augustine *Enchiridion ad Laurentium* 30 (PL 40.246–247).

[172]Peter Lombard *Sent.* 2, dist. 25, distinguishing *libertas a necessitate, a peccato, a miseria* (PL 192.1053).

[173]Bernard of Clairvaux *De gratia et Libero Arbitrio* VIII.24 (PL 182.1014). Cf. non compulsus est, sed consensit; see idem xii.39 (PL 182.1022).

[174]2 Cor. 3:5; Phil. 2:13.

ing good notions to us." He changes the will afterwards; he changes the effects, and once changed, consent may follow. So he says that God does four things in us. First he arouses by inserting good notions. Then he heals, that is, he changes the will. Third, he confirms, that is he leads to action. Fourth, he preserves, that we may not be lacking, that we may persevere and accomplish good work.[175]

[CONCLUSION]

35. To sum up, we also affirm that as regards sin, God is, as Epiphanius says, ἀναίτιον παντῶν κακῶν, that is, guiltless of all evils, since he is not the proper cause; and yet he does not sleep.[176] This word [*anaition*] also signifies blameless. We cannot draw God within law; what he does, he does with justice. For our part we add: it is a general belief to be retained in the church that nothing happens in the world, whether good or bad, outside God's providence. Human actions cannot exceed the bounds of divine providence, since "All the hairs of our head are numbered."[177] If sparrows, those tiny birds of lowest esteem, do not fall to the ground without the will of God, what shall we say of human affairs that are so much higher? Divine providence stretches as far as possible; if it has differing regard for the good and the bad, yet they are not accomplished without the providence of God, which is the divine will, by which things are well and firmly governed and directed to their proper ends. Nor should it offend us that he leaves some evils in the world, for although they are against particular natures, yet they make for the common good. If all evils were removed we would lack many good things. It is said that there would be no life for lions if there were no slaughter of sheep by which lions are fed; nor would there be the endurance of martyrs unless the cruelty of tyrants were permitted by God.

What Plato writes in the second book of *The Republic* seems to count against our position.[178] He says that God is the author of only a few things for humanity, because there are many evils among us and God causes none of them. By this he seems to compress divine providence into a narrow room. If he means effectual cause and is speaking of sins, we grant it; but meanwhile providence is not in a deep sleep. In the same place Plato has what must not

---

[175]Bernard of Clairvaux, *De gratia et libero arbitrio* XIV.46 (PL 182.1026).
[176]Epiphanius of Salamis (315–403), perhaps *Adv. Haereses (Panarion)* I.3.6 (PG 41.661). Martyr owned a copy of this work; see CSV 213.
[177]Matt. 10:30.
[178]Plato *Republic* II.379–380.

be granted in general by believers, for he denies that God comes to men in the likeness of strangers. But angels were entertained by Abraham and Lot in the form of guests.[179] When he says that God cannot be changed in substance, is it not true? but we cannot admit that he did not appear in certain forms at times. He talked with Moses from the burning bush; he declared himself on Mount Sinai by voices; he revealed himself to the prophets in a variety of forms. I think that Plato means those base mutations described by the poets, that he was changed into a swan, an eagle, or a bull; things that must not be attributed to God.[180]

36. When I said that all things whatsoever are ruled by divine providence, and that what Plato said presents no obstacle, it seems insufficient. Damascene is also against it, who said in his second book, chapter 29, that "those things not within us" are subject to the providence of God, adding that "things within us are not under God's providence but belong to our free will."[181] Will our actions therefore, which he says are within us, escape the providence of God? Let those believe this who choose. I do not. He adds something even harder, that "the choice of doing things is in us, but the perfection and accomplishment of good things is a cooperation of God and ourselves." Who will say it comes from us if we choose that the good should be done? The apostle says that "God works in us, to will and to perform."[182] Where Damascene takes such things away from divine providence, I cannot agree. He distinguishes providence as "good pleasure" and "permission";[183] I am not against these but affirm them both; providence not only rules the good but brings it about, while it permits evil, yet not so as to leave it completely on its own, for it puts it to use. He distinguishes this permission from good pleasure, holding that one dispenses and instructs, effecting the discipline of saints, when for a time they are left helpless. At other [285r] times it is called perfect permission, and in a sense without hope, when through their own default people perish and proceed beyond improvement. We also say that

---

[179]Gen. 18:2ff., 19:1ff.

[180]Plato's quarrel with the poets stems from his rejection of anthropomorphism, which debases the Idea of God; see p. 255, n. 160.

[181]Martyr quotes from the Greek, adding his own Latin translation. The key terms are: τα (οὐκ) ἐφ᾿ ἡμίν: "I mean those that are not in our hands: for those that are in our own power are outside the sphere of Providence and within that of our Free-will." Damascene *De Fide Orth.* 2.29, "De Providentia" (PG 94.964).

[182]Phil. 2:13.

[183]Damascene *De fide orth.*: κατ᾿ εὐδοκίαν, κατὰ συγχώρησιν. Martyr, SAM 2 (CP 1.17.38), had used this scholastic distinction between the will as signified and effectual: *aliam esse voluntatem signi, aliam vero efficacem, vel ut alij scribunt, beneplaciti.*

God leaves his elect for a time, but others forever. Moreover, he says that "by an inward cause" God wants men to share in the process of salvation, but that later he will punish them when they sin. He calls this "a following will," as though it follows through our own fault.[184] I say that the will of God is single, while objects are diverse. There are the elect, whom he wants to be saved; there are also reprobates, whom he wishes to be punished for their sins. But we should not linger on this step, for he will display his power through them. So I take providence to be universal, whatever Damascene says. Augustine also says so in the 58th sentence: nothing happens, either visibly or sensibly, that is not either ordered or permitted from the invisible or ideal court of the high Emperor, and so he excludes nothing from the providence of God.[185]

37. These are the points I judged relevant to this subject. Much more remains, but an end must be made. I am well aware that the distinguished Philip Melanchthon, whom I love and honor, seems to speak differently. But I appeal to the man himself in his earlier *Commonplaces*—read what is there on predestination and free will.[186] He says that the term "free will"—something I probably would not have said—is quite foreign to Holy Scripture, and from the judgment and meaning of the spirit. Further he says that the Platonic philosophy has compromised piety from the beginning of the church. In the conclusion to that place, he says that if we come to our own inward and outward doings and refer them to providence, all things come to pass as intended. But if outward actions are referred to the will, there we have freedom. If we consider the inward benefits which God requires, there is no freedom: if our emotions begin to rebel, they cannot be repressed. Ambrose says the same thing on Luke, and it is often cited by Augustine, that our heart is not in our own power.[187] There are also others who agree with them, including Zwingli and Luther, heroes of reformed religion; likewise Oecolampadius, Bucer, and Calvin. I could name others, but try not to overdo the supporters. I said that to speak properly, God is not the cause of sin, and that nothing occurs in the world, whether good or evil, outside divine providence. I am sorry if I have not hit the mark [scopus]. If anyone can show through cogent arguments that this opinion is unfaithful, or harmful to good behavior, I stand prepared to

---

[184]Damascene *De fide orth*: "Itaque prima illa voluntas, antecedens dicitur et beneplacitum, cujus ipse causa sit: secunda autem, consequens voluntas et permissio, ex nostra causa ortum habens"; the original has προηγούμενον θέλημα, καὶ εὐδοκία ... ἐπόμενον θέλημα, καὶ παραχώρησις (PG 94, 969–970).

[185]Augustine *Viginti unius sententiarum* 58 (PL 40.725ff).

[186]Melanchthon *Loci Communes Theologici* (1521): "The Power of Man, Especially Free Will" ed. W. Pauck, Library of Christian Classics, 19, SCM 1959) 23.

[187]Ambrose *De fuga saeculi* 1, in Augustine *De dono perseverantiae* 21 (ix), 32 (xiii), etc.

alter it. I have been verbose about this because it is a matter of great moment, and recurs often in Holy Scripture. Moreover, things that are set down fully are understood better than when they are treated sporadically here and there. So much on this: let us return to our narrative.[188]

[188]I.e., to the commentary on 2 Samuel, resuming with the beginning of chapter 17 (fol. 285 r). The Commonplace in LC/CP adds material, in §§38–42a, from a shorter scholium with the same title, *An Deus Sit Author Peccati* from SAM (1 Sam. 2, fols. 19 r–22 r), and from REG (1 Kings 1:16) §43, and GEN 18:22, §44. In addition, the CP, 205b–206b, ends its locus with our third "Summary."

PART FIVE

Free Will and Predestination

PETRI MARTYRIS
VERMILII
Locorum Communium
Theologicorum ex ipsius scriptis
sincere decerptorum,

TOMVS PRIMVS
IN QVATVOR CLASSES DISTINCTVS,
QVEM MOX SECVNDVS
SVBSEQVETVR.

*Cum INDICE quadrigemino: Auctorum, Titulorum,
Locorum Scripturæ, Rerum denique
& verborum.*

BASILEAE
AD PERNEAM LECYTHVM
M D XXC.

Title page from Loci communes, printed in Basel by P. Perna, 1580

About the Translations

Free Will and Predestination

DE LIBERO ARBITRIO. The relation between divine and human willing had been a hot topic throughout Martyr's life since his student days at Padua, as we have seen; it was still high on the agenda when Martyr first reached Strasbourg in 1542. His first book (1544; on the Apostles' Creed) spoke of the Christians' "happy freedom"—God "does not coerce and compel them in a way that would violate personality. He teaches them persuasively and effectively."[1] Bucer's commentary on Romans of 1536 had included a lengthy treatment of predestination, followed by Calvin's 1539 *Institutes*, revised during his Strasbourg residence. Calvin's debate with Jerome Bolsec sharpened the issue, while the Zurich theologian Theodore Bibliander (1500?–1564) opposed Calvin from an Erasmian position. Late in 1559 Bibliander challenged Martyr himself on the issue. Martyr was lecturing on the books of Samuel; he already had scholia on *De Praedestinatione* and *De libero arbitrio* in his 1558 commentary on Romans, as well as later scholia on *An Deus sit author peccati*.[2] Martyr's open lecture of January 25, 1560, constituted his formal response.[3] The Council retired Bibliander the next month, on the grounds of age and frailty.

[1]Peter Martyr Vermigli, Credo 47, in EW 57.
[2]See the third summary below; also J. C. McLelland, "The Reformed Doctrine of Predestination according to Peter Martyr," *Scottish Journal of Theology* 8, no. 3 (September 1955): 255ff., and PMRE 212–216. In a letter to Calvin from Strasbourg on March 8, 1555 Martyr had complained of Bibliander's denial of the eucharistic elements as "symbols of the Lord's body and blood," adding: "He does not honestly admit the doctrine of predestination"; Martyr, *Epist. Theol.*, DM 343–48.
[3]*De Libero Arbitrio*, included in Perna's additions to the LC (Basel, 1580–82) and in Marten's CP, add. 101–125. See BIB XIII.3. Our translation is based on the edition of Vautrollerius (London, 1583) fols. 971–989.

This historical setting provides more information about Martyr's opponents than we have for most of his scholia. His polemical monographs are explicit in naming the adversary: The *De Coelibatu sacerdotum et Votis monasticis* is against Richard Smith, his predecessor as regius professor in Oxford; the *Defensio ... de ss Eucharistiae Sacramento* has Stephen Gardiner in its title; the *Dialogus* on the two natures in Christ is aimed at Johann Brenz. But Martyr is capable of sustained argument, rebutting "they say," "some will object," and even "our adversaries maintain" without feeling the need to identify his opponents by name or by school. In his doctrine of providence he cites ancient schools of Stoics and Epicureans, and on freedom of the will he obviously has in mind modern Pelagians, Roman theologians in particular. Albert Pighius is mentioned by name in *Romans* often enough, and Tommaso di Vio Cajetan, Johannes Eck, Stanislas Hosius, and others only once or twice.[4] In the present lecture he studiously avoids naming Bibliander, who was the reason for its presentation.

Martyr's work on the cluster of problems before us contains a crucial key to its interpretation: Willing involves *power*, causation. Martyr handles the question in Aristotelian and Thomistic terms. He follows the Philosopher's distinction between the voluntary and the involuntary,[5] with its key definition: Compulsory acts [τα βιαια] are so "when the cause is in the external circumstances and the agent contributes nothing."[6] This leads into Martyr's favorite distinction between compulsion and infallibility: "The necessity that comes from God's foreknowledge and predestination, namely such a necessity as is not absolute but *ex hypothesi*, which we can term *consequentiae, infallibilitis et certitudinis*, but in no way *coactionis*."[7]

Aristotle's fourfold causality helped Martyr, as it did Aquinas,[8] with the thorny problem of *concursus*, the joint activity of divine and human wills. Concurrence is possible only if we acknowledge a distinction among causes, notably between primary (the ultimate or final cause) and secondary (mate-

---

[4]J. P. Donnelly provides a table of "references to contemporary authors" in CSV 38.

[5]Aristotle *NE* III.l; for Martyr, see LC 2.2.41–61.

[6]Aristotle *NE* 1110b2; see Martyr's "Free Will" §16, p. 306, below.

[7]P. Martyr Vermigli *De Praed.* 58; cf. "Free Will," §11, p. 297, and §16, p. 306, below; see McLelland, "Reformed Doctrine of Predestination"; J. Staedtke, "Der Züricher Prädestinationsstreit von 1560," *Zwingliana* 9 (1953) 536–546; PMRE chap. 5, "Zurich Theologian (1556/62)." The divine will is *simplex*, manifesting a *necessitas ex hypothesi et consequentiae/infallibilitis* because everything is ordered on the *hypothesis decreti divini*, whereas a *nec. coactionis et consequentis* would imply sheer necessity or fate.

[8]Aristotle *Meta.* V.2.1031a25ff.; Aquinas ST Ia.4.13 ad 1; 19, 6, 3, and ad 3: *causa prima et media*; cf QQ 23 (*De Prov*) 24 (*De Praed.*); SCG III.70ff.

rial, formal, efficient). Second causes became the touchstone of Reformed doctrine in both the doctrine of providence and the doctrine of predestination. The concept of concurrence guided the so-called Reformed scholastics of the following century in elaborating the doctrine of providence.[9] Karl Barth charges that this "divine accompanying" was forced into "purely formal concepts of God and his will and work," and resulted in "the tragedy of the Reformed doctrine of providence and more particularly of the divine *concursus.*"[10]

Martyr's lengthy lecture sums up his mature position on divine grace and human freedom. Augustine's anti-Pelagian writings offered him a wealth of definition and argument against his opponents, viewed as the latest brand of the Pelagian heresy. Quotations abound, taken from Augustine's *On Grace and Free-Will*, *Against the Two Pelagian Letters*, *On Rebuke and Grace*, and the paired *Predestination of the Saints* and *The Gift of Perseverance*; they are especially apparent in "Free Will," where there are over forty direct quotations from Augustine and other quotations from Prosper. They share common biblical passages: God both wills and works (Phil. 2:13), salvation depends not on our will or effort but on God's mercy (Rom. 9:17), for the elect are *vocati secundum propositum* (Rom. 8:28). There are also concepts such as operant and cooperant grace, *posse non/non posse peccare*, the *massa perdita*, and privative evil. As Augustine's classic work *De gratia et libero arbitrio* declares, innocents would require only a helping grace, but redeemed sinners need more, not only the *posse* but also the *velle*. For both theologians, "the real exercise of the will's freedom lies not in the capacity to choose but in the capacity to fulfill," hence the stress on effectual calling; grace relates not so much to the will's capacity as to its impotence.[11]

A final act for Martyr in the predestinarian debate arose through his former disciple and colleague Girolamo Zanchi, who had remained at

[9]E.g. "God's providence does not remove but posits second causes"; see Wolleb, *Compend. Theol. Chr.* (1626); "God concurs with creatures in the mode proper to the first cause and accommodated to the nature of second causes"; The divine will acts not "subjectively in second causes" but "effectively, as the first cause"; see J. H. Heidegger, *Corpus Theologiae Christianae* (1626); cited in H. Heppe, *Reformed Dogmatics: Set Out and Illustrated from the Sources,* rev. ed. by E. Bizer, trans. G. T. Thomson (London : Allen, & Unwin, 1950) 258 ff.; cf. *Reformed Reader*, vol. 1, ed. W. S. Johnson and J. T. Leith (Louisville: Westminster/John Knox Press, 1993) 174 ff.

[10] K. Barth, CD III.3.94 ff., 115 ff. Cf. C. Hodge, *Systematic Theology* (London: Nelson & Sons, 1873) 1:77 ff., 598 ff., on *concursus*. Barth's point is that the "absolute unlikeness of the two *causae causantes* should be brought into sharp relief, with the consequent rejection of any idea of an *analogia causae*" (103).

[11]See P. Lehmann, "The Anti-Pelagian Writings," chap. 8 of *A Companion to the Study of St Augustine*, ed. R. W. Battenhouse (New York: Oxford University Press, 1955) 203–230.

Strasbourg. In debate with Johannes Marbach, Zanchi prepared fourteen theses on the subject, visiting Martyr in Zurich to discuss them. Martyr endorsed them in the "Zurich Confession on Predestination" of December 1561 which he prepared at Henrich Bullinger's request. Jacob Hottinger calls the confession "a remarkable document for the history of the development of Reformed Church teaching, and a proof of Martyr's dominant influence in his Zurich College."[12] Zanchi's own theology is noteworthy for its strongly articulated doctrine of the divine attributes, from which both predestination and providence may be deduced.[13]

*   *   *

THE THREE SUMMARIES. *Free Will, Providence and Predestination*, and *Is God the Cause and Author of Sin?* are not necessarily by Peter Martyr. Rudolph Gualther found them among Martyr's papers and added them to his 1580 edition of the *Loci*,[14] but their authorship has been a matter of considerable debate. They were commonly ascribed to Bullinger, since they were in an unknown hand but with Bullinger's marginalia. In 1957 Peter Walser's research led him to attribute them to Vermigli. Joachim Staedtke challenged this and left the matter uncertain. Marvin W. Anderson noted the second summary's anomaly in bringing predestination within providence, whereas "Vermigli's understanding of predestination embraces an exclusively soteriological orientation." J. P. Donnelly reviewed the arguments, and on internal evidence concluded that Martyr was indeed their author.[15] This has been challenged in turn by Frank A. James III on the basis of his doctoral research on the *gemina praedestinatio*, leading him to suggest as author one of Martyr's students,

[12]The text of the Zurich Confession is given in J. H. Hottinger, *Historiae Ecclesiasticae Novi Testamenti* (Zurich, 1667) VIII.843–847. See McLelland, " Reformed Doctrine of Predestination," 267 ff.; P. Walser, *Die Prädestination bei Heinrich Bullinger im Zusammenhang mit seiner Gotteslehre* (Zurich: Zwingli-Verlag, 1957) 181 ff., "Das Zürcher Gutachten für Zanchius von 1561."

[13]G. Zanchi, *The Doctrine of Absolute Predestination Stated and Asserted*, trans. A. M. Toplady (London: Sovereign Grace Union, 1930). See O. Gründler, *Die Gotteslehre Girolami Zanchis* (Neukirchen-Vluyn: Neukirchener Verlag, 1965) 2: "Zanchis Lehre von Vorsehung und Prädestination," 97 ff. Cf. Muller, *Christ and the Decree*, 110 ff., "Christology and Predestination in the Theology of Zanchi."

[14]R. Gualther, appendix to the *Loci Communes* (Zurich: C. Froschauer, 1580): "accesserunt … nec antea publicati, Loci de Libero arbitrio, Providentia Dei, Praedestinatione, et Causa peccati." See BIB XIII.3, 100–101.

[15]P. Walser "Die fraglichen drei Traktate," in *Die Pradestination bei Heinrich Bullinger im Zusammenhang mit seiner Gotteslehre* (Zurich: Zwingli Verlag, 1957) 200–210; J. Staedtke, "Drei um strittene Traktate Peter Martyr Vermiglis," *Zwingliana* 11 (1962): 553–554; PMRE 89ff; CSV 117–18, and "Three Disputed Tracts" in *Essays Presented to Myron P. Gilmore*, ed. S. Bertelli and G. Ramakus (Florence: La Nuova Italia, 1978), 37–46.

someone who wished to summarize the master's doctrine on this cluster of important questions. As we noted, James agrees with Anderson's assessment that the phrase *pars providentiae* contradicts the soteriological nature of Martyr's doctrine of predestination.[16] The text states: "Predestination is part of divine providence, as it were [*pars quaedam providentiae divinae*]: for it is the strength and power of God by which he appoints and directs men to obtain eternal life through Jesus Christ." For Martyr, however, the "properly predestinated" are those elected to salvation; the impious are passed over because of their sins. James emphasizes the fact that Martyr moves predestination from its Thomistic locus in the doctrine of providence, to soteriology, following the "late Augustinian tradition" of Gregory of Rimini.[17] Anderson also points out the shift from "predestinate/reprobate" in the treatise (lectures on Romans, 1550; published 1558) to "regenerate/impious" in the 1560 lecture. Moreover, in the Zurich Confession of 1561 Martyr emphasizes predestination *in Christo*, recalling a theme familiar since his Oxford lectures.[18]

Against the James thesis, which denies Martyr's authorship, we note two points. First, the three are written in the first person; the third summary's introductory paragraph in particular explains Martyr's reasons for defending himself against the charge that he makes God the cause of sin. Of course, a student taking notes could have copied all three but confused the statement on providence. The second point concerns material in the scholium *De Providentia*, particularly Martyr's conclusion: "We have in a sense established the roots and foundation of predestination" ("Providence" §16). If we relate this to his explicit identification (in the lecture on Free Will) with Zwingli's teaching on providence, we can suggest a more complex view of the relationship between the two doctrines.[19] So there is evidence on both sides, and the matter remains unsettled. Our inclusion in the present volume allows readers to judge for themselves.

De libero arbitrio sums up the chief arguments from the 1560 Zurich lecture translated above. It begins with Peter Lombard's definition: A power of the will "by which the good is chosen when grace assists, or evil when grace

[16]See Introduction, pp. xxxiii ff.

[17]F. A. James III, "A Late Medieval Parallel, " in H. A. Oberman and F. A. James III, eds. *Via Augustini* (Leiden: Brill, 1991)

[18]PMRE 211ff., "Theology of Election." Cf. K. Sturm, *Die Theologie Peter Martyr Vermiglis während seines ersten Aufenthalts in Strassburg 1542–1547* (Neukirchen-Vluyen: Neukirchener Verlag, 1971) 189ff.

[19]"Free Will" §8, p. 303; cf. Muller, *Christ and the Decree*, 62ff: "Predestination in the Vermigli-Massonius *Loci Communes*."

fails." Its three main propositions rehearse the Augustinian themes of the lecture.

De providentia et praedestinatione recapitulates much of the scholium on providence as well as the *De Praedestinatione* (ROM 9; LC 3.1). Martyr begins with the divine purpose (*propositum Dei*), the free will of an omnipotent God. This is the only cause; more important is the effect of this purpose, namely the salvation of the elect. *Praedestinatio proprie* applies to the elect only; it is the first of a series of salvific events, followed by *vocatio, iustificatio,* and finally *glorificatio.* But because Martyr also relates reprobation, even if passively, to the initial *propositum Dei,* a form of double predestination results.[20]

The third and briefest topic, *An Deus Sit causa et author peccati,* summarizes the scholium *An Deus sit author peccati* (commentary on 2 Samuel 16:22) translated above. The problem of divine responsibility for human sin is the logical result of a strong doctrine of predestination, particularly its dual character; Martyr shows his unease by returning to the question several times throughout his writing career, as already noted. A gradual development in more philosophical terms is evident, with the latter scholia drawing heavily on scholastic concepts such as *causa removens prohibens.* This allows Martyr to hold "that God is not *per se* and properly the cause of sin; second, that nothing happens in the world, not even sins themselves, outside his will and choice or providence."[21] The second half of his formula means that providence will include divine willing as privation or the removal of obstacles to human sin. The "denial of sufficient grace," in Donnelly's opinion, "gave him a simple, clear, and pure position, but the price was high for it entails what many will deem a very harsh doctrine of predestination."[22]

---

[20] See McLelland, "Reformed Doctrine of Predestination," 259ff. As F. James, "Late Medieval Parallel," 183, points out, that article's view that Martyr does not teach double predestination requires qualification. James credits Gregory and Vermigli with "a passive approach to reprobation," whereas Calvin has "an active stress on condemnation"; even this asymmetrical or softer form implies *gemina praedestinatio.* The correlative question of whether this implies supralapsarianism remains debatable. Donnelly, *Calvinism and Scholasticism,* thinks so, while Muller and James soften this judgment considerably. See James, "Late Medieval Parallel," 184: "Vermigli's Christological orientation inclines him toward a more infralapsarian conception, while *sub specie aeternitatis* there is a form of supralapsarian will"; Muller, *Christ and the Decree,* 65: "This definition presses toward a purely soteriological and essentially infralapsarian definition of predestination and toward a discussion of the counsel or purpose of God behind the elective decree, the *propositum Dei.*"

[21] See "Author" §6, p. 333, below. The earlier treatise, *De Praed.* in ROM 1558, had acknowledged that "God in a sense (*quodammodo*) willed that first sin and was in a sense (*quodammodo*) the author"; see James, "A Late Medieval Parallel" 179.

[22] CSV 122; again, we may note the softer appraisal in Muller, *Christ and the Decree,* 62ff.

Common Places, Appendix

Free Will

[DEFINITION]

1. *[971]* The term "free will" [liberum arbitrium] is not found in Holy Scripture so far as I know. Yet what it means should not be taken lightly, for it is widely debated; it provokes considerable controversy these days and has always done so among scholars and theologians. Even philosophers never mentioned it when speaking of the soul, but instead put the word "choice" [*proairesis*].[1] For they place in the mind only understanding and will, while some add memory. Cicero also, an excellent author of the Latin language, never said *liberum arbitrium*. But in the book *On Fate* he repeatedly said *libera voluntas*, which is the same thing.[2] The Greeks called it *autexousion* [αὐτεξούσιον], a word compounded of *autos* [αὐτός] and *exousia* [ἐξουσία],

---

[1] προαίρεσις; Greek terms may be rendered in the original only the first time, as the context determines.

[2] E.g. Cicero *De Fato* chap. XI: Carneades "taught that the soul might possess free-will...."

A lecture given on January 25, 1560 (Martyr refers to the conversion of Saint Paul in §15). Its context in the predestinarian debate has been described in the introduction. The text is preserved in the material added by Peter Perna for his 1580–1582 edition of the *Loci Communes* (fols. 971–989). Page numbers are given in brackets, section numbers from LC (cf. CP, add. pp. 101–125. There is an earlier scholium, *De Libero Arbitrio* [DLA] in ROM 7:25, published 1558 (LC/CP 2.2.1–30), which Martyr uses as basis for the present lecture.

271

meaning precisely to have authority and power over oneself, so that you cannot be constrained; in this sense free will can be attributed to God, who cannot be compelled because he has no will that may be moved.[3] Nor can good angels sin or be turned away from God whom they have before their eyes; in this way are they said to have free will, and devils also. So far as I know, the term "one's own power" is not in Scripture. The Latin phrase *liberum arbitrium* consists of two words:[4] *arbitrari* means to weigh, perceive, suppose, or judge; we have already said that the adjective *liber* describes one who has authority over himself. Thus it appears that we have free will when the appetite is moved by itself toward what the understanding or power of knowing reveals to it. It is indeed in the will, but it takes root in the understanding since it is appropriate that something is judged and measured first, and then follows either refusal or endorsement.[5] Augustine often said that it is a faculty of both reason and will. And Damascene said that free will both judges and apprehends.[6] Judgment belongs to the function of understanding, but desire belongs to the will. Reason or understanding has the place of an advisor, but the will desires, accepts, or rejects.

2. Accordingly, we may define free will as a certain faculty of the will that follows the directive of the intellect to refuse or desire something by itself. When I say faculty I understand power only, in case someone thinks that I mean some quality, as if it were an additional habit, although Bernard said that free will is a free habit of his own mind.[7] Thus in our present discussion it is a faculty of willing, but not an absolute will, since we ourselves seek happiness and cannot do otherwise. It is said to be a faculty of will, since "purpose" [*proairesis*] derives from it. Whatever we choose, we do so for the sake of something else, not for itself but through some previous deliberation. For we do not choose unless things have been identified, and distinguishing must be done by the understanding. This is the definition of cause; if it is not enough, we will bring another, from the Master of the *Sentences,* book 2, distinction 25.

---

[3]Cf. Calvin *Inst.* II.2.4 on the key terms. His treatment parallels Martyr's, moving from philosophers through Fathers to establish definitions (*Inst* II.2, "Man in his present state, despoiled of freedom of will, and subjected to a miserable slavery").

[4]Reading: Latinum vocabulum [liberi] arbitrij.

[5]Martyr *NE* I.1, VI.2, follows Aristotle in giving reason priority over will: "The good is the object of every appetite." DLA begins in similar fashion: "Choice seems to consist in this, that we follow as we think good what the reason determines ... although the nature of free choice is clearest in the will, it has its roots in reason."

[6]Augustine *De gratia et libero arbitrio* 5 (iii) (PL 44.890); John of Damascus *De Fide Orth.* II.27 (PG 94.959ff.).

[7]Bernard of Clairvaux *De Gratia et Lib. Arb.* 2 (PL 182.1003).

He says that free will is a faculty of the reason and the will by which the good is chosen when God's grace assists, or evil when his grace is absent. The Master thought it well to add grace, lest he seem to agree with the Pelagians, yet he does not say justifying grace, but prevenient, which may move and arouse the mind.[8] If we then assent to God's word, regeneration follows.

I think this is enough to understand the nature of free will. But the things or objects to which this will applies must be identified. They are of two kinds. Some are of a lower order, subject to the senses and human reason, not exceeding our capacity or requiring supernatural light, such as whether I am teaching or not teaching, whether I stay or not, whether war is undertaken or not. These matters are subject to our senses and may be discerned by reason in either case. Other things are higher, of which we cannot even dream: for instance, to believe in Jesus Christ; to obey the commandments of God; to trust in him, to love him with all one's heart, all the soul, and all the strength; to obey the law through good deeds and the guidance of the Spirit of God. These are sublime matters, as Paul said: "The natural man does not perceive the things of the Spirit of God." Again, "The eye has not seen, nor ear heard, nor came it into man's heart, what God has prepared for those who love him," and so forth.[9]

3. Another distinction follows, concerning the human state and condition.[10] Adam enjoyed his own state before he sinned; then followed a pitiful corruption before men were regenerate, while they existed in mere darkness. The third condition consists in regeneration itself. The fourth is after regeneration, when men are now born anew and strengthened by grace. The fifth is that of the blessed, who are in heaven at the last. I do not need to discuss them all. Regarding the state of the first man, we have but little in Holy Scripture, except we know that God made him righteous and that he fell by his free will. Here we need not speak of the last, since it is of little relevance to our subject. [972] So three states remain to be considered: Before one is regenerate; how one stands in regeneration; and thirdly after regeneration. When David was given a choice by the prophet Gad, he was in the third condition; he was already regenerate and returned to favor.[11] But to clarify the whole subject we must speak of other things.

---

[8]Lombard, *Sent.* II, dist. 25 (PL 192.1052): "non justificantem, sed praevenientem." Calvin *Inst.* II.2.6, also approves of Lombard's distinctions.

[9]I Cor. 2:9, 14.

[10]Cf. DLA §2: "First we must distinguish the human state and condition. Surely at least four different states will be found."

[11]2 Sam. 24:12.

I maintain that those not yet regenerate have partial free will, namely in relation to those good things that are subject to the senses and do not exceed human capacity. Experience teaches that I can stand or sit, go away or remain. Such things are done in us by nature, the sinews and muscles and limbs being moved by deliberation; there are greater motions, but a certain power of restraining lies in the will or reason. Hypocrites often do such things; they too have awkward gestures, but led by a thirst for fame they control them by their reason,[12] for they judge that they cannot attain the glory of God through ordinary feelings. Yet this is not always possible; that is why I called it a partial free will, because the emotions and affections have such force that it is not within the power of reason to contain them. It should be noted here that when first aroused and brought into motion, these initial ideas or intrusions are not under control, nor is the restraining reason itself always in our power. Thus Ambrose said, as Augustine often alleged: "Our heart is not in our own power."[13] I take "is not" to mean "not always," since sometimes it is within our power; but there may be such a strong emotion of fear that those who have decided to remain firm in battle are moved to flight, since reason is not able to restrain it. This happened to the Canaanites in Joshua's time; although they wished to destroy the Israelites, they could not withstand the presence of Joshua, for as he had promised, God struck terror into them.[14] Therefore, freedom is partly in such affairs, and partly not. Nor does it hold for all ages, since children and fools are moved like animals rather than moved by themselves.

4. If asked whether we can do those things that may agree with the law of God through such partial freedom, I reply that we can use that term in certain ways when we understand it properly, since Scripture affirms it. Paul says to the Romans: "The Gentiles do by nature what the law requires."[15] For no nation is so savage or barbarous that it is not touched by some sense of right, justice, and honesty. On the other hand, if the law of God is understood properly and truly we cannot by such freedom perform what agrees with it. The law does not require of us mere externals, indeed that is the least concern; above all it requires good inward motives, that we should love God with all our heart, with all our soul, and with all our strength. This precept is as it were the soul and spirit of all others, so that whoever would obey other commands must do so with all the heart, all the soul, and all the strength with which he

---

[12] *Hypocritae* were mimes, who accompanied actors by supplying appropriate gestures.

[13] Ambrose *De Fuga Saeculi* 1, in Augustine, *Contra duas Ep. Pelag.* IV.30, *De bono persev.* 20, 32(13), 48 (19): "our heart and our thoughts are not in our own power...."

[14] Jos. 5:1.   [15] Rom. 2:14.

follows God.[16] With that mind he must refrain from robberies, uncleanness, and the like for the sake of God whom he loves with all the heart. We might say instead that by this freedom our works may agree with the civil or economic law, which has regard to outward acts and is not much concerned with the will.

When Paul says that the law is directed against the wicked, the ungodly, and murderers,[17] this does not imply that we can fulfill the law. One may also say that the law is not given for the just, since they are regenerate and free from the threat of damnation, having no law to accuse or condemn them, though not yet perfectly regenerated. Nevertheless, it cannot be deduced from this that by this liberty of which we are speaking men can fulfill the law. For that law as appointed may have many ends besides its fulfillment, namely that men may acknowledge their sins and the infirmity of their strength; that they may see what they ought to have done and be aroused to better things, and may come to Christ: God uses law as instrument to bring them into the way. In his book *On Grace and Free Will,* chapter 2, Augustine seems to teach so — that our free will follows logically from those precepts, otherwise they would be useless.[18] To this I say that free will is inferred from the law as it was given regarding man in his first state of perfect nature; also to the regenerate, that they may obey not with a perfect but an incomplete obedience. But what may be inferred from the laws concerning those who are not yet renewed? Human powers and faculties cannot be proved by this, except that they have a will that has some power to yield or to obey when moved by grace. For rebirth is not alien to the will, whose nature is such that it may be regenerated by God and obey him at least with an imperfect obedience.

When we look to outward things there is a kind of freedom, although not to fulfill the law which primarily requires those inward motions that originate from faith and the inspiration of the Holy Spirit. I agree, therefore, that this sort of liberty exists in some form, because experience teaches it, not because I am convinced by the argument that the law could not have been kept by a free will, that magistrates would punish offenders in vain, and laws would have been given in vain. For if this argument were firm, it would follow that while we are not regenerate we have free will even in things supernatural,

---

[16]Deut. 6:5. Cf. EW 143, thesis 41N9: "Although these words, 'You shall love the Lord your God with all your heart ... and your neighbor as yourself,' are not stated explicitly in any of the ten precepts, yet they are the form and measure of all."

[17]I Tim. 1:9.

[18]Augustine *De gratia et libero arbitrio* 2 (ii): "All such excuse is removed from them when the precept is given them…" (PL 44.883).

since God has given laws regarding such matters even to those not regenerated, and punishes them if they do not respect them. So I admit that in regard to outward things we have partial liberty of this kind; yet I could not be persuaded by those arguments without something more. For the magistrate himself will punish a robber or thief brought before him, provided they committed their crimes knowingly and willingly. At that point the magistrate will not inquire whether they had free will or were moved by an emotion that reason could not control. Indeed if they should die, God would punish those not yet regenerated who are without faith, hope, and charity, and would not consider whether in that state they could have them or not. God himself punished original sin; when we are born he does not ask whether we are without it or not. In the *Confessions*, Augustine says that infants also have their vices and sins at their age.[19] *[973]* For they are infected with envy. These are sins even when the infants cannot do otherwise; nor have they the reason to resist those motions.

[COMMAND AND FREEDOM]

5. The powers of free will are not to be deduced from the law and commandments of God. I grant that when something is commanded free will is consulted, because if we obey or resist we do so by the will. We do not assent or dissent with nostrils or fingers or other members of the body, but with our judgment. Yet this does not prove that we are able to do as much as is required of us. Therefore, while this reasoning does not persuade me to affirm such freedom, I grant it from experience; not experience in general, but what is witnessed in Scripture, which does not deceive. The first chapter to the Romans treats of those who were not reborn, who are said to have known the invisible things of God from creation—I mean the godhead and eternity, which David also affirms: "The heavens declare the glory of God," etc.[20] And in the same letter, the nations that do not have the law do by nature what the law requires. As regards what should be done, they were said to have knowledge of what is right [notitia rectitudinis]. For when they should have known the justice of God, and that those who do such things deserve to die, they not only do them but also agree with those who do them, and so are made inexcusable; they cannot pretend ignorance, since they knew that they did not perform even the little that they attempted.[21] Nor can they rightly excuse the weakness of their powers, since they themselves made it possible by the sin of Adam in whom

---

[19]Augustine *Conf.* I.7 (PL 32.665–666).
[20]Rom. 1:20; Ps. 19:1.
[21]Rom. 1:32. See "Nature and Grace" §6 , p. 18.

all have sinned. Also, Christ said that if you love only those who love you, publicans and prostitutes do the same.[22]

No one doubts that in general good manners are to be approved, while friendship is rightly honored; for those who betray or hurt a friend are condemned. Moreover, the Lord has said: "If you, being evil, can give good things to your children," and so on.[23] Nor do I doubt that the affection [ὀργή], of parents toward their children is good, by which they wish them well. For those who neglect their children or treat them with cruelty are severely censured. Moreover, when Paul was still an enemy of God and persecuting the church, he was more advanced in outward justice than most of his fellows, as he said to the Galatians. And he showed the Philippians that he was ἄμεμπτος (see Phil. 3:6), blameless as to the righteousness of the law.[24] Ethnic histories also show that Scipio, Pompey, Caesar, Cato, and Cicero did many things exceptionally well, speaking, commanding, and acting for the well-being of their countries and the cause of public good, though they were then strangers from Christ. As appears both from Holy Scripture and ethnic writings, some truth must be granted to such liberty, although degrees should be established for it, since it seems not to be given equally to everyone. The variety may be due to bodily temperament or to customs or education, to places or countries, to experience and similar things. Nor should we leave it unsaid that the notable acts recounted in the histories concerning pagans happened by some moving and special impulse of God, who wished such examples to occur so that republics and kingdoms might be preserved. To prevent everything from ending in confusion, it was fitting that some should be adorned with excellent qualities who might do good to others by holding office.

We concede that the spirit of prophesying and similar kinds of graces [charismata] are sometimes given by God to those without faith; even so, apart from justifying grace God may give not only a general influence but some spirits of fortitude or chastity and gravity and such like.[25] Therefore, this is the freedom that I think is given, even though considerable weakness and bondage go with it. There is first great blindness and darkness in the understanding, so that it hardly knows what should be done at any time; there is a great weakness in the will in resisting passion. Further, there is ongoing conflict between the superior part and the inferior, so that sometimes we cannot help but surrender; those who do fight cannot escape wounds that are often

---

[22]Matt. 5:46.   [23]Matt. 7:11.   [24]Gal. 1:13–14, Phil. 3:6.
[25]On "influxus communis" see "Providence" §7, p. 186.

deadly. To this is added the infirmity of the body, both corrupted and a burden to the soul, and often the reason why we cannot do those things we think should be done. What Paul says of the new birth is true, that they feel another law in their members, striving against the law of the mind and leading them captive where they do not want to go. The flesh so lusts against the spirit and the spirit against the flesh that they do not do what they intend; they do not do the good they desire but rather the evil they hate.[26] Therefore, what do we think happens in the unregenerate? Surely something even more severe.

Let us also consider the natural purpose which philosophers have discerned, that people should live according to reason and excellent virtue;[27] let us see how few have attained it, and so learn the weakness of human virtue even in what is within the capacity of human reason. Consider still another necessity to which those in this state are subject, namely sin. For whatever they do without the grace of God and faith, they necessarily sin. They are children of wrath, and since they do not believe in Christ, the wrath of God remains on them.[28] Thus they cannot do anything good that may please God, because he has regard to men rather than to their gifts. They are evil trees; therefore, they can bear no fruit that is not evil.[29] Paul called his Jewish good works not only dung but ruin, because they were offensive to him; further, what is of the flesh cannot but be flesh.[30] That the unregenerate are flesh needs no proof. Moreover, the book of Genesis, chapters 6 and 8, declares that the imaginations of men's own devising are evil, even from their infancy.[31] What is done by the unregenerate lacks the proper goal because it is not referred to God. So they cannot love God above all, which is nothing else than to refer all things to him; all their works are corrupt and therefore sins, since they are without faith. For whatever is not of faith is sin.[32] What God requires of us is impossible compared to that state of which *[974]* we speak, although it may be performed by the regenerate through an imperfect obedience.

Augustine acknowledged this necessity of sinning in his book *On Nature and Grace*, chapter 66, where he wrote that necessity to sin is the kind that comes not from our natural condition but from its corruption.[33] So the cry is

---

[26]Rom. 7:19, 23; Gal. 5:17.

[27]See Aristotle *NE* I.2.1094a18ff.

[28]Eph. 2:3; John. 3:36.

[29]Gen. 4:4; Matt. 7:18.   [30]Phil. 3:8; John 3:6.

[31]Gen. 6:3; 8:21.   [32]Rom. 14:23.

[33]Augustine *De natura et gratia* LXVI.79 (PL 44.286); Ps 25:17 Vulgate: de necessitatibus meis erue [educ] me; cf. Augustine *De natura boni* xvii: "Nothing is evil in anything save a diminishing of good" and *Enchiridion* 3.11: "Evil, then, is an accident, i.e., a privation of that good which is called health."

raised to the Lord: From necessity, O Lord, deliver us. In the same book, chapter 67, he teaches that certain things done from necessity, where one wants to do the right but cannot, should be condemned. But he holds them to be punishment for sins and not sins proper.[34] In the second disputation against Fortunatus the Manichean, he writes that the first man did not remain in free will; so are we now fallen headlong into necessity.[35] And in the book *On Nature and Grace,* chapter 46, he says: Not all necessity strives with the will, for we seek happiness, nor can it be otherwise.[36] Indeed even the will of the God of justice is not greater than necessity—the same author in *On Free Will,* third book, chapter 18, and also touched on in *Retractations,* first book, chapter 9.[37] In the book *On Nature and Grace,* chapter 66, he speaks of the unregenerate: "He is evil, nor can he be good, either because he does not see what should be done, or if he sees it, cannot do what he knows he should to be good." It is generally accepted that it was possible for the first man not to die, as it was possible not to sin; and when we will be in heaven [in patria] we will not be able to sin and to die; but while we are here it is not possible not to die, and not possible not to sin.[38] The same Father wrote in his treatise *On the Spirit and the Letter*: Free will is of no value except to sin, and is to be referred to the present state of humanity.[39]

The Milevitan Council condemned those who said that the grace of justification is given so that what is required by free will might be done more easily, as if free will could do this by itself even if with difficulty.[40] Holy Scripture also shows this necessity. For it is written to the Romans: "The wisdom or sense of the flesh is enmity against God and is not subject to the law of God, nor can it be." And in the same place, "what the law could not do, in that it was weak through the flesh," and so on.[41] Therefore, those who are not regenerate are under this necessity of sinning, to be understood generally and not of particular sins; for it is not necessary for them to be guilty of this sin rather than that. There is also another kind of necessity, related to the providence of God

[34]Augustine *De natura et gratia* LXVII.81 (PL 44.287).

[35]Augustine *Acta seu Disp. contra Fort.* Second Day 22: "nos in necessitatem praecipitati sumus" (PL 42.124).

[36]Augustine *De natura et gratia* XLVI.54 (PL 44.273).

[37]Augustine *De libero arbitrio* III.XVIII.50 (PL 32.1295); *Retract.* I.9.5 (PL 32.597–598).

[38]For the categories *posse / posse non / non posse (peccari, mori)* see Augustine, *De corr. et gratia* XII.33 (PL 44.936).

[39]Augustine *De spiritu et littera* XXXIII.58: free will as an intermediate power (PL 44.258).

[40]Council of Milevis (402), in the Code of Canons of the African Church, 93 (cxiiii), *Nicene and Post-Nicene Fathers,* vol. 14, ed. H. Percival (Grand Rapids: Eerdmans, 1983) 498.

[41]Rom. 8:3, 7.

and the predictions of prophets. But this is not an absolute necessity but relative, or as they term it a necessity of the consequence. I will speak later about that; at present I will not comment further.[42]

[WILL AND EMOTION]

6. We should also consider that in the various kinds of human willing there is an alternation of feelings [affectuum], so that each dominates another in turn, and the strongest are superior. There is also a difference among feelings, since some are more attractive and others more repulsive. The will has some freedom in this matter, sometimes giving in to one kind and sometimes to another. Nor should we forget that the will itself is by nature blind, and follows only what is proposed by the mind or understanding. Knowledge also is to be distinguished as relating to sense or reason or else to faith. The will assents to knowledge that is more vehement, nor is it in its power to react to one kind more than another. Some say that its power is to constrain the mind or reason, and that it inclines to the better sort of reasons and counsels, not allowing itself to be separated from them. But the will in itself does not know that something is good except insofar as reason has taught it.[43] Wherefore, I do not know a more powerful remedy than to call on God, that by his Spirit he will make the will's deliberation and counsel stronger, so that it contributes the more to our salvation and to his glory. It is his to inflame and enlighten that [glory] by which our will is moved above all else. For we all know that the will rules and commands human actions; but since it lies between knowledge and affection, we doubt whether it can decide by which it should be moved more strongly. When overcome by sins it surely becomes their servant; for Peter, the second letter, chapter 2, says: "Everyone is servant to that which overcomes him."[44] And it is written to the Romans: "We become the servants of him to whom we give ourselves in obedience"; again: "Whereas you were servants of sin, you were freed from righteousness." Christ also said: "If Christ has made you free, you will be free indeed."[45]

---

[42]Simplex, ex hypothesi, consequentiae. See "Providence" §13, p. 192, above. In the treatise *De Praedestinatione* (ROM 9 fin. 1558), the final section deals with the nature and implications of necessity; LC 3.1.49–58. The logical distinction is between implication that something is necessary (necessitas consequentis) and the necessity of the implication as a whole (necessitas consequentiae). Luther *De Servo Arbitrio* (1525) iv, WA 614–618, scorns the scholastic "absurd formula *all things take place by necessity of consequence, but not by necessity of the thing consequent.*"

[43]Martyr follows the "moderate realism" of Aquinas ST Ia.81.1; IIaIIae.2.10 and 23.6; cf. Aristotle *NE* VI.2.

[44]2 Pet. 2:19.

[45]Rom. 6:16, 20; John 8:36.

It follows, therefore, that people are not truly free before they are reborn. Besides all this there is the tyranny of the devil, who holds men captive before they are Christ's. For Christ said: "The strong man keeps his house in peace, holding the spoils captive, until a stronger comes, who takes them away." The second letter to Timothy has it: "They that speak against the truth are held captive by Satan at his will."[46] It is a common saying that the will is like a horse on which the Spirit of God and grace sits at one time, the devil at another; sometimes it is aroused by him and other times governed by grace. Its liberty therefore is ruined by its multiple bondage; it is strange that seeing how small is its freedom, especially in this state, the will is called free rather than bound. Considering this, Luther called *arbitrium* rather *servum* than *liberum*.[47] If one were in prison, bound with shackles and chains, would he be right to maintain that he is free because he can move his head and lift up his eyes? Our will can of course refuse spiritual things while it remains in this state; it can also choose things contrary to them, but it is unable on its own to seek or desire good things themselves. Seeing that it is so weak as to perform only certain external deeds of a lower kind, some have attributed to it in this first state the merit of congruity; that is, if it should do what is within its capacity, it would in one sense deserve grace, though not condign, as they say, but at least congruent.[48] Forget these fictions: Grace given because of works is not grace.[49] *[975]* I speak like this so as not to slacken the bridle for vices and crimes; for even those who are not regenerate will be far more severely punished if they do not perform those external things of which they are capable. But if any complain that in this way free will is too diminished, I say it is not so; while it is indeed reduced, much benefit is gathered from it. First, those who know these things are not puffed up or proud of their own strength, but are more strongly aroused to seek divine help, when they see themselves to be so weak. When later they are reborn and recognize the many evils from which they are delivered, they will be moved more fervently to give thanks to their deliverer. The Pelagians do not observe such things, thinking that before

---

[46]Matt. 12:29; 2 Tim. 2:26.

[47]Luther *WA* 18, 634ff., *De Servo Arbitrio* (1525): "Thus the human will is placed between the two like a beast of burden." Cf Calvin *Inst.* II.2.2: "The Philosophers ... place the will in the middle station between reason and sense." This simile goes back as far as Origen and was familiar among the scholastics; see H. A. McSorley, *Luther Right or Wrong?* (New York: Newman Press, 1968) 335ff.

[48]I.e., grace cannot be earned by natural merit either in strict justice (meritum de condigno) or as a matter of fitness (meritum de congruo). See *De Libero Arbitrio* in ROM 7:25, (LC/CP 2.2.1–30) §8; Aquinas ST 1.2ae, Q. 114, art. 3; Luther WA 769–771, *Bondage* VII.vi.

[49]Rom. 11:6.

regeneration they can merit grace by their own strength; thus by extolling themselves more than was fitting they destroyed themselves, and disturbed the church.

[MIND AS INSTRUMENT]

7. Another subject might be added, that God uses our minds as instruments; for "the heart of the king is in the hand of God, he bends it to the way he wills."[50] When Nebuchadnezzar reached the parting of two roads he stood in doubt which way to turn, whether against the Moabites or the Ammonites. He consulted by lots, which God influenced, to direct him to the Jerusalemites, who were to be punished for their sins, as we have it in Ezekiel.[51] In other prophets it is said that these monarchs are like an axe or staff in God's hand.[52] But since this divine use does not strengthen our minds, freedom towards these things under discussion is not completely removed, however small. In this way I admit it and have confirmed it from Holy Scripture. Thus for me, moral, civic, and economic knowledge holds and stays firm. Still, I may seem mistaken to some because I have said that the name *liberum arbitrium* is not found in the Latin translation of the divine writings, nor is the Greek word *autexousion*.[53] To be sure, I did not speak of the substance but of the words, and reaffirm what I said then. But I did not deny that *proairesis* or *proaireisthai* is found in Holy Scripture; if you ask whether these words mean the same as *autexousion*, I answer that they do not seem to.

In his second book, discussing free will and other things within us, Damascene uses the word *autexousion* when he defines *proairesis*, where he treats the will [περὶ τοῦ θελήματοῦ].[54] I will add the reason why they differ: *Autexousion* belongs to the genus of quality, since it is an affect and property of the will, but *proairesis* is an action. Everyone knows how property and action differ in themselves.[55] That *proairesis* is an action the same author shows in defining it. He says that *proairesis* means "to prefer one of two propositions before the other."[56] He also speaks of the will of the Lord, saying that will

---

[50]Prov. 21:1.   [51]Ezek. 21:21.   [52]E.g. Isa. 10:5.

[53]The key terms and their cognates appear in Greek in these two paragraphs: αὐτεξούσιον and προαίρεσις. See §§1–2, p. 271, above.

[54]The work is Περὶ τοῦ ἐφ᾽ ἡμῖν, τουτέστι, τοῦ αὐτεξουσίου; John of Damascus *De fide orthodoxa* II.25: "What is in our own power, that is, concerning free-will" (discussing Nemesius): sitne aliquid in nostra potesta (PG 94.956), and *De fide orthodoxa* II.30. See Aquinas SCG II.90 on the passage; Damascene following Gregory of Nyssa *De Prov.* viii.9, and Nemesius *De Nat. Hom.* xliv.

[55]See Aristotle *Categories* chap. 8 (9a28ff) on affective qualities, and chap. 9 (11b) on action.

[56]Damascene *De fide orth.* II.22 (PG 94.945): δύο [τὸ μὲν] προκειμένων, αἱρεῖσθαι καὶ ἐκλέγεσθαι τοῦτο πρὸ [τοῦ] ἑτέρου.

[θέλησις] is compatible since it is self-controlling [*autexousion*] while choice [*proairesis*] clearly is not. For it requires deliberation and implies previous ignorance, which cannot be ascribed to God. Furthermore, as we have it in Aristotle's *Ethics*, the third book, the word willing [βούλησις] concerns the end, but *proairesis* concerns whatever aims at the end.[57] Besides which, those things that we can do belong to *proairesis*, whereas willing concerns what is not to be done by us, such as when we want one athlete to overcome the other, or a ship to hold the right course. We can wish things like that but cannot choose them. In its own right and power the will sometimes wishes impossible things, such as not to die; but choice is directed only to possibilities. Therefore, they are different, with broader meaning for *autexousion*, since it matches not only *proairesis* but also *thelēma*; yet it is not their genus. But if you say that *autexousion* is inferred from *proairesis*, I grant it even though the words do not mean the same. I admit that the thing itself is found in Holy Scripture, although the word is not extant, just as the word *homoousion* itself is not in Holy Scripture, although the reality is present and demonstrated there. Since these words are not the same in any case, I could rightly say that the one is not in Scripture while the other may be found there.

I am not alone in saying this, for Johann Oecolampadius, a most learned man and well disposed toward our Zurich church, dealing with the text from the prophet Isaiah ("If you are willing, and listen to me," etc.), says: "The Pelagians as well as many fathers misuse this passage to affirm free will, saying 'If you are willing and not willing'; therefore our choice is free. To support this they draw a testimony from Jeremiah, chapter 21: 'Behold I set before you the way of life and of death.' So also in the 15th chapter of Ecclesiasticus and in the 30th of Deuteronomy.[58] We reply to this: if the argument is really about the name, that we identify will and free choice or self-determination [voluntas, et liberum arbitrium vel *autexousion*] (I have not yet found this term in the Scriptures), we allow them to use those names, because dissension is not the way of the church; for charity is more precious to us than syllables. For who does not know that to will means both to sin and to do well? But if under this pretense the glory and mercy of God are derogated, it is better to contradict men than to take part in blasphemy."[59] And a little later: "But they are not to be pitied,

---

[57]The distinction is between what is purposive (βούλησις) and what implies previous choice or preference (προαίρεσις): "Wish relates rather to the end, choice to the means"; see Aristotle *NE* 3.2.1111b26; cf. *NE* 3.3.1112a30.

[58]Jer. 21:8; Ecclus. 15:14; Deut. 30:15, 18.

[59]Johann Oecolampadius (1482–1531) was a Reformer of Basel and biblical scholar; see his *In Iesaiam Prophetam* 1:19 (Basel, 1525).

as I have said, as though they were kept in cruel bondage; for God allows the good to share in his liberty, and they are truly free in whom the Spirit of God is at work. He is more properly said to encourage the will than to set it aside. The apostle commends their excellence, saying 'Whoever is led by the Spirit of God,' etc.[60] For our works are so much the better as they proceed more purely from God. Not the slightest thought or endeavor in goodness comes from any other than God." And soon after: "To God is the glory, to us only confusion. Will you not say that those deprived of the Spirit of God, who offered them the strength not to fall, are surely servants carried headlong by their own fault, wherever their weakness leads them? O what miserable freedom is the freedom to sin! For God allows us to be sinful, and to be capable of turning away even from nature." Again: "Why do we boast of the freedom of the will, we whom Scripture condemns as servants of sin? In the eighth chapter of John: 'Whoever commits sin is the servant of sin.'" In that place just after: "Hence one who says 'if you are willing' is one who arouses and drives the will in us; whatever it is, 'It is not of him that wills, nor of him that tries, but of God that has mercy.'"[61] *[976]*

Again: "For following Adam's sin we are in our own nature such that being left to ourselves we grow numb, become deaf to the voice of the Lord, and fall into sin. Since not to will is in itself to be condemned, we are pushed into abandoning the Spirit of God and then we anger God, whose word we despise. Jeremiah also provides support for this statement in the 15th chapter: 'Be you converted, and I will restore,'" etc. And later: "Augustine reasoned like this, saying: 'give what you command, and command what you will,'" and so on.[62] We gather from these words that we are not to contend about the word, and may allow *liberum arbitrium* so long as it is the same as *voluntas*, and that freedom in spiritual matters is not attributed to it. We also take the will to be free only through grace; otherwise it is a slave. What I have proposed is also stated here, that these words *liberum arbitrium* and *autexousion* are not found in the sacred books.

8. I did not deny that *proairesis* is used and taught by philosophers; but I said that they place understanding and will in our mind, and perhaps memory. Not that they place free will there as a fourth or fifth power of the mind, but attribute *proairesis* to the will. I have never questioned whether these two words *liberum* and *arbitrium* are Latin, but hold that a compound of these two—*liberum arbitrium*—is not extant in Cicero, and I confirm this now. I

---

[60]Rom. 8:14.
[61]John 8:34; Rom. 9:16.
[62]Augustine *De spiritu et litt.* XIII.22 (PL 44.213), and *De praed. sanct.* XI.22 (PL 44.976).

might add further that it was not used by Caesar or Terence, or men of that age. This is enough in defense of the matters I declared at the beginning.

[THE UNREGENERATE WILL]

Now I come to substance, and ask how a will not yet regenerate stands in relation to divine and heavenly things. Everyone admits that in themselves such matters cannot be understood or desired by the unregenerate. They affirm that the Spirit of God, through the word, must be present to admonish, exhort, and persuade. Just as the senses cannot apprehend universals, so our mind cannot ascend to supernatural things while vitiated and corrupted. Some assert that it is enough to have the word and promises of God suggested to us by the Spirit. I deny it, for unless these powers are corrected, we are quite unable to understand and embrace things divine and heavenly. Nor is it within our capacity to be content with what is set before us; they must be proposed to us with force, efficacy, and power, so that the understanding may be affected with an uncommon light, and the will strengthened lest it submit to evil desires and temptations that call it away from spiritual things. When this is done it assents to the words and promises of God, and justification follows. The intellect is actively predisposed to such assent, willing and agreeing to what is proposed; but it remains passive toward that power of God, the force and efficacy which heals and converts it; for through him all this is received and comes about.[63] Nor should this seem absurd, since as Scripture says, we are drawn, indicating a kind of passion and disposition. It is also said that God stands at the door and knocks.[64] Hence those knocks and motions are received in the mind: yet this is no reason for us to make enthusiasts in faith. Enthusiasts are reproved who claim to experience I know not what inspirations and impulses to matters evil and forbidden, repugnant to the word of God. But we assign such efficacy to God as inclines the mind to the divine promises and words and occurs together with the word of God. In many, however, only an illustration or imitation or hint occurs, without any transformation, since the efficacy and power of spirit is not given to all, neither can all be made capable of the heavenly gifts that God himself grants, distributes, and adjusts as he sees fit. Hence there arise two kinds of calling. One is common, but the other is according to a purpose of which we will speak clearly in its place.[65] Those whom God endows with his gift and strength, as has been said,

---

[63]The pronoun *ipse* suggests that the subject is *intellectus*, whereas the margin has *voluntas*; cf. Thomas SCG 2.73ff., on active and passive willing. For the concept of intellectual predisposition see "Nature and Grace" p. 20, n. 6, above.

[64]Rev. 3:20.   [65]See §12, p. 299, below.

he does not compel or force, as if to corrupt the will or choice; rather he perfects it, since he adorns with form and fulfills matter but does not destroy it.[66]

Ulrich Zwingli, a godly and learned man who deserves well of the church, has noted this power of God in our conversion, on the letter to the Romans, expounding these words: "It is the power of God unto salvation to all who believe."[67] He says: "For when we could by no means be saved by our own power and strength, it was necessary to be saved by the power of God. He gave this power to us by Christ, who restored to life all who were dead in Adam. This place removes the freedom of the will, and the power of human strength," etc.[68] I understand this saying in regard to supernatural things, which exceed our capacity. The same Zwingli in his book *On True and False Religion*, the chapter *On God*,[69] writes as follows: ""Now the faithful (for this is the generally accepted term for believers or pious persons, or worshippers of the true God) are faithful by virtue of this one thing, that they believe in one only true and omnipotent God, and trust in him alone. Moreover, how it happens that the pious perceive God in this way, not in heathen fashion making any unknown power God, is easily explained by them. It happens through the power and grace of him in whom we believe; for as far as the capacity and nature of human beings are concerned, the godly differ not at all from the ungodly. Thus in the realm of error concerning gods, anything that could happen to one man could happen to any other, unless there were some higher power to call and attach to itself the human mind, which has no natural aversion to those who are most completely in error. Here then the first traces of faith and piety are revealed."

9. It is quite clear that in one sense the Pelagians appear to have acknowledged the grace of God; they made suggestions about those illuminations of the Holy Spirit and the like; but they neither recognized nor accepted this gift and efficacy of the Spirit in converting our souls. Augustine agreed, in *On the Grace of Christ* against Pelagius and Coelestinus, chapter seven:[70] "But see what [Pelagius] has given us whose expectation wavers. 'For God', he says, 'assists us through his teaching and revelation, while he opens the eyes of our heart, showing us the future, that we should not be absorbed in the present,

---

[66]potius perficit, quemadmodum forma ornat et absoluit materiam, non perdit. cf. Aquinas: Gratia naturam non tollit sed perficit; see, e.g., ST 1a.Q1.art. 8.ad 2; Q 62.Art. 5. resp.

[67]Rom. 1:16.

[68]Ulrich Zwingli *Opera, Comm. ad. loc.*, ed. M. Schuler and J. Schulthess (Zurich, 1836), VI.2.78; CR, vol. 90, provides only annotations.

[69]Zwingli *Opera* III.57, *De vera et falsa religione* chap. 3, "De Deo"; CR 90.3.642.

[70]Augustine *De gratia Christi* chap. VII (8) (PL 44.364).

[977] disclosing the snares of the devil, enlightening us with his manifold and ineffable gift of heavenly grace?' He concludes his statement with a kind of absolution: 'Does one who speaks like this seem to you to deny grace? Or does he confess our free will, and the grace of God?'" and so forth. Further, in the eighth chapter,[71] the same Augustine says: "Therefore, it is clear that [Pelagius] acknowledges this grace by which God points out and reveals what we ought to do, rather than bestow it and help us in our actions: since knowledge of the law is rather an aid to this, so that if the help of grace is lacking the commandment is transgressed," etc. In the tenth chapter, Pelagius is introduced, saying: "He works in us, to make us will what is good, what is holy, he arouses us who are given to earthly desires, after the manner of dumb animals who love only the present, by the greatness of future glory and the promise of its rewards. He stirs up our sluggish will to the love of God by the revelation of wisdom. He persuades us to all that is good (which you are not afraid to deny elsewhere)" and so on.[72] But in this same chapter 10 Augustine refutes him in these words: "But for our part we would wish him sometime to acknowledge that grace by which not only future glory in all its greatness is promised but also is believed and hoped for; by which wisdom is not only revealed but also loved, by which everything good is not only recommended but convincingly: for not all have faith," etc.[73]

Augustine again, *On Grace and Free Will*, chapter 16[74]: "It is certain that we keep the commandments if we will, but because the will is prepared by the Lord, we must ask from him such a force of will as makes us act through willing. It is certain that it is we who will when we will; but it is he who makes us will what is good, of whom it is said, as stated a little before, that the will is prepared by the Lord. Of whom it is said: 'His steps are directed by the Lord, and he ordains his way.' Of whom it is said: 'It is God that works in us both to will and to do.'[75] It is certain that it is we who act when we act; but it is he who makes us act by strengthening the will most effectively. Who said: 'I will make you walk in my statutes,'"[76] and so on. The same Augustine, to Boniface, against the two Pelagian letters, third book, chapter 9: He asks what it is in what follows, where they recount those things that they themselves believe, they admit to acknowledging "that grace assists every good purpose, but does

---

[71]Augustine *De gratia Christi*, chap. VIII.9 (PL 44.364).
[72]Augustine *De gratia Christi*, chap. X.11 (PL 44.365f).
[73]2 Thess. 3:2.
[74]Augustine *De gratia et libero arbitrio* XVI.32 (PL 44.900).
[75]Ps. 37:23; Phil. 2:13.
[76]In iustificationibus; Ezek. 36:27.

not put any desire for virtue into the reluctant [heart]," etc.?[77] Augustine wishes the Pelagians to acknowledge also that God puts zeal for the good into those who resist, which is impossible unless our mind is converted from evil and corruption and becomes good. This is the change which the Holy Spirit effects in us. By this are we pacified, who are hard and stubborn. The same Father said: "When God hardens it is only that he will not pacify, because unless we are pacified by him, we continue in our hardness."

The Holy Spirit causes us who are incapable of divine things on our own to become willing pupils of God. First Kings chapter 3 has it that Solomon sought from God an understanding or obedient heart.[78] This is what is said in the Gospels, that we are taught by God [Θεοδίδακτοι], as promised by the prophets.[79] God is the true schoolmaster, who not only instructs and teaches, but also causes us to learn, something that masters in externals cannot do. For God gives ears to hear, eyes to see, and a heart to understand. Thus in the Gospel, Christ said: "He that has ears to hear, let him hear."[80] Unless this is done in us, seeing we shall not see and hearing we shall not hear, nor shall we perceive by the heart. It is written in Deuteronomy 29: "He has not given you eyes to see, nor ears to hear, nor a heart to conceive, namely, what God did among you in the wilderness, and the words which he spoke."[81] The excellence of divine things shows why this should be done in us, as the Apostle Paul says: "Eye has not seen, nor ear heard, nor has it entered man's heart, what God has prepared for them that love him."[82] It is written in 1 Corinthians: "The natural man does not perceive the things which are of the Spirit of God, nor can he; for they are folly unto him."[83] The reason given why a natural man cannot understand or desire these things is that they are spiritual, and if spiritual they are discerned by the Spirit alone.

In 2 Corinthians: "We are not sufficient of ourselves to claim anything as coming from us alone, because our sufficiency is of God."[84] But if we cannot even think those things, how will we be able to understand them or desire them, so much greater and more difficult are they than thinking? Thus if the Spirit of God proposes the law to us or the promises or words of Holy Scripture and no change results, we will not be moved, because we are neither sufficient nor apt for them. It requires a previous conversion that may be called a kind of disposition. The Papists attribute this to human strength and

---

[77]Augusine *Contra duas Ep. Pel.* IV [sic], 2, 13 (PL 44.608, 610).
[78]1 Kings 3:9.
[79]διδακτοὶ Θεοῦ (John 6:45); Isa. 54:13. Cf. "Author," §27, p. 247, above.
[80]Matt. 13:9.   [81]Deut. 29:4.   [82]1 Cor. 2:9, 14.
[83]1 Cor 2:14.   [84]2 Cor. 3:5.

our own will, as if we could dispose ourselves to grace and faith. But this must be ascribed completely to the Spirit of God, not to human strength or will, as we have shown. Moreover it might properly be termed the health of the mind, the kind of healing that Augustine often mentioned in his book *On the Spirit and the Letter.*[85] In regard to sins we state first that human nature is corrupt and defiled: then we observe that evil acts break forth. On the other hand, we have to assume that some healing of the mind comes first; afterwards the assent of faith follows, confidence and love towards God, and acknowledgment of his words. But if such conversion or medicine has not preceded, we will fly from God, as was so well shown in the first man Adam as in a kind of type; when he had fallen into corruption and spiritual death after transgressing God's commandment, he fled from God and hid himself. And even though the Apostle Paul had heard and read many things about Christ in the law and the prophets, he turned away from him *[978]* and ravaged the church. For as he himself said to the Romans: "The mind of the flesh is hostile to God, and does not submit to God's law, indeed it cannot."[86] Since it is clear that this is God's gift, it relates to the prayers of the saints who say: "Illumine my eyes, lest they see vanity. Give me understanding, that I may learn or know your commandments." And to the Ephesians, Paul prayed God to enlighten their eyes that they might know what was the hope of their calling.[87] As to the will, David prayed: "Incline my heart to your testimonies" and "Create in me a clean heart, O God." His son Solomon prayed God to give the people an understanding heart.[88] Seeing that the saints pray in this way, what do they crave, what do they request? That God will reveal his word, or that his Spirit may knock? Yet he always does this by himself, as they themselves declare. But if they have it in their own power to give assent, why do they pray? Let them do it themselves, since they are able.

Now prayer is rightly made by the saints, therefore it is a sign to us that this is required from God, that he may change our minds. Augustine used this argument more than once. In his book *On Free Will*, chapter 14, he writes as follows:[89] "For if faith comes only from free will and is not given by God, why do we pray for those who will not believe, that they may believe? We would do this completely in vain unless we believe quite rightly that even wills that

[85]E.g. Augustine *De spiritu et littera* 5 (iii) (PL 44.203); on *gratia praeveniens et cooperans*, see Aquinas, ST IaIIae.Q 3.art. 3; Council of Trent, session 6, chap. 5.

[86]Rom. 8:7.

[87]Ps. 119:37, 73; Eph. 1:18.

[88]Ps. 119:36; 51:10; I Kings 8:58.

[89]Augustine *De gratia et lib. arb.* XIV.29 (PL 44.898).

are perverse and opposed to faith may be changed by the Almighty to believe. Human free will is clearly addressed when it is said: 'Today, if you will hear his voice, harden not your hearts.'[90] But unless God could also take away the hardness of heart, he would not say through the prophet, 'I will take from them their stony heart, and give them a heart of flesh.'"[91] The same Father to Boniface against the two Pelagian letters, first book, chapter 19, writes:[92] "For why has the Lord commanded us to pray for those who persecute us? Do we pray thus so that the grace of God may reward them for their goodwill, and not rather that their evil will may be turned into good? We believe that the saints whom he was persecuting did not pray for Saul in vain; it was revealed by a clear oracle that his will might be turned to the faith which he was destroying, and that his conversion came from above. How many enemies of Christ are daily drawn to him suddenly, by the secret grace of God?" In the same place, chapter 20, he declares how true it is that God converts and changes human wills, saying:[93] "We do not suppose this to be true by human conjecture but we discern it by clearest authority of Scripture. It is read in the books of Chronicles: 'The hand of God was also on Judah, to give them one heart, to follow the commandments of the king and princes in the word of the Lord.'[94] Likewise the Lord said through the prophet Ezekiel: 'I will give them another heart, and a new spirit will I give them; and I will take out of their flesh the heart of stone. And I will give them a heart of flesh, that they may walk in my precepts, and keep my judgments to do them.'[95] What is it that Esther the queen prays, saying: 'Give eloquent speech to my mouth, and make my words clear before the lion, and turn his heart to hatred of our enemies?'[96] Why does she say these words in her prayer to God, if God does not work his will in human hearts?" Certainly it happened just as she prayed, for like a fierce bull that king had his ferocity turned into compassion at first sight of her.

Finally, we must examine a place in the Acts of the Apostles, chapter 16, regarding Lydia, the woman who sold purple, whose heart God opened that she might heed what Paul said. No doubt there were many present, but only of that woman was it said that God opened her heart. My predecessor, Conrad Pellican, a most learned and godly man, has expounded this passage as

---

[90]Ps. 95:8.
[91]Ezek. 11:19.
[92]Augustine *Contra duas Ep. Pel.* I.XIX.37 (PL 44.568).
[93]Augustine *Contra duas Ep. Pel.* I.XX.38 (PL 44.568).
[94]2 Chr. 30:12.
[95]Ezek. 36:26.
[96]Esther 17:13 (LXX).

follows.[97] "Such repentance does not come by nature but by grace, whose heart," he says, "the Lord opened that she might heed what Paul said. For no one can put faith in the Gospel by his own strength, but by the gift of the Holy Spirit, not by our presumption. Therefore, hearing the promises of the Gospel, let us distrust the power of the flesh, and let us ask the Lord to open our heart, to grant the gift of the Holy Spirit so that what we have heard to be required might be believed in the heart and performed in deed." We read that it happened in this woman who sold purple; also the history of Samuel teaches so, the first book and tenth chapter, where it is written that those whose heart God had touched followed King Saul.[98] What Ezekiel said is also relevant, that he would take away the stony heart and give a heart of flesh. Paul taught in Philippians that "It is God who works in us, both to will and to accomplish, and that not for our but his own good pleasure." And to the Ephesians it is written that "we are saved by grace through faith, and that not of ourselves."[99] By this teaching our cooperation is removed, which is active: not indeed regarding the assent of faith but that change through grace of which we are speaking. It adds: "It is the gift of God." In 2 Thessalonians it is written, "Not all have faith,"[100] because such healing or medicine of the Spirit is not given to everyone; so it happens that not all assent to the promises of God. It is written in Ephesians, chapter 1: "We who believe, according to the working of his great might, which he accomplished in Christ, when he raised him from the dead."[101] These words show that it is the same power through which our will is changed and converted to believe, and Christ raised from the dead. Expounding this passage, Conrad Pellican says: "So God our father declares his power and goodness in us, since by a certain secret and ineffable power he has so transformed us from former habits that we spurn all else and trust in him alone, and condemning those things we see, hope from him those things we do not see," etc.[102] This agrees with what the Apostle writes in the same letter, chapter 2: "When we were dead through our sins, God made us alive together with Christ."[103] Just as a dead man can do nothing towards his own

---

[97]C. Pellican, *In sacrosancta quatuor evangelia et apostolorum acta* (Zurich: Froschauer, 1537), 157. Conrad Pellican (1478–1556) was Martyr's predecessor as professor of Hebrew. He had welcomed Vermigli when he first visited the city on his flight from Italy in 1542. Martyr held him in high regard; see Martyr's letter to Bullinger from Oxford, 14 June 1552 (DM 343) and his inaugural lecture on assuming the Zurich chair in 1556 (*Oratio*, LC app.).

[98]1 Sam. 10:26.　　　　　　　　　　[99]Phil. 2:13; Eph. 2:8.

[100]2 Thess. 3:2.　　　　　　　　　　[101]Eph. 1:19.

[102]C. Pellican, *In omnes apostolicas epistolas … commentarii* (Zurich: Froschauer, 1539), 370, on Eph. 1:15.

[103]Eph. 2:5.

raising up or resurrection, neither do we raise ourselves even though we call upon the words of God, unless spirit and life are first restored to us; *[979]* then we move and hasten to well-doing. In 1 Corinthians it is written: "For who sees anything different in you? And what have you that you have not received? And if you have received it, why do you boast as if you had not received?"[104] If we held that free will can receive the promises offered and assent to the words God proposes, one could easily answer: it is my free will that distinguishes me from others, because I will and they do not; I have assented, they have refused. So differences appear among us. And when Paul says "You have nothing that you did not receive" he does not mean creation but faith, Christianity, and regeneration. For he was dealing with the Corinthians who already professed Christianity.

10. Seeing that this healing of the mind depends on God, we rightly pray: "Heal me, Lord, and I shall be healed." And in the Psalms: "Restore us O God of hosts."[105] When God does so he takes from our hearts the veil that kept us from being fit for divine things: the nail of obstinacy and stubbornness is driven out by the nail of the word of God.[106] Christ said: "No man comes to me except my Father draw him."[107] Augustine speaks of this in his 26th treatise on John[108]: "Do not think that you are drawn against your will; the spirit is drawn also by love. [...] Nor should you say, how can I believe willingly, if I am drawn? You are drawn not only by will but by desire, for as the poet says, 'Everyone is drawn by his own pleasure.'"[109]

And he adds similes: "Show a green twig to a lamb and you lead him; show nuts to a boy and he is attracted. We are led without hurt to the body, drawn by cords of the heart." Explaining this leading further, he says: "What am I doing even now while I speak to you? I am pouring a clatter of words into your ears, but unless someone within reveals it, what am I saying? what do I mean? I tend the tree's exterior, the Creator is within. But neither he that plants nor he that waters is anything; it is God who gives the increase, and makes everyone teachable. Everyone? Those who have heard and learned from the Father come to Christ."[110] Treating the same subject against the two Pelagian letters, in chapter 19 he writes: "Who is drawn if already willing? Yet no one comes unless he is willing. Therefore, in marvelous ways he is led to will-

---

[104]1 Cor. 4:7.   [105]Jer. 17:14; Ps. 80:7.
[106]See "Resurrection," p. 48, n. 6
[107]John 6:44.
[108]Augustine *In Johannis Evangelium, Tract.* XXVI.4ff. on John 6:41–59 (PL 35.1608).
[109]Vergil, Eclogue 2: Trahit sua quemque voluptas.
[110]1 Cor. 2:7; John 6:45.

ingness by him who knows how to work within the very hearts of men. Not
that men should believe against their wills, which is impossible; but from
unwilling they are made willing."[111] I know that some would hold that everyone is led by God; some do not come because they do not choose, not because
they are not drawn. But such exposition does not agree with the discourse of
the Gospel. For some rejected the words of Christ, they murmured and went
their way, while the twelve clung to Christ, who seems to give as the reason
for this difference that no one comes to him unless the Father draw him. This
statement implies: They depart and do not come to Christ; therefore, they are
not drawn. The apostles adhere to Christ and follow him; therefore, they are
drawn. Thus these are led and those are not. As to the reason why one is led
and another not, Augustine says do not judge if you will not err. More might
be said of this leading, but I abstain.

I come to Paul and the prophet Isaiah, who compare us with God as if
he is the potter and we the clay, which is to be understood not only of our creation but also of our reformation; Paul used the same simile to the Romans.[112]
We should consider closely whether a potter not only forms and shapes the
clay but also softens, restores, and tempers it, relating to the change that we
speak of now. It is also said to the Romans: "It is not in him that wills nor him
that runs, but in God who shows mercy."[113] In these words Paul declares that
our salvation is wholly of him, and that we should not argue with him about
boundaries, as if to say this is mine and this his, but confess sincerely and truly
that our salvation is all from God. Oecolampadius, a man eminent in piety
and learning, commented on Isaiah 26, folio 156[114]: "Now we must not imagine that God prospers the endeavor while doing nothing. For a little later he
refutes this also, referring all our works to God. Nor do we grant him false
and unique titles as some flatterers do to kings; because through the authority
of kings many thousands are killed in battle, while meanwhile at home they
themselves have leisure for games and hunting." In *Of the Gift of Perseverance,*
chapter 2, Augustine says that we live rightly when we attribute everything to
God. He reports Cyprian as saying that nothing is of ourselves; therefore, we
may not glory in the least.[115] He said this not only for the sake of Christian
modesty but because it is the truth of the matter. If the exposition of those
words by some critics had been true, "It is not in him that wills nor him that

[111]Augusine *Contra duas Ep. Pel.* I.XIX.37 (PL 44.568).

[112]Isa. 45:69; Rom. 9:20.   [113]Rom. 9:16.

[114]Oecolampadius *In Iesaiam Prophetam* (Basel, 1548) fol. 156 on Isa. 26:7.

[115]Augustine *De dono perseverantiae* II.4 (PL 45.996); cf. Augustine *Contra duas Ep. Pel.* 25
(IX) (PL 44.618); Cyprian *De Oratione Dominica* XI–XII (PL 4.526–527).

runs, but in God who shows mercy," [as if] they are said because our will and strength are not sufficient without the mercy of God, then the sentence could have been inverted, as if to say: it is not in God who has mercy but the human will. For according to them the mercy of God is not sufficient unless we ourselves are willing. He thinks such an inversion cannot be allowed, as he teaches in his *Manual for Lawrence*, chapter 22, and more largely to Simplicianus, book 1, question 2,[116] where he writes like this: "If you mark those words diligently, 'Therefore, it is not in him that wills nor him that runs but in God who has mercy,' the apostle seems to have spoken not only because we may attain what we are willing by the help of God, but also in the sense in which he speaks in another place, 'Work out your own salvation with fear and trembling, for God is at work in us, both to will and to work for his good pleasure.'[117] Here he shows well enough that a good will is itself produced in us by the work of God. If it may be said, 'It is not in him that wills nor him that runs but in God who has mercy', since the human will alone is not enough for us to live justly and rightly unless helped by the mercy of God, it may also be said: [980] therefore it is not in the merciful God but in the human will, because the mercy of God is not sufficient on its own, without the consent of our will. Yet this is clear, that we will in vain unless God takes pity on us. Yet I do not know how this is meant: God takes pity in vain unless we are willing; for if God has mercy we also are willing. In fact our willing belongs to the same mercy. 'For it is God who works in us both to will and to do according to his goodwill.' If we ask whether a good will is the gift of God, it would be strange if anyone dared deny it," and so forth.

In the same question to Simplicianus he writes the same thing:[118] "But if such vocation produces a good will so that everyone who is called responds, how can it be true that 'Many are called, but few are chosen'?[119] If it is true, and if those who are called do not consequently obey their calling even if obedience is put into their will, it may rightly also be said: Therefore, it is not in God who has mercy, but in man that wills and runs, because the mercy of the one who calls is not enough unless obedience follows. But perhaps those who do not consent to this kind of call can adapt their will to another mode, so that it is also true, 'Many are called, but few are chosen.' Thus although many are called in one way, only those can follow their calling who are found fit to take

[116]Augustine *Enchiridion ad Laurentium* 32 [sic] (PL 40.247–248); Augustine *Ad Simplic.* 1.Q 2.12 (PL 40.117–118).
[117]Phil. 2:12–13.
[118]Augustine *Ad Simplic.* Q 2:13–114(PL 40.118–119).
[119]Matt. 20:16.

it up, because all are not affected in the same way. And is this no less true: 'Therefore, it is not in him that wills nor in him that runs, but in God that shows mercy', who calls in such a way as suits those who follow their calling? The call surely came to others, but because it was not such as would move them to become fit to take it up, they might well be said to be called but not chosen. But it is not equally true to say: 'Therefore, it is not in God who shows mercy but in man who wills and runs', because the effect of the mercy of God cannot lie in human power, if his mercy is vain when man is unwilling. If he would have mercy on them he is able to call them in a way suitable for them, that they might be moved and understand and follow. It is therefore true that 'Many are called, but few are chosen.' The elect were made agreeable to the call, but those who were not suited or prepared for their calling were not chosen because they did not follow even though called. It is true that 'it is neither in him that wills nor in him that runs, but in God who has mercy', because although he calls many yet he takes pity on those he calls so that they are fit to be called and to follow. But it is false to say: 'Therefore, it is not in God who has mercy, but in man that wills and runs.' For God does not have mercy on anyone in vain. Those on whom he has mercy he calls in the way he knows will agree with them, that they should not refuse the caller.

"Here some will say: why was Esau not called in such a way that he would obey? For we see that different people are moved differently to faith, though the same things were revealed or signified. For example, Simeon believed in our Lord Jesus Christ, who was still a tiny infant, knowing him through revelation of the Spirit.[120] Nathanael heard only one statement by him, 'Before Philip called you, when you were under the tree, I saw you,' and answered, 'Rabbi, you are the Son of God, you are the king of Israel.'[121] Much later, because Peter confessed he deserved to hear that he was blessed and that the keys of the kingdom of heaven were to be given him.[122] At the miracle performed in Cana of Galilee when Jesus turned water into wine, recounted by John the Evangelist as the first of Jesus' signs, his disciples believed in him.[123] Many were aroused to faith by preaching; many did not believe even when the dead were raised; the disciples were terrified by his cross and death, and faltered; yet the thief believed when he saw him not as preeminent in deeds but as his equal in the fellowship of the cross.[124] After his resurrection, one of the disciples did not believe the living members so much as the fresh scars.[125] Many of those who crucified him had seen him perform miracles yet

[120]Luke 2:25–26.   [121]John 1:48.   [122]Matt. 16:16–19.
[123]John 2:11.   [124]Luke 23:40–42.   [125]John 20:27.

condemned him, but they believed the disciples who preached of him and did similar things in his name. One is moved to faith in one way and someone else in another way; often the same thing spoken in one way moves one although spoken differently does not move him but moves someone else; therefore, who dares say that God lacked some way of calling Esau so that he might apply his mind and join his will to the faith by which Jacob was justified? But if there can be such great obstinacy of the will that the aversion of the mind is hardened against every kind of call, it must also be asked whether the hardness itself is a divine punishment. For when God forsakes by not calling in this way, how can one be moved to faith? And who will say that the omnipotent himself lacks the means by which one should be persuaded to believe," and so forth? Now it is clear what Augustine thought regarding that passage, "It is neither him that wills nor him that runs," and so on.

After these matters I refer to what Paul wrote, "And because you are sons, God has sent forth the Spirit of his Son into your hearts, crying Abba, Father."[126] But if the Spirit that God sent to men makes them cry out, it also makes them believe, and therefore, act and live well. For when it is said in the Prophet, "I will take from them that heart of stone and give them a heart of flesh," it is added: "And I will give my Spirit to them, and will cause them to walk in my commandments," etc. It is written also to the Romans: "As many as are led by the Spirit of God, they are the sons of God."[127] In this regard it should be noted that sometimes the saints are only passively subject to certain motions of the Holy Spirit. Some admit that our will is at times merely passive, for when troubles and anxieties force us to look for nothing but death, the spirit is sustained by God lest it surrender. What prevents our being no less passively subject to this change of which we are speaking? So I say that the will is the subject of both conversions, of healing and of faith; in regard to the first, it concurs only passively, but in regard to the second actively as well, because we believe willingly. There is no synergy in the first, but in the other there is cooperation. It is written to the Galatians: "But when it seemed good to him who had separated me from my mother's womb";[128] *[981]* it does not say, "When it seemed good to me." And to the Romans: "God distributed to every one the measure of faith"; concerning free gifts it is written that the Holy Spirit distributes them to every one as he wills.[129] He is no less our Lord of regeneration and God of faith than he is of free gifts. Therefore, he distributes both kinds as it pleases him. In the letter to the Philippians we read: "To them

---

[126]Gal. 4:6.   [127]Ezek. 11:19–20; Rom. 8:14.
[128]Gal. 1:15.   [129]Rom. 12:3; I Cor. 12:11.

was it given not only to believe but to suffer for Christ." And in second Timothy it is written: "For God has not given us the spirit of fear, but of power, and of love, and of a sound mind."[130] Christ said to the apostles: "To others, to whom it is said in parables, it was not given to understand; but to those who were his apostles was it given."[131] Many other testimonies of Scripture could be advanced in this way, but I will content myself with them; for if any will not believe all these, they will not credit even more.

[SYLLOGISM OF CHOOSING]

11. Many will say: If this is how things are, then we are like sticks and stones that are moved by God. But that is not the case, because when sticks and stones are moved they neither perceive nor understand nor choose. Further, if we are moved passively in anything like sticks and stones, we still should not be called so; for in this change under discussion we are not moved forcibly like stones and trees but by a motion appropriate to our purpose and perfection. What they object against us is not well reasoned, for it is an argument in the second figure of affirmative propositions, as if we should say:

Stones and sticks [lapides et trunci] are moved passively;
men are moved passively in this change or conversion;
therefore they are stones and sticks.

We might also say:

Stones and sticks are bodies, and also substances;
men are likewise bodies and substances;
therefore they are stones and sticks.

Everyone sees that the conclusions are not firm, and belong to the second figure of affirmatives.[132]

Nevertheless, the position which we hold concerning the conversion[133] or healing of the soul which occurs before we can believe or hope or expect heavenly things, does not support [Caspar] Schwenckfeld. He seems to put faith before the word of God, but we do not because we affirm that the word of God is an outward as well as an inward instrument of the Holy Spirit, by

[130]Phil. 1:29; 2 Tim. 1:7.
[131]Paraphrase of Matt. 13:11.
[132]In the second figure of the syllogism, the undistributed middle term is predicate in both premises: P–M/S–M//S–P, yielding an invalid consequence. Cf. Aristotle *An. Prior.* 1:17, 36a26ff., 2.19.66a25ff.
[133]Reading *de mutatione* for *Dei mutatione* (or *de immutatione*).

which he persuades and shows what is to be believed and done, and declares and reveals his efficacy in our conversion. We know that faith is by hearing, and hearing by the word of God. Paul says: "How shall they believe in him of whom they have not heard?" Elsewhere it is written: "Lord, who has believed our report?"[134] Schwenckfeld also seems to appoint the outward word to be a kind of effort of the faithful, and rejects the ministry. We abhor this opinion, for we affirm that both outward and inward word are instruments of the Holy Spirit, and do not doubt that the word precedes faith, at least by nature since it is its subject.[135]

[The Two Callings]

12. We conclude that before regeneration the will or choice can do nothing by itself in regard to divine and spiritual matters; the Spirit of God is required, since it proposes and teaches; nor is this enough unless it effects a change of soul. The Pelagians said that the grace of God is required, but only so that we may more easily believe and do well. The scholastics differ from them and have affirmed prevenient grace.[136] But we ask: what kind of grace is it? We think it not enough to answer, that by which the promises and words of God are offered us, either inwardly or outwardly. But a change or conversion should be introduced, nor should it be our will or choice to follow or cleave to the promises. Augustine reminds us that under the praises of nature lie hidden the enemies of grace.[137] Now that we have discussed the subject, there appear to be two kinds of calling [duplex vocationis genus], one ordinary and the other effectual. I prove this distinction first from Holy Scripture. Paul says: "Whom he has called, those he also justified";[138] this is the kind of call to which justification is joined. It is Paul's chain [cathena] to connect the links firmly. On the other side, Christ said: "Many are called, but few are chosen."[139] Here a calling is spoken of which is not followed by justification.

---

[134]Rom. 10:14, 17; Isa. 53:1; Rom. 10:16.

[135]Martyr reflects the image of Caspar Schwenckfeld common among the Reformers. In fact, Schwenckfeld would have agreed to the necessity of both outward and inward communication for faith to result, e.g. Schwenckfeld, *Corpus Schwen.* XII, 129; cf. VI, Doc. 256: "Those, on the other hand, who without distinction discard the ministry of the word ... despise ... Christ"; later, after 1526, he stressed the inward activity of Spirit much more. On outward and inward word, cf. Aquinas *De Veritate* xviii.3, and Martyr ROM 8:24.

[136]Lombard *Sent.* II, dist. 26 (PL 192.1055); Aquinas ST IaIIae.Q 111.3.

[137]Augustine; See *Contra duas Ep. Pel.* III.viii.24 (PL 44.606).

[138]Rom. 8:29.

[139]Matt. 20:16.

There is also a certain vocation called by Paul in particular "according to the purpose,"[140] which is shown to differ from the other common calling. It is proved by Scripture that there is a difference of vocations. Augustine confirms it in the first against the two Pelagian letters, chapter 19, where he writes[141]: "Not all who are called are called according to the purpose, for 'many are called, but few are chosen.' Those are called according to the purpose, therefore, who were chosen before the world was made." About this Augustine again, to Simplicianus at the end of the first book[142]: "Therefore, it remains that wills are chosen, but the will itself cannot be moved by any means, unless something happens to delight and attract the mind. But it is not in human power to cause this. What did Saul want except to attack and capture, to bind and stop the Christians? Did not his will rage? Was it not madness, blindness? Yet he was overthrown by a single word from above. Such a vision occurred so that his cruelty might be halted and his mind and will turned and corrected to faith. Suddenly, from a leading persecutor of the Gospel he became an even more outstanding preacher." Therefore, there are two vocations, one common and the other purposeful; to understand this we should know that this purpose is nothing else than a sure, firm, and steadfast decree of God, by which he foreknew and determined whom he would join to Christ, justify, and bless.

The calling appointed to this purpose *[982]* is effectual and converts men through the word of God, by the work of the Holy Spirit. But the other is general, by which the promises of God are offered through the outward or inward word, though not with such efficacy that souls are healed. Augustine understood this distinction well, writing as follows against Julian the Pelagian, fifth book, third chapter:[143] "Not all who are called are called according to the purpose; 'For many are called, but few are chosen.' Elsewhere he says: 'According to the power of God who saved us and called us with a holy calling, not according to our works but according to his own purpose and grace which were given us in Christ Jesus ages ago.'"[144] Augustine again, *On the Predestination of the Saints*, chapter 16:[145] "God indeed calls many predestined children of his to make them members of his only predestined son, yet not by that calling with which they were called who would not come to the wedding. The Jews

---

[140]Rom. 8:28. As the following paragraphs show, the *vocatio secundum propositum* was a favorite text of Augustine; e.g. Augustine *De gratia et lib. arb.* 33 (xvii), idem, *De corr. et gratia* 23 (ix), and of Martyr ROM 8:29.

[141]Augustine *Contra duas Ep. Pel.* II.x.22 [sic] (PL 44.586–587).

[142]Augustine *Ad Simplic.* I.Q 2.22 (PL 40.128).

[143]Augustine *Contra Iulianum Pel.* V.IV.14 [sic] (PL 44.792).

[144]2 Tim. 1:9.

[145]Augustine *De praedestinatione sanctorum* XVI.32–33 (PL 44.983–984).

also were called by that vocation, to whom Christ crucified is a stumbling block, and the Gentiles to whom Christ crucified is folly; but he calls the pre-destined by that calling which the Apostle distinguished, saying: 'He preached Christ the power of God and the wisdom of God to those who are called, both Jews and Greeks.'[146] He says 'To those who are called' in order to show that some were not called, knowing that there is a sure way of calling those who are called according to the purpose. He foreknew and predestined them to be con-formed to the image of his son; he meant this calling when he said: 'Not because of works but because of him that calls, she was told: the elder will serve the younger.'[147] Does he say: 'Not by works but by him that believes'? In fact he took this away from man so that all might be ascribed to God. There-fore, he said: 'But of him that calls,' not by any sort of call whatever but by that through which one becomes a believer. He also meant this when he said: 'The gifts and calling of God are irrevocable.'"[148] The same Father *On the Spirit and the Letter* chapter 34 mentions another difference of these vocations, that one recommends and the other convinces [suadeat et persuadeat], and says: "Now if anyone presses us to search the abyss as to why one is so persuaded as to yield and another not, only two things come to mind meanwhile which I should like to advance in response: 'O the depth of the riches!' and 'Is there any injustice with God?'[149] If this reply displeases him, he should seek the more learned, but let him beware lest he find the presumptuous."[150]

13. Augustine concludes the argument like this, knowing that some may be found who seek the cause of the difference in free will, whom he called pre-sumptuous. He writes in similar vein in chapter 9 of *The Predestination of the Saints*:[151] "Why it is not given to all should not disturb the believer, who holds that from one all surely go into well-deserved condemnation. Consequently even if none were delivered from it there would be no just cause for finding fault with God. So it is clear how great a grace it is that many are delivered. They learn from those who are not delivered what would be due to them-selves, that those who glory should glory not in their own merits, which they see equaled in those that are damned, but in the Lord," etc. Here Augustine plainly shows that whoever is delivered, not all are called by that calling which liberates; and this without any injustice on God's part. In the same book, chapter 8: "Why, they ask, does he not teach everyone? If we should say that those whom he does not teach are unwilling to learn, we will be answered:

---

[146]I Cor. 1:23–24.   [147]Rom. 9:12.
[148]Rom. 11:29.   [149]Rom. 11:33, 9:14.
[150]Augustine *De spiritu et littera* XXXIV.60 (PL 44.241).
[151]Augustine *De praedestinatione sanctorum* VIII.16 [sic] (PL 44.972).

What becomes of what is said to him, 'O Lord you will restore and revive us'?[152] Or else, if God does not make the unwilling willing, why does the church, according to the Lord's precept, pray for her persecutors?" etc.[153] Augustine does not rest on the answer that they are not taught because[154] they will not learn; for he says that God can make the unwilling willing.

In *To the Objections of the Gauls,* chapter 9, Prosper answers those who argue that whoever are called are not called in the same way, but some so that they might believe, and so on. The answer follows.[155] "If you understand by call nothing more than the preaching of the Gospel, it is false to say that it is preached differently to different people, since there is one God, one faith, one regeneration, one promise. But if we consider the effect of planting and watering,[156] one thing is done in those who heard the sound of words with the ears of the body and another in those whose inward understanding God has opened, and in whose heart he has put the foundation of faith and the fire of love," etc. Those two kinds of calling could not be more clearly expressed.

Zwingli, *On Providence,* tome 1, folio 370: "When that appointment or ordinance was decreed, that a man is now called by God not only by this general calling which signifies the outward preaching of the apostles, but also by that whereby the Spirit stirs the elect with desire to obey God, in command or promise," etc.[157] The same author on the letter to the Romans, chapter 8, tome 4, folio 428: "'To those who are called according to the purpose,' that is, called from the beginning. I understand these words to mean the inward call, that is election, not the call of an outward word; as if he should say: I have now declared that all things turn to good to the saints or those who are called. I approve this statement, for all things are established by the free election of God. God, who knew all things before they existed, also prescribed that they [the saints and the called] should be united with his son. Christ is the first-born, that is the natural and essential Son of God, and we are adopted. 'Whom he has appointed and preordained, those afterward he called by an inward

---

[152]Ps. 85:4–5.

[153]Augustine *De praedestinatione sanctorum,* VIII.15 (PL 44, 971f).

[154]Reading *quia* for *quid.*

[155]Prosper of Aquitaine (d. ca. 463), contemporary and defender of Augustine; Prosper,*Pro Augustino responsiones ad capitula obiectionum Gallorum calumniantium* 5 [sic] (PL 51.160). See *Ancient Christian Writers* 32, *Prosper of Aquitaine: Defense of St. Augustine,* ed. P. De Letter (Westminster: Newman Press, 1963) 144; translations below are from this volume. Cayré, *Manual of Patrology* 2:284, says that Prosper acquired "a deep and perhaps unrivalled understanding of St Augustine's ideas."

[156]1 Cor 3:7.

[157]Zwingli *De Providentia* chap. VI, "De Electione" (CR 93.3, SW 6.3), 178.

calling', that is, he draws inwardly, John 6; so he makes them faithful and draws them, that their mind may cleave to and trust him. Those whom he thus makes faithful, he also justifies through a firm faith, that is, of his Son," and so on.[158]

The same author in his book *On Providence*, tome 1, folio 368, says:[159] "For they saw that this matter was not just signified by symbols, but was done in plain sight, by which the sins of the whole world were expiated, although nothing was done about it. Only those repented whom the Holy Spirit enlightened, that they might know him to be the savior; and the Father drew them that they might come to him and embrace him; further, to know that outward things can do nothing but signify and show," etc. Conrad Pellican, on the first chapter to the Ephesians, interpreting these words, "Who has predestined us to the adoption of sons," writes as follows:[160] "In this matter the order must be noted, in which election holds first place, then adoption as sons, known as calling, while *[983]* the Lord draws to himself those endowed with his Spirit, yielding knowledge of himself; finally holiness of life follows," and so forth. Now through these excellent and learned men it is clear that this twofold vocation was not devised by me but was both received and put in writing by them; it happens that of those who are in the same assembly and hear the same Gospel, some believe and others deny it, some embrace and others mock. Again, those who question, scorn, and resist do so from their own wickedness, which God did not infuse in them; but[161] those who believe and accept do so by the effectual call of God, which is not given to all.

Thus Augustine, in *The Predestination of the Saints*, chapter 8, writes:[162] "Therefore, when the Gospel is preached, some believe and others do not; while the preacher speaks outwardly, those who believe hear the Father inwardly and learn; but those who do not believe hear outwardly but inwardly do not hear or learn. This means that it is given to the one kind to believe but not to the other, because 'no one', he says, 'comes to me unless my Father draw him.'"[163] The same Father in the same book, chapter 6:[164] "Many heard the word of truth, but some believe and others contradict. Some want to believe

---

[158]Zwingli, *Opera* VI.2, 106, *Comm.* on 8:28.

[159]Zwingli, *On Providence*, 165–166.

[160]C. Pellican, *In omnes apostolicas epistolas … commentarii* (Zurich: Froschauer, 1539) 367, on Eph. 1:6.

[161]Reading *autem* for *aut*.

[162]Augustine *De praedest. sanctorum* VIII.15 (PL 44.972).

[163]John 6:44.

[164]Augustine *De praedest. sanctorum* VI.11 (PL 44.968–969).

and some do not. Who does not know this? Who can deny it? Yet since the will of some is prepared by the Lord and the will of others is not, must we not especially distinguish what comes from God's mercy and what from his judgment? 'What Israel sought,' said the Apostle, 'it did not obtain, but the elect obtained it. The rest are blinded; as it is written, God gave them a spirit of stupor, eyes that should not see and ears that should not hear, to this very day,'" and so forth.[165] There is therefore a great difference among hearers, which Augustine, as we know, relates to the diversity of callings. Why God proportions and distributes them so, he teaches in the same book, chapter 8, in these words:[166] "Why he does not teach everyone, the apostle has shown as much as he thought fit to show, for 'desiring to show his wrath and to make known his power, endured with much patience the vessels of wrath made for destruction, in order to make known the riches of his glory for the vessels of mercy, which he prepared for glory,'" etc.[167] Clearly the reason is derived from the final cause, because God resolved to manifest not only his goodness but also his justice and severity. But some will say: if this is the case God will not be universal but particular. This cannot be denied in the sense that we see how he rules according to his will, and distributes these two kinds of vocation. But we will speak of this later, when we come to Predestination.[168]

[The Limits of Freedom]

14. Meanwhile let us turn to those who say that they seek only a little thing, that the free will they wish to be allowed is but a tiny spark [scintillula]. We grant this so far as sound piety permits, namely in those matters subject to human sense and reason not exceeding the capacity of our natures. We also concede it—so far as human infirmity allows to those who are renewed, while we live here. But we cannot grant it to those who are not renewed in relation to heavenly goods and spiritual matters, because it is the kind of spark that would breed not light but smoke, by which men would soon become proud and detract from the grace and mercy of God. For they would boast that they differ from others by this little spark, and do not want to be distinguished by divine mercy and grace alone rather than free will or gifts and virtues. Augustine wrote of these matters in *On the Predestination of the Saints*, chapter 5:[169] "Are men distinct from one another by those gifts which are common to

[165]Rom. 11:8.
[166]Augustine *De praedest. sanctorum* VIII.14 (PL 44.971).
[167]Rom. 9:22–23.
[168]See §§16ff. below, on Prosper of Aquitaine.
[169]Augustine *De praedestinatione sanctorum* V.10 (PL 44.968).

all? First he says 'For who sees anything different in you?' and then adds, 'What have you that you did not receive?'[170] For someone might boast over another and say: my faith, my righteousness, or something else distinguishes me. The good teacher prevents such thoughts, saying: 'What have you that you did not receive?' And what separates you from another that did not come from him? To whom he has not given what he gave you,' and so on.

They say: what a poor thing which we suppose does nothing on its own. But we could say the same about grace, since it does nothing for us unless the consent of our mind is added. Surely it is absurd for us to bring something active to change or regeneration, since no one does anything toward his own begetting. If this is true in physical and carnal affairs, how much more should it be granted in spiritual, which are far beyond our power? Oecolampadius sees this; interpreting the words "And say to them, return unto me" in the first chapter of Zechariah, he writes: "Jeremiah said, 'Turn me back, O Lord, and I shall be restored, for you are the Lord my God; for after you had turned me I repented.'[171] I could not beget myself to a physical life when I did not exist: how will I beget myself to a spiritual life? So John said: this birth is from God.[172] Therefore, those who oppose us on this point contend not only against us but against the grace of God. They adopt what the Holy Spirit avoided, for these things are taught so that we may know that the city is built by the mercy of God. From this they infer that from our physical birth we are allowed a kind of freedom by which we may be converted and build the city of God by our own strength," etc.[173] Oecolampadius does not deny that we have a certain freedom ever since birth, but denies that it is such as to convert us.

They also say that to them God resembles those trustworthy guides who show the way to travelers, advising and urging us to choose the safe way and avoid the dangerous and deadly. If they are not heeded they are not to blame, but have done their part. Such a similitude has no place here, because those who show the way do not have it in their power to persuade or to change the will of those making the journey. But God can do these things if he will, and does so toward those whom he calls effectually. They also affirm that no one is so corrupt and lost that by his own free will he may not seek happiness and the grace and favor of God, *[984]* that it may be well with him. I acknowledge that in general all the unregenerate desire happiness; but if this happiness were laid before them, which we may gain through Christ, through faith in him and

---

[170]I Cor. 4:7.

[171]Jer. 31:18.   [172]John 3:5.

[173]Oecolampadius *In Minores, Quos vocant Prophetas* (Geneva, 1568), "In Zach." 1.3.169.

through the cross, I maintain that it is not within their choice to desire it; rather will they spurn and reject it.

15. A saying of Nazianzen is introduced: "Everything that is right comes from God, and is given to those whom he calls, and who do not reject his call."[174] But if this is understood properly, it counts for us. I take the word κατορθώμενον ["right action"] to mean the duties of believing, hoping, loving God and our neighbor, and of right living. I acknowledge that they come from God and are given to those he calls. If they have been called effectually and are whole, they eagerly assent and agree, which they could not have managed before they received preparation or wholeness. Chrysostom is also quoted, who says: "God truly draws, but draws him that is willing [βουλόμε-νον]," etc.[175] We do not reject this saying either, but should consider that since the divine attraction causes the change, man is found to be unwilling at the very start. When changed by God and healed he is made willing, and willingly drawn to further matters such as believing, hoping, and loving God himself; nevertheless, at that first moment when he began to be drawn he was not willing. Therefore, Augustine well said against the two Pelagian letters, chapter 19, that Christ used the proper word for drawing and not leading [trahendi non ducendi]; for those are led who are already willing, but those are drawn who were not willing; so he said we are drawn and not led, lest we imagine ourselves to have a good will when we begin to be moved by God.[176]

If one asks whether Paul was drawn by free will at his conversion—an event celebrated annually on this very day[177]—I say that the proposition is ambiguous and cannot be satisfied by a simple answer. If asked through which part of the spirit God began to heal Paul and convert him, I gladly concede it to be the free will, that is the will and understanding which concur passively in this renewal. But if I am asked whether Paul was drawn by free will as the active principle by which he might cooperate in his initial renewal and preparation, I deny that the drawing was by free will, especially regarding the first moment of change. There is an obvious reason why I will not admit such freedom in this case, because from the beginning he lacked both the Spirit and grace; without them no strength is sufficient for heavenly and spiritual matters. But they say that since the promises are offered us when we are not yet reborn, we must strive to believe. This is easily commanded but impossible to

---

[174]See Nazianzen *Orat.* 37.13 on Matt. 19:11: ἐπὶ τοῖς κατοπθώμασιν (ob recte facta); PG 36, 297.

[175]Chrysostom *Hom.* 55.1 on Matt. 26:24 (PG 57.541).

[176]Augustine *Contra duas Ep. Pel.* I.37 (XIX) (PL 44.568).

[177]January 25. See introduction for the context of the lecture.

do, for unless we are reformed by the Spirit we will struggle against it and not for it, and will run away, just as Paul and Augustine were against the true faith before they were converted and made whole.

16. They say that we look for violent motion, which is not true; we do not look for force, but we preach the efficacy of divine power. Aristotle defines compulsion in *Ethics* 3 as that which is moved by external principle and does not contribute anything;[178] but our will is not like that. To show what it contributes we must use a physical simile: through transmutation matter first takes on new form and is moved by an efficient cause. It confers a new subject, for it is subject to those motions; thereafter it has power or ability in relation to these forms; even so the human mind is the passive subject of this conversion and healing. It has a certain power or ability, not active but passive when compared with God, since it can be changed actively by him. For we are created rational, in the image and likeness of God. A passive power of this kind may be rightly called, in the scholastic manner, a power of obedience [potentia obedientialis]; because we are capable of a divine change when God wills to effect it. Accordingly, we will understand Augustine correctly when he says that to be able to have faith, hope, and charity comes from nature, but to have them from grace. For we have it from nature that we can be changed passively by God, but that we are changed in fact is of grace.

In his book *Of Rebuke and Grace,* chapter 11, Augustine rightly said that free will is insufficient unless it is changed by the omnipotent God, and that there would be no need of power if it were enough to apply persuasion or revelation of the good.[179] Thus power is required so that the change might be marveled at. The same Father, *Of the Grace of Christ* against Pelagius and Coelestinus, chapter 24, wrote well:[180] "Let them therefore read and understand, let them observe and acknowledge that it is not through law and doctrine sounding outwardly, but by an inward and secret, a marvelous and ineffable power that God works in human hearts not only revelations of truth but also good wills." They object to us from John: "God has given them power to become sons of God."[181] Yet they add nothing, for John is speaking of the regenerate or believers, since it is immediately added: "even to those who believe in his name," and also "those who are born of God." If you want to take

---

[178]Violentum; Aristotle *NE* III.1, 1110b2: "when the cause is in the external circumstances and the agent contributes nothing."

[179]Augustine *De correptione et gratia*, I.xi.31 (PL 44.935).

[180]Augustine *De gratia Christi*, I.xxiv.25 (PL 44.373).

[181]John 1:12.

this in regard to those who are not renewed, we reply that they had that power by predestination before all eternity, although they do not yet possess it in fact. What is written in Zechariah also seems against us: "Return to me," and in Ezekiel chapter 18, "Make yourselves a new heart."[182] Here we seem to concur actively ourselves. Yet as I said at the beginning, we must make distinctions in the drawing, considering the origin of the motion at the time we are resistant; then God converts, changes, and heals us, making willing out of the unwilling. Still, while we live here we are not perfectly converted to God, nor are we so compliant, tractable, or docile towards his commandments as we should be: therefore we are summoned as already being coworkers with God, to be converted more and more to him, and to make new hearts for ourselves day by day.

There is another sort of cavil. First they affirm that the law is the revealed will of God, and also powerful and invincible; they ask why all may not [985] perform it. If God, they inquire, directed the sea to stay within its bounds and to split apart, and it was done because he willed it so; if when he ordered the dead man to be raised up his will was not empty but issued in action; why then doesn't his will have effect, since it is in the law? Obviously not because of his weakness, but because God seems to have so ordered these affairs that he left us to do what he himself did not. I reply: God wants his commandments kept not through the strength of the will alone but through grace by which we are first healed and afterward led to such obedience. Moreover, I agree when it is said that the law is God's will—but not any kind of will. This will may be called the approving will of God, the will of his good pleasure, and a prevenient will. But it is not a creating, regulating, deciding, and effective will toward all, but toward those for whom God planned; just as we say about sin that he did not will it since he forbids it, is offended by it, and punishes it, yet his will toward it is not such that he effectively and forcefully denies it, by ordering or decreeing; otherwise he would not permit it but prevent it. Nor are any wills so perverse that God cannot change them.

Further it is asked whether we are able to resist the call of God. We may, especially the ordinary and general kind, indeed we run away from it before we are regenerated, as did Adam at the beginning, and Paul for a long time. Even afterwards, when we are healed and prepared, we often fall, as we know happened to Peter and to David. But if you ask whether the call prevails when it is effectual and according to the purpose, I say yes. For it was said to Paul in the very hour of his conversion: "It is hard for you to kick against the goads."

---

[182]Zech. 1:3; Ezek. 18:31.

Not that any force is introduced into the will, since that is impossible; although it is written in Luke 14: "Compel them to come in."[183] But there it refers rather to the goodness of God, which is importunate in calling them, and if it can be put like this, uses some persistence; it works not only through exhortation but by blame and affliction. Augustine applied this to the edicts of Christian princes, who decree grievous punishments against heretics—exile, imprisonment, beating, and so on.[184] And although faith is voluntary, God still drives us to it by ways and means like this. It is also objected: "How often would I have gathered your children together, as a hen gathers her chickens?"[185] Augustine replies: "Yet those whom I would gather, I did so even against your will." This Father, however, seems to have spoken harshly against Adimantus the Manichean, chapter 26, where he wrote, "It is in the power of man to change the will for the better."[186] Yet he answered this in his *Retractations*, book I, chapter 22, where he says: "But that power is nothing unless given by God, of whom it is said: 'He gave them power to become sons of God.'[187] For since it is in our power to act when we will, nothing is so much within our power as the will itself; but the will is prepared by the Lord,[188] and by that means is given power. So we should also understand what I said afterwards, that it is in our power either to be engrafted by the goodness of God or to be cut off by his severity, because there is within our power only what follows our will; when armed by the Lord with strength and power, the work of piety is easily performed, which was hard and impossible before," and so on.[189] Therefore, let this rule and exposition stand for all the passages from Augustine where he seems to attribute to free will more than he should in regard to heavenly and supernatural goods. We must answer that this holds only for wills already prepared and healed. This Father never withdrew this rule, but made it firm and certain in his *Retractations*. Also in chapter 10 of the same book[190] he showed that whatever he wrote about free will against the Manicheans was said in order to show that there is not some kind of first evil principle opposing the good God, from which initial evil sins might flow: the origin of sins is from the will. Hence it was inappropriate for that treatise to

---

[183]Acts 26:14; Luke 14:23.

[184]Augustine *De civ. Dei* XXI.11 (PL 41.725–726): Tullius (Cicero) distinguished eight kinds of legal punishment.

[185]Matt. 23:37.

[186]Augustine *Contra Adim.* I.26 (PL 42.169).

[187]John 1:12.

[188]Prov. 8:35 (LXX).

[189]Augustine *Retract.* I.22.4 (PL 32.620).

[190]Augustine *Retract.* I.10.1 (PL 32.599); Augustine *De Genesi contra Manichaeos, libri duos.*

say much about the grace of God's preparing and healing, although he was not completely silent. He spoke of free will as it was in predetermined nature rather than as it is now in defiled and corrupted nature.

We are also blamed for doing evil by denying free will, giving opportunity to those who seek it, and surrendering to the Papists. But I do not remove freedom in general; I acknowledge it in externals and what is within human capacity. Moreover I grant it partially to those who are prepared, healed, and converted by the grace of God, as will be noted soon. Nor is the slander of the Pharisees of much weight: they are blind and leaders of the blind and therefore should be ignored. "Every plant which the heavenly Father has not planted will be rooted up."[191] Besides, they are asking whether God does enough for all to suffice for their salvation. Some affirm it, but it does not seem so to me. For I know from Holy Scripture that those of Tyre and Sidon would have believed if they had seen what Christ did in Chorazin, Bethsaida, and Capernaum.[192]

Prosper noted this also in *To the Objections of the Gauls*, where he commented in chapter 10 on their objection to Augustine's teaching that the grace of the Gospel was withdrawn from some by God.[193] He writes as follows: "Whoever says that the Lord withholds the preaching of the Gospel from some lest they are saved through it, can meet the unjust charge by invoking the authority of the Savior himself. He did not want to perform his works among people who he said would have believed had they seen the signs of his miracles. He forbade his apostles to preach the Gospel to some nations,[194] and still allows other nations even now to live without his grace. Yet we actually know with firm faith that the church will spread to all parts of the world," etc. On this point also the same Father, *To the Extracts of the Genoese*, question 8, writes:[195] "What else can we say of Tyre and Sidon but that it was not given them to believe, while the Truth himself states that they would have believed if they had seen *[986]* such miracles as were done among those who did not believe? Let those who slander us explain if they can why this was refused them, and let them show why the Lord worked miracles among those who would not profit from them. Though we ourselves cannot fathom the reason for God's action nor the depth of his decree, we know for certain that what he has said is true and what he has done is right. Not only the people of Tyre and Sidon but also those of Chorazin and Bethsaida might have been converted

---

[191]Matt. 15:13.   [192]Matt. 11:21.
[193]Prosper of Aquitaine *Ad capitula Gallorum* art 10, qual., 160 (PL 51.172).
[194]Matt. 10:5.
[195]Prosper of Aquitaine *Ad excerpta Genuensum* exc. 8, answer (PL 51.198).

and have come from unbelief to faith had the Lord chosen to do this among them. No one can suspect of falsehood what Truth itself says: 'No one comes to me unless it is given him by my Father'; and 'To you is it given to know the mystery of the kingdom of heaven, but to them it is not given';[196] again: 'No one knows the Son except the Father, nor the Father except the Son; and anyone to whom the Son chooses to reveal him'; again: 'As the Father raises the dead, so the Son gives life to whom he will'; and: 'No one can say "Jesus is Lord" but by the Holy Spirit.'[197]

Moreover, Prosper shows that the preaching of the Gospel has not always been given to all nations nor in all times, even though it is necessary for salvation. To the objection against Augustine that in his opinion all are not called to grace, Prosper gives answer in *To the Objections of the Gauls*, chapter 4: "Suppose even that the whole world had now received the Gospel, every nation and every country (that it will be so is infallibly foretold), yet there can be no doubt that from the time of the Lord's resurrection until today many have departed this life without having known the Gospel. Of these we may say that they were not called, since they never heard of the hope to which we are called. And if anyone claims that the universality of the call was always so public and so full that, from the Lord's ascension into heaven there was not a single year in which the preaching failed to reach everyone, then let him explain how the Asiatics were called; for as it is written, the apostles were forbidden by the Holy Spirit to preach the word of God in Asia or among the Bithynians, to whom they tried to go, and the Spirit of Jesus did not allow them.[198] Let him also explain the warning of the Truth itself saying: 'This Gospel will be preached throughout the whole world, as a testimony to all nations, and then the end will come.'[199] For the certainty of that word is surely shaken—God forbid anyone to say so!—if the world is filled with the Gospel for four hundred years, and yet the Lord's coming is still delayed," and so forth.[200]

This Father in a letter to Rufinus, regarding the passage, "Who desires that all should be saved":[201] "At the very moment when proclamation was sent to all men, the apostles were forbidden to visit certain regions by him who will have all men to be saved and come to the knowledge of the truth. Many of course were detained and went astray in that delay of the Gospel, dying without having known the truth, and without the sanctity of regeneration.[202]

---

[196]John 6:44; Matt. 13:11.   [197]Matt. 11:27; John 5:21; I Cor. 12:3.
[198]Acts 16:6–7.   [199]Matt. 24:14.
[200]Prosper of Aquitaine *Ad capitula Gallorum* art. 4, 143 (PL 51, 159).
[201]I Tim. 2:4.   [202]Reading *consecratione* for -*is*.

Therefore, let Scripture tell what happened: 'When they had passed through the region of Phrygia and Galatia, they were forbidden by the Holy Spirit to preach the word in Asia. And when they had come to Mysia, they attempted to go into Bithynia but the Spirit of Jesus did not allow them.'[203] Is it any wonder that at the very beginning of the preaching of the Gospel the apostles could go only where the Spirit of God wanted them to, when even now we see that many nations only begin to share in Christian grace, while others still have not a glimpse of this good? Or should we say that the wills of men obstruct the will of God, that those people are of such wild and fierce ways that they do not hear the Gospel because their ungodly hearts are not ready for its preaching? Who else changed their hearts but he who has made every heart?[204] Who softened this unyielding hardness to the way of obedience, but he that is able from stones to raise up children to Abraham?[205] Or who will give preachers a bold and unshaken firmness but he who said to the apostle Paul: 'Do not be afraid, but speak and do not be silent; for I am with you and no man shall attack you to harm you; for I have many people in this city'?[206] I think no one will dare to say that there is any nation in the world, or any region on earth[207] that should be passed over, in which the tabernacles of the church should not be established," etc.[208]

It is clear how many reasons [Prosper] brings to prove that the preaching of the Gospel necessary to salvation has been lacking in many nations and many ages. So it cannot be said that God did what was sufficient for human salvation. But to show his mind more fully let us add what he wrote in the 4th chapter of *To the Gauls*: "Whoever says that all are not called to grace is above reproach if he speaks only of those to whom Christ has not been announced. For we know that the Gospel is meant to reach all parts of the world, but we do not think it has already been preached everywhere, nor can we say that the call of grace is present where there is not yet regeneration by the mother church," and so on.[209] In his *To the Extracts of the Genoese*, question 6: "Just as we cannot complain that in past ages God left all nations to walk in their own ways, so we would have no right to complain if grace ceases and we perish along with those whose condition is the same as ours. Just as then grace chose a few the world over, so now it saves countless from all humankind, 'not according to our works but according to his own purpose and grace, which

---

[203]Acts 16:6–7.   [204]Ps. 32:15   [205]Matt. 3:9
[206]Acts 18:9–10.   [207]Reading *terrae* for *rerrae.*
[208]Prosper of Aquitaine *Ep. ad Rufinum de Gratia et Lib. Arb.* §§14–15, 32–33 (PL 51.85–86).
[209]Prosper of Aquitaine *Ad capitula Gallorum* art. 4, qual. (PL 51.171).

was given to us in Christ Jesus ages ago,'" etc.[210] Now it is clear from the writings of this man that the grace of God sometimes stopped, nor did everyone always have equal calling to salvation; thus it is not so universal as some maintain, but rather particular.

Some choose an escape, saying that those to whom the Gospel was not preached had a sufficient call from God, since they were taught by the elements, the spheres of heaven, and other created things *[987]* about the only true God whom they should have worshipped; so that as is said to the Romans, they are held to be inexcusable.[211] Just how true this is the same Prosper showed in the letter to Rufinus, where he writes: "It is no secret that countless thousands of men in various ages were left to their own errors and impieties and died without any knowledge of the true God, as Paul and Barnabas declare in the Acts of the Apostles, saying to the Iconians: 'Brothers, why are you doing this? We also are mortal, men like yourselves, preaching to you that you should turn from these vain things to the living God who made heaven and earth, the sea, and all that is in them. In past generations he allowed all nations to walk in their own ways, yet he did not leave himself without witness, for he did good to them and gave from heaven rain and fruitful seasons, satisfying their hearts with food and gladness.'[212] Certainly, had natural reason or the use they made of God's gifts been enough for them to attain eternal life, then in our day also, the light of reason, the mildness of the climate, and the abundance of crops and food would save us; because making better use of nature we would honor our Creator on account of his daily gifts. But let such foolish and harmful opinion be far from the minds of the faithful and those redeemed by the blood of Christ! Nothing sets human nature free apart from the one mediator between God and men, the man Christ Jesus.[213] Without him there is no salvation: he also renews us and not we ourselves," etc.[214]

So this Father has confirmed that it was not enough to be called to salvation by elements and creatures; for if this kind of calling had ever been effective it should be so today also, seeing that the human condition is not better or worse since the coming of Christ than it was before. He also maintains as the highest truth that there can be no salvation unless by faith that accepts Jesus Christ our Savior. In regard to Paul who in the letter to the Romans renders the nations inexcusable because of their natural knowledge: I answer first that excuse is quite cut off from them because they did not keep faithfully the

---

[210]2 Tim. 1:9; *Respons. ad excerpta Genuensium* exc. 6, An.; (PL 51.194–195).
[211]Rom. 1:18.   [212]Acts 14:15ff.   [213]1 Tim. 2:5.
[214]Prosper of Aquitaine *Ep. ad Rufinum* §§11–12 (PL 52.83–84).

little they knew from the divine creation about holding fast to one God alone; nor did they follow the justice which their mind perceived.[215] They also became inexcusable because they trusted their own strength so much that they thought they needed only to be shown and know what should be done, and that possessing this they could fulfill the justice they understood by themselves. Thus when they had received from God some knowledge of justice and righteousness from creation, and had formed their lives in opposition to it, they were quite empty of excuse. We should also consider that the nations lacking the word of God and the preaching of the Gospel did not enjoy the divine drawing to Christ. For as explained, if we think of ordinary calling, it consists in the word of God outwardly preached or else inwardly and effectually revealed through the Spirit; whether the nations had this is uncertain and cannot be proved. So we cannot assert that God acted toward all in ways sufficient for their salvation. He did not call everyone by the preaching of the Gospel, nor was the healing of their souls always effective among those to whom he gave it. Yet they say: but when God calls he does not pretend but calls in truth. Nor do we say that God plays; we say that he calls truly because it is he himself that calls. For they are not revelations of good things and motions toward doing well unless they come from the true God; whatever he proposes, such as commands and promises, are true and not prone to falsehood. Thus he truly calls even those whose vocation is not effectual. Nor is he frivolous in so calling, since he has his own purposes. While not to be fathomed by us, yet as Scripture teaches he sometimes acts in judgment, so that as we said, men may be made inexcusable, and that the faithful and elect may more clearly perceive in those who are called like this what great benefit they have received in comparison, and may understand that for their own part they might have been called in the same way since they made common cause with them. This kind of calling also serves to blind and harden men for their punishment, as we read in Isaiah when he was sent. God says: "Blind their eyes, make their hearts heavy and fat, lest they turn and be healed," and so on.[216]

They also object against us that humans are so made by him that they are not to be led like donkeys by beating and whipping. I do not deny this: as I have often said, I do not make such effectual calling a matter of force or separate from the word; as I say, through it those who are converted are not only advised but convinced [*suaderi, persuaderi*].[217] Christ indeed said that his

---

[215]For this argument, see Martyr "Nature and Grace" §§6 ff., p. 24.

[216]Isa. 6:10.

[217]Cf. Augustine *De praedestinatione sanctorum* VIII.16 (PL 44.972).

sheep hear his voice,[218] but we must consider that first they are and become his sheep before they hear, just as trees must be good before they bear good fruit. Even so, some imagine that the matter is to be so divided that it is God's to give and ours to receive. I admit that it is we who receive the gifts which God offers; but we do not receive them by ourselves: in fact we would refuse them except that by changing us he causes us to receive them. So God does both, for he offers his gifts and causes us to receive them. That is not within human power; for sometimes a father offers his children something, but cannot change their will so that they become willing to receive what he offers.

Finally, in order to show that the divine drawing is universal, they like to propose what is written in the twelfth chapter of John: "When I am lifted up from the earth, I will draw all men unto me."[219] But they are deceived; for that universal must be limited to the children of God, not only those at present but those already predestined before the world was made. In chapter 11 the same Evangelist described them when he said that Caiaphas prophesied that Jesus should not only die for the people but should gather together the children of God who were dispersed, not just of Jews but of the nations. When Chrysostom [988] interpreted those words he said that the universality must be referred to both peoples, namely to Gentiles and to Jews.[220] For those who desired later to be admitted to Christ were Greeks. While he lived Christ did not admit Gentiles into his company, but showed that he would admit all kinds of people when he had been exalted by the cross and by his death. Thus not all people are being considered here, but rather their various kinds. But to return to that preparation or healing of the soul which I said our mind meets only passively, I say that I have clearly proved it by Scripture and also by the witness of the Fathers. Now I add that this is not foreign to scholastic theologians, for they also grant that there are habits and theological virtues infused by God which we receive only passively. And in defining them they say that they are good qualities of the mind, which God works in us without our help; so he bestows on us the spirit of wisdom, the spirit of counsel, the spirit of courage and others of that kind.[221]

In *Of Grace and Free Will*, chapter 17, Augustine wrote:[222] "Therefore, he operates without us so that we may will; but when we will, and so will that we act, he cooperates with us. We ourselves, however, can do nothing to effect

---

[218]John 10:27.   [219]John 12:32.

[220]Perhaps Chrysostom *Hom*. LXVII, on John 12:25 (PG 50.371–372).

[221]'Habits are qualities, the subject of which must be *in potentia*: the *habitus supernaturales* are not acquired but infused; see Lombard *Sent*. III, dist. 33 (PL 192.822–823).

[222]*De gratia et lib. arb*. XVII.33 (PL 44.901).

good works of piety without his either working that we may will, or cooperating when we will. It is said of his working so that we may will: 'It is God who works in us even to do.'[223] Concerning his coworking with us when we will and act through willing, the apostle says: 'We know that all things work together for good to those who love God.'"[224] While we are prepared and healed by God like this, he does not remove the will from us, but allows us to choose well; nor does he remove intelligence but allows us to understand rightly. Indeed it is the will itself that elicits the act of willing, yet God gives it strength to do so. Augustine writes, *Of the Spirit and the Letter*, chapter 3:[225] "We affirm that the human will has divine help in the pursuit of righteousness, not only because man is created with a free will or because of the teaching which instructs him how he ought to live; but because he receives the Holy Spirit by whom the mind finds a delight in and love of that supreme and unchangeable good which is God, even now while he still walks by faith and not yet by sight.[226] By this down payment [arrha] as it were, of the free gift, he may conceive an ardent desire to cleave to his Maker, and burn to enter on a participation in that true light, that it may go well with him, from him through whom he exists. For free will counts for nothing except to sin, if the way of truth is hidden. And when his duty and his proper aim begin to become known, he neither does his duty nor pursues it nor lives rightly, unless he takes delight in and has love for it. Now in order that such a course may be cherished, 'the love of God is poured into our hearts,' not through the free will which arises from ourselves but 'through the Holy Spirit who is given to us,'"[227] and so forth. By these words he shows that free will does not originate in us so as to share in the mind's healing, but is effected by the Holy Spirit, so that afterwards we may do well by loving God and living uprightly. Grace does not wait on our will, for if so we might look to ourselves before there was strength to desire spiritual and supernatural goods.

The Council of Orange, canon 4, condemned that opinion which believes that divine grace waits for the human will, if indeed it precedes and does not introduce force.[228] To explain this more clearly, an analogy of the Lord's resurrection is of great help. He was raised from the dead in terms of his humanity; this raising from the dead involved human nature only passively. We have already expounded how in outward things subject to human

---

[223]Phil. 2:13.   [224]Rom. 8:28.

[225]*De spiritu et littera*, III.5 (PL 44.203).

[226]2 Cor. 5:7.   [227]Rom. 5:5.

[228]The Council of Orange 529 CE condemned semi-Pelagianism and endorsed a modified Augustinian position on sin and grace, based on propositions from Augustine and Prosper.

capacity, our will is to be allowed some freedom as regards heavenly and supernatural things, which is afterwards denied it unless God converts and prepares it.

[THE REGENERATE WILL]

17. We should now consider the state of the regenerate, who are given freedom in heavenly and supernatural things, so far as the weakness of this life allows. Prosper wrote on the subject in the letter to Rufinus about free will.[229] "They wish to refer this to all who labor in the uncertainty of this life and are burdened with sins, so that those who are willing to follow the meekness and humility of the Savior and accept the yoke of his commandments will find rest for their souls, and hope of life eternal. But those who refuse to do so miss salvation through their own fault—had they wanted to, they could have attained it. But let them hear what is said by the Lord to those who act of their own free will: 'Without me you can do nothing.' And: 'No man comes to me unless my Father who sent me draws him.' Again: 'As the Father raises the dead, so also the Son gives life to whom he will.' Again: 'No one knows the Son except the Father, and no one knows the Father except the Son, and anyone to whom the Son chooses to reveal him.'[230] Since all these sayings are unchangeable and cannot be twisted and interpreted in another sense, who can doubt that free will obeys the invitation of God's calling only when his grace has aroused in someone the desire to believe and to obey? Otherwise it would be sufficient to teach him and there would be no need to produce in him a new will. As it is written: 'The will is prepared by the Lord'; and the apostle: 'God is at work in you both to will and to accomplish, according to his good will.'[231] According to which good will if not the one which God produces in them, as to give them to accomplish what he gave them to will?" and so on.

18. The same Prosper writes on the matter in the place already noted:[232] "Yet if we consider with eyes of faith [pio intuitu] that part of the sons of God who are chosen for works of piety, will we not find that their free wills are not suppressed but renewed? No doubt when unaided and left to itself free will acted only for its own destruction: for it had blinded itself but could not enlighten itself. But now the same will is turned back, not destroyed, and given new desires, new tastes, new actions; its health is entrusted not to itself but to its physician. For even now it is not so perfectly healthy [989] as to be

---

[229]Prosper of Aquitaine *Ep. ad Rufinum* §5 (PL 51.80). The reference is Matt. 11:28–30.
[230]John 15:5; 6:44; 5:21; Matt. 11:27.
[231]Phil. 2:13.
[232]Prosper of Aquitaine *Ep. ad Rufinum* §17 (PL 51.87).

proof against what caused its past illness, nor can it by its own strength abstain from what is unhealthy. Accordingly, man who was evil in his free will has been made good in that same free will; through himself he was evil, he is good through God. God has restored him to his original dignity by a new beginning, not only forgiving him the guilt of his willing and doing evil, but also enabling him to will and to do what is good, and to persevere in it. 'For every good gift' (the apostle James says) 'and every perfect gift is from above, and comes down from the Father of lights,'" etc.[233] By these words we see that no little power is to be attributed to free will, that is, a will now reformed. Therefore, I state that the regenerate can know spiritual things, can also choose and to some extent perform them; for they are not now merely and only human but people of God; they are engrafted into Christ, they are his members and therefore partakers of his freedom. It is said to them: "Work out your salvation with fear and trembling."[234] They are no longer enemies of God, but friends of God and of Christ; therefore he has made known to them what he has heard from his Father. "Now they have the laws of God written in their hearts, and within them."[235] They are not at the very start of being led, where the movement begins, but have progressed further, and from unwilling are made willing. Augustine's simile on John agrees well with them, about the green bough shown to the lamb, and the child to whom nuts are offered; at first they would not go but afterwards they are led with great delight.[236] It may also be fitly said of them: if you are not drawn, pray that you may be. When they are children, they are led by the Spirit of God, and so led as to do what is right on their own. In the letter to Rufinus, Prosper wrote of this, saying: "'For all have not faith, nor do all believe the Gospel,'[237] but believers are led by the Spirit of God, while unbelievers turn away by their own free will. Therefore, our turning to God is not of ourselves but of God, as the apostle says:[238] 'By grace are you saved through faith, and this not of yourselves, but it is the gift of God; not of works, lest anyone should boast,'" etc.[239] The regenerate can arouse in themselves the gifts and grace of God, as Paul wrote to Timothy, in the second letter.[240] They also adapt themselves to the Holy Spirit so that they possess and use the more excellent and profitable spiritual gifts, as the Corinthians are advised by Paul in the first letter.[241] Those that are renewed do works that are pleasing to God: Abraham is commended by God

[233]James 1:17.   [234]Phil. 2:12.   [235]Jer. 31:33.

[236]Augustine *In Joann.*, Tract. 26.5 (PL 35.1609). Cf p. 292, n. 107, above.

[237]2 Thess. 3:2; Rom. 10:16.   [238]Eph. 2:8–9.

[239]Prosper of Aquitaine *Ep. ad Rufinum* §6 (PL 51. 81).

[240]2 Tim. 1:6.   [241]1 Cor. 12.

because for God's sake he spared not his only son. The alms of the Philippians were called a fragrant odor before God.[242] It is written to the Hebrews, chapter 13, that good deeds and hospitality are sacrifices that please God. They are now good trees, and therefore it is no wonder that they bring forth good fruit;[243] they will be accepted even by Christ when he is judge at the last day. The regenerate come to be called perfect, prepared for every good work, yet still have need of the special help of God in everything that is to be done well.

Prosper wrote about this in the letter so often mentioned: "Therefore, whomsoever God's grace justifies, it does not make better from good, but good from bad; later, when they make progress it will make the good better, not by taking away their free will but by setting it free. [...] When the mercy of Christ enlightened it, it was rescued from the kingdom of the devil and placed in the kingdom of God where it may remain. But even provided with this capacity it is not strong enough, unless it is also given perseverance by him who gave it diligence."[244] Yet those who are converted, prepared, and healed have not complete freedom of the will while they live here. They see a law in their members at war with the law of the mind: they do not do the good which they want but the evil they hate, nor can they fulfill God's law completely: they serve the divine law with their mind, but with their flesh the law of sin. The spirit lusts against the flesh and the flesh against the spirit, so that they do not the things which they would.[245] More often than not results do not correspond with their intentions, while grave faults occur, as happened to Peter and David. They cannot be without sins, for John said: "If we say that we have no sin, we deceive ourselves, and the truth is not in us." And James wrote: "We all offend in many matters."[246]

19. There is nonetheless a difference between sinners and the regenerate; for the former delight and rejoice in sins while the faithful sorrow and lament, praying daily: "Forgive us our debts," and so on. They also exclaim: "O unhappy man that I am! Who will deliver me?"[247] And seeing themselves imperfect, having only the first-fruits of the Spirit, they wish that their last days had come, so that in truth they may become fully perfect in the final regeneration.

---

[242]Gen. 22:16–7; Phil. 4:18.
[243]Heb. 13:16; Matt. 7:17.
[244]Prosper of Aquitaine *Ep. ad Rufinum* §9 (PL 51, 83).
[245]Rom. 7:19, 23, 25; Gal. 5:17, Matt. 26:29.
[246]I John 1:8; Jas. 3:2.
[247]Matt. 6:12; Rom. 7:24.

Finally, those who distinguished three kinds of freedom seem to have spoken correctly. One is the freedom from constraints of necessity and is common to both godly and ungodly, for the human will cannot be constrained. Another that they posit is freedom from sin which the unrighteous by no means have while the regenerate enjoy it in part, as was noted already. The third freedom is from anxiety, which the wicked lack, but which we have to a certain extent.[248] For though tossed by various misfortunes, yet by hope we are saved from both sin and anxiety; when we have reached the fatherland, we will have complete freedom. Let these things do in regard to free will.

---

[248]The *triplex libertas* is *ab necessitate cogente...ab peccato...ab miseria*. Cf. Bernard of Clairvaux, "Author," p. 256, n. 164.

Common Places, Appendix

Three Summaries

1. Free Will

What is put forward to be known concerning free will is no light affair, but of great importance. For those of us who are renewed by the grace of Christ, well aware of the feebleness and infirmity of free will, will not become proud, nor exalt ourselves by its power. Rather will we be urged more strongly to seek God's help. When we proceed further and understand from what evils and dangers we are delivered, we will be moved more earnestly to give thanks to our deliverer. Moreover, the honor will be attributed to God, to whose goodness, mercy, and liberality we owe [990] whatever will be ascribed to our power and ability. The Apostle required above all that we should not glory, but should yield everything to God.[1] Also, giving free will so much as some demand brings free justification into doubt, while free election and predestination cannot stand.

Free will [Liberum arbitrium] is a certain power of the will, which partially follows knowledge, but either refuses or desires something on its own.

---

[1] 1 Cor. 4:7.

Included in the material added by Rudolph Gualter to the 1580 edition of the *Loci Communes* are three brief topics, summaries of longer treatises. Their authorship is disputed (see "The Three Summaries." on p. 268); they are written in the first person but not in Martyr's hand. *De libero arbitrio* summarizes the "Free Will" lecture translated above. The opening paragraph is italicized in the original.

320

[DEFINITION]

It is held to be a power of the will: but that is insofar as free choice [*proairesis*] is drawn from it. The Master of the Sentences, book 2 dist. 25, said that it is a power of reason and of will by which the good is chosen when grace assists, or evil when grace fails.[2]

The things to which the will is applied are of two kinds. Some are subject to the sense and reason; others exceed our capacity, since they are divine and supernatural.

Human states and conditions are also differentiated. Some are not yet renewed, but are still strangers from Christ. Others are regenerated.

[PROPOSITION 1]

Those who are not yet renewed have in part a free will towards things subject to sense and reason and which do not exceed our capacity, and in part they have not. They have it because it is in our power to walk, to stand, to sit, to study, to buy and sell, to travel, etc. And often reason may restrain outward motions, or else arouse them. To some extent they have not [free will]; because often so much disturbance is aroused, and so many impulses, that it is not in reason's power to restrain them. Thus they are terribly angry, they tremble, they are disturbed; sometimes they cannot move from their spot, and seized by too much fear must flee, as the Canaanites could not stand against the Israelites. Also, initial motions are not in our power.

By such freedom as we allow, men are able to do those things which agree with civil and economic laws. Therefore, civil and moral science remain sound, and the authority of the magistrate is not threatened but confirmed. Also, they are able to do many outward things which may seem to agree with the law of God, as hypocrites do: but in fact such doings are not according to the law of God. For divine law requires faith, good inward impulse, and that it be done with all the heart, with all the soul, and with all the strength.

The freedom we are discussing is posited because I am led by experience, which has support from Scripture. Paul speaks to the Romans of the wicked and those not regenerate, yet he grants that they could have known God from creation. Also he acknowledged that they knew many just, right and honest things. While still unregenerate, Paul himself advanced in the Jewish religion above his fellows, so that he lived blamelessly.[3] And there are many notable examples of Gentiles.

[2] Peter Lombard *Sent.* II.25.1 (PL 192.706).
[3] Rom. 1:18; Gal. 1:13–14.

[Difficulties That Hinder Freedom]

This freedom that I admit in regard to moral and economic affairs encounters several problems. In reason there is darkness, in the will no small infirmity. Since there is perpetual conflict between the rational part and the duller powers of the mind, wounds cannot be avoided, and reason is often overcome; infirmity of the body results. If this is spoken of the regenerate, spirit strives against flesh and flesh against spirit, so that you do not those things that you would; and if they perceive a law in their members rebelling against the law of the mind, and if they do not the good which they would but the evil which they hate, how much more does this hold for those that are not renewed?[4]

We add that while they are not regenerate, there is a certain necessity of sinning: not such that the will is thereby constrained to will anything unwillingly (for that is impossible) but a necessity by which they cannot do otherwise while they remain in that state. The things they do, since they are not done by faith, must be sins: for whatever does not come from faith is sin. Since they are still evil trees, they cannot bear other than evil fruit. The thoughts and imagination of man are evil from his youth. The wisdom of the flesh is hostile to God, it is not subject to the law of God, neither can it be. And while they are like this they do not love God above all things. Therefore, since all the actions which they do are not referred to him they must be sins.[5]

Add to this that whoever sins is the servant of sin, as Christ said. Paul says in the letter to the Romans: "His servant you are, to whom you have given yourselves to obey." Also: "Then shall you be free indeed, when the Son shall make you free." Peter also said that one becomes the servant of him by whom he is overcome.[6] Therefore, in this state, while men are without Christ, they are not truly free.

Another difficulty arises from the devil, who always seeks whom he may devour, because being strongly armed, he holds them until someone stronger comes.[7]

It is also said to Timothy that at his own pleasure he holds captive those that resist the faith.[8] Therefore, I acknowledge the freedom we have discussed, although it is weakened by great difficulties.

---

[4] Gal. 1:17; Rom. 7:19, 23.
[5] Rom. 14:23; Matt. 7:17; Gen. 8:21; Rom. 8:7.
[6] John 8:34ff; Rom. 6:16–17; 2 Pet. 2:19.
[7] 1 Pet. 5:8.
[8] 2 Tim. 2:26.

Another subject could be added, that God uses our minds as instruments to perform the counsels of his providence. For "the heart of the king is in the hand of God, he turns it wherever he will." As in Ezekiel, God directed Nebuchadnezzar against the Jerusalemites rather than the Moabites or Ammonites; on his own he was in doubt. And the prophets said, "these monarchs are in the hand of God as a saw and staff."[9] Since such means used by God towards them does not destroy the liberty which I have proposed, nor does it force human will or constrain it, it remains sound, as I have explained. For the things which these men do they do willingly, at a nod from God.

[PROPOSITION 2]

I say that these who are unregenerate are not free but unfit in regard to spiritual things, such as to believe in Christ, to hope, to love God above all things, to obey the law of God in faith. In order to will and receive such things, the Holy Spirit must be present, who through the word outward [*991*] or inward, or both together, may illumine the mind, encourage, warn, exhort, and persuade the will.

Some will affirm that this is not enough, though I deny it. For unless these powers are amended and healed, we shall not take hold of or embrace things divine: nor is it in our power that what is proposed to us will satisfy. The understanding must be endowed by the Holy Spirit and not with a common light, and the will confirmed, lest it be drawn aside and yield to convenience or wrong opinion, by which it is diverted from spiritual things. When this is done the mind assents to the words and promises of God, and from such assent or faith justification follows, by the mercy of God through Christ. To this assent the mind submits itself actively: for it is we that both will and consent, when we believe those things that are proposed. But to that efficacy and power of the Holy Spirit by which our mind is prepared, changed and disposed, the mind concurs passively.[10] For it receives them, and they are in it by the spirit of God. This should not seem absurd, for the Scriptures say that we are drawn to Christ by the Father; but drawing signifies a passion and a kind of disposition. Also God stands at the door and knocks; and those blows happen and are received in the mind.[11]

This efficacy of the Holy Spirit, I maintain, inclines our minds and hearts to embrace the words and the promises of God. Yet by this efficacy of

---

[9]Prov. 21:1; Ezek. 21:21; Isa. 10:15.
[10]See pp. 266–267 on concurrence.
[11]John 6:44; Rev. 3:20.

the Spirit no compulsion is forced on the mind, nor should it be inferred as though what they will they choose against their will, or believe unwillingly: but with a pleasant and gentle persuasion, it makes willing of unwilling; and it is so far from corrupting or defiling the will that it rather perfects it. This is what is meant, that "God works in us both to will and to perform"; moreover, "not all have faith."[12] For those not so prepared do not believe. Scripture testifies plainly enough that the will is prepared by the Lord; without doubt that means to put zeal for virtue into those who resist from the beginning.

This change of our mind, when from evil it is made good, happens so that our otherwise hard heart should be softened and become a heart of flesh: for God promised through Ezekiel that we may become teachable for spiritual things. Thus Solomon prayed God that he would give him a hearing heart, implying that his heart, corrupted by nature, was deaf to them.[13] This is to become instructed by God [θεοδίδακτον], this is to hear from the Father and learn, and to have hearing ears, without which "seeing we shall not see, and hearing shall not hear." For these divine and celestial things are such that "eye cannot see, ear cannot hear, nor can there arise in the human heart what God has prepared for them that love him."[14] The natural man does not perceive what belongs to God. We are not sufficient of ourselves to think that anything comes from ourselves. "Our sufficiency is of God"; unless our mind is thus prepared and healed, we will stray from the Divine, as Adam did; we persecute and hate, as Paul did. Hence we pray: "Give me understanding, that I may learn thy commandments. Open my eyes."[15] Paul to the Ephesians wished that their eyes might be opened, so that they might see what should be the hope of their calling. David: "Incline my heart to your testimonies. Create in me a clean heart, O God."[16] God opened the heart of the woman that sold purple, that she might give ear to those things that were spoken. Those whose heart God had touched followed Saul. "By grace you are saved through faith, and that not of yourselves."[17] Here our cooperation regarding that healing is denied. Also to the Ephesians: We believe "according to the working of his mighty power, which he accomplished in Christ, when he raised him from the dead.... When we were dead in trespasses and sins, he quickened us with Christ."[18] The dead have no power to prepare themselves nor regenerate themselves. We have our preparation from God; otherwise, we might have gloried in it: "What have you that you did not receive?" For who sets you apart?

---

[12]Phil. 2:13; 2 Thess. 3:2.
[13]Ezek. 6:26; 1 Kings 3:9.
[14]John 6:45; Matt. 13:9,14; 1 Cor. 2:9.
[15]2 Cor. 3:9; Ps. 119:18, 34.
[16]Eph. 1:18; Pss. 119:36; 51:11.
[17]Acts 16:14; Eph. 2:8.
[18]Eph. 1:19; 2:1.

Someone might say: free will does so. We pray for the faithless, that God will open their heart. "No one comes to me, unless my Father draws him."[19] But whoever is said to be drawn, it shows that he was unwilling before, otherwise he would not be said to be drawn, but rather to be led. Therefore, he that is drawn was unwilling at first, but in that change he becomes willing from being unwilling. Afterward willingly and of his own accord he followed the drawing. I might add that it should not be understood, as some think, that all are drawn, because the meaning [ratio] of the text will not allow that. A reason was given why those who murmured should depart and why the apostles should remain and cleave to Christ, namely because these were drawn, and the others were not.

For God, we are like clay; the potter, however, not only fashioned the clay but softened and tempered it. "It is neither in him that wills, nor in him that runs, but in God that shows mercy."[20] Here everything is attributed to God; especially in regard to predestination, and that first healing of the mind, which is done by the Holy Spirit through the word of God. God turned the heart of king Ahasuerus from ferocity to good will towards Esther: He gave to Saul another heart.

[Two Callings]

Hence there are two kinds of calling. For some are called in such a way that they are enlightened by outward preaching, they are moved by certain suggestions, they are persuaded and aroused a little to it. Besides what I have said, others are prepared and made gentle, they receive hearing ears, and from unwilling become willing; their stony heart is taken away, it is changed and healed. The first kind is simply named calling: the second is calling according to the purpose.[21] Paul said: "Whom he has called, those he also justified." This calling always has faith and justification joined with it, and depends on election; for Paul said: "Whom he has predestined, them also has he called." And in the second to Timothy: "Who has called us with his holy calling, not according to our works, but according to his own purpose and grace, which was given to us through Christ Jesus ages ago."[22] Here he said that this calling is confined to eternal predestination.

[992] Another saying also pertains to this: "The gifts and calling of God are without repentance." But of the first kind is said: "Many are called, but few are chosen."[23] God distributes these kinds of callings as he will, for with

---

[19] 1 Cor. 4:7; John 6:44.   [20] Rom. 9:16, 20.

[21] Primum genus appellatur vocatio simpliciter: alterum vocatio secundum propositum.

his own he may do what seems good to him, without injury to anyone. Is your eye evil because I am good? May I not do what I will with my own? Augustine well said: Why this man is drawn, and not that, do not judge if you will not err. If he wished, God could have healed the mind of Esau as he did of Jacob; but to the one he would give, to the other he would not. And in Deuteronomy 29 it is written, "To this day the Lord has not given you a heart to understand, or eyes to see, or ears to hear."[24]

Those prepared like this by God are those to whom he has given power to become his sons. For being healed they believe and are born of God. Whenever the Fathers, especially Augustine, seem to attribute anything to free will regarding these spiritual and celestial things, they should be understood of a free will that is healed, changed, and already prepared. If it is asked whether we can resist the calling of God, I say that we can, and that from the beginning on occasion we resist it for a while. After we are renewed we sometimes acted against the calling of God, and fell surely and heavily, as did Peter and David. When God has fully decided to change someone, and from unwilling to make him willing, his will is altogether fixed, without forcing. Wherefore it is said to Paul, "It hurts you to kick against the goads."[25]

If effectual calling is not given to all, it will seem that God has not done for everyone as much as was sufficient to salvation. I accept this, for Scripture also says that "they of Tyre and Sidon would have repented in ashes and sackcloth, if those things done in Chorazin and Bethsaida had been done in them."[26] Therefore, God did not grant them the things he knew could have moved them to repentance. Experience shows that many ages have passed in which the word of God was not preached to the nations, and many are the places in new India that even today have heard nothing of salvation through Christ. Yes and the apostles, in Acts 16, were forbidden to preach in Asia and to go into Bithynia.[27] Therefore, we to whom it is given ought specially to give thanks to God.

No doubt some things are done in our mind by God without expecting our consent and will, for faith and diverse gifts of the spirit in which our former consent is not required are infused in us by God. By this alteration God does not take understanding from us but allows us to understand rightly: he does not take willing from us but allows us to will well. He himself converts and heals us. But when we are renewed, we are also said to convert ourselves, and become more and more perfect, as we will soon mention.

[23]Rom. 11:29; Matt. 22:14.
[24]Deut. 29:4.
[25]Acts 26:14.
[26]Matt. 11:21.
[27]Acts 16:6.

[PROPOSITION 3]

Those renewed to spiritual works that may please God have a free mind, that they may perform those things at least with an initial kind of obedience. Therefore, they have the power to know, judge, and choose spiritual things, and do them to a certain extent: because they are not mere men but men of God, they are engrafted in Christ, they are his members and are made partakers of his freedom. To them is it said that they work their salvation with fear and trembling; they are no longer servants but friends, and therefore, they have known the things that are of God; they have a fleshy, not a stony heart; they have the laws of God written in their hearts, they are led by the spirit of God; they can stir up the grace which they have in them, they can apply themselves to better spiritual gifts.[28] So the work of Abraham is praised by God. The alms of the Philippians were an odor of sweet fragrance. Since they are good trees, they can bring forth good fruit;[29] and their work will be commended in the day of judgment. They have been brought to that point where they may be called perfect, and prepared to every good work:[30] yet in such a way that in every good work which they do, they need not only the general influence of God but also the special help of the Holy Spirit. Restored in this liberty, however, they are not so renewed as not to feel some law in their members contrary to the law of the mind, that they do not do the evil which they hate, and so fulfil the law as the law requires. There is still striving between the flesh and the spirit, such striving that they do not do what they would; nor are they so free, but that "in the mind they serve the law of God, but in the flesh the law of sin."[31] Also events and successes are not in their own power. Grievous faults also happen at times, nor are they free from sin. John said: "If we shall say that we have no sin, we deceive ourselves, and the truth is not in us." James: "We all offend in many things."[32]

Yet this is the difference between the wicked and the regenerate, that the former delight themselves in sins and are not sorry, rather are they occupied in them willingly and of their own accord. But the regenerate lament, sorrow, sigh, mourn and perpetually cry: "Forgive us our sins." And since they have the firstfruits of the Spirit, they wish that their last hour were come. So much of free will.

---

[28]Phil. 2:12; Jer. 31:33; Rom. 8:14; 2 Tim. 1:6.
[29]Gen. 22:17; Phil. 4:18; Matt. 7:17.
[30]2 Tim. 3:17.
[31]Rom. 7:19-25; Gal. 5:17.
[32]1 John 1:10; James 3:2.

2. PROVIDENCE AND PREDESTINATION[33]

The doctrine of providence and predestination is most profitable. The fountain of our salvation is revealed in it. It leads us to attribute all our goodness not to our own selves but to the ministration and dispensation of God: we may see in the reprobate what might have been with justice done to us also, if the divine mercy had not intervened by his predestination. By this faith that we are predestined we receive great comfort in adversities. From it Saint Paul gave reasons to the Romans. From this ground also we have certainty of our salvation, which would be uncertain if it depended on the quite unstable free will, and not on the steadfast predestination of God.

[DEFINITION]

[*993*] The providence of God is his ordained, unmovable, and perpetual governance [administratio] of all things; by it he specifically directed all things that he established to their proper ends. Therefore, it is not a bare understanding, but also a will is added to it, which directs all things according to its judgment.

This power cannot be separated from God. For he disposes kingdoms at his own pleasure. "All the hairs of our heads are numbered." "Two sparrows do not fall to the ground without the will of the Father." Whoever is killed by accident, God is said to have delivered him into the hand of another. Princes are in his hand like a staff and a saw. "He upholds all things by the word of his power."[34] To the Hebrews and Ephesians: "He works all things, according to the counsel of his will."[35] Therefore, the Holy Spirit said, "Cast your care upon God, and he will support or nourish you." Peter: "He cares for us." "He that touches you, touches the apple of my eye."[36] This is a great comfort for the godly, that they know themselves to be in the hand of God.

Let the wicked do what they will, they can do nothing that does not accord with the providence of God, as Peter said in Acts: Herod and Pilate agreed "to do whatever your hand and your plan had decreed to do." Job said: "The Lord gave, the Lord has taken away."[37]

---

[33]*De providentia et praedestinatione*, a summary of "Providence" above, and *De Praedestinatione* (ROM, 1558, cap. 9 fin.; LC/CP 3.1). The opening paragraph is italicized in the original.

[34]Dan. 2:21; Matt. 10:29–30; Ex. 21:13; Isa. 10:5.

[35]Heb. 6:17; Eph. 1:11.

[36]Ps. 37:5; 1 Pet. 5:7; Zech. 2:8.

[37]Acts 4:27; Job 1:21.

[CHANCE AND PROVIDENCE]

Things that seem to happen by chance are governed by providence. Joseph said: "God sent me ahead into Egypt." God said that he sent Saul to Samuel, although it might seem that he came by chance. Christ said: "A man shall meet you bearing a pitcher of water."[38]

The breadth of this providence is declared: "If I ascend into heaven, you are there; if I go down into hell, you are there. If I take the wings of the morning," etc.[39]

The decrees of providence are immutable. "I am the Lord, and do not change." "With God there is no variation or shadow of change." "The counsel of the Lord abides forever."[40]

The providence of God does not remove human election or destroy chance, because things are to be understood according to the nature of proximate causes. Causes may be called contingent in regard to human choices and the effects of nature because the fact that they occur one way as well as another is not against the will, and the order of nature is not against it. Further, the providence of God does not govern things except according to their own natures. He governs contingent and voluntary causes in such a way that they may work both by chance and by will. But if the things themselves are referred to God, there is only a hypothetical necessity, as there is a necessity of prediction.[41] It was necessary that the Scriptures should be fulfilled, and that Christ should have suffered. Now there is a greater power in providence than in predictions. For predictions do not act in creatures as does the providence of God: although neither does it violate the natures and properties of second causes.

In relation to the providence of God, things are certain from eternity. For all things are numbered by it. But in our will and mind they are not certain. Still, in regard to ourselves they may be called both voluntary and contingent, though in regard to God nothing is fortuitous or contingent. God said in Isaiah: "All things that I will, I do," etc. Paul: "He accomplishes all things according to the counsel of his will."[42]

Since the providence of God is like this, there is room for counsels and admonitions, deliberations and corrections, since it has decreed to attain the ends which it prescribed by these means. For instance when it has determined

[38]Gen. 45:8; 1 Sam. 9:16; Mark 14:13.
[39]Ps. 139:8–9.
[40]Mal. 3:6; James 1:17; Isa. 46:10.
[41]On absolute and hypothetical necessity, see "Providence," §13.
[42]Isa. 55:11; Eph. 1:11.

to change an evil will, it proceeds to convert it by these means. Therefore, such means are instruments of God.

[PREDESTINATION]

Predestination is part of the providence of God, as it were: [43] for it is the strength and power of God by which he appoints and directs men to obtain eternal life through Jesus Christ.

By predestination the natures of things are not changed, in terms of necessity, contingency, and deliberations, as we said in regard to providence.

Even if everything is present to the foreknowledge and eternity of God, creatures which have had a beginning are not coeternal with God as if to coexist with his eternity. Paul said, "We were chosen before the foundation of the world was laid." And of Jacob and Esau it is said: "Before they had done either good or evil, Jacob have I loved, but Esau have I hated."[44]

Those who affirm that with God things are appointed only in respect of his foreknowledge err greatly, for the Scriptures interpose his will. A sparrow falls not without the will of the Father: the will (I say) not new, but eternal. Seventy years were prescribed to the captivity of Babylon; fifteen years were added to Hezekiah's life. Christ: "My hour is not yet come." "I will have mercy on whom I will have mercy." "They believed, as many as were ordained," and so on. Christ was crucified according to God's fixed counsel.[45]

Some say that predestination is a preparation of grace, or foreknowledge, or a preparation of divine gifts by which those who are delivered are truly delivered; but others are left in the mass of perdition.[46] Some say that it is a purpose to have mercy, others a preparation of grace in the present and glory in the future. But I say that it is the most wise purpose of God, by which he firmly decreed before all ages, to call those whom he loved in Christ into the adoption of children, into justification through faith, and at length into glory through good works, that they may be conformed to the image of the Son of God, and that in them the glory and mercy of the Creator may be declared.

Predestination is unchangeable. "The foundation of God remains sure." "The Lord knows who are his." The certainty of salvation proceeds from it. Therefore, when Paul had spoken of predestination he said: "Who will accuse

---

[43]For the problem which the phrase *pars providentiae quaedam* poses for Martyr's doctrine of predestination, see xxxiiiff.

[44]Eph. 1:4; Rom. 9:11ff.

[45]Matt. 10:29; Jer. 25:11; Isa. 38:5; John 7:6; Ex. 33:19; Acts 13:48, 2:33.

[46]On the *massa perditionis* see Augustine, *Ench.* xxvi–xxvii.

us? Who will condemn? Who shall separate us from the love of God?" "I am the Lord, and do not change."[47]

[REPROBATION]

Reprobation is the most wise purpose of God by which he firmly decreed before all ages, without any injustice, not to have mercy on those whom he did not love, but passed them over, so that by their just condemnation he might declare his wrath towards sins, and show his power and glory.

Sins are not the cause of reprobation, for some are exempted from the love of God and are forsaken, but they are the cause of damnation. Thus if the Fathers sometimes say "Sins are the cause of reprobation," they understand it in regard to final condemnation, imposed wholly on account of sins.

God predestined us to this end, that while we live we should work well. For it is said to the Ephesians that he has ordained good works, that we should walk in them.[48] Yet good works or faith cannot be causes of predestination: they are its effects. To those he has decreed to bless he has predestined to give faith and good works. It is said to the Romans, regarding the twins when they had as yet done neither good nor evil: "The elder will serve the younger.... Jacob I loved, Esau I hated.... Not of works, but by him that calls.... It is not in him that wills, nor in him that runs but in God that shows mercy....I will show mercy on whom I will show mercy.... He has mercy on whom he will, and whom he will he hardens."[49] The arguments of Paul would count for nothing if the predestination of God depended on faith or else on works that were foreseen. I obtained mercy so that I should be faithful, I did not obtain mercy because I would be faithful. So many as were ordained to eternal life believed.[50] They believed because they were ordained; they were not ordained or predestined by God because they believed. Our justification depends on the election or predestination of God. "Whom he predestinated, those he called; whom he called, those he justified."[51] But if predestination depended on free will we would be justified by free will.

Divine and human election have different modes. Men love and choose those in whom they find virtues or some good. But God cannot find any good in men that he himself has not given them. Therefore, if he chose those whom he will in Christ, they do not have it from themselves that they are in Christ,

---

[47]2 Tim. 2:19; Rom. 8:32; Mal. 3:6.
[48]Eph. 2:10.
[49]Rom. 9:11-18.
[50]Acts 13:48.
[51]Rom. 8:30.

but they will receive it from God himself. So to be in Christ is not the means or cause of predestination, but the effect.

Christ is the chief and principal effect of predestination; God gave him so that through him he might save the predestined. Through him as by a channel, other effects of predestination are derived to us by the mercy of God.

If election depended on works foreseen, it would not have been so hard with Paul that he should cry: "O the depth of the riches," etc.[52]

The doctrine of predestination does not open a window to idleness but rather to diligence, and an attempt at right living. For when we believe that we are predestined, we know that we are predestined to good works; so let us study to make our calling certain and to live according to the nature of the predestined.

At first it seemed absurd that some should be created by God to perish. Yet Scripture says that the potter makes some vessels to honor and some to dishonor, and that God appointed Pharaoh to show his power in him. It is also said that to show his wrath he suffered with much patience the vessels of wrath prepared to destruction. Also: he makes the wicked for the day of trouble.[53]

Not all those who are called are predestined. For Christ said: "Many are called, but few are chosen."[54] But they contend that the calling is universal and that God would wish everyone saved. If it is understood as universal calling because it is offered to all and no one is excluded by name, it is true. If it is also called universal because the death of Christ and his redemption is sufficient for the whole world; that also is most true. But if this universality is meant so that it is in everyone's hand to receive the promises, I deny it: because to some it is given, to others it is not given. As if we did not see also that for a long time the very preaching of the Gospel was not given to many places, ages, and nations. God would have all to be saved, provided they believe. He gives faith to whom it seems good to him. For he may justly do with his own what he will.

The certainty of our salvation depends on this, for when we see that we are both called and also believing, we have an earnest [arrham] or sure pledge of our salvation, the spirit of God bearing witness with our spirit that we are sons of God.[55] Yet the sense of our calling and of our faith is not the cause of predestination, but its sign.

Like providence, predestination brings no constraint or violence to the human will. Whatever we do, we do it willingly and of our own accord.

[52]Rom. 11:33.
[53]Prov. 16:4; Rom. 9:17ff.
[54]Matt. 22:14.
[55]Rom. 8:16.

3. WHETHER GOD IS THE AUTHOR OF SIN[56]

I know that I am charged with making God to be the author of sin; that is not true, as will be made clear. By my teaching I try simply to show how the Scriptures must be understood when they seem to state this. Also what Augustine meant, who said that God bends human wills to both good and evil. Similarly, how Zwingli and Oecolampadius and other excellent men, professors of the Gospel, should be understood when they seem to assert the same thing.

[994] I hold the cause of human sin to be the will or free will of the first humans, who fell voluntarily and obeyed the suggestion of the devil rather than the commandment of God: afterwards original sin is transferred from them to all descendants. Therefore, we have vice and corruption enough in ourselves. As to sinning, God did not instill in us any fresh wickedness, nor does he introduce depravity. Therefore, I take our wills to be the cause of sin, not God.

Scripture says, to the Romans: "God gave up the heathen to a base mind, and to dishonorable passions."[57] In Second Samuel it says that God stirred David up to number the people. In the same history David said that God commanded Shimei to curse him. In that book, chapter 12, God said to David through the prophet: "I will take your wives and give them to your neighbor and he will lie with them. You did it secretly, but I will do this thing before all Israel, and in daylight."[58] It is said by others that these sayings must be related to permission, which I do not completely deny; for if God wished he could have prevented these offenses, but he would not. Yet I add that we should not grant a kind of permissiveness by which God is held to deal so casually, and gives up the governance of things so that he does nothing about sins themselves.

First, he removes his gifts and his grace from certain individuals because they abused them; by such a just removal of grace in punishment for former sins, they are without help and fall into worse things. David knew well enough that God sometimes withdraws his grace, saying "Turn not thy face from me. Take not thy Holy Spirit from me."[59]

---

[56]Summary of *An Deus Sit Author Peccati* translated above. The opening paragraph is italicized in the original; LC App. p. 994. In his English translation Anthony Marten separates it from the text, placing it before the scholium with the same title from 2 Sam. 16:22 (CP 1.17) with the text as appendix-; see pp. 176, 205–206.

[57]Rom. 1:26, 28.

[58]2 Sam. 24:1; 16:5ff.; 12:11ff.

[59]Ps. 51:11.

Second, God punishes sins with sins, as appears to the Romans[60] and in the places already quoted: insofar as sins are punishments they pertain to justice, and have regard to the good. Hence it is not improper for God in this way to punish former sins by sins.

Third, he rules and governs sins themselves; he does not allow them to range as far as our evil will desires. He restrains and checks them, not permitting them to rage against everyone and in every age. Moreover, he directs them to perform his counsels, namely testing the just and scourging the wicked and so on. Hence Scripture says that fierce and cruel tyrants are in the hand of God, like staves, hammers and saws.[61]

Fourth, God sends other occasions which provoke to good things if they happen to good men, but because they happen to the wicked are by their fault soon taken for the worse and made occasions for sin. So Paul says that "by the law sin was increased."[62] And the words of God spoken to Pharaoh by Moses were an occasion to draw from him blasphemies and hardness of heart. God saw that this would happen, but did not restrain his own word when he knew that Pharaoh would do worse by it; nevertheless he had the evil in himself, he did not receive it from God.

Fifth, since the defect of sin is only in human actions deprived of proper direction, human actions themselves cannot be sustained, preserved, and moved without the common influence of God, by which all things are governed and preserved. For it is truly said: "In God we are, we live, and are moved."[63] Therefore, the defect which is properly sin does not proceed from God; but the action, which is something natural in which the defect lodges, cannot be drawn out without the common influence of God.

These are the things which I said God does concerning sin by his providence and guidance, although he is not the true and proper cause of sins. By this interpretation we may understand rightly what those passages of Scripture and sayings of the Fathers mean, in which God seems to be made the cause or author of sin.

---

[60]Rom. 1:24ff.
[61]Isa. 10:5,15.
[62]Rom. 5:20.
[63]Acts 17:28.

About the Translator

*J*OSEPH CUMMING MCLELLAND received his Ph.D. in historical theology from New College, Edinburgh, in 1953 for a dissertation on Peter Martyr's sacramental doctrine. He was Robert Professor of History and Philosophy of Religion and Christian Ethics at the Presbyterian College, Montreal, from 1957 to 1964, McConnell Professor of Philosophy of Religion at McGill University from 1964 to 1993,and dean of the faculty of religious studies at McGill from 1975 to 1985. He served as president of the Canadian Theological Society (1968-69) and editor of *Studies in Religion/Sciences Religieuses* (1973-77). He is now emeritus professor of McGill University and The Presbyterian College. A symposium at his retirement has been published as *The Three Loves: Philosophy, Theology and World Religions,* edited by Robert C. Culley and William Klempa, 1994. His books and articles on philosophical and historical theology include *God the Anonymous: A Study in Alexandrian Philosophical Theology* (1976) and *Prometheus Rebound: The Irony of Atheism* (1988). His works on Vermigli include *The Visible Words of God* (1957), *Peter Martyr Vermigli and the Italian Reform* (editor, 1980), *Life, Early Letters and Eucharistic Writings of Peter Martyr* (with G. Duffield, 1989), and *Early Writings* (vol. 1 of the Peter Martyr Library, 1994). He serves as consulting editor of *The Blackwell Encyclopedia of Medieval, Renaissance, and Reformation Thought* and as a general editor of the Peter Martyr Library series.

Scripture References

Index

93580400R00217

Made in the USA
Columbia, SC
12 April 2018